The Legal
Environment
of Social Work

The Legal Environment of Social Work

Revised Edition

Leila Obier Schroeder, MSW, JD

NASW PRESS

National Association of Social Workers
Washington, DC

Ann A. Abbott, PhD, ACSW, *President*
Sheldon R. Goldstein, ACSW, LISW, *Executive Director*

Linda Beebe, *Executive Editor*
Nancy A. Winchester, *Editorial Services Director*
Fran Pflieger, *Staff Editor*
Patricia D. Wolf, Wolf Publications, Inc., *Project Manager*
Anne Grant, *Copyeditor*
Annette Hansen, *Proofreader*
Susan J. Harris, *Proofreader*
Bernice Eisen, *Indexer*

© 1995 by the NASW Press

Library of Congress Cataloging-in-Publication Data

Schroeder, Leila Obier, 1925-
    The legal environment of social work / Leila O. Schroeder.
        p.   cm.
    Includes bibliographical references and index.
    ISBN 0-87101-235-9
    1. Social workers--Legal status, laws, etc.--United States.
I. Title
KF3721.S37   1995
344.73'0313--dc20
[347.304313]   95-18029
                                                                CIP

Printed in the United States of America

For Martin

Contents

Preface

This book attempts to give you a perspective on the legal environment in which social work operates. Naturally, it is selective. It cannot discuss the whole of either the law or social work. Nor does it try to answer specific legal questions, because the law is constantly changing. If you are alerted to the problems—the crucial issues—the book accomplishes its purpose. There are numerous references to the social work and legal literature for those who want to delve into an area further. This book updates the law in the earlier edition of this book and adds mention of new legislation, such as the Americans with Disabilities Act, that will be of interest to social workers.

Part I introduces you to the legal system and its impact on the profession through the organization of social agencies and professional licensing—in other words, the legal environment that makes social work possible as an organized activity. It also includes a brief introduction to the criminal justice system and the juvenile courts, those components of the legal system with which social workers have the most contact.

Part II discusses special problem areas for clients. Some of these, such as filiation and adoption, are properly the concerns of those in child welfare. Others raise important questions for those interested in the delivery of services within complex organizations. All try to suggest avenues for social work intervention through creative use of the legal system.

I am particularly grateful to Charmaine Dimattia, who has done a remarkable job of typing the manuscript, adding to existing material, and juggling footnotes. She was a tremendous help.

—*Leila Obier Schroeder*

PART I

The Legal System and Its
Impact on the Profession

To the end it may be a

government of laws and

not of men.

—JOHN ADAMS

1

The Nature of Law

Organized societies develop rules to govern themselves. These rules create and protect certain rights, providing remedies for their abuse and a method to resolve disputes when they are jeopardized. Physical protection is a paramount reason for the creation of these rules, but the concepts of property and personal status are important as well.

Societal rules that establish correlative rights and duties between individuals and between an individual and the state provide a framework of rights and duties. (*Correlative* rights and duties are mutual and reciprocal, so that if I have a duty not to trespass on your land, you have a correlative right that I not do so.) These rules help to avoid the violence and chaos that would result if individuals set and attempted to enforce their own laws. The rules of a society are applied through its legal system.

As educated individuals, we understand many things about the legal system in the United States. We know that we must register in order to vote in elections; that we must verify the seller's title to a property when we buy a house; and that we cannot be forced to testify in a criminal trial if we would incriminate ourselves. However, as social workers, we need more specific legal information because our profession operates as a legally recognized activity and because our professional activities often serve individuals whose legal rights have been ignored or abused.

Law is a useful tool in social engineering. If, as Alexander de Tocqueville asserted, political questions in this country end up in court, the significance of law as a weapon for social change cannot be overestimated. The more clearly social workers understand this, the more creative they can be in using law to remedy social ills.

Events occurring throughout the centuries of Western civilization highlight how legal rules have been refined in practice and demonstrate that mature societies as well as developing ones need the order and security that an organized legal system imposes.

In Old Testament times in Israel, the injunction to leave gleanings in the fields, which allowed the poor such as Ruth and Naomi to feed themselves, is an example of an early public welfare system. The Ten Commandments that Moses brought down from Mt. Sinai are examples of laws governing interpersonal relationships.

Hammurabi, king of Babylon from 1955 B.C. to 1913 B.C., devised an early civil code regulating property rights and family relationships. Although the code's governing principle was retaliation—an eye for an eye and a tooth for a tooth is an idea of retribution with us to this day—its protection of the weak and poor from the rich and powerful was particularly just and humane.

In 450 B.C., when Romans wanted the law written down rather than trust the memories or whims of judges, they created the Twelve Tables. These were at first simple written rules for a basically agricultural community, but Roman law gradually became more sophisticated, adding law for conquered territories and establishing equality under the law for plebeians as well as patricians. From 528 to 534 A.D., Justinian, an emperor of Roman Byzantium, directed the compilation of the *Corpus Juris Civilis.* The foundation of European law for the next thousand years, it still supports the civil law system now operating in most of Europe and in many other parts of the world, including Louisiana and Puerto Rico.

Roman civil law was private law that governed relations between individuals, not those between individuals and the state. It included *matters of status,* such as relationships between parent and child and husband and wife, and other rights and duties of private citizens.

The common law, which is the basis for the Anglo-American legal system, developed in England after the Norman Conquest. As judges heard disputes, they created substantive rules for deciding similar cases. They used canon (religious) law, local customary law, and other accepted standards when they could and created new rules for unique situations. The emerging principle of *stare decisis,* "the decision stands," obliged later judges to use existing precedents to settle disputes before them. In this fashion, a body of positive law was established.

In civil law systems a judge is not bound by *stare decisis.* The judge applies written principles to the facts but may look to prior cases with similar facts in doing so. If there is no written principle, which is unusual, the case is decided according to *equity,* that is, by fair and impartial decision. In the United States a judge who is examining a set of facts against the constitutional principle of *due process of law* is engaging in a kind of civilian method of interpretation.

DEFINITION OF LAW

What is this law that was so long in developing? Blackstone, an 18th-century English jurist, defined *law* as "a rule of civil conduct prescribed by the supreme power of the state, commanding what is right and prohibiting what is wrong" (Jones, 1973). Article 1 of the Louisiana Civil Code states, "Law is a solemn expression of legislative will." Both these definitions express the basic idea that law is a body of rules created by whatever authority has the power to do so, whether legislative body or judge. The laws are made known either through publication of statutes or through written opinions of judges.

However, these definitions are inadequate. Who commands? What if the legislative will is arbitrary and capricious? The Soviet legal system had well-defined rules of civil conduct, prescribed by the supreme power, yet under them, political dissenters might be incarcerated in mental hospitals for their beliefs.

The Justinian compilation reduced the doctrines of law to a simple precept: *Honeste vivere, alterum non laedere, sum cuique tribuere,* that is, "to live honorably, not to injure others, to render to every man his due." If this is a reasonable basis for a legal system, consider whether ours accomplishes these goals.

Natural Law

The doctrine of natural law, a legal philosophy that presupposes certain immutable laws, responds to the need for a standard of justice and a method for evaluating positive law. Our law contains features of natural law: "We hold these truths to be self-evident; that all men are created equal; that they are endowed by their creator with certain unalienable rights; that among these are life, liberty, and the pursuit of happiness." The social work principle of self-determination follows natural law philosophy in its relation to the formal ideal of human dignity.

But to whom are "these" truths self-evident? Are all men created equal or only white men? What about women? Is there a place for civil disobedience or passive resistance in a legal system? Does our Constitution provide a satisfactory method for evaluating a law that has a negative impact on some individuals? Because the nature of law is not easily defined, legal philosophers continue to examine it (see, for example, Bodenheimer, 1962).

Substantive Law

Over the centuries, Western nations, states, and empires tried and discarded various legal systems, eventually developing common substantive rules. *Substantive law* is that which creates and defines the rights and duties of an individual. Examples typical of most legal systems are the right to dispose of property by sale, the obligation of parents to support their children, and the duty of the state to protect the helpless from exploitation. Meanwhile, *procedural law* formulates the rules by which the substance is tested in court.

Contract

One of the divisions of the substantive law developed to handle frequent concerns is contract. *Contract* is a binding agreement to do or to refrain from doing some lawful thing. For such an agreement to be legally (as opposed to morally or socially) binding—enforceable by law so that its breach may incur money damages or an order for specific performance—certain elements must be manifested. First, there must be an agreement between parties legally capable of making it. Then the agreement must cover some bargained-for element that has a legal object. Finally, there must be *consideration*, what each party gives up in order to get something from the other party.

Contracts need not be written; we enter contracts every day without giving them a great deal of thought. A purchase at the supermarket is a contract. If you are planning to set up a private social work practice, you will encounter myriad situations—leasing an office, hiring a receptionist, having a telephone installed—all of which involve entering into contracts.

Consider an employment contract: The employer and the prospective employee must *agree* on the terms of employment, hours to be worked, rate of pay, and other specifics of the position. The *consideration* is the promise that the employer makes to the employee to hire and that the employee makes to the employer to work—that is what has been bargained for. Hiring someone to work for pay is a *legal object*; you cannot make an enforceable agreement to break the law. A *capable party* does not refer to an individual's ability; legal capacity refers to age, mental competence, and the legal authority of an artificial person, such as a corporation, which has been granted legal authority to function.

The use of the term *contract* as it currently prevails in social work does not refer to a legally enforceable agreement. Agreements between student and supervisor or worker and client on common goals and how they are to be accomplished are often described in the literature as contracts. Maluccio and Marlow (1974) discussed contract from a social work viewpoint. The article emphasizes the need for clarity in defining goals in social work practice, a useful discussion of the need for explicit contract terms. In law if the terms of a contract are so ambiguous that there is no concurrence of wills, there is no contract (see also Murdaugh, 1974; Seabury, 1976). These agreements are commendable, but law is very precise in its use of language. To speak of such an agreement as a contract when no legal sanctions punish its breach is inaccurate—no matter how valuable it may be to set goals and conscientiously work together toward them.

Torts

This division of the substantive law imposes legal responsibility for reparation for harm done to another person. There is no agreement here, but rather a proscription by society as a whole of certain harmful behavior and the imposition of sanctions for that harm, usually money damages. An act may be both a crime and a tort. *Tort* is the civil remedy available to the injured party, as opposed to criminal sanctions, which are enforced through the district attorney in the name of the state.

The theory of tort allows restitution to the victim or through an *injunction*, an order of a court that the offensive behavior be discontinued. To prove that you deserve redress in a tort case, you must prove that (1) another person had a duty to take reasonable care in the situation; (2) the other person breached that duty, causing you injury; and (3) failure to honor that duty was a direct cause of the injury.

Because society is constantly changing its assessment of which harmful behaviors entitle the victim to damages, torts is a dynamic field. Invasion of privacy could not be imagined two centuries ago in a rural society when individuals longed for neighbors. Today, as technology has increased, invasion of privacy is recognized as a tort. Similarly, in a simpler society purchasers could go directly to sellers for reparation for harm caused by a defective product; today, they must seek out manufacturers and even retailers who may be hundreds of miles away.

Although social workers recognize the harm they may cause, some wrongs cannot be redressed by money damages. Ingratitude, for instance, is not a harm the law would recognize, although some forms of emotional abuse, difficult as that is to define, are recognized as a legal wrong.

An example of the dynamic nature of torts is the recent development of the tort of wrongful life. *Zepeda v. Zepeda*, the first case to allow damages for "wrongful life," was decided as recently as 1963 (see chapter 9). Similarly, a dramatic explosion in product liability occurred when asbestos suppliers, car manufacturers, and other commercial entities were found liable for large compensatory and punitive damages for the harm caused by their products.

Malpractice—the practice of a profession so negligently as to harm a client—is a tort. Social workers who are negligent, even those not in private practice, may be responsible for money damages in an action in tort; damages have been awarded against social workers in public agencies for negligent practice.

In addition to private law, such as contract and tort, which governs the relations between individuals, public substantive law may govern relations between individuals and the state. Government income maintenance programs, criminal law, and child protection services are examples of public law. It is important to understand the concepts that protect the individual against arbitrary enforcement of substantive laws by the state. Two vital instruments for protecting individual rights are due process and equal protection.

Due Process

Due process, like the pursuit of happiness, is a phrase with an old and noble history. The barons who forced the Magna Carta on King John demanded due process in their dealings with the king. In the United States the phrase is included in both the Fifth and Fourteenth Amendments to the Constitution. It has been the vehicle for gradual implementation of basic rights whose fullest enjoyment is a social work goal.

Due process has both substantive and procedural aspects. *Substantive due process* requires *nexus*—a connection—between the means selected to correct a particular evil and the end to be achieved, and the means must be inherently fair. The concept is vague and flexible, permitting courts to adjust the law to changing moral attitudes in society. Substantive due process is not applied much in the 1990s as a constitutional doctrine. The courts generally defer to the wisdom of lawmakers, unless the means they call for are arbitrary and capricious.

Procedural due process has to do with how a party to a lawsuit or an administrative proceeding is treated and how legislation affects such proceedings. It includes an individual's right to timely legal notice of proceedings, the opportunity to cross-examine witnesses, the right to the assistance of an attorney at trial—in other words, it requires fair play in the methods by which legal rights and obligations are implemented.

To illustrate the difference between procedural and substantive due process, suppose the legislature wished to reduce the number of automobile accidents. One tactic would be to forbid all blue-eyed people to drive. Because this would greatly cut down on the number of drivers, it would reduce the number of accidents, but the means is both arbitrary and capricious. It would violate *substantive* due process because there is no rational connection between eye color and the incidence of automobile accidents.

Cutting highway speeds to 55 miles per hour to reduce accidents is also arbitrary, but it is not capricious. Although there is no great difference between 56 miles per hour and 55 miles per hour, the rule is not inherently unfair, as is the rule banning blue-eyed drivers.

A substantively sound statute making it a crime to drive a car faster than 55 miles per hour could not provide, on the other hand, that anyone caught speeding would be put in jail for six months with no trial; the denial of a trial would be denial of *procedural* due process. Nevertheless, although severe, the penalty of six months in jail for driving one mile over the speed limit could be imposed after a trial if society considered the evil great enough to justify the penalty.

Goldberg v. Kelly (1970) illustrates how due process is used to decide a case:

Goldberg v. Kelly
397 U.S. 254, 90 S. Ct. 1011 (1970)
Brennan, J.
The question for decision is whether a state which terminates public assistance payments to a particular recipient without affording him the opportunity for an evidentiary hearing prior to termination denies the recipient procedural due process in violation of the due process clause of the Fourteenth Amendment .

· · · · ·

The constitutional issue to be decided, therefore, is the narrow one whether the due process clause requires that the recipient be afforded an evidentiary hearing before the termination of benefits. . . . The district court held that only a pre-termination evidentiary hearing would satisfy the constitutional command, and rejected the argument of the state and city officials that the combination of the post-termination "fair hearing" with the informal pre-termination review disposed of all due process claims.

· · · · ·

Appellant does not contend that procedural due process is not applicable to the termination of welfare benefits. Such benefits are a matter of statutory entitlement for persons qualified to receive them. Their termination involves state action that adjudicates important rights. The constitutional challenge cannot be answered by an argument that public assistance benefits are " 'a privilege' and not 'a right.' " The extent to which procedural due process must be afforded the recipient is influenced by the extent to which he may be "condemned to suffer grievous loss. . . ." and depends upon whether the recipient's interest in avoiding that loss outweighs the governmental interest in summary adjudication.

· · · · ·

It is true, of course, that some governmental benefits may be adminis-
tratively terminated without affording the recipient a pre-termination
evidentiary hearing. But we agree with the district court that when wel-
fare is discontinued, only a pre-termination evidentiary hearing provides
the recipient with procedural due process. . . . For qualified recipients,
welfare provides the means to obtain essential food, clothing, housing,
and medical care. . . . Thus the crucial factor in this context—a factor not
present in the case of . . . virtually anyone else whose governmental entitle-
ments [are] ended—is that termination of aid pending resolution of a con-
troversy over eligibility may deprive an eligible recipient of the very means
by which to live while he waits. Since he lacks independent resources, his
situation becomes immediately desperate. His need to concentrate upon
finding the means for daily subsistence, in turn, adversely affects his abil-
ity to seek redress from the welfare bureaucracy.

Moreover, important governmental interests are promoted by affording
recipients a pre-termination evidentiary hearing. From its founding the
nation's basic commitment has been to foster the dignity and well-being of
all persons within its borders. We have come to recognize that forces not
within the control of the poor contribute to their poverty. This perception,
against the background of our traditions, has significantly influenced the
development of the contemporary public assistance system. Welfare, by meet-
ing the basic demands of subsistence, can help bring within the reach of
the poor the same opportunities that are available to others to participate
meaningfully in the life of the community. At the same time, welfare guards
against the societal malaise that may flow from a widespread sense of
unjustified frustration and insecurity. Public assistance, then, is not merely
charity, but a means to "promote the general welfare, and secure the bless-
ings of liberty to ourselves and our posterity." The same governmental
interests which counsel the provision of welfare, counsel as well its uninter-
rupted provisions to those eligible to receive it; pre-termination evidentiary
hearings are indispensable to that end.

Appellant does not challenge the force of these considerations but ar-
gues that they are outweighed by countervailing governmental interests in
conserving fiscal and administrative resources. These interests, the argu-
ment goes, justify the delay of any evidentiary hearing until after discontinu-
ance of the grants. Summary adjudication protects the public fisc by stopping
payments promptly upon discovery of reason to believe that a recipient is no
longer eligible. Since most terminations are accepted without challenge, sum-
mary adjudication also conserves both the fisc and administrative time and
energy by reducing the number of evidentiary hearings actually held.

We agree with the district court, however, that these governmental inter-
ests are not overriding in the welfare context. The requirement of a prior

hearing doubtless involves some greater expense, and the benefits paid to ineligible recipients pending decision at the hearing probably cannot be recouped, since these recipients are likely to be judgment-proof. But the state is not without weapons to minimize these increased costs. Much of the drain on fiscal and administrative resources can be reduced by developing procedures for prompt pre-termination hearings and by skillful use of personnel and facilities. . . . Thus, the interest of the eligible recipient in uninterrupted receipt of public assistance, coupled with the state's interest that his payments not be erroneously terminated, clearly outweighs the state's competing concern to prevent any increase in its fiscal and administrative burdens.

· · · · ·

We also agree with the district court, however, that the pre-termination hearing need not take the form of a judicial or quasijudicial trial. We bear in mind that the statutory "fair hearing" will provide the recipient with a full administrative review. Accordingly, the pre-termination hearing has one function only: to produce an initial determination of the validity of the welfare department's grounds for discontinuance of payments in order to protect a recipient against an erroneous termination of his benefits. . . . Thus, a complete record and a comprehensive opinion, which would serve primarily to facilitate judicial review and to guide future decisions, need not be provided at the pre-termination stage.

The opportunity to be heard must be tailored to the capacities and circumstances of those who are to be heard. It is not enough that a welfare recipient may present his position to the decision maker in writing or second-hand through his caseworker. Written submissions are an unrealistic option for most recipients, who lack the educational attainment necessary to write effectively and who cannot obtain professional assistance. Moreover, written submissions do not afford the flexibility of oral presentations, they do not permit the recipient to mold his argument to the issues the decision maker appears to regard as important. Particularly where credibility and veracity are at issue, as they must be in many termination proceedings, written submissions are a wholly unsatisfactory basis for decision. The second-hand presentation to the decision maker by the caseworker has its own deficiencies. . . . Therefore a recipient must be allowed to state his position orally. Informal procedures will suffice; in this context due process does not require a particular order of proof or mode of offering evidence.

· · · · ·

In almost every setting when important decisions turn on questions of fact, due process requires an opportunity to confront and cross-examine adverse witnesses. . . . Welfare recipients must therefore be given an opportunity to confront and cross-examine the witnesses relied on by the department.

"The right to be heard would be, in many cases, of little avail if it did not comprehend the right to be heard by counsel. . . ." We do not say that counsel must be provided at the pre-termination hearing, but only that the recipient must be allowed to retain an attorney if he so desires.

• • • • •

Finally, the decision maker's conclusion as to a recipient's eligibility must rest solely on the legal rules and evidence adduced at the hearing. . . . To demonstrate compliance with this elementary requirement, the decision maker should state the reasons for his determination and indicate the evidence he relied on. . . though his statement need not amount to a full opinion . . . and, an impartial decision maker is essential. . . . We agree with the district court that prior involvement in some aspects of a case will not necessarily bar a welfare official from acting as a decision maker. He should not, however, have participated in making the determination under review.

Affirmed.

Black, J. dissenting

In the last half century the United States, along with many, perhaps most, other nations of the world, has moved far towards becoming a welfare state, that is, a nation that for one reason or another taxes its most affluent people to help support, feed, clothe and shelter its less fortunate citizens. The result is that today more than 9 million men, women, and children in the United States receive some kind of state or federally financed public assistance in the form of allowances or gratuities, generally paid them periodically, usually by the week, month, or quarter. Since these gratuities are paid on the basis of need, the list of recipients is not static, and some people go off the lists and others are added from time to time. These ever-changing lists put a constant administrative burden on the government and it certainly could not have reasonably anticipated that this burden would include the additional procedural expense imposed by the Court today.

• • • • •

In my judgment there is not one word, phrase, or sentence from the beginning to the end of the Constitution from which it can be inferred that judges were granted . . . legislative power. True, Marbury v. Madison . . . held, and properly, I think, that courts must be the final interpreters of the Constitution, and I recognize that the holding can provide an opportunity to slide imperceptibly into constitutional amendment and law making. But when federal judges use this judicial power for legislative purposes, I think they wander out of their field of vested powers and transgress into the area constitutionally assigned to the Congress and the people. This is precisely what I believe the Court is doing in this case. Hence my dissent.

• • • • •

Particularly do I not think that the Fourteenth Amendment should be given such an unnecessarily broad construction. That amendment came into being primarily to protect Negroes from discrimination, and while some of its language can and does protect others, all know that the chief purpose behind it was to protect ex-slaves. . . . The court, however, relies upon the Fourteenth Amendment and in effect says that failure of the government to pay a promised charitable installment to an individual deprives that individual of his own property, in violation of the due process clause of the Fourteenth Amendment. It somewhat strains credulity to say that a government's promise of charity to an individual is property belonging to that individual when the government denies that the individual is honestly entitled to receive such a payment.

· · · · ·

This decision is thus only another variant of the view often expressed by some members of this Court that the due process clause forbids any conduct that a majority of Court believes "unfair," "indecent," or "shocking to their consciences. . . ." Neither these words nor any like them appear anywhere in the due process clause. If they did, they would leave the majority of justices free to hold any conduct unconstitutional that they should conclude on their own to be unfair or shocking to them. Had the drafters of the due process clause meant to leave judges such ambulatory power to declare laws unconstitutional, the chief value of a written constitution, as the founders saw it, would have been lost. In fact, if that view of due process is correct, the due process clause could easily swallow up all other parts of the Constitution. And truly the Constitution would always be "what the judges say it is" at a given moment, not what the founders wrote into the document.

· · · · ·

The procedure required today as a matter of constitutional law finds no precedent in our legal system. Reduced to its simplest terms, the problem in this case is similar to that frequently encountered when two parties have an ongoing legal relationship which requires one party to make periodic payments to the other. Often the situation arises where the party "owing" the money stops paying it and justifies his conduct by arguing that the recipient is not legally entitled to payment. The recipient can, of course, disagree and go to court to compel payment. But I know of no situation in our legal system in which the person alleged to owe money to another is required by law to continue making payments to a judgment-proof claimant without the benefit of any security or bond to insure that these payments can be recovered if he wins his legal argument. Yet today's decision in no way obligates the welfare recipient to pay back any benefits wrongfully received during the pre-termination evidentiary hearings or post any bond.

The Court apparently feels that this decision will benefit the poor and needy. In my judgment the eventual result will be just the opposite. . . . In the next case the welfare recipients are bound to argue that cutting off benefits before judicial review of the agency's decision is also a denial of due process. Since, by hypothesis, termination of aid at that point may still "deprive an eligible recipient of the very means by which to live while he waits". . . I would be surprised if the weighing process did not compel the conclusion that termination without full judicial review would be unconscionable. After all, at each step, as the majority seems to feel, the issue is only one of weighing the government's pocketbook against the actual survival of the recipient, and surely that balance must always tip in favor of the individual. . . . Thus the end result of today's decision may well be that the government, once it decides to give welfare benefits, cannot reverse that decision until the recipient has had the benefits of full administrative and judicial review. . . . [T]he inevitable result of such a constitutionally imposed burden will be that the government will not put a claimant on the rolls initially until it has made an exhaustive investigation to determine his eligibility.

· · · · ·

[The dissenting opinions of Justice Stewart and Chief Justice Burger are omitted.]

This case is a landmark in public welfare law. The basis of the decision is procedural due process: The justices are not declaring the particular statute providing and terminating public welfare benefits to be arbitrary and capricious. Rather, they fault the way the statute is administered—the agency's failure to provide a hearing when the client disputes the basis for termination of benefits. As Justice Brennan points out, termination involves state action, and the due process clause of the Fourteenth Amendment forbids any state to "deprive any person of life, liberty, or property without due process of law." When an adjudication may deprive the client of the very means of subsistence, procedural due process now requires a pretermination hearing.

The Court formerly used a right–privilege distinction in determining whether an individual was deprived of liberty or property without due process. In *Goldberg* the Court found an "entitlement," which is treated like a property right that the government may not terminate without notice and a hearing.

The case also illustrates how members of the Supreme Court may disagree in interpreting the Constitution. Although the dissenting justices are no less concerned about individuals suffering from "brutal need," they do not read the Constitution as requiring a pretermination hearing.

Note that *Goldberg* does not say that a welfare grant can never be terminated without a hearing. If there are no disputed matters of fact—if the state statute has been amended, for instance, or the regulations concerning levels of need or age at termination revised—there may be no dispute and no need for a hearing.

Because the Supreme Court decides only the legal issues before it and not the facts, which are determined at the trial level, its opinions do not speculate on how the holding may apply to other situations. However, the opinion may be used as a precedent in cases dealing with other rights that are allegedly protected from arbitrary state action by procedural due process. For instance, do foster parents have a protected right to a continuing relationship with a foster child? *Smith v. Organization of Foster Families* (1977), which is excerpted in chapter 9, answers this question.

Equal Protection

The equal protection provided by the Fourteenth Amendment does not require that each person be treated absolutely the same. Classifications cannot be entirely neat and tidy. Classifying is inherently arbitrary, because each individual or each piece of property or each activity, although unique, cannot be treated as a separate class. To provide equal protection, classifications must have a "rational basis." But this is not always enough to support a challenged classification. When a law impinges on a freedom as basic as freedom of speech or freedom of travel, or when it is based on a suspect classification such as race or religion, there must be not merely a rational basis but also "a compelling state interest" for any discrimination in classification. For example, a statute that taxed four-wheeled vehicles on one basis and motorcycles on a different basis might be upheld if the state can show a "rational basis" for the difference. However, a classification dealing with people and based on race will be subjected to strict scrutiny. Note that, contrary to what might be expected in something as vital as the right to public assistance, "in the area of economics and social welfare, a State does not violate the Equal Protection Clause merely because the classifications made by its laws are imperfect" (*Dandridge v. Williams,* 1970). For instance, in *Dandridge v. Williams* maximum grants to public welfare clients were upheld against the argument that they treated larger families unequally.

In the 1970s the Supreme Court moved away from an either–or approach to a more flexible analysis of the nature of the unequal classification challenged and the rights affected, and the government interests (such as economy of administration) used to support the classification. This is apparent in cases challenging gender classifications and those that disadvantage illegitimate children. Without holding that gender and illegitimacy are "suspect" classes, the court requires that the classification serve important government objectives and be substantially related to those objectives in order to withstand the equal protection challenge.

Brown v. Board of Education of Topeka (1954) illustrates the use of the equal protection clause in deciding a case that challenged a state's classification by race.

Brown v. Board of Education of Topeka
347 U.S. 483, 74 S. Ct. 686 (1954)
Mr. Chief Justice Warren delivered the opinion of the Court.

These cases come to us from the States of Kansas, South Carolina, Virginia, and Delaware. They are premised on different facts and different local conditions, but a common legal question justifies their consideration together in this consolidated opinion.

In each of the cases, minors of the Negro race, through their legal representatives, seek the aid of the courts in obtaining admission to the public schools of their community on a nonsegregated basis. In each instance, they had been denied admission to schools attended by white children under laws requiring or permitting segregation according to race. This segregation was alleged to deprive the plaintiffs of the equal protection of the laws under the Fourteenth Amendment. . . . The plaintiffs contend that segregated public schools are not "equal," and that hence they are deprived of the equal protection of the laws. . . . Reargument was largely devoted to the circumstances surrounding the adoption of the Fourteenth Amendment in 1868. . . . An additional reason for the inconclusive nature of the amendment's history, with respect to segregated schools, is the status of public education at that time. In the South, the movement toward free common schools, supported by general taxation, had not yet taken hold. Education of white children was largely in the hands of private groups. Education of Negroes was almost non-existent, and practically all of the race were illiterate. In fact, any education of Negroes was forbidden by law in some states. Today, in contrast, many Negroes have achieved outstanding success in the arts and sciences as well as in the business and professional world. It is true that public school education at the time of the amendment had advanced further in the North, but the effect of the amendment on northern states was generally ignored in the congressional debates. Even in the North, the conditions of public education did not approximate those existing today. The curriculum was usually rudimentary; ungraded schools were common in rural areas; the school term was but three months a year in many states; and compulsory school attendance was virtually unknown. As a consequence, it is not surprising that there should be so little in the history of the Fourteenth Amendment relating to its intended effect on public education.

In the first cases in this Court construing the Fourteenth Amendment, decided shortly after its adoption, the Court interpreted it as proscribing all state-imposed discriminations against the Negro race. The doctrine of "separate but equal" did not make its appearance in this Court until 1896 in the case of Plessy v. Ferguson, *supra, involving not education but transportation. . . . In more recent cases, all on the graduate school level, inequality was found in that specific benefits enjoyed by white students were denied to Negro students of the same educational qualification. . . . In none of these cases was it necessary to re-examine the doctrine to grant relief to the Negro plaintiff. And in* Sweatt v. Painter, *supra, the Court expressly reserved decision on the question whether* Plessy v. Ferguson *should be held inapplicable to public education.*

In the instant cases, that question is directly presented. Here, unlike Sweatt v. Painter, *there are findings below that the Negro and white schools involved have been equalized, or are being equalized, with respect to buildings, curricula, qualifications and salaries of teachers, and other "tangible" factors. Our decision, therefore, cannot turn on merely a comparison of these tangible factors in the Negro and white schools involved in each of the cases. We must look instead to the effect of segregation itself on public education.*

In approaching this problem, we cannot turn the clock back to 1868 when the amendment was adopted, or even to 1896 when Plessy v. Ferguson *was written. We must consider public education in the light of its full development and its present place in American life throughout the nation. Only in this way can it be determined if segregation in public schools deprives these plaintiffs of the equal protection of the laws.*

Today, education is perhaps the most important function of state and local governments. Compulsory school attendance laws and the great expenditures for education both demonstrate our recognition of the importance of education to our democratic society. It is required in the performance of our most basic public responsibilities, even service in the armed forces. It is the very foundation of good citizenship. Today it is a principal instrument in awakening the child to cultural values, in preparing him for later professional training, and in helping him to adjust normally to his environment. In this day, it is doubtful that any child may reasonably be expected to succeed in life if he is denied the opportunity of an education. Such an opportunity, where the state has undertaken to provide it, is a right which must be made available to all on equal terms.

We come then to the question presented: Does segregation of children in public schools solely on the basis of race, even though the physical facilities and other "tangible" factors may be equal, deprive the children of the minority group of equal education opportunities? We believe that it does.

In Sweatt v. Painter . . . *in finding that a segregated law school for Negroes could not provide them equal educational opportunities this Court relied in large part on "those qualities which are incapable of objective measurement but which make for greatness in a law school." In* McLaurin v. Oklahoma State Regents . . . *the Court, in requiring that a Negro admitted to a white graduate school be treated like all other students, again resorted to intangible considerations: ". . . his ability to study, to engage in discussions and exchange views with other students, and, in general, to learn his profession." Such considerations apply with added force to children in grade and high schools. To separate them from others of similar age and qualifications solely because of their race generates a feeling of inferiority as to their status in the community that may affect their hearts and minds in a way unlikely ever to be undone. . . . Whatever may have been the extent of psychological knowledge at the time of* Plessy v. Ferguson, *this [that segregation has a detrimental affect upon colored children] is amply supported by modern authority. Any language in* Plessy v. Ferguson *contrary to this finding is rejected.*

We conclude that in the field of public education the doctrine of "separate but equal" has no place. Separate educational facilities are inherently unequal. Therefore, we hold that the plaintiffs and others similarly situated for whom the actions have been brought are, by reason of the segregation complained of, deprived of the equal protection of the laws guaranteed by the Fourteenth Amendment.

Bolling v. Sharpe (1954) reached the same conclusion for public schools in the District of Columbia, using as a constitutional rationale that racial segregation is a denial of due process of law as guaranteed by the Fifth Amendment. (The court used the Fifth rather than the Fourteenth Amendment because the Fourteenth applies to states; the District of Columbia is part of the federal government.) The *Bolling* court said, "The equal protection of the law is a more implicit safeguard of prohibited unfairness than 'due process of law,' therefore, we do not imply that the two are always interchangeable phrases. But, as this court has recognized, discrimination may be so unjustifiable as to be violative of due process" (p. 497). The court then added,

Segregation in public education is not reasonably related to any proper governmental objective, and thus it imposes on Negro children of the District of Columbia a burden that constitutes an arbitrary deprivation of their liberty in violation of the due process clause. In view of our decision that the Constitution prohibits the state from maintaining racially segregated public schools, it would be unthinkable that the same Constitution would impose a lesser duty on the federal government. (p. 499)

The Supreme Court decision in *Brown* was unanimous, holding that classification by race is inherently unequal. Although the decision applies only to public schools, it is used as a precedent.

Brown illustrates that constitutional interpretation is not static. The Court recognized that times had changed since the Fourteenth Amendment had been ratified. Although many questions that come to the Court were never considered by its framers, the language of the Constitution lends itself to meeting the needs of a dynamic society.

In deciding *Brown*, the Court had to deal with a precedent, *Plessy v. Ferguson*. It could have distinguished the precedent from *Brown* by saying that *Plessy* applied to transportation, not to education. Courts often make such distinctions when they wish to reach a result more in keeping with current equities without overruling a prior case, but if the Supreme Court had distinguished *Plessy* in *Brown*, cases challenging discrimination in public transportation inevitably would have followed, so *Plessy* was expressly overruled.

The Court was not unmindful of the difficulties that complete integration of public schools would entail and asked the attorneys to return with suggestions. A second *Brown* decision determined that integration of public schools would follow "with all deliberate speed." The problem of fully integrating public schools remains to this day.

The *Brown* decision on inequality in public schools raises important questions: Is it a denial of equal protection for students to attend public schools that are less than adequate because of limited financing? Are students for whom English is a second language denied equal protection of the law if they are not provided with special language classes? In thinking about these questions, consider whether a "right" or a "privilege" is involved and whether the classifications serve important governmental objectives. You must also take into account whether the Court is interpreting a statute, presumably enacted for modern concerns and easily amended, or a provision of the Constitution.

ADVERSARIAL SYSTEM

The lawyer is a counselor—a role social workers understand. The lawyer helps the client identify the legal problem, search for the facts needed to clarify it, and begin work on it. As with social work some people make better clients than others because they are better able to follow advice and have an appropriate degree of intellectual capacity to grasp the problem, mental and physical energy to work on it, and objectivity about it.

Lawyers are also advocates. They muster their clients' best arguments to vindicate their rights. Lawyers engage in social action when their experience shows them that changes are needed. On some rare occasions, as in *Brown* or *Goldberg v. Kelly*, a lawyer's advocacy can change the legal (and social) system. When professional social workers undertake social action, they are recognizing that the best solution to a client's problem may lie less in accommodation to an unsatisfactory social system than in change of the system itself.

Important as it is, the adversary role is one of the most misunderstood aspects of the legal profession. In the arena of the courtroom, attorneys must be champions for their clients, advocating their interest as foes of the opposing party, although not in an emotional way (Steele, 1972). In so doing they may not use illegal, immoral, or unethical methods, but the psychological and sociological implications of their course of action do not concern them. Their function is to win—to minimize their client's loss of property or liberty.

Once a lawyer chooses to represent a particular client, all value judgments are irrelevant. Lawyers are bound by the law to assert the law on behalf of the client. Because society has made the value judgment that this is the lawyer's responsibility, he or she will try to give an abusive parent the best representation possible, even if this means returning a child to the client's home. The objective of the attorney is not to determine what is best for all parties or what solution would best benefit society but to win for the client.

To work effectively with attorneys, you must understand the role of lawyers and the methods they use to win cases. You will deal with them in juvenile courts, in probation and parole cases, and in many family matters. A lawyer can explain how you can present your analysis and diagnosis convincingly using legally admissible evidence to counteract an opposing attorney's advocacy of a position you know to be harmful to the client.

This is not to say that an attorney does not compromise, but the art of compromise, one of the attorney's strongest skills, is used only if it will bring the best solution for the client. Ultimately the client decides whether to sue, defend, or compromise (Mueller & Murphy, 1965; Smith, 1968).

HOW TO FIND THE LAW
Legal Research

To understand and appreciate the legal environment in which social work exists and is practiced, it is important to become acquainted with the raw material of the law: statutes and cases. These give a feel for the law and an appreciation of how lawyers think, because studying cases and statutes is the way law students study. Good legal research involves identifying the real issue, an activity not unfamiliar to social workers, who know that the problem a client presents is often not the real one.

In private law schools, permission is required to use the law library, but libraries in state-supported law schools are often open to the public. Some large cities have extensive legal collections in their public libraries. State agencies may also have law libraries open to the general public or may retain legal staff employees may consult.

Any nonlawyer who is planning to do in-depth legal research should first read a text on the subject (see, for instance, Price, Bitner & Bysiewicz, 1979). Once familiar with how materials are indexed, you can find additional cases, statutes, and law review articles on a given subject. All *reported* cases—cases that have been printed in bound volumes—are indexed in encyclopedias and digests. By checking a number of key words in an index, a researcher can find all the relevant cases in the country. The task in legal research is therefore to identify the key words that best define the problem.

A lot of legal research is now done on computers. To learn how to do that, read *How to Find the Law* (Cohen, Berring, & Olson, 1980).

Briefing Cases

Law students learn to identify legal problems by *briefing* the cases they read, summarizing very concisely the facts important to the court's decisions. These facts may amount to no more than a few lines in a case many pages long. The student then finds the *issue*, the question the court has been asked to decide. The brief concludes with the *holding*, what the court decided and why. The "why" of the holding is important because this becomes a rule of law that may apply to other similar cases. For instance, a brief for *Brown v. Board of Education* might be as simple as this:

Facts: *Negro students from four states sought the aid of the courts in obtaining admission to the public schools of their community on a nonsegregated basis.*

Issue: *Does the precedent of* Plessy v. Ferguson, *which created the doctrine of "separate but equal," apply to public education?*

Holding: *The doctrine of "separate but equal" has no place in public education. Separate educational facilities are inherently unequal. Therefore, the plaintiffs and others similarly situated for whom the actions have been brought are, by reason of the segregation complained of, deprived of the equal protection of the law guaranteed by the Fourteenth Amendment.*

Among other things this brief tells you that the race of the plaintiffs is crucial to the decision, because it is racial discrimination that is complained of. It also tells you that the plaintiffs are students actively suffering from discrimination at the hands of the state, not people who believe abstractly that segregated schools are wrong. It tells you of an existing precedent that must be overruled if the court is to find for the plaintiffs. And the holding refers you to the provision of the Constitution that the court used to reach this rule of law.

In reading a case, always look at the *citation*, the numbers and letters telling you where the full report of the case is to be found. For instance, the first citation for *Goldberg v. Kelly* is 397 U.S. 254; this tells you that the case can be found in volume 397 of the United States Reports and begins on page 254. The case was decided in 1970.

Cases are reported in series that carry different names. Cases decided by the federal courts of appeals are found in the Federal Reporters; the first series of these will be cited, for example, as 144 F. 34 (1906) and the second as 14 F.2d 299 (1926). The date is not necessary to find the case but it can be important if you are wondering whether the case has value as a precedent. You can check that by referring to *Shepherd's Citations* in a law library. Shepherd gives you information about whether a case has been overrruled and which cases have cited the case you are looking up.

Cases decided in federal district courts are reported in the Federal Supplement, cited as F. Supp. State cases are published in regional reporters. Once you do any legal research, you will quickly discover which reporter has the federal cases from your state. (Louisiana cases are cited in the Southern Reporter.) Some reporters have a second or even a third series, each starting with volume one, once the previous volumes have reached a certain number.

You will recall that *Goldberg v. Kelly* had a second citation to 90 S. Ct. 872. This is what is called a parallel citation, meaning that the same case is printed in another reporter, in this case, the Supreme Court Reporter. The full case is found in both places.

HOW TO FIND A LAWYER

For most people recommendations of a lawyer come from family and friends. Legal clinics occasionally advertise in newspapers, but advertising by lawyers was unusual in the past. Now that the Supreme Court has decided that lawyers may advertise, it is much more common, with some lawyers using television, particularly to tout expertise in tort, especially accident, litigation.

The local bar associations in larger cities have lawyer referral services. Anyone wishing to find a lawyer can call the bar association, describe the problem briefly, and ask for a referral. Usually these services depend on lawyers registering themselves for referral, listing their specialties. For a set fee the client may have a brief consultation with the lawyer to learn whether the problem is a legal one, whether the lawyer can and will handle it, and what it might cost if necessary to litigate.

There are also directories of lawyers; *Martindale-Hubbell Law Directory* (1994) is one. It and others will be found in any large public library or in a law library. The volumes of these directories list lawyers by name and locality, give their educational background, mention the type of clients the lawyers see, and indicate their colleagues' opinion of their ability by the listing of a rating.

A large community will probably have a legal aid office that handles civil matters for indigent people; those accused of crimes may ask the court to appoint a lawyer. This will be discussed in more detail later.

REFERENCES

Bodenheimer, E. (1962). *Jurisprudence: The philosophy and method of the law.* Cambridge, MA: Harvard University Press.

Cohen, M. L., Berring, R. C., & Olson, K. C. (1980). *How to find the law.* St. Paul, MN: West Publishing.

Jones, G. (Ed.). (1973). *The sovereignty of the law. Selections from Blackstone's "Commentaries on the Laws of England."* Toronto: University of Toronto Press.

Maluccio, A. N., & Marlow, W. D. (1974). The case for the contract. *Social Work, 19,* 28–36.

Martindale-Hubbell law directory. (1994). New Providence, NJ: Reed Publishing.

Mueller, E. E., & Murphy, P. J. (1965). Communication problems: Social workers and lawyers. *Social Work, 10,* 97–103.

Murdaugh, J. (1974). Student supervision unbounded. *Social Work, 19,* 131–132.

Price, M. O., Bitner, H., Bysiewicz, S. R. (1979). *Effective legal research* (4th ed.). Boston: Little, Brown.

Seabury, B. A. (1976). The contract: Uses, abuses, and limitations. *Social Work, 21,* 16–21.

Smith, A. D. (1968). A study of the lawyer–social worker professional relationship. *Research Contributions of the American Bar Foundation, 6.*

Steele, W. W., Jr. (1972). Understanding the advocacy process. *Social Work, 17,* 108–109.

STUDY QUESTIONS

1. Can the Supreme Court affect the conduct of hearings in government social agencies?

2. Is government classification according to race subject to strict scrutiny when a court looks at it in terms of equal protection?

3. What is the nature of the adversary role of attorneys?

2

Lawmaking

Substantive law is found in constitutions, codes, statutes, ordinances, and cases. Judges do not advise that a law denies equal protection or due process until an actual case appears before them. For individuals who cannot afford to go to court to protect their substantive or procedural rights, society provides limited legal assistance.

JUDICIAL AND ADMINISTRATIVE LAWMAKING

Because the common law is a precedential system, in tort and contract disputes the judge will often use a decision in an earlier case as a guide. In common-law jurisdictions where there is no relevant statute and no precedent, the judge will formulate a rule by determining what would best serve the interests of justice. Recent invasion-of-privacy rules are examples of judge-made law.

In Louisiana and Puerto Rico, jurisdictions with a civil law tradition, judges interpret general concepts, much as judges elsewhere interpret constitutional provisions. In both the common-law and civilian traditions, judges interpret the written law according to their own understanding of it, that understanding being influenced by their background, personality, integrity, and intellect.

Administrative agencies such as federal and state health departments are created by legislative bodies to perform functions defined in the enabling clauses of a given statute: "protect our natural resources," "promote a clean environment," "provide for dependent children." Because the drafting of complex rules is beyond the time, energy, and technical expertise of most legislators, the authority to study problems and promulgate rules having the force of law in such areas as taxation and conservation or even setting policy in providing for people who are poor or ill is turned over to the agency. The 1912 law creating the Children's Bureau is typical. It demonstrates how:

- Enabling statutes empower agencies to carry out new programs.
- Purpose clauses give the reason for the new legislation, what it is intended to do.

42. U.S.C.A. § 191.

There shall be established in the Department of Health, Education, and Welfare a bureau to be known as the Children's Bureau.

42. U.S.C.A. § 192.

The Children's Bureau shall be under the direction of a chief, to be appointed by the President, by and with the advice and consent of the Senate. The said bureau shall investigate and report to the Secretary of Health, Education, and Welfare, upon all matters pertaining to the welfare of children and child life among all classes of our people, and shall especially investigate the questions of infant mortality, the birth rate, orphanages, juvenile courts, desertion, dangerous occupations, accidents and disease of children, employment, legislation affecting children in the several states and territories. But no official, or agent, or representative of said bureau shall, over the objection of the head of the family, enter any house used exclusively as a family residence. The chief of said bureau may from time to time publish the results of these investigations in such a manner and to such extent as may be prescribed by the Secretary.

This short piece of legislation created an administrative agency with broad powers and a mandate to study many areas of American life. From such short statements comes the authority to create large agencies.

The growth of administrative agencies and administrative law is endemic to the 20th century. Because the "purpose" clauses of enabling statutes are frequently quite short, they only hint at the extent to which agencies may develop and what policies these agencies can establish.

In theory, lawmaking belongs entirely to the legislature. In practice, agency rules have the force of law. Because administrative agencies are creations of the legislative branch, they can exercise only the authority the legislature gives them. The rules they make pursuant to that authority must offer the same due process protections as any other law.

Proposed agency rules must be made public to allow opportunity for them to be challenged; if the final rules are broken, there must be opportunity for a hearing before any sanction is applied. Courts will not disturb agency decisions if there is substantial evidence to support the decision, even though the facts could also support another finding. *Substantial evidence* means that there is enough evidence to support the decision but not necessarily enough to dismiss any other finding.

Because the agency has been set up to find facts and weigh them according to specified rules, the court will not substitute its judgment for that of the agency.

COURT SYSTEM

Judges clearly make laws when their decisions expand the common law to create a new right or obligation, as with invasion of privacy or product liability. Judges also make law when they overrule precedents or find statutes unconstitutional, as did the justices in *Brown v. Board of Education of Topeka (1954)*.

When judges adopt a new procedural rule, they make law, as did Florida's fourth circuit court of appeals when it changed the Florida contributory negligence rule to one of comparative negligence (*Jones v. Hoffman*, 1972). Contributory negligence bars a person from recovering any damages if the injured person has been even slightly negligent. The comparative negligence rule reduces damages in proportion to the degree of negligence of the injured person. Most states have adopted the comparative negligence rule. (See *Li v. Yellow Cab Co. of Calif.*, 1975, and *Profitt v. State of Colorado*, 1971.)

Another example of judicial lawmaking is the erosion of the doctrine of sovereign immunity, a doctrine itself originally derived from jurisprudence. (*Jurisprudence* is the body of judicial decisions.) The doctrine of sovereign immunity protects the sovereign—the state—from suit when its institutions and agents are guilty of negligence. Louisiana has rejected the doctrine as unfair and tending toward governmental irresponsibility (*Board of C. of P. of New Orleans v. Splendour S. & E. Co.*, 1973), as have several other states.

A similar construct is *charitable immunity*, which protects from suit charitable institutions such as schools, hospitals, and social agencies. In *Myers v. Drozda* (1966) a Nebraska court discussed the bases for this immunity. The *trust fund theory* considers the assets of the charity as held in trust for the benefit of the public and asserts that payment of a damage claim would dissipate the assets of the trust. The *implied waiver theory* is that an individual, in dealing with a charitable organization, assumes the risk and waives any right to sue for damages. The court held that neither theory responds to the realities of the present day, because many beneficiaries of charitable institutions pay directly for services and indirectly through taxation and because the availability of insurance protects the institutions from damage claims. In *Flagiello v. Pennsylvania Hospital* (1965) Pennsylvania supreme court justice Musmanno commented on the argument that precedents granting charitable immunity should not be overruled because of the doctrine of *stare decisis*:

> *Stare decisis channels the law. It erects lighthouses and flies the signals of safety. The ships of jurisprudence must follow that well-defined channel which, over the years, has been proved to be secure and trustworthy. But it would not comport with wisdom to insist that, should shoals rise in heretofore safe course and rocks emerge to encumber the passage, the ship should nonetheless pursue the original course, merely because it presented no hazard in the past. The principle of stare decisis does not demand that we follow precedents which shipwreck justice.* (p. 205)

Court Hierarchy

Most states have a three-tiered hierarchy of courts. A litigant begins a lawsuit with a petition in the district court, the trial court of general jurisdiction: a court that tries cases of all sorts. A party who loses there may appeal as a matter of right to the next level, typically a court of appeal, where the case usually ends.

However, all states have a final appellate court, usually called the supreme court. By statute there may be an automatic right of appeal in some cases, for instance, in election contests or in criminal cases where the penalty is severe. Other cases are heard when the court grants a writ of *certiorari*, a writ of review, because it wishes to clear up a conflict in interpretations in the lower courts, or to give guidance in a new or confusing area of the law.

There are also specialized courts and courts of limited jurisdiction. Most city courts and small claims courts hear only cases involving claims for small amounts of money, typically $1,000 or $2,000, and traffic cases and misdemeanors. Juvenile and family courts are specialized courts, as are probate courts, which have jurisdiction not just over the probate of wills but also over the guardianship of minors and people with mental disabilities. They are not set up to hear breach of contract cases and negligence actions. State legislation creates the various courts and jurisdictions.

Jurisdiction

Jurisdiction is the authority of a court to hear and decide a case. It is based on two elements: subject matter jurisdiction and personal jurisdiction. *Subject matter jurisdiction* comes from the statute giving a court authority to hear certain kinds of cases. A juvenile court would have subject matter jurisdiction over charges of the neglect, abuse, or delinquency of children but could not hear negligence claims arising from automobile accidents. *Personal jurisdiction* arises when the defendant, whether a natural person or an artificial one such as a corporation, is notified that a lawsuit has been filed, usually by service of process, that is, receipt of written notice by the defendant. (Personal jurisdiction over the plaintiff occurs when the plaintiff files the action and thus submits to the court's jurisdiction.)

All facts are determined at the trial level, whether the trial is in a regular court, a specialized court, or an administrative agency. The factfinder may be the judge or a jury. At the trial level rules of evidence keep information that is immaterial or irrelevant out of the proceedings. Using the rules, the judge will determine the *credibility* of witnesses, that is, whether their statements are to be believed. In appellate courts, the judges only decide legal questions, without hearing witnesses or any other factual evidence. The attorneys prepare appellate briefs arguing the legal issues they wish the court to decide, for instance, whether the plaintiff or defendant received due process.

Federal courts, where many of the cases of interest to social workers are heard, have federal question and diversity jurisdiction. *Federal question jurisdiction* depends on whether a claim is based on federal statutes or arises under the Constitution, that is, questions of federal law. *Diversity jurisdiction* requires that the parties be citizens of different states. Under diversity jurisdiction federal courts can hear the same kinds of cases that a state court hears, such as breach of contract or negligence, if the claim reaches the jurisdictional amount, presently $50,000. A person from Ohio who wishes to sue a person from Michigan for $7,000 in damages arising from an automobile accident will have to go to court in either Ohio or Michigan. There is diversity, but the claim does not reach the jurisdictional amount.

It is usually presumed that a litigant is in the right court, that is, the one with jurisdiction; however, if jurisdiction is challenged, the issue must be resolved at once. A court cannot hear a dispute in a matter over which it has no jurisdiction. Courts are required to notice for themselves the absence of subject matter jurisdiction. Pleadings in all courts must allege the jurisdictional basis for the action.

Diversity jurisdiction was designed to give out-of-state litigants a neutral forum. However, once a federal court accepts a diversity case, it will apply state law, so that the accident of diversity does not give the out-of-state litigant an advantage. Congress periodically considers doing away with or further limiting diversity jurisdiction because of the amount of litigation it promotes.

Administrative Agencies

Social work is practiced primarily under the auspices of federal or state agencies. If you are curious about the authority of a public agency, you may check the statute setting it up either in the *United States Code* (cited as U.S.C. with volume number first and section number following) or the state code. As the statute creating the Children's Bureau illustrates, the enabling legislation may not spell out operating procedures for the agency. For these, you must check the published regulations of the agency.

Rules for federal agencies are found in the Code of Federal Regulations (cited as C.F.R. with volume number preceding and section number following). When an agency first promulgates regulations, they are published in the *Federal Register* to give any interested parties an opportunity to comment on them. Then they are published in C.F.R. Some states have a publication similar to C.F.R., but many simply print the regulations and keep them at the state office (the primary office in the state capital), or for an agency like the welfare department, in county offices.

Regulations are detailed, as anyone who has tried to cope with state revisions to a manual knows. Some laws rival regulations in their detail. For instance, civil service statutes may regulate in minute detail the rights and duties of a Civil Service Commission and state employees. Teacher tenure laws are often detailed, as are revenue and taxing statutes. A law setting up a department of vital statistics will spell out exactly how a birth certificate must be filled out, who is responsible for completing it, and how it can be corrected if it contains an error.

The federal Administrative Procedure Act of 1946 regulates how federal agencies conduct their activities. Some states have similar acts, defining rule making, rules of evidence for hearings, and procedures for adjudication proceedings.

The pretermination hearing mandated by *Goldberg v. Kelly* (1970) is a form of administrative agency lawmaking. The pretermination hearing is an evidentiary one. The hearing is a dispute-resolution mechanism by which disputed facts are determined. As in a court of law, the facts determine the outcome. As the Supreme Court said in *Goldberg*, these hearings do not have to be as formal as those conducted in a court of law.

METHODS OF SETTLING DISPUTES

The procedural aspects of lawsuits are usually of no concern to anyone who is not a lawyer. There are exceptions: It is important for everyone to understand that statutes of limitations limit the time within which actions must be brought, so that a person does not wait too long before discussing the problem with a lawyer. How many copies of a petition must be filed, where an action begins, how to serve opposing parties, and whether the action is in contract or tort are all of interest to the lawyer, not the litigant. From the earlier discussion of due process, we know that procedural fairness—notice, the right to appeal, and (in criminal cases) the right to assistance of a lawyer—is required in all legal proceedings.

It is important for social workers to respond to every legal document they receive. In *Walden v. Wishengrad* (1984) a child protection caseworker brought a civil rights case that was dismissed. She was arrested on a warrant and sat in a jail cell for an hour before testifying. The warrant was issued because she had previously ignored a subpoena ordering her to testify in a child abuse case. She sued the attorney for the Department of Social Services, the department, and the county, alleging the court held that the attorney was entitled to absolute immunity. Social workers must respond to subpoena and not ignore any legal papers received.

Civil Suits

The ordinary civil suit is the proceeding most people will confront if they have any contact with the legal system at all. The probate of a will, the tort claim for damages caused by an automobile accident, eviction of a tenant for nonpayment of rent, and a doctor's suit against a former patient for nonpayment of medical fees are all civil suits. The right jurisdiction—filing in a court with subject matter jurisdiction and making sure the opposing party is properly served—is vital.

A good client must tell the attorney everything about the transaction or dispute. As a social worker, you will understand this. We all appreciate that a fact or an opinion that seems irrelevant to a layperson may be crucial to understanding a situation. The lawyer will ask numerous questions and will request all written documents having to do with your case. It is critical that you or your client answer all questions truthfully and fully. Do not conceal any unfavorable information; doing so will only hurt your case.

Class Actions

Class actions are civil suits brought by one or more people for themselves and as representatives for others who were similarly injured by the same defendant. There must be a fact or a question of law common to every member of the class so that the dispute can be settled in one lawsuit.

The purpose of class action suits is the efficient use of court resources. When the number of people constituting a class is so large that it is impracticable or impossible to bring them all together, the class action settles all their claims in one lawsuit, and the decision becomes *res judicata,* "the thing is judged." This doctrine puts an end to litigation. Once a party has had its day in court, the decision is final—there is no opportunity to litigate the identical claim again. The Supreme Court has limited the use of this procedural device in a diversity action by holding that each member of the class must demand the jurisdictional amount (*Zahn v. Int'l Paper Co.,* 1973). *Zahn* illustrates the advantages of a class action: Property owners led by Zahn alleged that a New York corporation had discharged waste into a creek, polluting a lake that bordered their property and damaging the value and the utility of the property. The costs of having experts verify the pollution and the property damage—not to mention the other costs of litigation—would have been too great for a single property owner to bear. A recent class action suit, *Abbott v. Owens-Corning Fiberglas Corp.* (1994), was an appeal by more than 1,000 plaintiffs who filed product liability actions against approximately 70 manufacturers, suppliers, and distributors of asbestos-containing products for injuries from exposure to them. The defendants used the doctrine of *forum non conveniens,* which asserts that although the court may have jurisdiction, it is not a convenient forum. The case was reversed and remanded to determine whether the defendants' contact with the forum state satisfied the federal due process requirements.

The jurisdictional amount can be a problem in welfare litigation and other areas of concern to social workers. Civil rights statutes that give a federal court federal question jurisdiction have been used successfully in getting these disputes to court (Subrin & Sutton, 1973). Subrin and Sutton pointed out the ethical dilemma of a public lawyer when actions that would benefit the class as a whole will painfully delay relief for a particular client. Class actions have been brought to declare that mental hospitals and schools for people with mental disabilities deny a right to treatment. These cases did not seek money damages for the members of the class, but asked the court for sweeping orders that the state improve conditions in the institutions. Class actions have also been brought by inmates of penitentiaries and jails, alleging conditions so poor as to violate the Eighth Amendment's prohibition against cruel and unusual punishment.

Criminal Charges

A criminal charge is begun either by the filing of an information—a formal accusation of crime sworn to by the indictment of a grand jury—or by the prosecutor on the reasonable belief that a crime has been committed by the individual charged. The *grand jury* consists of 23 people who review evidence presented by the district attorney (for state matters) or federal attorney and decide whether there is enough evidence to bring the accused to trial. (The grand jury should be distinguished from the *petit jury*, a group empaneled by the court at the request of one or both parties to decide the facts in civil as well as criminal cases.)

A cautionary note that may be unnecessary: Never ignore any criminal charge. See a lawyer at once. Even for a traffic summons, if you fail to appear at the appointed time to resolve the matter, the judge may issue a bench warrant for your arrest so you will be in custody when your presence is again required.

Arbitration

Arbitration is a method of dispute resolution that does not involve the court system. Arbitration may be required by law or by a contract between the parties. Long-term contracts occasionally contain an arbitration clause. Parties must select a person to hear the dispute within the terms of the law or of their agreement. They then submit the disputed question to the arbitrator.

Submitting disputes to an arbitrator is usually less expensive and time-consuming than taking a contract dispute to court. The National Labor Relations Act of 1935 provides for the submission to arbitration of disputes arising under a labor contract. Because the recommendations of the arbitrator are not binding it is not true arbitration, but its effects are similar to the extent that the parties follow its suggestions and its sanctions are effective. Appeals of adverse social security or VA disability determinations are a form of dispute resolution. Although they take place under oath, the proceedings are typically informal. The hearing officer can hear evidence that might be inadmissible in a court procedure. The officer makes a determination based on evidence presented.

COST OF LEGAL PROCEEDINGS

Legal proceedings carry with them certain costs: attorney's fees, court costs (such as filing fees, the costs of transcribing testimony, and administrative overhead), and fees to experts for examining documents and sites or testifying about the psychological condition of a party. Payment of the attorney's fees can sometimes be arranged through a contingent-fee contract. In this arrangement the plaintiff pays the expenses of the lawsuit, including filing fees and other costs, and the attorney receives as a fee a percentage of the recovery. If there is no recovery, the attorney gets no fee. Contingent-fee contracts are not uncommon in workers' compensation and tort cases. A person injured in an automobile accident who cannot afford hourly lawyer's fees can benefit from a contingent-fee contract. Parties to a lawsuit pay their own fees; therefore, litigation can be expensive even if you win. When an attorney suggests compromise, consider it carefully, if only to avoid the costs of a lawsuit.

The Civil Rights Attorney's Fees Awards Act of 1976 provides that in proceedings brought in vindication of civil rights, such as employment discrimination on the basis of race, "the court, in its discretion, may allow the prevailing party, other than the United States, a reasonable attorney's fee as part of the costs." New consumer legislation also provides for payment of attorney's fees, and the judge in most civil cases has discretion to order the loser to pay the fees of the winner's attorney. *Maine v. Thibout* (1980) and *Maher v. Gagne* (1980) upheld attorney's fees in litigation about Aid to Families with Dependent Children payments.

Suit in *Forma Pauperis*

For those who cannot afford any court costs, a suit in *forma pauperis* may be the solution. By undertaking the suit as a pauper, the plaintiff is relieved of the obligation of paying court costs.

The suit in *forma pauperis*, created by statute, applies only to proceedings brought by natural persons. It is possible for a low-income client to combine a contingent-fee arrangement with a private attorney and a suit in *forma pauperis*.

The Supreme Court has upheld, against the allegation of discrimination because of poverty, the payment of a filing fee by indigent people seeking discharge in bankruptcy (*United States v. Kras*, 1973). The Court contrasts this with *Boddie v. Connecticut* (1971), which allowed a person unable to pay the filing fee in a divorce action to proceed in *forma pauperis* because of the fundamental interests involved in getting a divorce and the state monopoly of the means to resolve the dispute. *Ortwein v. Schwab* (1973) upheld the filing fee requirement for indigent people seeking to appeal the decision of a welfare agency.

Legal Aid

Understanding the legal problems of clients is of little value if you have no resources with which to help them. Because many social work clients are indigent, the usual stumbling block to resolving their legal problems is inability to pay the court costs. The legal aid offices in most large cities act as a kind of law firm in general civil practice for those at or below the poverty level who cannot pay attorney's fees. (*Trujillo v. United States*, 1974, said, however, that legal aid societies are not required to pay client court costs.) Legal aid offices do not usually take cases that could be handled by private attorneys on a contingent-fee basis.

The first legal aid office, the Legal Aid Society of New York, was incorporated in 1876 as an outgrowth of the activities of Arthur von Briesen, who gave advice and legal assistance to new immigrants from Germany (Bamberger, McCalpin, & Theophilus, 1966). The societies struggled with inadequate financing for over half a century, until the Office of Economic Opportunity (created by the Economic Opportunity Act of 1964) attempted to provide justice for all by supporting existing legal aid societies and setting up new ones. Federal financing of legal aid has been controversial; in 1974 Congress created the Legal Services Corporation Act, which transferred the multimillion-dollar federal program to a congressionally chartered nonprofit corporation (Arnold, 1974, 1975). The need for these services is readily apparent to anyone who works with clients unable to pay to defend their legal rights effectively.

Legal aid in Europe is also in a state of flux. The trend there has been to provide a system of "judicare" that uses state funds to pay private attorneys selected by indigent parties (Cappelletti, 1974). None of the systems used in Europe is entirely adequate; both European and American approaches are open to criticism.

Merket (1990) discussed the history of the legal aid system. Since the federal government has started supporting them as part of the war on poverty, it is no longer a service available only to urban poor people. Domestic relations is still a significant part of the workload, but there are now cases involving welfare benefits, food stamps, social security, public housing, and other entitlements.

Cousins (1993) wrote on civil legal aid in European countries. As in the United States, the largest area of the caseload is family law (Young, 1991). The Netherlands and the United Kingdom have more-developed systems than other countries. However, all schemes emphasize legal advice and representation rather than preventive legal services.

PREPAID LEGAL SERVICES

Medical insurance has diminished the burden of medical expenses for many Americans. Prepaid legal services or other comparable coverage has not developed to the same extent. In 1970 the American Bar Association selected the Bar Association of Shreveport, Louisiana, to implement a plan for members of Local 229 of the International Laborers Union of North America. The plan, the first in the country to provide broad coverage, paid a percentage of listed expenses in four areas: advice and consultation, office work, judicial and administrative proceedings, and major legal expenses (Hallauer, 1973). By 1988, 42 states had coverage. Dahlgren (1994) wrote that nationwide coverage is estimated at 18.5

million people and involves approximately 20,000 lawyers. Social workers can appreciate the preventive aspects of legal advice on contracts, property transactions, and tort claims, and so should welcome this trend toward legal support for clients whose income is too high for them to receive free legal aid but too low for them to bear the costs of litigation (Cole & Greenberger, 1974).

REFERENCES

Arnold, M. R. (1974). President Nixon approves legislation creating a National Legal Services Corporation. *American Bar Association Journal, 60,* 1045–1049.

Arnold, M. R. (1975). And finally, 342 days later . . . . *Juris Doctor, 5,* 32–37.

Bamberger, E. C., Jr., McCalpin, F. W., & Theophilus, W. (1966). Legal aid: Opportunity or octopus? A seminar on legal services for the poor. *Washington and Lee Law Review, 23,* 235–273.

Cappelletti, M. (1974). Legal aid in Europe: A turmoil. *American Bar Association Journal, 60,* 206–208.

Cole, G. F., & Greenberger, H. L. (1974). Legal services for welfare recipients. *Social Work, 19,* 81–87.

Cousins, M. (1993). Civil legal aid in France, Ireland, The Netherlands, and the United Kingdom—A comparative study. *Civil Justice Quarterly, 12,* 154–166.

Dahlgren, J. (1994). Consulting the future. *American Bar Association Journal, 80,* 77–78.

Hallauer, R. P. (1973). The Shreveport experiment in prepaid legal services. *Journal of Legal Studies, 2,* 223–242.

Merket, P. P. (1990). At the crossroads of reform: The first fifty years of American legal aid, 1876–1926. *Houston Law Review, 27,* 1–44.

Subrin, S. N., & Sutton, J. (1973). Welfare class actions in federal court: A procedural analysis. *Harvard Civil Rights–Civil Liberties Law Review, 8,* 21–76.

Young, M. W. (1991). English and American legal aid. *Cornell International Law Journal, 24,* 379–405.

STATUTES CITED

Administrative Procedure Act of 1946. Ch. 324, 60 Stat. 237, 5 U.S.C.S. §551.

Civil Rights Attorney's Fees Award Act of 1976. P.L. 94-559, 90 Stat. 2641, 42 U.S.C.S. 1988 et seq.

Economic Opportunity Act of 1964. P.L. 88-452, 78 Stat. 508, 42 U.S.C.S. §2701.

Legal Services Corporation Act of 1974. P.L. 93-355, 88 Stat. 378, 42 U.S.C.S. §2996.

National Labor Relations Act of 1935. Ch. 372, 49 Stat. 449, 29 U.S.C.A. § 158 et seq.

STUDY QUESTIONS

1. Is it true that because of the costs, poor clients of social agencies cannot sue to vindicate their rights?

2. Can social agencies create rules that have the force of law?

3. What branches of the court hierarchy are of most concern to social workers?

3

Organization of Social Agencies

Most social work is conducted in public and private agencies. Public social agencies are created by federal or state laws that spell out the organization of the agency and its authority. The laws themselves may be quite short, giving little indication of the size and complexity to which agencies must grow.

NONPROFIT CORPORATIONS
Except for social workers in private practice as sole practitioners or in partnerships or corporations that make a profit, most social work in private agencies is conducted in nonprofit corporations. (The American Red Cross—a corporation created by congressional charter—is a notable exception.)

Corporate Form
A corporation is an organization created in compliance with the requirements of state law as either a for-profit business or a nonprofit corporation, such as a college, school, country club, professional association, fraternity or sorority, or social agency. That a social agency charges for services does not affect its status as nonprofit, because the distinguishing feature is whether the corporation is organized to make a profit for shareholders. In a nonprofit corporation, the board of directors sets policy and a board-appointed executive and other employees hired by the executive manage day-to-day operations.

The corporate entity is created once it complies with state law and when a state officer issues it a charter. A corporation is an artificial person with many of the powers of a natural person. Thus, a typical incorporated social agency could sue and be sued, acquire property, and carry on any activities not forbidden by law. It would also be bound as an employer by laws like the Social Security Act of 1935 and the Fair Labor Standards Act of 1938.

The rights of a nonprofit corporation include certain tax exemptions and mailing privileges; the duties include providing the services for which the corporation was organized. In *Senior Citizens Stores, Inc. v. United States* (1979), a Texas nonprofit corporation lost its exemption from federal income taxes. It had been organized to provide training, jobs, recreation, living accommodations, and a general improvement in the physical and mental conditions of senior citizens by selling used clothing, furniture, and household appliances to the general public, but the court found the retail sales operation to be an end in itself rather than a means of accomplishing a charitable goal. In *National Retired Teachers Ass'n. v. U.S. Post. Serv.* (1979), nonprofit organizations sought an order declaring invalid a Postal Service regulation that prohibited them from mailing material about a separate but affiliated nonprofit organization that could not itself qualify for the lower rates. The court upheld the regulation. The availability of tax exemptions and mailing privileges must be checked at the time the agency is incorporated; the *Senior Citizens Stores* case illustrates how exemptions can be reexamined.

The Internal Revenue Service (IRS) determines whether an agency is entitled to the tax exemption. In *Eastern Kentucky Welfare Rights Org. v. Simon* (1974), a class of health and welfare organizations sought injunctive relief from an IRS policy that allowed private nonprofit hospitals to qualify as charitable without providing free or reduced-rate services to people unable to pay. The court upheld the power of the IRS to define *charitable* in terms of community benefit and promotion of health, saying, "The term charitable is thus capable of a definition far broader than merely the relief of the poor" (p. 1287). This relieved nonprofit hospitals from the obligation to provide free services to poor people. Further controls on nonprofit corporations are spelled out in 26 U.S.C.A. § 504, which provides for a tax on public charities on excess expenditures used to influence legislation.

Nonprofit agencies are not exempt from federal social welfare legislation. In *Richland County Ass'n for Retarded Citizens v. Marshall* (1981), houseparents were receiving a monthly salary less than that required by the Fair Labor Standards Act. The federal court held the Fair Labor Standards Act applicable to the private nonprofit corporation, which provided services for people with mental disabilities.

Nonprofit corporations do, however, have the same constitutional protections as natural persons. *Family Counseling Serv., Etc. v. Rust* (1978) held that a regulation of the Nevada State Board of Marriage and Family Counselor Examiners prohibiting advertisement of the cost and availability of counseling services violated the First Amendment. The court made the following statement:

> *Defendants do not assert that there is anything misleading about advertising the costs of a consultation session. Moreover, in this age of spiraling divorce, alcoholism and suicide rates, there is obviously a great need for basic truthful information regarding the availability and terms of counseling services. Those individuals on fixed or limited incomes have a right to know that they may avail themselves of counseling services without charge or at a reduced fee.* (p. 77)

Charitable Immunity

Administrators of social agencies traditionally drew comfort from the belief that the doctrine of charitable immunity barred negligence actions against their agencies, but 37 states have now abolished the doctrine because courts and legislatures feared that irresponsibility would follow from immunity (see, for example, *Garlington v. Kingsley,* 1974). This trend reinstates the principle that liability follows negligence, an idea discussed in chapter 2 under judicial lawmaking. With the demise of charitable immunity, agencies need to be sure they have sufficient liability coverage.

The *Harvard Law Review* (Note, 1987) discussed the history of charitable immunity and arguments for abandoning it. By 1986, 33 jurisdictions had abrogated the doctrine for some kinds of charities, and 16 of the 33 had abandoned it altogether. However, Bush (1988) discussed the Texas limited statutory re-creation of the common law doctrine of charitable immunity.

Cy Pres Doctrine

Administrators trying to change the direction of an agency to meet current needs occasionally find their hands tied by the provisions of wills and charters that direct the agency's funds and resources toward formerly laudable but now antiquated goals. A deceased benefactor, for instance, may have left valuable real estate to "be used to train orphaned boys in agriculture." If that real estate is now in downtown Houston and the agency has no orphaned constituents who wish to become farmers, what can the administrator and the board do? Over the years courts and legislatures have developed a doctrine that lets a charity ignore the literal provisions of a will or donation in order to meet current needs. The following case illustrates this cy pres doctrine.

Ada C. Pollock-Blundon Ass'n. Inc. v. Heirs of Evans
273 So.2d 552 (La. App. 1st Cir. 1973)
Ellis, J.

Plaintiff Ada C. Pollock-Blundon Association, Incorporated is a non-profit corporation which was organized for the purpose of maintaining and operating a school and home for Negro children. Over the years, the nature of its operation has changed, and today it operates a home for children referred to it by the Family Court for the Parish of East Baton Rouge.

In 1937, while the school and home were being operated, it received a donation from Alice A. Evans and Mary M. Evans of an undivided interest in a tract of land in East Baton Rouge Parish. The donation was made subject to the following conditions:

> *A part of the consideration of this sale is that the interest in said above described lands herein conveyed by the vendors to the purchaser and the land that shall be taken and received by the said purchaser, if and when said purchaser shall partition said land in kind with its co-owner or co-owners, shall be named and known as The Olin Hetser Evans Memorial Plantation for Colored Children, and said property shall be farmed by colored children, and the acreage is not to be dimished (sic), and no part of the property is ever to be mortgaged or encumbered in any manner whatsoever.*

On November 21, 1938, by the act of partition with its co-owners, plaintiff acquired full ownership of 113.12 acres of land in Section 53 and 70, Township 6 South, Range 1 East. Thereafter, the said property was, in fact, farmed by the children in the home, on a part time basis, until about 1950, when the entire tract was leased to Thomas F. Wallace for agricultural purposes. The lease remained in effect until 1970, when it expired. No farming operations have been conducted on the property by the children since the time of the lease.

The property has become quite valuable, being worth over $300,000 and, because of the change in the nature of their operation and the social changes which have occurred since the time of the donation, plaintiff now wishes to sell or lease the said property without restriction to use of the funds for the furtherance of its present operation.

To this end, it has brought this suit under the provision of R.S. 9:2331, asking that the court apply the cy pres doctrine so as to free the property from the said conditions and restrictions.

· · · · ·

It provides, in effect, that when circumstances have changed since the making of a conditional donation inter vivos for charitable, educational, or eleemosynary purposes, and the donor is deceased, and the change is such as to render compliance with the conditions "impractical, impossible, or illegal," the court may direct that the said donation be administered in a manner consistent with the general purpose thereof, and free from the said conditions.

· · · · ·

Turning now to the question of the propriety of the action of the district court in relieving the donation of its conditions, we note first that it is not claimed that compliance with the conditions is illegal or impossible. We are dealing solely with the question of impracticality.

The testimony in the case indicates that opportunities for Negroes have increased manyfold since 1937, and that they have made spectacular advances both socially and educationally. It may very well be that at the time of the original donation, there was great value in training in agricultural pursuits. This is no longer the case. Plaintiff has further shown that there is little likelihood that operation of the farm by the children in the home could be done profitably. It is shown that the highest and best use of the property is for residential, rather than agricultural, purposes.

We conclude that it is indeed impractical to carry out the original condition imposed relative to cultivation of the property by colored children. As noted above, the other conditions are regarded in law as not written. It is clear that the basic intention of the donors in the original donation was to assist the plaintiff in bettering the condition of children, and that this intention can be best carried out, in the light of present circumstances, by permitting the sale or lease of the property, free from all restrictions and conditions, and the application of the funds derived therefrom to the furtherance of the present aims of the plaintiff.

The association sued the heirs of the original donors, because they were the only ones with standing to challenge the planned use of the land. Omitted portions of the opinion deal with the Louisiana statute of limitations, the court recognizing that because more than 10 years had passed since the charity had farmed the land, a protest about its misuse would come too late. The court also said that because a prohibition against mortgaging or encumbering the property would take property out of commerce, it was to be considered as not written.

But the heart of the decision was the present impracticality of the terms of the donation. The court looked to the intention of the donor, found it to be bettering the condition of children, and determined that a different use of the land would further that intention.

Some cases turn not on the impracticality of the donation but on its illegality. *Guillory v. Adm'rs of Tulane Educ. Fund* (1962) considered provisions of Paul Tulane's will leaving a sum of money to be used for educating white men. Guillory argued that this racial and gender discrimination was illegal because Tulane had become a public institution as a result of its involvement with the state through tax benefits and scholarship provisions. The federal court disagreed, holding that Tulane remained a private university that could discriminate if it desired—but also holding that the federal courts could not enforce a discriminatory provision in a will. This left the university free to admit anyone, regardless of race or sex, solely on the basis of merit. The experience of the city of Philadelphia in dealing with Stephen Girard's will, in which he left money to establish a school for poor, white male orphans, is another example of the power of the courts to help an agency change direction as times and conditions change (Keats, 1978).

Social workers rejoice at the charitable motives that cause people to give. It is reassuring that the conditions of these gifts are not engraved in stone; modern uses for them can be found.

LIABILITY OF BOARD MEMBERS

A lay board serves public relations and educational as well as oversight functions for the agency. The good performance of the board depends on its members' knowledge of the agency's services, its current needs for personnel and funds, and its long-range goals. Many business corporations provide orientation programs for directors; social agencies should do no less.

An even more important reason for training board members is their personal liability for any violation of their duties as directors (Zelman, 1977). Directors are "fiduciaries." A *fiduciary* is one in a trust relationship with another to whom he or she owes the highest duty, as for instance an attorney to a client or a guardian to a ward. The efforts of directors must therefore be in the best interest of the agency they serve. Fiduciaries are not responsible for errors of judgment, but if fraud or injury could have been prevented by their more careful attention to duty, they are culpable.

Directors of business corporations have recently been the target of suits by disgruntled stockholders complaining of mismanagement or gross negligence in their oversight of corporate activities. An example is *Cottle v. Slover Communications, Inc.*, a shareholder-derivative action challenging a merger. As is true of business corporations, directors of nonprofit corporations may be sued for gross mismanagement—not by shareholders, because there are none, but by the funding source or the government. If directors mismanage the agency, enabling an employee to abscond with funds, allowing taxes to go unpaid, or misusing federal or state funds, they may be liable. There should be some preparation for this responsibility.

Preparing board members will help them understand the agency's need for professional services. Agency executives cannot expect board members who are lawyers, accountants, or architects to give large amounts of valuable professional advice free to the agency. The board member who understands the need for these services can interpret for funding sources such as the United Fund why such funding items are included in the agency budget. In *United Way, Etc. V. Department of Industry* (1981), the appellate court affirmed the order of the Labor Industry Review Commission requiring the United Way of Greater Milwaukee to pay workers' compensation to a man who was injured making a parachute jump at the kickoff promotion for the annual fund drive. He did not maintain a separate business and was held to be a statutory employee of the charity.

Well-informed board members may be able to arrange for the agency to secure student legal services from law schools (Allison, 1973). This arrangement serves many functions, among them informing potential lawyers of the services traditionally offered by community agencies so that they can provide better legal counsel in areas of potential agency liability.

Social agencies can be engaged in an extraordinary range of litigation. In *Homemakers H. & H. C. S., Inc. v. Chicago Home for Friendless* (1973), for instance, an agency got caught up in a trademark dispute. More common are civil rights suits like *Perez v. Sugarman* (1974), a suit against four municipal employees and two private child care institutions by a mother who alleged that her children had been detained by the institutions for over two years without her consent and without benefit of a court order or a hearing.

FOUNDATIONS

Some social agencies are supported by funds from private foundations (Pekkanen, 1979, 1980). In 1969 Congress overhauled the tax law relating to foundations to correct loopholes through which foundations were used as tax-avoidance devices. Administrators of agencies using such funds are well advised to hire tax attorneys and certified public accountants to handle the problems associated with such funds.

Jackson v. Statler Foundation (1974) is instructive. This was an action against 13 charitable foundations in Buffalo, New York, alleging racial discrimination in their refusal to hire the plaintiff as a director of their foundations, to give scholarships to his children, and to grant money to his foundation. The plaintiff was a *pro se* litigant, which means that he acted as his own attorney. In *pro se* cases the courts give a generous construction to the petition even if it does not follow all the procedural requirements of ordinary lawsuits. To prove a discrimination case, the plaintiff had to prove *state action,* that is, some involvement by the state in the contested behavior. The court found state action in the tax exemptions that the foundations enjoyed. To appreciate the importance of this decision, consider Judge Friendly's comments in dissent:

> *The Panel's fundamental error is its loose characterization of the "state action" doctrine. In holding that the federal and state tax exemptions provided to charitable foundations render them subject to civil rights suits challenging their policy decisions in the selection of beneficiaries, the panel relies primarily on three-judge court cases that have struck down tax exemptions for institutions practicing the crudest form of racial discrimination—the exclusion of blacks from attendance in schools or membership in clubs of a public nature. In these cases, however, the plaintiffs had sued federal or state officials to force revocation of tax benefits. The challenged action was clearly government action; the only question was whether that action sufficiently promoted private racial discrimination to render the decisions impermissible for a government officer. . . . In this case, by contract, the plaintiff has sued the foundations themselves. . . . A holding that an otherwise private institution has become an arm of the state is much broader and can have far more serious consequences than a determination that the state has impermissibly fostered private discrimination. The foundation might be exposed to damage claims for prior discriminatory conduct and could be required by a court to make decisions not only as to the disposition of its charitable donations but in the selection of its employees in accordance with the restrictions properly imposed on governmental agencies. . . . The implications of this decision for institutions receiving tax benefits of various sorts are staggering. Simply because of tax exemptions, private social agencies, community centers, institutions of higher education, homes for the young and the aged, endowed by private donors for the sole or preferential benefit of particular creeds or races, must open their doors equally to all, with every decision subject to judicial reexamination, even though this may impair or destroy the very purpose which led the donor to endow them. (pp. 637–638)*

REFERENCES

Allison, J. L. (1973). A legal service for social agencies. *Social Work, 18,* 103–104.

Bush, D. J. (1988). The constitutionality of the Charitable Immunity and Liability Act of 1987. *Baylor Law Review, 40,* 657–687.

Keats, J. (1978). Legacy of Stephen Girard. *American Heritage, 29,* 39–47.

Note. (1987). The quality of mercy: "Charitable torts" and their continuing immunity. *Harvard Law Review, 100,* 1382–1399.

Pekkanen, J. (1979). The great givers, part I. *Town & Country, 133,* 141–148.

Pekkanen, J. (1980). The great givers, part II. *Town & Country, 134,* 37–44.

Zelman, W. N. (1977). Liability for social agency boards. *Social Work, 22,* 270–274.

STATUTES CITED
Social Security Act of 1935. Ch. 351, 49 Stat. 620.

Fair Labor Standards Act of 1938. Ch. 676, 52 Stat. 1060, 29 U.S.C.A. § 201 et seq.

STUDY QUESTIONS
1. Why should social workers be familiar with the existence of nonprofit corporations as legal entities?
2. Why should social agencies provide training for their board members?

4

The Employment Relationship

The employment relationship arises through an employment contract. Not all contracts have to be in writing to be enforceable, so absence of a written document setting out their obligations and rights does not mean that employees and employer have not entered into a contract. The board of directors of the agency will hire a director and give that person authority to hire and fire other employees in the name of the corporation.

Often specific laws, such as civil service regulations, limit employment contracts, and employees cannot waive benefits provided by law, for instance, the employer's obligation to remit social security taxes or to provide a safe workplace. Civil service regulations governing the amount of vacation time or sick leave an individual will accrue may become part of the contract even though not specifically negotiated.

Congress and some states have enacted social legislation to protect employees. Although several statutes were enacted during the Great Depression of the 1930s, many are more recent. Social agencies—whether government or private nonprofit—were not originally covered to the same extent as other employers, although coverage has since been broadened in all areas. The sole practitioner in private practice who employs others will be subject to the statutes.

CIVIL RIGHTS ACT
The first civil rights acts were passed immediately after the Civil War to help emancipated slaves obtain their newly won rights. The act under

which most current litigation is brought was passed in 1964 and addresses discrimination in a variety of guises. The famous "public accommodations" provision of Title VI regulating local restaurant and motel businesses that "affect commerce" was challenged promptly and was upheld in *Katzenbach v. McClung* (1964) and *Heart of Atlanta Motel, Inc. v. United States* (1964).

Today Title VII of the act is much more prominent. It says in part:

Sec. 703(a) It shall be an unlawful employment practice for an employer

(1) to fail or refuse to hire or to discharge an individual or otherwise to discriminate against any individual with respect to his compensation, terms, conditions, or privileges of employment, because of such individual's race, color, religion, sex, or national origin; or

(2) to limit, segregate, or classify his employees or applicants for employment in any way which would deprive or tend to deprive any individual of employment opportunities or otherwise adversely affect his status as an employee, because of such individual's race, color, religion, sex, or national origin.

The act was amended in 1972 to change the definition of employer to cover government entities.

The Civil Rights Act of 1991, known as the Government Employee Rights Act of 1991, prohibits discriminatory practices and provides for confidential counseling when it is requested by an employee alleging a violation of rights. A chapter in the act, which deals with federally assisted programs, defines program to mean an instrumentality of the state or local government; public system of higher education; local educational agency; and organizations engaged in providing education, health care, housing, social services, or parks and recreation.

The Civil Rights Act of 1964 is used to challenge discriminatory practice in both private and public employment. In *Griggs v. Duke Power Co.* (1971) Chief Justice Burger, writing for a unanimous court, discussed the use by a company of a generalized intelligence test for employment that had a disproportionate impact on prospective black employees (they scored poorly). The Court held that although the act does not preclude the use of testing, tests used must be a demonstrably reasonable measure of job performance. *Griggs* thus created the job-related requirement for testing practices.

The decision was narrowed by the holding in *Washington v. Davis* (1976), a case challenging the use of a test of verbal skills that excluded a large number of black applicants for the position of police officer in the District of Columbia. The Court held that Title VII did not prevent the government from seeking to upgrade the communicative abilities of its employees, particularly when the job required special ability to communicate orally and in writing.

Tests are not the only requirements for employment that can be challenged under Title VII. In *Dothard v. Rawlinson* (1977) a woman applying for the position of correctional counselor in the Alabama state penitentiary system was rejected because she did not meet the height and weight requirements for the job. The Supreme Court held that because the height and weight requirements were not shown to be job-related, there was a prima facie case of discrimination. However, the Court further considered that because an estimated 20 percent of male prisoners in the Alabama prison system were sex offenders, the regulation, although it effectively allowed women to compete equally with men for only 25 percent of the correctional counselor positions, was directly job-related, a bona fide occupational qualification.

Title VII also applies in the academic setting. *Sweeney v. Bd. of Trustees of Keene State College* (1979) had a long history in the courts. Finally, the court of appeals upheld as not clearly erroneous the district court's conclusion that the basic reason the college had failed to promote a female college professor was because of her sex, that the reasons advanced by the college were merely pretexts for sex discrimination, and that the professor would have been promoted in a certain academic year but for the fact that she was a woman.

The statute under which many challenges to job terminations may be brought is 42 U.S.C. § 1983, which reads as follows:

Every person who, under color of any statute, ordinance, regulation, custom, or usage of any state or territory or the District of Columbia, subjects, or causes to be subjected, any citizen of the United States or other person within the jurisdiction thereof to the deprivation of any rights, privileges, or immunities secured by the Constitution and laws, shall be liable to the party injured in an action at law, suit in equity, or other proper proceeding for redress.

Under this statute, employees can sue for reinstatement by alleging that a constitutional right, such as freedom of expression under the First Amendment, has been denied (Stevens, 1980). In *Phillips v. Adult Prob. Dept., City & County of San Francisco* (1974), a deputy probation officer was suspended when he refused to remove a poster complimentary to H. Rap Brown, Angela Davis, and Eldridge Cleaver, who were at the time fugitives sought by the Federal Bureau of Investigation. The court of appeals affirmed the trial court's summary judgment of dismissing his action, holding that government interests in promoting the efficiency of public services outweighed the plaintiff's rights to constitutionally protected expression. Similarly, in *Harnett v. Ulett* (1972), appealing a jury verdict against a probationary psychiatric social worker discharged by a mental hospital for making calls to the Legal Aid Society on behalf of patients, the court of appeals affirmed, because there was no implied promise of retention and no allegation of conduct impugning the employee's reputation of honesty, integrity, or morality. It is interesting to note that plaintiff Harnett attempted to introduce the testimony of three professors of social work asserting that in making the phone calls, she was in conformance with her ethical responsibilities as a social worker. The court of appeals sustained the trial judge's ruling to exclude the testimony, confirming the trial judge's wide discretion in determining whether to admit or exclude expert testimony.

Several letter-writing cases illustrate the protection of First Amendment rights of expression. In *Atcherson v. Siebenmann* (1979) a juvenile probation officer sued the judge of the family court for reinstatement, back pay, and costs and attorney's fees; all were awarded. Although the facts are so convoluted that the case is best read in its entirety, basically, the plaintiff had written to the judge, accusing coworkers of falsifying their expense accounts. The trial judge ruled that the defendant's letter did not fall within the category of protected speech because it contained allegations that might interfere with the "maintenance of discipline by immediate superiors or harmony among coworkers." On appeal, this ruling was rejected because the "First Amendment protection of a public employee's speech depends upon a balancing of the employee's interest as a citizen in commenting on the matter at issue against the interests of the employing governmental entity in the efficient operation of public services" (605 F.2d 1058, at 1063). However, the court did hold that the judge had a *qualified immunity* defense against liability for damages, that is, he was protected from a lawsuit to avoid limiting his discretion in carrying out his duties.

In *Alicea Rosada v. Garcia Santiago* (1977) a social worker alleged that the secretary of social services of Puerto Rico had violated his First and Fourteenth Amendment rights by transferring him because he had written a letter criticizing the way the food stamp distribution program was administered. The court of appeals remanded the case for a determination of whether the transfer amounted to a *constructive discharge*— such a drastic change in the conditions of employment as to amount to termination—and for a determination of the amount of compensatory damages to which the worker was entitled. In *Wilderman v. Nelson* (1972) the court of appeals reversed the summary dismissal of a Section 1983 action brought by a welfare caseworker discharged during a probationary period. The plaintiff had written a memorandum complaining of a regulation directing that employees lose two hours of vacation time for each day they arrive late for work. The action had been dismissed without a trial of the merits of the claim because a probationary employee may be discharged within the probationary period without a hearing. The higher court held that the absence of a tenure "right" is immaterial to a claim of retaliation for exercise of the constitutionally protected right of free speech. In addition, when there is a genuine dispute regarding a free speech claim, summary judgment without full exploration of the issue is improper.

AGE DISCRIMINATION IN EMPLOYMENT

The Age Discrimination in Employment Act, passed in 1967, makes it unlawful for an employer who has 25 or more employees on each working day in each of 20 or more calendar weeks per year to refuse to hire or to discharge any person or to otherwise discriminate against a person with respect to compensation, terms, conditions, or privileges of employment solely because of that person's age. The protected ages are 40 through 70 years. There are certain exemptions in the act, the most important of which is the "bona fide occupational qualification," which permits an employer to select a younger applicant if age is a bona fide occupational qualification: A movie director need not hire a 45-year-old actress if the part calls for a teenager.

The exemption most often has been litigated in the area of safety, when an employer alleges that the slowing of reflexes with age can be dangerous to the public. This allegation has been upheld in the case of bus drivers (*Hodgson v. Greyhound Lines, Inc.,* 1975), but the burden of proof is on the employer to show that age is a detriment to proper performance on the job. Because age is unlikely to be a particular qualification in hiring social workers, except perhaps in work with teenage gangs, an employer covered by the act could hardly justify hiring a younger worker over an older one, unless there are other qualifications of education and experience that justify the choice.

The Older Americans Act was amended several times during the 1980s. These amendments tightened up the administration of community service projects and added provisions relating to coordinating administration of employment services to people in need to increase job opportunities.

REHABILITATION ACT OF 1973

The Rehabilitation Act of 1973 forbids discrimination on the basis of handicap in any program receiving federal funds. It is discussed in detail in chapter 13, which deals with the sociolegal problems of special groups. In addition, the Americans with Disabilities Act of 1990, also discussed later, is important.

Social workers have traditionally been sensitive to the needs of people with disabilities, one of which is the need for employment. Social workers should not expect many problems in this area of the employment relationship.

AMERICANS WITH DISABILITIES ACT OF 1990

The Americans with Disabilities Act of 1990 requires employers to make reasonable accommodation to the disabilities of current and prospective employees. Thus, lowering or raising a desk to accommodate a person using a wheelchair may be required. The law does not require employers to go to great expense to accommodate a person with disabilities. Social workers who are used to working with people with disabilities may be able to help them explain to potential employers how to accommodate a given disability (for example, installing a ramp is a common accommodation for people who use wheelchairs).

OCCUPATIONAL SAFETY AND HEALTH ACT

The Occupational Safety and Health Act (OSHA), passed in 1970, applies to employers "engaged in a business affecting commerce." This language implies that Congress has used the broadest interpretation of the commerce clause of the Constitution in its effort to reach all employers. If an employee uses supplies that have moved in interstate commerce, the employer will be covered. Furthermore, because the health and safety of employees affect their purchasing power, they have an indirect impact on interstate commerce. The act says that

> the basic duties imposed on an employer are that he: . . . shall furnish to each of his employees employment and a place of employment which are free from recognized hazards that are causing or are likely to cause death or serious physical harm to employees. (§ 654)

A workplace may be inspected for compliance with the safety standards promulgated by the secretary of labor. If a violation is found, the employer may be fined and given time to correct the violation. Challenges to the fact of violation or the amount of a fine are heard before an administrative law judge of the Occupational Safety and Health Review Commission—an example of administrative law at work—and may be appealed to a federal court of appeals.

There have been several important challenges to the act. In *Atlas Roofing Co. Inc. v. Occupational Safety & Health Review* (1977), a company objected that the finding of the fact of violation was not made by a jury. The Supreme Court held unanimously that the lack of a jury trial was not a violation of the Seventh Amendment because Congress can create new "public rights" and can establish an administrative remedy enforceable in an administrative tribunal without a jury trial. Another challenge came in *Marshall v. Barlow's Inc.* (1978), which called inspections of the workplace without a warrant a violation of the Fourth Amendment's prohibition of unreasonable search and seizure. Upholding the challenge, the Supreme Court held that searches without warrants are generally unreasonable for commercial premises and private homes, except for "closely regulated" industries. Therefore, an administrative warrant is necessary for such a search.

The requirement of probable cause is not as difficult a standard to meet here, however, as it is for search of a home. Probable cause in OSHA cases may be based not only on specific evidence of violation, but also on a showing that reasonable legislative or administrative standards for conducting an inspection are satisfied. Three dissenters were concerned that removing the element of surprise in inspection of workplaces might lead to a loss of protection for employees. However, a report by an employee of a suspected safety violation would constitute probable cause, so the act may retain its protective mechanism.

The U.S. Department of Labor in 1973 promulgated regulations that permit employees not to work because of a reasonable apprehension of death or serious injury, coupled with a reasonable belief that no other alternative is available (29 C.F.R. § 1977.2(a)). Employers may not discriminate against employees who exercise that right. The secretary's authority to establish such a regulation was upheld by a unanimous Court in *Whirlpool Corporation v. Marshall* (1980).

In practice, the Occupational Safety and Health Commission, created by the act, focuses its inspection efforts on the areas of greatest danger to employees. Industries that have a high incidence of employee injuries or that are targeted as particularly dangerous, such as manufacturing, construction, and logging, receive the greatest attention.

FAIR LABOR STANDARDS ACT

The Fair Labor Standards Act was passed in 1938 under the congressional authority to regulate interstate commerce. Its purpose is to provide a minimum wage and a maximum workweek excluding overtime for employees engaged in commerce or in the production of goods for commerce. Previously, Congress and several of the states had tried unsuccessfully to regulate working conditions, particularly the use of child labor, but the Supreme Court had held all such efforts as infringing on the constitutional freedom of contract. The 1938 act survived constitutional attack, and its coverage has broadened ever since.

Because coverage at first depended on the activities of employees, many cases went to the Supreme Court. A 1961 amendment (P.L. 87-30, 75 Stat. 65) broadened the act to provide *enterprise coverage.* A covered enterprise is one that has "employees engaged in commerce or in the production of goods for commerce, including employees handling, selling, or otherwise working on goods that have been moved in or produced for commerce by any person" (§ 203(s)). If one employee meets the statutory test, all employees are covered. The act was further amended in 1966 (P.L. 89-601, 80 Stat. 830, and P.L. 89-670, 80 Stat. 943) to include state employees in hospitals, elementary and secondary schools, and institutions of higher education. The enterprise coverage concept was challenged in *Maryland v. Wirtz* (1968) and was upheld over a dissent by Justice Douglas. Justice Douglas considered the amendment a serious invasion of state sovereignty not consistent with constitutional federalism.

The Fair Labor Standards Act was further broadened in 1974 (P.L. 93-259, 88 Stat. 55) to include public agencies, both federal and state, including agencies of the political subdivisions of a state. In *National League of Cities v. Usery* (1976), this amendment was challenged. The Supreme Court overruled *Wirtz* and struck the amendment down as a violation of the Tenth Amendment, adopting Justice Douglas's earlier argument. The Court spoke of interference with state sovereignty in determining wages paid to those employed to carry out government functions, such as fire and police protection. The limits of state sovereignty were not defined, although the Court gave examples such as determining the location of the state capital.

A subsequent case, *Garcia v. San Antonio Metro. Transit Auth.* overruled *National League of Cities* to permit federal regulation of wages and hours of state employees. Although *Garcia* was a 5 to 4 decision, it demonstrates how the Supreme Court can change its thinking and is not bound by precedent. It is unlikely that administrators of state social services agencies would pay less than minimum wage, but it is desirable to check with a state labor department if you have questions about wages, hours, or what records have to be kept.

The Fair Labor Standards Act contains the Equal Pay Act of 1963, which prohibits discrimination in working conditions, including pay, on the basis of sex. Several federal court cases have enforced this provision against public employers, including *Pearce v. Wichita County, City of Wichita Falls, Etc.* (1979) and *Usery v. Charleston County Sch. Dist., Etc.*

(1977), citing the *severability* clause in the Fair Labor Standards Act, the narrow holding in *National League of Cities,* and that the ability to pay female employees less than male employees for equal work is not among the "functions essential to the separate and independent existence" of the states. (Severability clauses are clauses stating that if any portion of the statute is invalid, the remaining parts can be enforced separately.) The cases held that the Equal Pay Act applies to states and their political subdivisions under the commerce clause. The Tenth Amendment does not bar exercise of that power. Recent amendments to the Equal Pay Act (29 USC § 206) provided for a minimum wage of $4.25 an hour and made special provisions for employers in American Samoa and Puerto Rico and for employees in domestic service.

In *Fitzpatrick v. Bitzer* (1976) the Supreme Court held that the principle of state sovereignty embodied in the Eleventh Amendment—and the amendment itself—is limited by section 5 of the Fourteenth Amendment, the enforcement provision. Title VII is an exercise of this enforcement power. Power reserved to the state by the Tenth Amendment is likely to be similarly limited. Therefore, a public employer may not discriminate on the basis of sex in payment of wages, although this area is not covered by the minimum wage and overtime provisions of the rest of the Fair Labor Standards Act. Thus, the U.S. Constitution is paramount. Provisions of the Fourteenth Amendment forbidding a state to deprive any person of due process and equal protection apply.

The history of the labor movement in the United States is a book in itself. Social work reformers participated in this movement, as witnessed by the creation of the Children's Bureau in 1912 to investigate the condition of child labor. And Frances Perkins, Franklin D. Roosevelt's secretary of labor, drew on her social work experience in helping to pass New Deal legislation (Martin, 1976).

The National Labor Relations Act of 1935 has been amended many times. It guarantees to workers the right to organize unions and to bargain collectively and, by creating the National Labor Relations Board, puts government in the business of ensuring that these rights are respected. The board has considerable discretion in determining unfair labor practices, although the courts may disagree with it. In *National Labor Relations Board v. Yeshiva University* (1980) the Supreme Court held that the faculty of a private university were managerial employees not subject to collective bargaining under the act. The board found the university guilty of an unfair labor practice for refusing to bargain with the Yeshiva University Faculty Association. The Court's 5 to 4 decision affirmed the refusal of the U.S. court of appeals for the second circuit to enforce the board's order. In *N.L.R.B. v. Cooper Un. for Advancement of*

Science (1986), the court held that full-time faculty members were not managerial employees and thus were entitled to protections of the National Labor Relations Act when they did not exercise effective recommendations or control in academic or nonacademic areas and were not managerial or supervisory employees.

However, *N.L.R.B. v. Florida Memorial College* (1987) held that a private college's faculty was not managerial or supervisory and was therefore not excluded from the bargaining requirements of the act. The court found that the faculty asserts insufficient control in terms of almost every relevant criterion examined by the Court in *Yeshiva*.

Glen Manor Home for the Jewish Aged v. N.L.R.B. (1973), the board's assertion of jurisdiction over nonprofit nursing homes, was held not to be an abuse of discretion. The court's language in the case is instructive:

Because of several factors, including limited resources and manpower, the board for the first 15 years of its existence determined on an ad hoc case-by-case method whether to assume jurisdiction in a particular case. This was replaced in 1950 with the pronouncement of a series of "yardsticks" to determine whether the board would assume jurisdiction in a specific type of case. These standards, issued in a series of 1950 decisions by the board, were essentially dollar volumes. The board held that if these dollar volume minimums of the value of inflow or outflow were exceeded in a particular case then it would take jurisdiction. In other cases it would decline to act. Different yardsticks were promulgated for different industries. The yardsticks were raised in 1954 and then lowered in 1958. . . . In 1959, Congress validated this board practice, extending over a span of 20 years, of declining jurisdiction in certain cases, by the enactment of § 14(c)(1) of the act. . . . This amendment authorizes the board to decline jurisdiction by "rule of decision or by published rules." There is no statutory jurisdiction over non-profit hospitals. . . . The board originally exercised no jurisdiction over proprietary hospitals, either . . . but asserted jurisdiction over them in 1967. . . . On the same day, the board asserted jurisdiction for the first time over proprietary nursing homes . . . and announced a gross volume of business yardstick of $100,000.

• • • • •

The board did not exercise jurisdiction over non-profit nursing homes until, in 1968, a district court held that the board could not constitutionally assert jurisdiction over proprietary nursing homes while renouncing jurisdiction over non-profit nursing homes. (p. 1148)

An interesting question is whether social workers should unionize (Alexander, 1987; Alexander, Lichtenberg, & Brunn, 1980; Deutsch,

1944; Shlakman, 1950; Tambor, 1973). Is a professional organization the appropriate vehicle for bettering working conditions and professional practice in general, or is a union better able to resolve employment problems? If unions become common, the problem of public employee strikes is inevitable. As of 1988, Alaska, Hawaii, Illinois, Minnesota, Montana, Ohio, Oregon, Pennsylvania, Vermont, and Wisconsin permitted strikes by public employees (Lewin, Feuille, Kochan, & Delaney, 1988; Podgers, 1980). The 18th edition of the *Encyclopedia of Social Work* (Alexander, 1987) provided the history of social workers' activity in unions but reported that unionization among social workers remains understudied and underpublicized. However, indications are that union participation by professional social workers is increasing. Social workers face a peculiar dilemma when the issue of strikes is raised because they must decide whether to go on strike and leave their clients without services.

EMPLOYEE BENEFIT LAWS
Employee Retirement Income Security Act
The Employee Retirement Income Security Act of 1974 comprehensively regulates employee benefit plans maintained by an employer engaged in commerce or in any industry or activity affecting commerce (Alperin, Eisenstat, Kreusch, & Netzorg, 1975). The statutory requirements for plans are detailed, including standards for eligibility to participate and for vesting of benefits, minimum funding standards, and standards of conduct for those serving in a fiduciary capacity to a plan. Because the employer receives tax benefits for contributions to a plan, the act ensures that the employees will have the benefit of those contributions at the time of retirement.

Social Security
Employees of state and local governments are not covered by the Social Security Act of 1935, although the state and the federal government may voluntarily agree to coverage; state contributions are paid directly to the Treasurer of the United States. A social worker employed by a state or federal agency may obtain coverage by working at covered employment after retiring from government service. The social worker who has a part-time private practice may acquire coverage by paying self-employment taxes on income from that practice.

Work performed for a nonprofit religious, charitable, educational, or other tax-exempt organization is now covered, with certain exceptions. A nonprofit agency should have its legal counsel check the statute to see whether it is exempt. Even if it is possible to waive coverage, employees generally find the benefits desirable. An employer who provides good medical and retirement benefits through private benefit plans should consider providing this extra protection even if it is not mandatory.

Coverage is obtained—and remitting taxes is required—if an employee earns at least $100 in a calendar year. Certain individuals are exempt, for instance, an ordained minister who has elected to be exempt or a student working for a university where he or she is enrolled and regularly attends classes.

Social Insurances

Retirement, survivors', and disability benefits as well as unemployment compensation are also provided in the Social Security Act. Covered employers must remit taxes for their employees. The social insurances are discussed again in chapter 12, which deals with the economic problems of clients. Problems that affect the relationship of a dependent to a covered wage earner are important to social workers.

Unemployment Compensation

The unemployment compensation program is a federal–state program operating in all states. As with other social legislation, its coverage has been gradually broadened over the years. The employer pays a federal tax on the base pay of all covered employees. Of that tax, 2.7 percent is forgiven if the employer pays a state unemployment compensation tax where the state has enacted a program, as all states have. The state tax can be reduced according to the *experience rating* of the employer, that is, the ability to maintain a stable work force. The employer gets an employer number from the Internal Revenue Service; the forms for remitting income, social security, and unemployment compensation taxes then come automatically.

In 1972 employment for religious, charitable, educational, and other tax-exempt organizations and for state and local government agencies became covered by unemployment compensation. There remain exemptions. Domestic employees are not covered unless they earn at least $1,000 during the quarter. Agricultural workers are not covered unless their employer paid a total of $20,000 or more to employees and had 10 or more nonalien employees.

The purpose of unemployment compensation is to provide a subsistence allowance for employees who lose their jobs through no fault of their own. In some states even an employee who leaves a job to accompany a spouse who has been transferred to another community may be eligible for benefits. If your client has lost or quit his or her job, check to see whether he or she is eligible. Benefits are not paid automatically. A former employee must file a claim with the employment security office, must register for work, and must be available for and able to work. An employee who leaves a job because of a disabling illness is unable to meet the "able to work" requirement and cannot receive benefits.

Workers' Compensation

The Industrial Revolution initiated the machine age, which brought us the comfort, ease, and mechanical marvels of modern society. It also initiated many of the accidents associated with industrialization that lead to the death and disability of employees.

Industrial accidents are an unavoidable risk of doing business. The cost of payments to injured workers can be passed along to the consumers of goods and services, much as the cost of replacing obsolete machinery and equipment is.

The need to compensate employees for injuries emerged when other programs of health and disability insurance did not materialize. All states now have workers' compensation programs to compensate employees for accidents and diseases arising out of and in the course of employment.

A client who has lost a job because of accident or illness should be encouraged to apply for workers' compensation promptly. The agency will determine whether the illness or accident is job-related and therefore covered.

Typical programs have a schedule of benefits for certain injuries and provide for periodic payments to compensate for wage loss. All statutes provide medical benefits: hospitalization, doctor's care, and medical expenses necessary for rehabilitation such as prostheses. Same states limit the extent of covered medical care.

The workers' compensation program in most states is administered by a board or commission. A number of states do not cover employers with fewer than a designated number of employees. Some states cover only hazardous or ultrahazardous businesses, with the classification occasionally left to litigation. Most statutes exclude domestic employees and workers engaged in casual employment not customarily performed in a particular employer's trade, business, or occupation. Charitable and nonprofit organizations may be expressly excluded from coverage or excluded as providing employment not carried on "for pecuniary gain." Most states offer limited protection for public employees.

Workers' compensation is usually financed by private insurance. Some statutes make insurance coverage elective. The employer would then self-insure, paying any award directly.

The laws in each state differ. Executives of social services agencies should consult with legal counsel to determine whether they are covered and how they should procure coverage, by purchasing insurance or as a self-insurer.

Compensation statutes schedule certain benefits to the dependents of deceased employees. Who is or who is not a dependent is determined by state law, although the law itself may contain unconstitutional classifications. In *Weber v. Aetna Casualty & Surety Co.* (1972) the Supreme Court held that the Louisiana workers' compensation statute, which denied coverage to unacknowledged illegitimate children, violated the equal protection clause of the Fourteenth Amendment.

The Supreme Court, in *Wengler v. Druggists Mutual Ins. Co.* (1980), held that the part of Missouri's workers' compensation statute that denies a husband compensation for his wife's death unless he is either mentally or physically incapacitated, whereas a wife qualifies without having to prove actual dependence on her husband's earnings, was unconstitutional, setting an important precedent.

Louisiana permits an *executive officer* suit by an injured employee against a superior whose negligence contributed to the injury in addition to the recovery against the employer through workers' compensation. *Phillips v. Phelps* (1979) was a suit for damages suffered by a correctional officer who was attacked and beaten by a prisoner when the officer sought to give the prisoner a mop for cleaning up. At the trial the jury awarded the plaintiff $137,000 against the officials responsible for providing safe working conditions. The verdict was reversed on appeal on the grounds that the plaintiff had negligently violated regulations by opening the cell door while alone. The Louisiana legislature has since made workers' compensation the exclusive remedy for an employee injured on the job.

REFERENCES

Alexander, L. B. (1987). Unions: Social work. In A. Minahan (Ed.-in-Chief), *Encyclopedia of social work* (18th ed., Vol. 2, pp. 793–800). Silver Spring, MD: National Association of Social Workers.

Alexander, L. B., Lichtenberg, P., & Brunn, D. (1980). Social workers in unions: A survey. *Social Work, 25,* 215–223.

Alperin, S. N., Eisenstat, D. H., Kreusch, G. A., & Netzorg, G. W. (1975). The Employment Retirement Income Security Act of 1974: Politics and problems. *Syracuse Law Review, 26,* 539–669.

Deutsch, A. (1944). American labor and social work. *Science and Society, 8,* 283–304.

Lewin, D., Feuille, P., & Kochan, T. (1988). *Public sector labor relations.* New York: Free Press.

Martin, G. (1976). How Miss Perkins learned to lobby. *American Heritage, 27,* 64–71.

Podgers, J. (1980). Public sector labor disputes: A balancing act for judges. *American Bar Association Journal, 66,* 548–550.

Shlakman, V. (1950). White collar unions and professionals. *Science and Society, 14,* 214–236.

Stevens, G. E. (1980). Private expression in public employment: "Intramural" speech and the Constitution. *American Business Law Journal, 17,* 535–541.

Tambor, M. (1973). Unions and voluntary agencies. *Social Work, 18,* 41–47.

STATUTES CITED

Age Discrimination in Employment Act of 1967. P.L. 90-202, 81 Stat. 602, 29 U.S.C.A. § 621 et seq.

Americans with Disabilities Act of 1990. P.L. 101-336, 104 Stat. 327, 42 U.S.C.S. 12101.

Civil Rights Act of 1964. P.L. 88-352, 78 Stat. 241, 42 U.S.C.A. § 2000e-2.

Employee Retirement Income Security Act of 1974. P.L. 93-406, 88 Stat. 829, 29 U.S.C.A. § 1001 et seq.

Equal Pay Act of 1963. P.L. 88-38, 77 Stat. 56, 29 U.S.C.A. § 206 et seq.

Fair Labor Standards Act of 1938. Ch. 676, 52 Stat. 1060, 29 U.S.C.A. § 201 et seq.

Government Employee Rights Act of 1991. P.L. 102-166, 105 Stat. 1088.

National Labor Relations Act of 1935. Ch. 372, 49 Stat. 449, 29 U.S.C.A. § 158 et seq.

Occupational Safety and Health Act of 1970. P.L. 91-596, 84 Stat. 1590, 29 U.S.C.A. § 651 et seq.

Rehabilitation Act of 1973. P.L. 93-112, 87 Stat. 355, 29 U.S.C.A. § 701 et seq.

Social Security Act of 1935. Ch. 351, 49 Stat. 620.

STUDY QUESTIONS

1. What is the Civil Rights Act and does it cover social workers in public agencies?

2. What is the purpose of the Fair Labor Standards Act and does it apply to public agencies?

3. How does workers' compensation concern social work practice?

5

Practice Settings

Social work is an organized activity recognized by society and carried out in a variety of settings. The traditional settings were federal or state agencies and nonprofit corporations supported by local monies or funds from an endowment, from a foundation, or from community drives such as the United Way. These agencies still provide services of the widest possible variety: from traditional family service to practice in family courts; from public assistance and placement of children to supervision of homemaking services and counseling in nursing homes.

The private practice of social work has increased dramatically. Anyone contemplating private practice should consult *Social Work in Private Practice* (Barker, 1992) for a more in-depth discussion of the legal isssues mentioned here such as financing, contracting with clients, and other concerns. These subjects were also briefly discussed in *Who We Are* (Gibelman & Schervish, 1993), a study of the social work labor force as reflected in the membership of the National Association of Social Workers. Hopps and Collins (1995) discussed practice settings and the legal regulation of practice. All 50 states and the District of Columbia currently regulate the profession. According to Gibelman and Schervish (1993), the primary practice areas of professionals are mental health, children, medical clinics, and family services.

CONSTRAINTS OF PUBLIC SETTINGS

The social worker in public settings carries out programs created by the public through elected representatives. Although members of the public are rarely aware of the intricacies of social programs, the programs do represent the choice, considered or not, of the voters. Inadequate financing or discriminatory programs may represent the wishes of an electorate choosing among the conflicting demands for tax money. The social worker who protests is risking a less-than-enthusiastic response; Harris (1974a, 1974b) presented a chilling report of what happened to one public employee, a teacher, when he protested the Vietnam War.

The Hatch Act

Beyond the legal and financial constraints on social workers in government settings, the Hatch Act of 1939 imposes a further restraint on freedom of political expression. The act considerably limits the participation in political activities of employees of public agencies that receive federal funds. For instance, they may neither run for political office themselves nor campaign actively for others.

United States Civil Service Comm'n v. National Assn. of Letter Carriers (1973) upheld the constitutionality of the act, reaffirming a holding in a challenge to the act shortly after its passage in 1939. The Supreme Court emphasized that it is in the best interest of the country for federal employment to depend on meritorious performance rather than political service. Because employees retain the right to vote as they choose and to express opinions on political subjects and candidates, the act's restrictions on active participation in partisan political activities do not violate First Amendment rights of freedom of expression and association.

In an appendix to the *Letter Carriers* opinion, the Court set out that portion of United States Civil Service Commission Form 1236 (Political Activity and Assessment, September 1939) that details permissible and impermissible activities. For instance, a public employee could vote at a primary meeting or caucus but could not participate in deliberations. An employee could be a member but could not act as an officer of the caucus or a political club, or address it. An employee could make political contributions but could not solicit or collect them. Employees may vote as they please, free from interference, solicitation, or dictation by a fellow employee or superior and may express their opinions privately on political subjects but may not run for national, state, county, or municipal office. Justice Douglas, in dissent, complained that the prohibitions were so ambiguous as to have a chilling effect on an employee's activities, although his real quarrel was with the statute's effect on First Amendment rights to speak, to petition government, and to assemble.

The Hatch Act certainly does limit freedom of speech, but none of the constitutional rights is absolute. The political activities of federal or state employees are governed differently than those of private citizens, but because there is no absolute right to government employment it may carry restrictions.

The Hatch Act does not prevent social workers from engaging in social action. Giving testimony before legislative committees on social programs and lobbying for social legislation are not proscribed. However, active support for a particular candidate—say, one who promises to push national health insurance—is prohibited.

Congress amended the Hatch Act effective January 1, 1975. The act still prohibits management from requiring employees to contribute to or work for a particular candidate, and state and local employees covered by the Hatch Act are still prohibited from using the authority of their position to influence an election, but covered employees no longer include those "employed by an educational or research institution, establishment, agency, or system which is supported in whole or in part by a state or political subdivision thereof, or by a recognized religious, philanthropic or cultural organization."

A 1993 amendment again eased the proscriptions of the act. Employees may now take an active part in political management or in political campaigns, although employees are still prohibited from coercing subordinates, soliciting funds, and running for office. There are also prohibitions against engaging in political activity while on duty, in a government office, wearing a uniform or an official insignia, or using a government vehicle. If you work in a federally supported agency and want to participate in a campaign, be sure to check the current Hatch Act rules. If you are a state employee, ask the state Civil Service Commission about relevant state law. Many state laws on political activity by state employees are less restrictive than the Hatch Act, so you may have more scope for political activity.

Broadrick v. Oklahoma (1973), heard along with the *Letter Carriers* case, affirmed the constitutionality of the state civil service acts' prohibiting of various political activities. The challengers did not question Oklahoma's right to place evenhanded restrictions on employee partisan political conduct, conceding that the restrictions served important interests by ensuring job security, providing an environment free from the vicissitudes of the election process, and protecting employees from political extortion. Their complaint was that two paragraphs were vague and overbroad. Justice Douglas, again dissenting, wrote,

> *These people are scrubwomen, janitors, typists, file clerks, chauffeurs, messengers, nurses, orderlies, policemen and policewomen, night watchmen, telephone and elevator operators, as well as those doing some kind of administrative, executive or judicial work. . . . A bureaucracy*

that is alert, vigilant, and alive is more efficient than one that is quiet and submissive. It is the First Amendment that makes them alert, vigilant, and alive. It is suppression of First Amendment rights that creates faceless, nameless bureaucrats who are inert in their localities and submissive to some master's voice. (p. 2920)

Justice Brennan also wrote a dissenting opinion, in which Justices Stewart and Marshall joined. His concern was that critical phrases of the Oklahoma act were not defined and that, in contrast to the elaborate regulations defining the prohibitions of the Hatch Act, Oklahoma had merely five rules, which he felt did not provide explicit guidance.

It would be naive to deny that social workers need protection from political and other forms of harassment and discrimination. Consider *London v. Florida Dep't of Health & Rehab. Serv.* (1971). The only black social worker in a Florida county was transferred to another county after numerous complaints by public officials that he was "belligerent and antagonistic"; the circuit court said that these complaints were engendered by his civil rights activities. However, for several months after his transfer, the social worker was warned that his work was deficient, and he was then dismissed for inefficiency. Both the district and circuit courts found evidence to demonstrate that his dismissal was based on his work record and was not racially motivated. The circuit court expressed concern about the possibility of continuing discrimination but felt that the trial court was in a better position to judge this.

Although state civil service acts limit political activity by social workers, they also protect social workers from employers who demand political allegiance. For instance, *Illinois State Employee Union, Council 34, Etc. v. Lewis* (1972) held that a state employee may not be discharged solely for refusing to transfer his political allegiance from one party to another (Maher, 1974). *Branti v. Finket* (1980) held that the First and Fourteenth Amendments prohibited a new public defender from dismissing two assistant defenders solely because of party affiliation.

Civil Service Rules

Civil service commissions manage the merit selection and retention of federal and state employees. Federal grants to states for social programs mandate merit selection for employees of the programs, and state and local governments recognize merit selection as an efficient way to create and maintain a trained bureaucracy.

In addition to the limits on employee rights that the civil service laws create, there are corresponding protections against arbitrary discharge. In *Sampson v. Murray* (1974) and *Arnett v. Kennedy* (1974), the Supreme

Court refused to support injunctions against the discharge of employees without a pretermination hearing. *Sampson* involved a probationary federal employee; *Arnett,* a nonprobationary one. For both, the Court held that without a showing of irreparable injury, the postdischarge hearing provided all necessary due process, allowing back pay and reinstatement for an employee wrongfully discharged.

In *Larry v. Lawler* (1978), an individual rated ineligible for federal employment because of alleged alcoholism and abusive behavior challenged not the postdischarge hearing itself but how it was conducted, alleging that it violated due process. The Civil Service Commission had given him a summary of its investigation but did not grant an oral hearing to rebut the charges. The court first determined that Larry's interest rose to the level of a constitutionally protected "liberty" or "property" interest because he had been totally debarred from federal employment for up to three years. The commission was required to expunge his record.

In *Herzbrun v. Milwaukee County* (1974), suspended and discharged county welfare department employees attacked the constitutionality of a county civil service rule under which they had been disciplined. The employees had engaged in a massive disruption of the telephone communications system of a welfare office after a dispute between the union local and the county. The court held that the rule was not unconstitutionally overbroad:

> *It is clear that both the federal statute considered in* Arnett v. Kennedy *and the county rules before us here are directed at employees' behavior including a wide spectrum of harmful, constitutionally unprotected conduct, not intended to convey any message and manifestly subject to state regulation.* (pp. 1194–1196)

Free speech protections do not cover disruptive behavior.

PITFALLS OF PRIVATE PRACTICE

The social worker engaged in private practice, even part-time, has the same legal problems as workers in nonprofit social agencies. The social worker with even a part-time receptionist or typist has all the obligations of an employer. (Accountants and attorneys who advise the private practitioner are usually self-employed independent contractors, so the practitioner is not responsible for remitting taxes on their behalf.)

Contracts

The factor of legal capacity to contract may concern the social worker who treats minors. In all states, minors can *disaffirm* their contracts—that is, free themselves from the obligations—simply on the basis of their minority. This long-established policy is designed to protect minors from their own irresponsibility and the overreaching of adults. Minors may not disaffirm contracts for "necessaries" such as food, clothing, and shelter but may be able to disaffirm and avoid fees for casework services unless a court determines that the services were necessary. It is better practice, for this and many other reasons, to see a minor only with the consent of a parent or legal guardian.

Another contractual element to consider is "legal object." Where a state license is required to protect the public from practice by untrained individuals rather than as a revenue-raising measure, you may not be able to collect for services if you are not licensed and you may be subject to state action for unauthorized practice. Similarly, a nonphysician who performed an emergency appendectomy that saved a person's life would not recover an agreed-on fee in a lawsuit. A contract for an unlicensed social worker to provide services as a licensed professional would have an illegal object and would be unenforceable.

Other illegal contracts are those in restraint of trade. Partial restraints of trade that are reasonable both as to time and geography are permissible if they are ancillary to another contract. For example, a social worker, on retiring, decides to sell her private practice to another social worker and agrees not to practice for a limited period of time in a circumscribed area. This would be permissible: The restraint is ancillary to the sale of the practice. If the seller violated the agreement not to practice, a court could issue an injunction to stop and award the buyer monetary damages. Contracts with such restraints of trade are rare in social work but do exist in other professions and in trades and businesses, where the courts examine them carefully to determine their legality.

Leases

One contract of special concern to social workers in private practice is the lease. A lease of office space is a contract between the worker and the landlord, whereby the worker agrees to pay a certain rent in return for peaceful possession of the premises. A lease may be on a month-to-month basis or for a fixed term, usually a year or longer. When signing a lease for a fixed term, check whether you must give a certain period of notice before vacating, whether the premises can be subleased, and so on. If your private practice does not work out, you may be unable to terminate the lease and could be responsible for paying rent on unused space, unless the lease permits someone else to assume the obligation. Also find out what the lease provides concerning occupancy at night or on weekends. If the office is in a large building, will there be someone on duty to direct clients? Is the office heated and cooled? Who pays the utilities? What are the responsibilities for repainting or other repairs if the premises are damaged by clients? These questions should be answered before you sign a lease. Asking a lawyer to read the lease before you sign it is advisable.

Zoning

Zoning is comprehensive municipal regulation of land use within designated geographical areas; it includes restrictions on building use. Where zoning restricts certain areas to residential uses, commercial use is limited or forbidden. Many zoning ordinances prohibit any commercial activity in residences, so before you turn the den or front bedroom into an office, consider the zoning restrictions.

Malpractice

Malpractice is negligence in the practice of one's profession. Although state and federal employees often have a qualified immunity against errors of judgment (*Downs v. Sawtelle*, 1978; but see also *Frank v. State*, 1980), the private practitioner has no such protection and must carry insurance to protect against liability. (The National Association of Social Workers sponsors a professional liability policy underwritten by the American Home Assurance Company that covers damages arising out of the performance of professional services.)

One way to protect against malpractice loss is to keep careful records that reflect the services rendered. Good records also support the amount of fees, because they show the number of visits, their length, and other information on which the fee is based. One problem with social work records is whether they contain information that will be damaging to the client if the records are subpoenaed. Privileged communication laws in some states prevent the production of such evidence without the client's consent. However, a client who sues a social worker for malpractice is presumed to have waived the privilege, and workers may use client records in their own defense.

Malpractice cases do arise. In *Horak v. Biris* (1983), a former client sued a social worker who had had sexual relations with the client's wife when both had come for marital counseling (see Jones, nd). The trial court dismissed the husband's case on the basis of a prior decision, but the appellate court held that his charges of mishandling of the transference phenomenon and the sexual relations stated a cause of action for malpractice. The decision notes the *NASW Code of Ethics* (National Association of Social Workers, 1979). It also notes the possibility of license revocation if a social worker is found to be unfit or incompetent by reason of gross negligence. In discussing vendorship, Shatkin, Frisman,

& McGuire (1986) noted that the major impact was an increase in the number of social workers in solo private practice.

Insurance Reimbursements
Although the Internal Revenue Service allows clients to deduct charges for mental health services provided by social workers, insurance carriers do not always recognize social worker fees as reimbursable. The attempt to obtain third-party vendor status and recognition can be a long struggle (Kurzman, 1973). The modern mental health care delivery system depends so heavily on clinical social workers that they should be covered by insurance plans (Fishman, 1976).

To receive third-party reimbursement, social workers must meet the licensing, regulation, and certification requirements of their state (Biggerstaff, 1995). As of 1994, 31 states and the District of Columbia had vendorship laws that support third-party reimbursement for social work services (Goldstein & Beebe, 1995; Whiting, 1995).

The third-party reimbursement provided in the Civilian Health and Medical Program of the Uniformed Services (CHAMPUS, 1958) is by far the clearest example of a comprehensive plan. This program, administered by the U.S. Department of Defense, provides medical care to active and retired members of the uniformed services (U.S. Army, U.S. Navy, U.S. Air Force, Public Health Service, Coast Guard, and National Oceanographic and Atmospheric Administration), to their dependents, and to dependents of retired and deceased personnel. The Federal Employee Health Benefits Program now permits payment for services by a qualified clinical social worker, that is, one licensed or certified by the state where he or she practices, or, if there is no state licensing, certified by a national professional organization (Federal Employee Health Benefits Act of 1959).

In 1974 an agreement between Bankers Life of Iowa and the National Association of Social Workers granted vendor status to social workers ("Social Workers Gain Third Party Status," 1974) who were licensed or registered in California, Illinois, Kansas, Kentucky, Louisiana, Maine, Michigan, New York, Oklahoma, Rhode Island, South Carolina, Utah, Virginia, and Puerto Rico. In 1978 Blue Cross and Blue Shield of Utah recognized the clinical social workers in Utah as independent third-party vendors ("New Vendorship Breakthrough," 1978).

In *Wheelahan v. State of Louisiana through the Louisiana Claims Review Board* (1979), a state employee sought reimbursement for money paid to a social worker who had treated her for a nervous disorder. The employee's argument—that the benefits plan of state employees must conform to the insurance code, which does permit reimbursement of social workers—was denied on the basis that her employer, not she, was the policyholder. The court indirectly held that the plan was not subject to the insurance code. There was no coverage for payment to a social worker who rendered services to employees of the State of Louisiana.

That situation has been changed. Louisiana's state employees may now recover for treatment by social workers. However, the client must go through the Louisiana Biodyne Incorporated group, which lists those social workers approved for reimbursement. Check your own state's regulations if you have state employees as clients.

In *Blue Shield of Virginia v. McCready* (1982), the Supreme Court held that a subscriber who was not reimbursed under a group health plan for costs of treatment by a psychologist had standing to seek treble damages for defendant's alleged violations of the Sherman Act (which outlaws antitrust violations). The insurance carrier had refused to reimburse subscribers for psychotherapy performed by psychologists unless such claims were billed to a physician, but provided reimbursement for comparable treatment by a psychiatrist. Cases like this clearly open up avenues of reimbursement.

INTERNATIONAL SOCIAL WORK
Historical Roots

American social workers learned the historical roots of their profession by studying the pioneering work of charity organizations in Great Britain and Europe. Sidney and Beatrice Webb and others documented the need for social legislation; their example inspired pioneers in American social work. However, actual practice across national boundary lines is rarer than theoretical interchange; it usually occurs in relief operations following wars and natural disasters, when social workers, under the auspices of the International Red Cross or the United Nations, operate within the legal jurisdiction of those organizations, and the agency settles problems of logistics, nationalities, and other legal questions. (Witner, 1944, analyzed the aspects of local custom that workers in these situations should take into account to be effective.)

Foreign Adoptions

Another area in which social workers have international dealings is the adoption of foreign children (Pettiss, 1958). Although foreign adoptions require the same careful practice as domestic ones do, there are additional legal constraints of quotas and immigration procedures for children brought into the United States (Johnson, Edwards, & Puwak, 1993). Intercountry adoptions greatly increased when, in the Refugee Relief Act of 1953, Congress allowed nonquota visas for orphans. The admission of foreign orphans is now handled by the Immigration and Naturalization Service of the U.S. Department of Justice. Once children are admitted to this country, the adopting parents must comply with the adoption law in their home state. A hearing before the U. S. House of Representatives (1991) discussed Romanian adoptions and the many legal problems associated with them.

The number of social workers trained in this country who practice in foreign countries is unknown. Social workers and other professionals have long been interested in foreign institutions and have sought to transplant attractive ones to this country. The institution of ombudsman is an example. An ombudsman oversees public administration, accomplishing by power of persuasion and prestige of office beneficial changes in practices of the state and its agents. Very occasionally, the ombudsman will recommend social legislation to alleviate abuses. An ombudsman is thus a watchperson against abuses and arbitrary behavior by public administrators (Gelhorn, 1966; Payne, 1972). Other foreign institutions may or may not transplant as easily as has the ombudsman. When social workers trained in this country transplant their services to other countries, similar questions must arise about American institutions (Weber, 1974).

With the use of computer systems, transferring technology from one country to another may become possible and even frequent. Chatterjee (1995) discussed the possibilities of technology transfer in personal social services.

FUNDRAISING

Many social workers practice in private agencies supported by United Way campaigns or private fundraising. Although not fundraisers themselves, social workers should assure themselves that the agency's fundraising is not fraudulent. A North Carolina law regarding the solicitation of funds for charitable purposes sets a three-tiered definition of "reasonable fees" to decide the legality of the fundraiser's fee. In *Riley v. National Fed'n of the Blind of N.C.* (1988), charitable organizations, professional charitable solicitors, and others challenged the law. The Supreme Court subjected the law to strict scrutiny and found the definition of reasonable fee was not tailored narrowly enough to the state's interest in preventing fraud; other provisions, including the licensing requirement for professional fundraisers, were also found unconstitutional.

REFERENCES

Barkan, T. W. (1973). Private casework practice in a medical clinic. *Social Work, 18,* 5–9.

Barker, R. L. (1992). *Social work in private practice* (2nd ed.). Washington, DC: NASW Press.

Biggerstaff, M. A. (1995). Licensing, regulation, and certification. In R. L. Edwards (Ed.-in-Chief), *Encyclopedia of social work* (19th ed., Vol. 2, pp. 1616–1624). Washington, DC: NASW Press.

Blomquist, D. C., Gray, D. C., & Smith, L. L. (1979, October). Social work in business and industry. *Social Casework, 457–462.*

Chatterjee, P. (1995). Technology transfer. In R. L. Edwards (Ed.-in-Chief), *Encyclopedia of social work* (19th ed., Vol. 3, pp. 2393–2397). Washington, DC: NASW Press.

Cohen, M. (1966). The emergence of private practice in social work. *Social Problems, 14,* 84–93.

Fishman, B. (1976). Third-party reimbursement for mental health care delivered by clinical social workers: The case for its expansion. *Clinical Social Work Journal, 4,* 302–318.

Gelhorn, W. (1966). The Norwegian ombudsman. *Stanford Law Review, 18,* 293–321.

Gibelman, M., & Schervish, P. H. (1993). *Who we are: The social work labor force as reflected in the NASW memberships.* Washington, DC: NASW Press.

Goldstein, S. R., & Beebe, L. (1995). National Association of Social Workers. In R. L. Edwards (Ed.-in-Chief), *Encyclopedia of social work* (19th ed., Vol 2, pp. 1747–1764). Washington, DC: NASW Press.

Harris, R. (1974a, June 17). Annals of law. *New Yorker,* pp. 37, 83.

Harris, R. (1974b, June 24). Annals of law. *New Yorker,* pp. 37, 79.

Hopps, J. G., & Collins, P. M. (1995). Social work profession overview. In R. L. Edwards (Ed.-in-Chief), *Encyclopedia of social work* (19th ed., Vol. 3, pp. 2266–2282). Washington, DC: NASW Press.

Johnson, A. K., Edwards, R. L., & Puwak, H. (1993). Foster care and adoption policy in Romania: Suggestions for international intervention. *Child Welfare, 72*(5), 489–506.

Jones, J. B. (1987). Social worker malpractice. *American Law Reports, 4th ed., 58,* 977–983.

Kurzman, P. (1973). Third-party reimbursement. *Social Work, 18,* 11–12.

Maher, T. F. (1974). Freedom of speech in public agencies. *Social Work, 19*, 698–703.

National Association of Social Workers. (1979). *NASW code of ethics.* Washington, DC: Author.

New vendorship breakthrough is made in Utah. (1978, September). *NASW News,* p. 13.

Payne, J. E. (1972). Ombudsman roles for social workers. *Social Work, 17*, 94–100.

Perlis, L. (1978, May). Industrial social work—Problems and prospects. *NASW News,* pp. 3, 8.

Pettiss, S. T. (1958). Effect of adoption of foreign children on U.S. adoption standards and practices. *Child Welfare, 37*, 27–32.

Shatkin, B. F., Frisman, L. K., & McGuire, T. G. (1986). The effect of vendorship on the distribution of clinical social work services. *Social Service Review, 60*(3), 437–448.

Smith, A. D. (1970). The social worker in the legal aid setting. *Social Work Review, 44*, 155–168.

Social workers gain third party status from Bankers Life. (1974, November). *NASW News,* pp. 1, 12.

Tropp, E. (1974). Expectation, performance, and accountability. *Social Work, 19*, 138–148.

U. S. House of Representatives, Committee on the Judiciary, Subcommittee on International Law, Immigration, and Refugees. (1991, June 5). Hearings.

Weber, S. (1974). Social work in Scotland: Lessons for America. *Social Work, 19*, 298–304.

Whiting, L. (1995). Vendorship. In R. L. Edwards (Ed.-in-Chief), *Encyclopedia of social work* (19th ed., Vol. 3, pp. 2427–2431). Washington, DC: NASW Press.

Witner, H. L. (1944). A theoretical basis for foreign relief and rehabilitation operations. *Smith College Studies in Social Work, 14*, 273–310.

STATUTES CITED
CHAMPUS. P.L. 85-861, 72 Stat. 1445, 10 U.S.C.A. 1079, 5 U.S.C. 301 (1958).

Federal Employee Health Benefits Act of 1959. P.L. 86-382, 73 Stat. 708, 5 U.S.C.A. 8901 (11).

Hatch Political Activity Act of 1939. Ch. 410, 53 Stat. 1147, 6 U.S.C.A. 1501.

Refugee Relief Act of 1953. Ch. 336, 67 Stat. 400.

Sherman Anti-Trust of 1890. Ch. 647, 26 Stat. 209, 15 U.S.C.S. § 1 et seq.

STUDY QUESTIONS

1. What should concern you if you decide to go into private practice?

2. What are some of the constraints of working in a public setting?

6

The Legal Environment of the Profession

As an activity matures from an occupation into a profession, it slowly acquires the trappings of its new status: formalized education, a title, legal protection of that title, and an obligation to the society that sanctions use of the title to conduct activities for the general good. A profession has a transmissible body of specialized knowledge, and it usually insists on governing itself under a code of ethics that contains sanctions imposed by peers against unethical behavior (Gilbert & Specht, 1976). A profession requires its practitioners to take responsibility for their judgment in professional matters beyond the obligation of the merchant not to purvey a shoddy product.

Professional and occupational licensing originated in Europe (Gartner, 1975; Weinberger & Weinberger, 1962). In the Middle Ages guilds developed standards and protections for their members. The activities of the guilds and other groups evolved into state recognition that certain functions were exclusive to these groups—the precursor of licensing. Through apprenticeships the guilds guided and governed the activities that became our modern trades and occupations. The professions of medicine, law, and theology have long been recognized, although apprenticeship and self-study to achieve professional status have almost disappeared. Formal training in an institution of higher learning is almost invariably required, although some denominations allow clergy to qualify through self-study and one or two states allow lawyers to apprentice as preparation for the bar examination.

LICENSING

Education for Social Work

Social work became a recognized profession only in the 20th century, with professional education now carried out in colleges and universities. Formalized professional training began in 1898 when the New York Charity Organization Society launched the School of Applied Philanthropy, which later became the Columbia University School of Social Work. Social work education is now standardized and accredited by the Council on Social Work Education, which monitors the quality of existing programs and grants approval for new ones.

Professional social work education has occurred primarily at the master's and doctoral levels, although there is now provision for undergraduate social work education. Students then come to postgraduate training with a basic understanding of social work and some skills in methodology (Dyer, 1977). Students with undergraduate degrees in social work present a challenge to professional schools, which must build on these students' existing knowledge while at the same time educating students who do not have that knowledge and experience.

In 1991 the NASW Academy of Certified Baccalaureate Social Workers was established to provide objective testing and certification of social workers who had a bachelor of social work degree. This led to the Council on Social Work Education's Curriculum Policy Statements on the baccalaureate degree programs in social work education.

The profession is legally regulated in all 50 states and the District of Columbia. There was intensive NASW action at the state and national levels to achieve this goal. Some employees of public agencies, such as mental hospitals, are called social workers although they are not so trained. This occurrence is rare and will become rarer as true professionals assume these jobs and the more-demanding ones in other settings.

Forms of Regulation

Laws regulating social work take several forms: Licensing regulates the right to practice and may be voluntary or compulsory; registration acts typically to protect the use of certain titles such as "social worker," "certified social worker," and "registered social worker." Licensing has an element of exclusivity that raises the problem of defining what is exclusive to a practice. The relative ease or difficulty of definition influences the kind of regulation selected. If the problem of definition is insurmountable, protection of a title for those who have received a certain level of professional training is a compromise. If regulated practice can be defined, this implies the ability to recognize good practice and the authority to exclude those not trained to perform it and requires a board of examiners to enforce the standards ("Competitor's Right," 1957; *Virginia Academy of Clin. Psychol. v. Blue Shield of Va.,* 1980). A District of Columbia statute (D.C. Code 82-3308.1-6) regulates social work strictly. It requires a degree, an examination, and post–master's degree experience under supervision.

In 1995 all 50 states, as well as Puerto Rico, the Virgin Islands, and the District of Columbia, regulate the practice of social work (American Association of State Social Work Boards, 1993). Since the mid-1980s, there has been a dramatic increase in regulation because of the efforts of NASW and its local chapters.

Title 37 of the Louisiana Revised Statutes (37 LSA-R.S. 37:2701-2718) is a typical law; it regulates the practice of *board certified social work,* which is defined as

> *a practice of service in which a special knowledge of social resources, social systems, human capabilities, and the part that past experiences play in determining present behavior is directed at helping people to achieve more adequate, satisfying, productive, and self-realizing social adjustments. The application of social work principles and methods includes, but is not restricted to, casework and the use of social work methodology of nonmedical nature with individuals, families, and groups and other measures to help people modify behavior or personal and family adjustment; providing information and referral services; explaining and interpreting the psychosocial aspects in the situation of individuals, families, or groups; helping communities to analyze social problems and human needs and the direct delivery of human services; and education and research related to the practice of board certified social work.* (37:3703[2])

Opinions may differ as to whether this is a valid definition of social work practice. It is possible that an individual practicing without a license could simply claim not to be a board certified social worker, just as an unlicensed individual could give legal or medical advice. The licensing board must decide whether to enjoin such practices and seek other sanctions. Regulation may simply require some professional education, without defining the activity regulated.

In Louisiana, being grossly negligent as a board certified social worker may be grounds for denial, revocation, or suspension of a certificate (§ 2713(6)). Is good practice well enough understood that negligence can be easily recognized? For instance, is it negligent practice to save a marriage that only feeds the neurosis of one partner (Briar, 1975; Malcolm X, 1964)?

ETHICS

One hallmark of a profession is a codified system of ethics. These codes go beyond proscription of grossly negligent practice or felonious behavior and require of the professional a higher level of trustworthiness in dealing with clients than is required in the "arm's length" transaction of commercial contracts. The *NASW Code of Ethics* (NASW, 1994) serves as a guide for the social worker, who, by studying it, by observing other professionals, and by accepting the tutorial experience of supervision, learns appropriate professional behavior.

One ethical responsibility is the social worker's obligation to refuse to provide services beyond his or her expertise (Levy, 1974). An internist does not perform brain surgery; a lawyer with a domestic relations practice does not accept a complicated antitrust case. Responsible professionals select the method of treating the diagnosed problem most suitable for its resolution and frankly discuss with clients the limitations of their own skill and available resources. This means, too, that they must continue to evaluate emerging techniques and methodology (Marshall, 1980; Wood, 1978). Currently, 25 states require continuing education of social workers, a further incentive to learn more about new techniques and methodologies.

The delegate assembly of NASW adopted a revised code of ethics in November 1979, which was revised again in 1990 and in 1993 (NASW, 1994). Unless the provisions of this or a similar code are incorporated into state laws, even if only by reference, their observance is voluntary, not mandatory. Mandatory observance of an ethical code is necessary if a profession is to carry out its self-regulating function. Ethical violations should be sanctioned by loss of license or loss of membership in the professional association. It should be noted that NASW members must affirm in writing their adherence to the *NASW Code of Ethics* and face sanctions and possible loss of membership if they are found to have committed ethical violations.

Professional Organization

NASW was created on October 1, 1955, from the merger of seven organizations: (1) the American Association of Social Workers (successor to the first formal social work organization, the National Social Workers Exchange, established in 1917), (2) the American Association of Medical Social Workers, (3) the American Association of Psychiatric Social Workers, (4) the American Association of Group Workers, (5) the Association for the Study of Community Organization, (6) the National Association of School Social Workers, and (7) the Social Work Research Group. Although NASW membership is not required for a social worker to practice (as membership in the American Bar Association or the American Medical Association is not required for lawyers and physicians, respectively), membership allows social workers to share professional interests and concerns with others committed to working toward professional recognition and improvement.

During the 1970s, societies for clinical social work were developed (Pharis, 1973); California formed the first in 1966. Fourteen societies have since formed, growing rapidly, and 10 more states are now forming societies to counteract threats to private practice and to guarantee insurance coverage of the clinical social worker as a vendor of services. Most societies work toward legal regulation. A national organization—the National Federation of Societies for Clinical Social Work—was founded by the societies in California, Illinois, Kentucky, Louisiana, New York, and Texas. The minimum requirement for membership in these societies is the master of social work degree, with different societies adding other requirements, such as current practice and supervised post–master's degree experience. NASW was created in part to counteract the fragmentation of numerous professional organizations. The proliferation of clinical social work societies seems a return to the pre-1955 situation.

SANCTIONS AGAINST SOCIAL WORKERS

Sanctions against unethical behavior include license revocation, censure by a professional association, or a grievance hearing by a group authorized to examine complaints of clients. The action taken depends on whether professional organizations have set sanctions and on the determination of governing boards to enforce them. State laws provide that boards of the professional organizations control by revoking licenses or censuring after a hearing.

A malpractice suit for monetary damages is a sanction not only for unethical practice but also for negligence. An agency or other employer may sanction workers by suspension or discharge. The following case was brought by a worker faced with a choice of unethical practice or discharge for insubordination.

Parrish v. Civil Service Comm'n. of County of Alameda
57 Cal. Rptr. 623, 425 P.2d 223 (1967)
Tobriner, J.
In the present case an Alameda County social worker, discharged for "insubordination" for declining to participate in a mass morning raid upon the homes of the county's welfare recipients, seeks reinstatement with back pay on the ground that such participation would have involved him in

multiple violations of rights secured by the federal and state Constitutions. He urges that his superiors could not properly direct him to participate in an illegal activity and that he could not, therefore, be dismissed for declining to follow such directions.

For the reasons set forth in this opinion we have decided that the county's failure to secure legally effective consent to search the homes of welfare recipients rendered the mass raids unconstitutional. We have determined further that, even if effective consent had been obtained, the county could not constitutionally condition the continued receipt of welfare benefits upon the giving of such consent. We have therefore held, for these two independently sufficient reasons, that the project in which the county directed the plaintiff to take part transgressed constitutional limitations. In light of plaintiff's knowledge as to the scope and methods of the projected operation, we have concluded that he possessed adequate grounds for declining to participate.

On November 21, 1962, the board of supervisors of Alameda County ordered the county welfare director to initiate a series of unannounced early-morning searches of the homes of the county's welfare recipients for the purpose of detecting the presence of "unauthorized males." The searches were to be modeled on a Kern County project popularly known as "Operation Weekend."

Because the social workers lacked experience with the techniques employed by the fraud investigators they received special instruction in the procedures to be followed. Their superiors instructed them to work in pairs with one member covering the back door of each dwelling while the recipient's own social worker presented himself at the front door and sought admittance. Once inside, he would proceed to the rear door and admit his companion. Together the two would conduct a thorough search of the entire dwelling, giving particular attention to beds, closets, bathrooms, and other possible places of concealment.

Plaintiff was one of the social workers chosen to participate in the first wave of raids. Upon learning the nature of the proposed operation, he submitted a letter to his superior declaring that he could not participate because of his conviction that such searches were illegal. After plaintiff had explained his position to the division chief and the welfare director, he was discharged for insubordination.

"Insubordination can be rightfully predicated only upon a refusal to obey some order which a superior officer is entitled to give and entitled to have obeyed." Plaintiff contends that his superiors were not entitled to compel his participation in illegal searches and urges that such participation might have exposed him to severe penalties under federal law.

On the basis of the foregoing analysis we conclude that the searches contemplated and undertaken in the course of the operation in the present case must be deemed unconstitutional unless the county can show compliance with the standards which govern searches for evidence of crime. The county concedes that it sought no warrants for these searches and that it lacked probable cause to arrest any person in any of the homes searched, but contends that the searches took place pursuant to effective consent, freely and voluntarily given.

Our first task is to analyze the county's argument that the raids entailed no unlawful searches because the authorities instructed the searchers to refrain from forcing their way into any home. They were, instead, to report any refusal of entry to their superiors for such further action as might be deemed appropriate. The record indicates that, under the county's established practice, a reported refusal to entry could serve as a basis for terminating welfare benefits. The record also establishes that welfare recipients must depend to a remarkably high degree upon the continued favor of their social workers, who are vested with wide discretion to authorize or prohibit specific expenditures. Accordingly, we must determine whether the threat of sanctions necessarily implicit in a request for entry under such circumstances vitiated the apparent consent which the searchers sought to secure from the occupants.

The persons subjected to the instant operation confronted far more than the amorphous threat of official displeasure which necessarily attends any such request. The request for entry by persons whom the beneficiaries knew to possess virtually unlimited power over their very livelihood posed a threat which was far more certain, immediate, and substantial. These circumstances nullify the legal effectiveness of the apparent consent secured by the Alameda County searchers.

Even if we could conclude, however, that the consent secured by the Alameda County searchers constituted a knowing and fully voluntary waiver of Fourth Amendment rights, that conclusion would not establish the constitutionality of the operation involved in this case. That operation rested upon the assumption that a welfare agency may withhold aid from recipients who do not willingly submit to random, exploratory searches of their homes; from its inception, the operation contemplated the use of such searches to threaten the withdrawal of welfare benefits from anyone who insisted upon his rights of privacy and repose. In light of the resulting pressure upon welfare recipients to sacrifice constitutionally protected rights, the ultimate legality of the operation in which the plaintiff refused to participate must turn on whether the recipient of welfare benefits may be conditioned upon a waiver of rights embodied in the Fourth Amendment.

Although we can conceive of unusual situations in which the government might properly predicate continued welfare eligibility upon consent *to unannounced early morning searches, the record fails to develop any justification for such a condition here. Under some circumstances the county might be able to establish that a requirement of consent to such searches would facilitate the detection of frauds which deplete the welfare fund. As noted above, we would then be called upon to decide whether the benefits derived from the imposition of such a condition outweighed the corresponding impairment of constitutional rights. We could not resolve this issue upon the record now before us, because the evidence adduced in the present case fails to establish the incidence of welfare fraud or the efficacy of mass morning raids in reducing such fraud.*

In any event the instant operation does not meet the last of the three requirements which it must satisfy: so striking is the disparity between the operation's declared purpose and the means employed, so broad its gratuitous reach, and so convincing the evidence that improper consideration dictated its ultimate scope, that no valid link remains between that operation and its preferred justification.

The record clearly shows that the Alameda County director was anxious to include non-suspect homes in order to provide a dramatic public demonstration of the efficiency of the Alameda County welfare program and the low incidence of fraud.

However laudable the goal of the Alameda County authorities to persuade the public that the incidence of welfare fraud falls below popular estimates, we cannot accept the view that they were free to advance that objective by indiscriminate raids upon the homes of persons selected solely because their honesty could be exploited to dramatize the point.

Since the record establishes that the information known to plaintiff at the time he made his decision gave him reasonable grounds to believe that the operation would be unconstitutional, that he did so believe, and that the operation, as ultimately conducted, was in fact unconstitutional, we need not consider how we would decide this case had any one of these elements been missing.

We fully recognize the importance of ferreting out fraud in the inexcusable garnering of welfare benefits not truly deserved. Such efforts, however, must be, and clearly can be, conducted with due regard for the constitutional rights of welfare recipients. The county welfare department itself has now abandoned the technique of investigation which it pursued here; we may thus rest assured that it will develop other more carefully conceived procedures. It is surely not beyond the competence of the department to conduct appropriate investigations without violence to human dignity and within the confines of the Constitution.

The judgment is reversed and the case is remanded to the trial court with directions to enter judgment in accordance with this opinion.

The social worker, on principle, refused to participate and risked his job in the process. This case dramatically illustrates that the sanction of discharge for insubordination cannot be based on failure to obey an illegal or unconstitutional order.

PRIVILEGED COMMUNICATION

One ethical requirement of the profession is that social workers must hold confidential all communications of a client unless the client authorizes the transfer of communications to another professional person or agency. This differs from privileged communication, a legal rule protecting the confidences that a client shares with certain professional persons in a professional relationship. The privilege protects such communication from admission in court without the permission of the person holding the privilege, the client, who can authorize the professional person to testify. The privilege arises from society's belief that certain favored relationships should be protected so that individuals may seek advice freely without jeopardizing their legal rights. The most common privilege is that of attorney–client. Others may include husband–wife, physician–patient, priest–penitent, accountant–client, and journalist–news source, depending on the state. Without societal recognition of the necessity for confidentiality in these communications, they would not exist.

Although social work communications are privileged in 32 states (see Louisiana Rev. Stat. § 2714), social workers *can* be compelled to testify concerning matters learned from clients. Privileges are not favored, because they may bar from court certain information bearing on the truth of the matter being tried (Arnold, 1970; Bernstein, 1977a; Schwartz, 1989). The advantage of the privilege is that both client and worker are freed from the specter of subpoena of the worker to testify: The confidentiality of the relationship is inviolate. Although the social worker may be ethically or even legally bound not to disclose communications of the client, on occasion the communications of a client may disclose threats to the safety of others. In such a situation the *Tarasoff* case held the therapist obligated to the larger society (Schroeder, 1979).

In Louisiana, communications are not privileged when the social worker's client is a minor who may have been the victim of a crime or of neglect. Because much of the social work activity that relates to court proceedings does involve children, these limitations may be in the best interest of society. For instance in *Cronier v. Cronier* (1989), a married couple had been granted a separation and the husband appealed the trial court's restrictions of his visitation with his two-year-old daughter. The court of appeals held that "good cause" existed for requiring the social worker and clinical psychologist to disclose results of their investigations of child abuse. Although the Department of Health and Human Resources has statutory privilege, it must comply with a subpoena if the court refuses to quash it.

A social worker who receives a subpoena should check to see whether the client has consented to the testimony. If not, the social worker should ask the client's attorney whether a motion to quash the subpoena can be filed. In any case, the social worker must respond to the subpoena.

Community Serv. Soc. v. Welfare Insp. Gen. (1977) was a giant step toward legal recognition of the privilege. A community service and social work agency applied for an order quashing a subpoena served by the welfare inspector general, who was investigating whether a public assistance recipient had received welfare funds under false pretenses. The recipient had spoken with a certified social worker, and such communications are privileged by statute in New York unless the privilege is waived by the client. The court held that because the information sought as to the recipient's marital status and employment was not information that revealed contemplation of a crime or harmful act, which would not be privileged under the statute, the order was granted. The court added the following:

> *The statutory privilege conferred on communications between a social worker and client must be afforded the same standing as that given traditional similar privileges provided by statute, such as the privilege respecting communications between attorney and client, physician and patient and clergyman and penitent. To constitute a waiver there must be a clear relinquishment of a known right.* (p. 95)

A caveat is in order: *Belmont v. California State Personnel Board* (1974) is instructive. The Department of Social Welfare suspended a group of psychiatric social workers for five days for willful disobedience of an order to furnish the department with information on their patients for inclusion in its computerized system of record keeping. The patients were receiving welfare assistance. The workers brought a mandamus action asking the court to review the order. The court held that the social workers were not entitled to invoke the statutory privilege despite their objections that the patients had not been asked for permission to use the information or told that the information would be fed into a computer system. The court said,

> *More appropriately, the handicapped persons are "clients" of the state and its Department of Social Welfare acting through its employees, psychiatric and other social workers. . . . And as we shall now point out assuming, arguendo, a conflict between appellants' allegiance to a code of ethics and their duties as employment, or suffer disciplinary action.* (p. 109)

The court held that the social workers were not entitled to invoke the privilege when required to furnish information to be fed into the department's computer system.

The 1975 federal rules of evidence provide that privileges are governed by principles of common law, which, of course, did not traditionally recognize a social work privilege. The rules provide that if a social worker is subpoenaed to testify in a case in federal court concerning information received in confidence from a client, the court may order the testimony. A worker who refused to obey the court's order could face a contempt of court citation and imprisonment. Social workers faced with this dilemma must decide the course of conduct according to their own standards of professional ethics; this is a moral question.

SOCIAL WORKER AS EXPERT WITNESS

Although court appearances are rarely pleasant, one rewarding experience for the social worker can be testifying as an expert witness. Expert witnesses, because of special training and expertise, can be permitted to testify not just to facts within their knowledge, as most witnesses must, but also to their opinions about those facts and about hypothetical situations. The expert can draw inferences that an ordinary witness cannot. Thus, an expert engineer witness would be allowed to speculate on the condition of a tire and why it blew out in an accident without having been present when the tire blew. Social workers may be asked to testify in disputes involving interpersonal relationships and family situations, such as custody battles, child abuse cases, and adoption placements.

To testify as an expert witness, you must be qualified by educational background and professional experience. If the judge is not satisfied with your qualifications, you can testify only to facts within your own knowledge. For instance, "the mother constantly fidgeted in her chair" and "everything in the office was in a neat line; no papers were on the desk; there was no disorder of any kind" are observed facts. One qualified as an expert might infer from those facts that the mother was anxious or the person occupying the office seemed obsessive.

As an expert you may also give your opinion about hypothetical situations and inferences about unobserved facts, although the first situation is more common. The opposing attorney will always try to undermine the weight of your testimony, so you must be able to marshal the facts on which you base your conclusions and be prepared for questions like "Don't you think it is natural for a person to be nervous when a social worker has come to interview her about her children?" and "Are you suggesting that there is something wrong with being neat and orderly?"

Answer questions truthfully, but do not volunteer extra information that might make the answer legally objectionable. If a question cannot be answered with the simple "yes" or "no" demanded, ask whether you can explain your answer. Above all try to have a detailed conference with the attorney who needs your testimony. You will have a better understanding of the use that is to be made of your testimony. Opposing counsel may ask whether you have discussed your testimony, hoping to imply that it is coached and so to *impeach* your testimony—to show that it is not worthy of belief. It is perfectly natural for a witness to discuss testimony with the attorney before trial, and you should answer truthfully if you have done so (Bernstein, 1977b). Gothard (1989, 1995), a judge and social worker, has written about the social worker as expert witness and the legal issues regarding confidentiality and privileged communication.

SOCIAL ACTION

A professional person owes to the profession and to society a commitment to work for those changes that experience reveals are necessary for the good of society. Needed changes may be structural or functional; they may involve an attitude change or social legislation. Social workers have been advocates for needed social change throughout the 20th century, advising on legislation and lobbying for disadvantaged groups that have no other champions. They should be alert to opportunities for social action (Grinnell & Kyte, 1974).

Social action is not without dangers. One social worker, a chief probation officer, challenged the racially discriminatory admission policy of certain facilities for children by advocating litigation to desegregate these facilities. His participation was in direct disobedience of an order of his superior, the juvenile court judge, who recommended his discharge for insubordination. The U.S. court of appeals for the fifth circuit initially ordered his reinstatement on the grounds that the firing interfered with protected First Amendment rights. A rehearing *en banc*, that is, before the entire panel of 13 judges, upheld the firing because of the importance of a cooperative and confidential relationship between the judge and the chief probation officer (*Abbott v. Thetford*, 1977).

REFERENCES

American Association of State Social Work Boards. (1993). *Social work laws and board regulations: A state comparison study.* Culpeper, VA: Author.

Arnold, S. (1970). Confidential communication and the social worker. *Social Work, 15,* 61–67.

Bernstein, B. E. (1977a). Privileged communications to the social worker. *Social Work, 22,* 264–268.

Bernstein, B. E. (1977b). The social worker as an expert witness. *Social Casework, 58,* 412–417.

Briar, S. (1975). Protecting the public and private interest [Editorial]. (1975). *Social Work, 20,* 174.

Competitor's right to enjoin unlicensed professional practice. (1957). *University of Chicago Law Review, 24,* 714–722.

Dyer, P. M. (1977). How professional is the BSW worker? *Social Work, 22,* 487–492.

Gartner, A. (1975). Four professions: How different, how alike. *Social Work, 20,* 353–358.

Gilbert, N., & Specht, H. (1976). Advocacy and professional ethics. *Social Work, 21,* 288–293.

Gothard, S. (1989). Power in the court: The social worker as expert witness. *Social Work, 34,* 65–67.

Gothard, S. (1995). Legal issues: Confidentiality and privileged communication. In R. L. Edwards (Ed.-in-Chief), *Encyclopedia of social work* (19th ed., Vol. 2, pp. 1579–1584). Washington, DC: NASW Press.

Grinnell, R. M., Jr., & Kyte, N. S. (1974). Modifying the environment. *Social Work, 19,* 477–483.

Levy, C. S. (1974). On the development of a code of ethics. *Social Work, 19,* 207–216.

Malcolm X. (1964). *The autobiography of Malcolm X as told to Alex Hailey.* New York: Grove Press.

Marshall, E. (1980). Psychotherapy works, but for whom? *Science, 207,* 506–508.

National Association of Social Workers. (1994). *NASW code of ethics.* Washington, DC: Author.

Pharis, M. E. (1973). Societies for clinical social work. *Social Work, 18,* 99–103.

Schroeder, L. O. (1979). Legal liability: A professional concern. *Clinical Social Work Journal, 17,* 61–67.

Schwartz, G. (1989). Confidentiality revisited. *Social Work, 34,* 223–226.

Weinberger, P., & Weinberger, D. (1962). Legal regulation in perspective. *Social Work, 7,* 67–75.

Wood, K. M. (1978). Casework effectiveness: A new look at the research evidence. *Social Work, 23,* 437–458.

STUDY QUESTIONS

1. What are some advantages of licensing social workers?

2. Does the practice of social work carry with it the legal protection of the privileged communication status?

7

The Criminal Justice System

rimes are acts of commission or omission prohibited by the penal laws. They may be *mala in se,* wrong in themselves, such as murder or rape, or *mala in prohibita,* not necessarily immoral but wrong because prohibited, such as exceeding the speed limit. Crimes are either felonies or misdemeanors; the former are the more serious. You can usually distinguish between the two by the penalty: A felony is punishable by death or imprisonment in a penitentiary; a misdemeanor is punishable by fine or imprisonment in an institution other than a penitentiary. The criminal justice system includes the laws that declare certain acts criminal, the courts that try people accused of committing these acts, and the institutions that enforce the laws and punish offenders. Different states have different criminal laws and procedures.

Society, through its elected representatives, has declared certain acts to be inimical to its safety and peace or to be flagrant abuses of the rights of others. The sanctions for these acts contain elements of retribution and vengeance as well as of deserved punishment, deterrence, and rehabilitation. Does society select appropriate sanctions?

We as social workers are interested in the definition of crimes and their sanctions, from murder and rape to possession of marijuana and nonsupport of family. We are concerned with the impartial administration of justice, so that race, poverty, or other characteristics will not disadvantage those who come in contact with the system. And we are concerned with the effectiveness of penal and correctional institutions as agencies for rehabilitation.

Social workers work in courts, halfway houses, prisons and reformatories, probation and parole agencies, and child protection centers; they come to understand and appreciate the problems and potentials inherent in each response to the breakdown of law and order. Many if not most of these agencies have been established for rehabilitation, an activity in which social workers often play a major role. In addition, there is now new interest in an old setting for social work: police departments. After a promising start in the early decades of the 20th century, the use of police departments as practice settings for social work faded (Roberts, 1976; Woolf & Rudman, 1977). Police departments seem to be one component of the criminal justice system where social workers who are experts in crisis intervention might be particularly effective (Carr, 1970; Henderson, 1976; Michzels & Treger, 1973; Treger, 1995).

Most criminal justice agencies suffer from a chronic lack of funds and personnel. However, within this limitation social workers learn special techniques for working with people whose social problems are compounded by their confrontation with the law. This chapter discusses rehabilitation programs, the response of the courts to constitutional challenges to the operation of the criminal justice system, and some of the special problems of criminal offenders.

HOW THE SYSTEM WORKS

Any study of the criminal justice system in this country should begin with the document that limits the ways state and federal governments may control crime and correct those convicted of it: the Constitution of the United States. The relevant passages are the following:

Article IV

Section 1. Full faith and credit shall be given in each state to the public acts, records, and judicial proceedings of every other state. And the Congress may by general laws prescribe the manner in which such acts, records and proceedings shall be proved, and the effect thereof.

· · · · ·

Section 2.1. The citizens of each state shall be entitled to all privileges and immunities of citizens in the several states.

· · · · ·

2. A person charged in any state with treason, felony, or other crime, who shall flee from justice and be found in another state, shall on demand of the executive authority of the state from which he fled, be delivered up to be removed to the state having jurisdiction of the crime.

Bill of Rights

Amendment IV. The right of the people to be secure in their persons, houses, papers, and effects, against unreasonable searches and seizures, shall not be violated, and no warrants shall issue, but upon probable cause, supported by oath or affirmation, and particularly describing the place to be searched, and the persons or things to be seized.

Amendment V. No person shall be held to answer for capital, or otherwise infamous crime, unless on a presentment or indictment of a grand jury, except in cases arising in the land or naval forces, or in the militia, when in actual service in time of war or public danger; nor shall any person be subject for the same offense to be twice put in jeopardy of life or limb; nor shall be compelled in any criminal case to be a witness against himself, nor be deprived of life, liberty or property, without due process of law; nor shall private property be taken for public use without just compensation.

Amendment VI. In all criminal prosecutions, the accused shall enjoy the right to a speedy and public trial, by an impartial jury of the state and district wherein the crime shall have been committed, which district shall have been previously ascertained by law, and to be informed of the nature and cause of the accusation; to be confronted with the witnesses against him; to have compulsory process for obtaining witnesses in his favor, and to have the assistance of counsel for his defense.

. . . . .

Amendment VIII. Excessive bail shall not be required, nor excessive fines imposed, nor cruel and unusual punishments inflicted.

Article IV not only requires states to honor the decisions of courts in other states, it also provides for extradition, the method by which a person accused of a crime who flees across state lines may be returned to the accusing state. The Uniform Criminal Extradition Act, originally drafted in 1936, is now in effect in 47 states, Puerto Rico, and the Virgin Islands (*Uniform Law Annotated,* 1994).

Some extradition cases are difficult. *California v. Superior Court of California* (1987) was a custody dispute. After the mother remarried, took the children to Oregon, and kept them from seeing their father, he and their grandfather brought the children back to California. They were charged with kidnapping in Louisiana, and their extradition from California was requested. The state executive branch asked the Supreme Court if it had to comply with the extradition request. The Supreme Court held that the asylum state was bound to deliver the accused men up to the demanding state without inquiring into whether the charge was sufficient. The Louisiana court will decide whether the California custody decree gives the father lawful custody under full faith and credit.

The Bill of Rights, the first 10 amendments to the Constitution, limits the power of the federal government in several areas. The Fourteenth Amendment, not part of the Bill of Rights, extends federal protection of due process and equal protection to the states. The Supreme Court has come to use the Fourteenth Amendment as a means to apply the Bill of Rights to the states, by interpreting due process and equal protection to include the Bill of Rights. Thus, in Application of *Gault* (1967), the Supreme Court gave the Sixth Amendment's right to notice, to cross-examination of witnesses, and to counsel to a juvenile appearing before an Arizona state court, under the due process clause of the Fourteenth Amendment.

ARREST, ARRAIGNMENT, AND TRIAL

Arrest is the procedure by which an individual is taken into custody and jailed. In rare instances, people will turn themselves in when they hear the police are looking for them. For less-serious accusations a summons may be issued by mail or hand delivery, as is typical for traffic offenses. If the accused does not appear for trial, the judge issues a bench warrant, and the police bring the accused into court.

Arrest by Warrant

When a *complaint* has been filed, that is, a charge has been made before a magistrate by either the victim or the police investigating the crime that a particular individual committed an offense, the magistrate issues a warrant identifying the individual as the one responsible for the offense and authorizing his or her arrest. Under the Fourth Amendment, warrants can only be issued on *probable cause.* The courts have struggled over what constitutes probable cause. Generally it now means information that would lead a cautious person reasonably to believe that the accused committed a crime.

Arrest at the Scene

A police officer who sees a crime committed, receives information about a crime and sees a person who fits a description of the criminal, or suspects from the circumstances that a crime has been committed may make an arrest without a warrant. In all these cases the officer has probable cause for the arrest. In *Colorado v. Bannister* (1980), upholding the search of an automobile that had been stopped for a traffic violation where stolen objects were in plain view, the Supreme Court set out the exceptions to the prohibition against a search without a warrant. The court noted that the contents in plainview within an automobile can be seized when a car is stopped for speeding. Investigations at airports, immigration stops, and "stop and frisk" actions are preventive police work. The police can also search without a warrant as an incident to an arrest.

An individual also may be taken into protective custody without being arrested. For instance, children can be removed from surroundings detrimental to their welfare.

Probation and parole officers have limited arrest power. They are deemed peace officers and can arrest without a warrant if they have reasonable cause to believe the parolee violated or is attempting to violate a condition of parole. Social workers acting in these capacities should ask legal staff of their employer for definite guidelines concerning their arrest authority. False arrest may constitute a tort.

Warrants to allow authorities to gather evidence of a crime also cannot be issued without probable cause. The Supreme Court has held that evidence seized by state officers during a warrantless and therefore illegal search is inadmissible in a state court proceeding, although a warrant is not required to search the person of someone who has been arrested legally (Schroeder, 1985).

As the *Bannister* exceptions suggest, probable cause to arrest, search, and seize is becoming easier to prove when defendants move to exclude evidence. Defendants can challenge suspected illegal procedures by motions before trial as well as at trial. Certainly individuals can refuse to allow police to search their homes without a warrant, but resisting arrest is a crime even if the arrest should later be declared unjustified.

Indictment

An indictment from a grand jury is required for all felonies. A grand jury, usually 23 people, hears the district attorney present the evidence and decides whether the evidence is sufficient to hold the individual for trial. The indictment is not a finding of guilt. The grand jury is a protection for the individual, a barrier to protect a citizen from the expense, trauma, and risk of a trial stemming from arbitrary action by the prosecutor.

Bail

Before trial and sometimes immediately after arrest, the accused may be released on bail or on his or her own *recognizance,* which means that the accused is trusted to appear for trial without the posting of bail. *Bail* is the security an accused person deposits with the court—usually cash—

to be released from jail while waiting for trial. The procedure is known as *posting bond*. The money is forfeited if the accused fails to appear for trial. The Eighth Amendment forbids excessive bail, so the judge adjusts the amount according to the seriousness of the crime and the likelihood that the accused will appear.

Any amount of bail may be excessive for the individual who has little money. Because a professional bondsperson charges a percentage of the amount of the bond, accused indigent people usually stay in jail until trial, unable to find witnesses who can aid in their defense and unable to provide for their families. The Vera Foundation of New York did an extensive study on the feasibility of pretrial parole (Ares, Ranken, & Sturz, 1963) using a questionnaire designed to elicit factors—marital and family relationships, employment history, willingness of friends to guarantee that the accused would go to trial, duration of present employment, employer's willingness to take accused back, prior convictions—that measured ties to the community and suggested whether the accused might be a good prospect for release without bail. The results showed that those released when enough factors were present did appear for trial and had a lower rate of conviction than those who remained in jail. The Bail Reform Act of 1984 accomplishes much the same purpose for those individuals accused of federal crimes. Yet pretrial parole systems for those almost certain to appear for trial are by no means universal.

Preliminary Hearing
After arrest, an individual is brought to the police station and photographed, fingerprinted, and, unless immediately granted bail, jailed. There must be a prompt preliminary hearing to determine whether there is evidence sufficient for the state to hold the individual. This hearing is not a trial.

The Plea
At the *arraignment,* the accused is brought before the court to hear the charge read. The arraignment follows the formal accusation, which may be presented by information filed by the prosecutor or by indictment. The accused then responds to the charge with a plea of "guilty," "not guilty," "nolo contendere," or "not guilty by reason of insanity." *Nolo contendere* means that the accused is not contesting the charge and has the same effect as a plea of guilty, although some states may not count a nolo plea in cumulating offenses under a habitual offender law.

Trial
The Sixth Amendment mandates a speedy public trial. In 1974 Congress passed the Speedy Trial Act, reducing the period between arrest and

indictment to 35 days and requiring that the trial be held within one year. If the accused requests delays—to give the attorney more time to prepare a defense, for example, or to find witnesses—the time limits do not apply. The limits also do not apply if a delay is caused by the mental incompetence or physical disability of the accused.

Violation of the act brings mandatory dismissal of the case. The judge can dismiss without prejudice, depending on the seriousness of the charge. This means no rights or privileges of the party are waived or lost. The act is designed to curb abuses caused by court congestion or dilatory prosecutor practices.

During the trial the defense attorney will introduce motions, object to certain testimony, and do all that is possible to prevent the prosecution from meeting its burden of proving the crime beyond a reasonable doubt and to present the accused in the best possible light. The attorney for an accused may also negotiate with the prosecutor an arrangement whereby the accused pleads guilty to a lesser offense than originally charged or pleads guilty in return for the prosecutor's recommendation of a moderate sentence. Plea bargaining saves the state and the accused the expense of trial and is common when the evidence against the accused is not overwhelming, but the chance of conviction is substantial. The *Yale Law Journal* (Easterbrook, 1992; Schulhofer, 1992; Scott & Stuntz 1992a, 1992b) published papers from a symposium on punishment in which the pros and cons of plea bargaining were discussed. A plea bargain can be considered a kind of contract. Defendants may accept these bargains because of the threat of harsher penalties after trial. Although the speakers at the symposium recognized that both trials and plea bargains are flawed, they alleged that plea bargaining is, for the most part, efficient and fair.

Diversion

In a *diversion*, charges are suspended for a specified time on condition that the accused refrain from criminal activity and participate in a rehabilitation program. If the accused complies, the charges are dismissed (Birns, 1976). This diverts from the criminal process first offenders and people suffering from social and emotional problems that may respond to treatment.

The disadvantage of the diversion for the offender is that the right to a speedy trial is waived and all conditions of the diversion must be fulfilled; the advantages are that both the state and the accused are spared the expense of a trial and that, once the program is completed, the accused has no criminal record.

LEGAL REPRESENTATION

Right to Representation

This discussion thus far has presupposed that an accused has an attorney, something not always true for people who are indigent. In 1932 the Supreme Court held, on the basis of the Sixth Amendment, that the state must provide an indigent person accused of a capital crime with a lawyer if he or she is not able to afford one (*Powell v. Alabama*, 1932). However, it was not until 1963 that the Supreme Court, in the *Gideon v. Wainwright* case, extended this right to counsel to indigent people accused of crimes other than capital crimes (Lewis, 1964); 10 years later the right to counsel was extended to people accused of misdemeanors punishable by a loss of liberty (*Argersinger v. Hamlin*, 1973).

After *Gideon* the organized bar was asked to represent indigent people accused of crime free of any fee for services and in many cases themselves paying the expenses of experts, printing, and travel. As the burden to these appointed lawyers increased, states devised various methods to handle this responsibility. These methods included panels of volunteer lawyers (often young lawyers who wanted the trial experience) supported by court funds, set fees for court-appointed lawyers (usually considerably lower than normal charges), and the development of public defender programs (Richards, 1994). According to Mounts (1982), as recently as 1961 there were public defender offices in only 3 percent of the nation's counties. She also discussed cases where attorneys have been relieved of assignments because they were too overburdened to adequately represent the defendants. Ogletree (1993) commented on the need to develop motivations that will sustain public defenders through trying times.

Public Defense

When legal systems require that an accused have a "fair" trial, justice seems less than fair if the accused faces the resources of the prosecutor unrepresented. The need for a public defender was noted in the United States at the end of the 18th century, and by the end of the 19th century, several states had considered such laws, although none had passed. In 1913 Los Angeles County established the first public defender for criminal cases. Several cities and states followed suit, and the movement spread, but it was not until the *Gideon* decision that public defender systems began to develop extensively nationwide.

Public defender programs allow lawyers to become skilled in trial work and familiar with criminal law and procedure—something largely untrue of lawyers with practices devoted to civil matters. Unfortunately, public defender offices usually operate with limited funds, especially for investigation and experts, and very large caseloads. In addition, public defenders insulate prominent members of the bar from the inadequacies in the criminal justice system. Still, lawyers in private practice continue to provide charity to the community by shouldering a large part of the representation of indigent accused people; they realize that fair trials for all benefit the entire community.

Public defender offices are often overloaded—so much so, in fact, that in *State v. Peart* (1993) the district court ordered the legislature to provide funds for additional facilities, attorneys, and staff, to reduce the public defender caseload. The Louisiana supreme court held that the constitutional requirement that the legislature provide a uniform system for securing and compensating qualified counsel for indigent defendants *was not a right that an individual defendant was entitled to enforce.* The case points out that other states have faced a crisis in funding the indigent defense system where lawyers are overloaded with cases and undersupplied with investigators and other personnel.

A small percentage of social workers are working in court practice settings (Gibelman & Schervish, 1993). These workers understand better the public defender's concern with acquittal and reduction of the charges to a minimum offense, and barring these, sentencing. Although sentencing seems to conflict with their own focus on rehabilitation, rehabilitation follows only if there is conviction and sentencing. Currently, NASW lists only 1,323 social workers in public defender offices; therefore, it appears that there has been a decline in the use of them since 1975.

CRIMINAL RESPONSIBILITY

An element of most crimes is *mens rea,* the guilty mind. The legal capacity to commit a crime (as distinguished from the physical capacity to pull the trigger, wield the knife, or steal the money) is an essential element of responsibility for the crime (see *State v. Brown,* 1979). Thus, a small child may deliberately kill someone and yet not be guilty of a crime, being legally too young to commit intent. The element of legal intent may be lacking because of insanity, mental retardation, distortion of perception caused by an addiction, or any other factor that leads the jury to conclude that the individual could not form the specific intent.

There are several tests for the effect of insanity on criminal responsibility (Caplan, 1984; Winock, 1985). Most popular is the M'Naghten rule, which is in use in about 30 states and Great Britain:

If the circumstances indicate that because of a mental disease or mental defect the offender was incapable of distinguishing between right and wrong with reference to the conduct in question, the offender shall be exempt from criminal responsibility.

Known popularly as the "right and wrong" test, the M'Naghten rule is often criticized as simplistic in this day of advanced psychological knowledge and new understanding of human behavior. The rule announced in *Durham v. United States* (1954) sets out another principle.

An accused is not criminally responsible if his unlawful act was the product of mental disease or mental defect.

The chief criticism of the Durham rule is that it leaves "disease," "defect," and "product" undefined. In fact, the District of Columbia circuit, which created the Durham rule, now uses the American Law Institute (ALI) test discussed later in this section (*Bethea v. United States*, 1976). The Durham rule was modified by the "irresistible impulse" test, which asks whether there was

an impulse to commit an unlawful or criminal act which cannot be resisted or overcome by the patient because insanity or mental disease has destroyed the freedom of his will and his power of self-control and of choice as to his actions. (Black's Law Dictionary, 1968)

The ALI rule is applied in one form or another in all federal courts and in many states:

A person is not responsible for criminal conduct if at the time of such conduct as a result of mental disease or defect he lacks substantial capacity either to appreciate the wrongfulness of his conduct or to conform his conduct to the requirements of law.

Clark (1992) discussed the various insanity defenses and wrote, "The M'Naghten test is the accepted standard in approximately one-half of the jurisdictions that allow the insanity defense" (p. 164).

To prove that a client lacks criminal responsibility, the attorney may introduce expert testimony as to intelligence quotient, psychological condition, or psychiatric evaluations of a disease or defect—provided, of course, that money is available for experts. A social history also may be introduced.

Criminal responsibility is different from *competence to stand trial*, which means that the accused is able to comprehend the significance of the trial and can assist counsel in the defense. An individual who killed someone during a psychotic episode may not be guilty because of insanity, but may be perfectly able to assist counsel with the defense because in the interim tranquilizing drugs have produced a remission in the psychosis.

The existence of a "synthetic sanity" induced by drugs presents a dilemma to the defense attorney, who may want the jury to see the accused in a psychotic state. The Supreme Court of New Hampshire, for instance, has held that, on request by the defendant, the jury can view him or her without medication as long as the defendant was found to have been without medication at the time of the crime (*State v. Hayes*, 1978). However, the New Mexico court, in *State v. Jojola* (1976), held that the defendant had no absolute right to be tried free from the influence of the drug Thorazine, which was given to sedate him emotionally.

In *Ake v. Oklahoma* (1985) the Supreme Court held that when the defendant makes a showing that his sanity at the time of the offense will be a significant factor at trial, due process requires a state to provide a psychiatrist's assistance if the defendant cannot afford a psychiatrist.

Those defendants found incompetent to stand trial are usually sent to a secure hospital until they reach competence. Some defendants who are incompetent by reason of insanity may wish to stand trial or plead guilty rather than be in a state mental institution indefinitely. The fifth circuit has held that the due process clause entitles a person acquitted of a crime by reason of insanity to a hearing before commitment, whereas the equal protection clause requires the state to afford that person substantially the same protections, with certain qualifications, as are granted to persons committed under civil statutes (*Jackson v. Foti*, 1982). In this case, the individual's schizophrenia was in remission but because the doctors were unwilling to guarantee that he would not commit another violent act, he was recommitted to the forensic unit. The court said he must have a hearing on his current mental condition and continued propensity for committing dangerous acts.

A person who is deaf and mute and thus unable to comprehend the proceedings or communicate with the attorney may be perfectly sane and of normal intelligence, but may not be tried if unable to assist counsel with the defense. Because the criminal justice system cannot hold such an individual indefinitely, it must try to teach someone with such disabilities a sign language or other method of communicating so that the trial can proceed.

SENTENCING

Shortly after conviction, the defendant is sentenced. Except in those rare instances where the jury has sentencing power—usually only capital cases where it decides between execution or life imprisonment—sentencing is within the discretion of trial judge. Occasionally, the legislature restricts this discretion by mandating a certain sentence for crimes that have received considerable public attention like armed robbery or drug dealing. Usually the trial judge has the flexibility to determine the rehabilitative goals immediately after conviction. However, there is an emerging trend for more determinate sentences, by which anyone convicted of a crime is required to serve a specific sentence. This trend, along with recommendations for abolition of parole, reflects dissatisfaction with present rehabilitative measures as well as concern with the increase in crime.

Because of disparities among sentences imposed by federal judges on similarly situated offenders, Congress passed the Sentencing Reform Act of 1984, which created the United States Sentencing Commission as an independent body in the judicial branch with power to promulgate binding sentencing guidelines for all categories of federal offenses according to specific detailed factors. The constitutionality of the commission was upheld in *Mistretta v. U.S.* (1989), which discusses in detail the doctrine of separation of powers. There have been some complaints that local judges are better able to determine an individual's potential for rehabilitation and so better able to fashion the sentence; judges do occasionally look for mitigating circumstances that can shorten the sentence. Social workers may know of these circumstances, such as a history of abuse as a child. (For insight on how the Sentencing Act applies to juveniles, see *United States v. R.L.C.*, 1992.)

Probation and parole bring social work into the criminal justice system in ways crucial to clients. Social workers are often the professionals to whom probationers and parolees are entrusted for rehabilitation and supervision. Their responsibilities are great. The presentence investigation and other reports that social workers make may be crucial to the judge's decision to grant probation or the executive branch's decision on parole. The convicted person may have few rights to the information contained in these reports and no opportunity to correct or contradict any discrepancies in it ("Employment of Social Investigation Reports," 1958). Legal writers have expressed concern about this, and there is a movement to permit the defendant or the attorney to see the report or parts of it. Any social worker doing presentencing investigations should learn the local rule and let informants know whether the information is confidential or whether it may be revealed.

Probation and Parole

Probation is a matter of "grace"; a convicted person stays on probation only as long as he or she meets the conditions imposed when it is granted. The responsibility for seeing that these conditions are met, and for reporting to the court if they are not, usually rests with the social worker supervising the convicted person.

Judges can put numerous conditions on probation. In *United States v. Stine* (1982) the court of appeals held that requiring the defendant to submit to psychological counseling did not violate his constitutional right to privacy because it was reasonably related to the purpose of probation.

Parole is similarly a matter of grace. Some courts have questioned whether revoking probation or parole after a violation of the imposed conditions requires the application of the same due process standards that apply to criminal proceedings. The matter was settled by two Supreme Court decisions: *Morrissey v. Brewer* (1972) for parole; *Gagnon v. Scarpelli* (1973) for probation. In *Morrissey,* the Court attempted to delineate precisely what process is due to parolees, recognizing that the whole range of criminal due process rights should not be required, but recognizing also that even a conditional freedom from prison is a valuable privilege that should not be revoked unjustifiably.

In determining what process is due in parole revocations, and by extension in probation revocations, the Court stated that there are typically two important stages in the process: the first involves the arrest and detainment of a parolee, usually at the direction of a parole officer; the second occurs when parole is formally revoked. Due process requires a preliminary hearing to determine whether there is cause to believe that the parolee or the probationer has violated the conditions of parole or probation. This preliminary hearing should be held reasonably near the place where the alleged violation was committed within a reasonable time after the arrest, with advance notice to the parolee or probationer of the time and place of the hearing and of the alleged violations. Parolees or probationers are entitled to speak in their own behalf, present witnesses and evidence in their favor, and in some circumstances cross-examine witnesses. They are not entitled to remain at liberty on bail, as are those not yet convicted. Due process does not require that the parolee or the probationer be represented by counsel at all preliminary or final hearings, but it does require that counsel be permitted, or for an indigent person appointed, in those hearings where it would be fundamentally unfair for counsel not to be present.

The responsibility of the parole officer, who may initiate revocation proceedings, to the parolee is great, and the responsibility may influence the kind of casework attempted or even possible in this setting. If you counsel parolees or probationers, you must delineate the limitations on your authority in counseling at the beginning of the relationship (Ankersmit, 1976; Sheridan, 1967).

In this situation your responsibility to the general public is also great, because usually you are the primary representative of society, determining whether the probationer or the parolee is a threat. In *Rieser v. District of Columbia* (1977) the father of a woman who was raped and murdered by a parolee who worked in her apartment complex won damages under the District of Columbia Wrongful Death Act from the owners of the apartment complex where his daughter had lived, the parolee, the parole officer, and the District of Columbia. The parolee had a long history of assaults on women, and the parole officer did not adequately discuss his history with his employer at the apartment complex. The negligent performance of this ministerial duty constituted the breach of a duty owed to the deceased. The case cites other negligent omissions in the provision of public services.

In *Martinez v. California* (1980) the Supreme Court held that parole officials were not liable for the death of a 15-year-old girl murdered by a parolee, because a California statute immunizes parole officers from tort liability for their decisions. Convicted of attempted rape, the man had been sentenced to 1 to 20 years, with a recommendation that he not be paroled. He was released five years later and five months after his release he tortured and killed the girl. Her survivors sued, alleging that the officials knew or should have known that his release created a clear and present danger of such an incident. The Supreme Court rejected the arguments that the Fourteenth Amendment invalidates the California statute and that the officials were liable under the Civil Rights Act of 1964. Although the release from prison was "state action," the act of murdering the girl was not. No caveat is necessary to urge parole officials to use extreme care in making parole decisions. The statute granting immunity frees them to take the calculated risks that may lead to rehabilitation of a prisoner.

Work Release and Restitution

Alternatives to regular sentencing that may lead to better rehabilitation include work release, diversion, and restitution. Work release programs that permit the inmate of a correctional institution to leave during the day to take employment are designed to reintegrate the convicted person into the community ("Project: Temporary Release," 1974). Work release, which is a privilege, not a right, has certain basic characteristics: The inmate is released only to hold employment during working hours and must return to confinement during nonworking hours. Inmates must pay their room, board, and other expenses, although they may keep any funds earned over those expenses. Their employment conditions are identical to those of other personnel of the employer (Waldo, Chiricos, & Dobrin, 1973). In 1913 Wisconsin was the first state to implement a work release program; many states have followed. The federal work release statute, enacted in 1965 (18 USCA § 3603[f]), provides for probation officer supervision and reports to the attorney general about the person while he or she is on work release.

Because of their rehabilitative potential, such programs should be carefully considered when social workers must recommend plans for prisoners, although it requires great care to select only those prisoners who will benefit. State law sets standards for the selection of participants, usually excluding prisoners with a history of violent behavior, drug or alcohol abuse, or sex crimes. If you are employed in a correctional institution, be alert to this possibility for appropriate inmates.

Restitution, the process by which the criminal pays the victim back for the pecuniary loss the criminal act has caused, has been investigated as a rehabilitative tool (Hudson, Galaway, & Chesney, 1977; Read, 1977). The Supreme Court has held that a federal trial judge who suspends a sentence under the Federal Youth Corrections Act may also impose a fine, require restitution, or both as conditions of the youthful offender's probation (*Durst v. United States,* 1978). The virtues of this sentencing device are that criminals do not lose their jobs and become a burden to society and that victims receive some recompense for their loss.

In *Bearden v. Georgia* (1983) the Supreme Court held that a sentencing court cannot revoke probation for failure to pay a fine and make restitution when the probationer lacks financial resources, although willful refusal to pay when the probationer has resources or failure to make sufficient efforts to seek employment or borrow money may justify imprisonment. Deprivation of liberty because of inability to pay would be contrary to the fundamental fairness required by the Fourteenth Amendment.

Part-time imprisonment under work release or restitution programs gives the judge latitude in sentencing criminals who have strong ties to the community. The convicted person serves time at night or on weekends and retains a job or stays in school during weekdays. These programs are particularly appropriate for first offenders and nonviolent criminals (Balkin, 1980; Parisi, 1980).

As crime, and especially violent crime, increases, we see an alarmed public responding with demands for harsher prison sentences. In some states certain serious crimes, like armed robbery, carry long sentences with no probation, parole, or pardon. Thus, even the criminal who is rehabilitated in prison has no hope of early release. Sentencing devices that do have merit should be publicized, because the crimes committed by parolees certainly get publicity. If the sentencing devices are not accomplishing their rehabilitative purposes, we need to find new ones that do. The Omnibus Crime Control and Safe Streets Act of 1968 created the Law Enforcement Assistance Administration (LEAA), which awarded grants for innovative programs in criminal justice. The act also provided grants for training, law enforcement, and other criminal justice purposes; an amendment to the act in 1979 created a National Institute of Justice.

LEAA was disbanded during the first Reagan administration; however, during its existence, it funded many diversion and alternative programs.

SEX OFFENDERS

A particularly vexing problem for the criminal justice system is how to handle those who commit sex crimes. Although experts may be convinced that voyeurs or exhibitionists will not become violent, the general public can be particularly incensed by such crimes, especially when children are involved. Several states have passed statutes that permit an individual convicted of a sex crime to be held indefinitely for "treatment." Because facilities generally cannot treat all types of mental conditions, they are unlikely to be any better than prisons and jails for sex offenders; they may simply reward conformity rather than foster real psychological growth (Stanford, 1979).

In *Specht v. Patterson* (1967) the Supreme Court held that an individual committed indefinitely under the Colorado Sex Offenders Act was entitled to fundamental due process rights—right to counsel, to be heard, to offer evidence, and to confront and cross-examine witnesses—before sentencing. In *United States ex rel Stachulak v. Coughlin* (1975) the defendant was charged with indecent solicitation of a child, a misdemeanor that carried a maximum $500 fine and less than one year imprisonment. The state of Illinois brought a proceeding that culminated in the offender's indeterminate commitment under the Sexually Dangerous Persons Act. The act was first passed in 1938 and was amended in 1955. Its purpose is to provide treatment for people with mental disorders lasting for more than one year who have a propensity toward sexual assault or molestation of children.

After five years in the psychiatric division of the Illinois State Penitentiary, a maximum-security penal institution, defendant brought a habeas corpus action. The court added to the due process requirements of *Specht* the necessity of proof beyond a reasonable doubt that an accused is a mentally disordered sex offender. Similarly, the California court required in *People v. Burwick* (1975) proof beyond a reasonable doubt before commitment as a mentally disordered sex offender and in *People v. Feagley* (1975) held that hospital confinement without treatment for such offenders was cruel and unusual punishment.

RIGHTS OF CONFINED INDIVIDUALS

An individual does not lose all constitutional protections once incarcerated. One may lose liberty and, in the case of capital punishment, life, but only with the protection of due process. A convicted criminal retains the right to communicate with an attorney on many matters relating to incarceration and appeal, and in *Johnson v. Avery* (1969) the Supreme Court held that prison officials who fail to provide an effective legal services program for inmates cannot forbid "jailhouse lawyers" from rendering legal assistance to fellow inmates.

An exciting use of the legal system to improve prisoners' rights can be seen in recent charges that subhuman conditions in many prisons violate the Eighth Amendment's prohibition of cruel and unusual punishment. The cases detail overcrowding, homosexual assaults, use of inmate guards, poor food, and lack of recreation and work—a litany all too familiar to those working in correctional facilities. In *Newman v. State of Ala.* (1977) the court said,

> *The Eighth Amendment to the Constitution of the United States, reinforced by the Fourteenth Amendment, prohibits the imposition of cruel and unusual punishment. It is much too late in the day for states and prison authorities to think that they may withhold from prisoners the basic necessities of life, which include reasonably adequate food, clothing, shelter, sanitation, and necessary medical attention. . . . It should not need repeating that compliance with constitutional standards may not be frustrated by legislative inaction or failure to provide the necessary funds.*

The opposing argument offered by states in these cases is that the federal courts cannot order states to spend money because of the Eleventh Amendment, which says

> *The judicial power of the United States shall not be construed to extend to any suit in law or equity, commenced or prosecuted against one of the United States by citizens of another state, or by citizens or subjects of any foreign state.*

The federal court answered this argument in *Williams v. Edwards* (1977):

> *The appropriations statute is not "inexorably condemned" because the legislature could choose to close the unconstitutional facilities rather than appropriate funds needed to bring them to habitable standards. Nothing in the order requires the legislature to apply its funds other than as it wishes. That it has shown the wisdom to choose rehabilitation and expansion of facilities for Angola prison, as well as other Louisiana prison facilities, attests to its good judgment. . . . It requires only that if the State of Louisiana continues to operate the Angola prison it must do so in accordance with the Constitution and laws of the United States and the State of Louisiana.*

Anderson v. Vasquez (1992) held that denial of conjugal visits to death row inmates did not violate equal protection rights, and failure to have sperm preserved for artificial insemination did not amount to cruel and unusual punishment.

The courts are reluctant to interfere with administrative discretion in maintaining prison discipline and managing prisons. Solitary confinement is permissible for a breach of prison rules, so long as it does not violate the Eighth Amendment. A prohibition against prisoners forming a union is permissible. Officials can place reasonable restrictions on mail and visitors that are compatible with efficient prison administration but cannot entirely prohibit prisoners' use of the mail system. Prisoners have the right to communicate in person and by mail with attorneys. Although the courts traditionally uphold freedom of religion, economic considerations mandate practices that infringe on certain religious rights. Thus, prison officials can refuse to provide pork-free meals or late meals during Ramadan for Black Muslim prisoners and can refuse to pay for visits by a rabbi for a single Jewish prisoner. In *Roseborough v. Scott* (1994), an inmate charged that the policy on hair length and facial hair violated freedom of religion. The case was remanded to test the sincerity of the inmate's belief. *Ennis v. Barg* (1993) held that permitting religious tapes to come from sources other than directly from the publisher did not violate equal protection by treating them differently than other cassettes. Procedural due process can be used to challenge transfer of a prisoner to a mental hospital: The involuntary transfer denied a liberty interest protected by the Fourteenth Amendment (*Vitek v. Jones,* 1980). State prisoners formed a class in *Baugh v. Woodard* (1987) to challenge on due process grounds Bureau of Corrections procedures for transferring prisoners to correctional mental health facilities. The court held that the hearing conducted promptly after transfer but before admission and psychiatric treatment would comply with due process.

Many civil rights lost during confinement may remain lost after release. Property rights are not among them, although there are reasonable restraints on the disposition of property acquired in prison through occupational therapy and prison labor. However, confinement does entail difficulties in the management of other property, which may have to be handled by family members or an agent.

A change in social status is a common effect of conviction. Being a felon may limit employment opportunities; prohibit entrance to such professions as law, medicine, or social work; and deny other occupational licenses. However, expungement, removal of the case from the records, is possible. In many states, a spouse's conviction of a felony and incarceration are grounds for a divorce (see, for example, LA.C.C. 103, 1990).A lengthy sentence may be grounds for a declaration that a child is abandoned and free for adoption. (D.C. Code § 16-304 and comments to it indicate that abandonment may be grounds for adoption without parental consent.)

The ordinary civil rights of holding elective office, serving on a jury, and voting are often lost when one is convicted of a felony. The Supreme Court has held that a state may constitutionally disenfranchise former felons (*Richardson v. Ramirez*, 1974). These particular disabilities frequently have nothing to do with protecting the public and merely serve to penalize the individual and inhibit efforts at rehabilitation. This may be a fertile field for social action.

EXPUNGEMENT OF ARREST AND CONVICTION RECORDS

After serving a sentence the criminal has paid the debt to society and is, one hopes, rehabilitated. However, the stigma of a criminal conviction remains. Statutes permitting the expungement of arrest and conviction records free the offender from one disability: the necessity to discuss a conviction of crime or delinquency with future employers, insurance agents, military recruiters, and others. Some statutes provide that after a period of time with no recurrence of criminal behavior, the individual may request expungement and in some instances may also apply for an automatic pardon. If the record has been expunged, a former offender is able to state truthfully that there is now no criminal record and has the same chance to serve in public office, apply for admission to the armed services, and compete for employment as those without a record.

Because soliciting information about arrests and convictions from job applicants is now prohibited, this may not be the barrier to employment that it once was. In *Doe v. Utah Dept. of Public Safety* (1989), the court held that the department could not ask about or obtain expunged convictions. Therefore, any social worker who has a client with an arrest or criminal record may want to explore the availability of expungement.

The following case discusses some of the difficulties in correcting criminal justice records.

Dale Menard, a 19-year-old college student, had a summer job in Los Angeles. At 11:30 P.M. he waited in a park for a friend who was to drive him to his room in a nearby suburb. The friend failed to arrive. Menard dozed, walked around, and waited some more. At 3 A.M. he was approached by two police officers, who confronted him with a wallet containing $10 found near a park bench. Although his friend arrived and corroborated his story, Menard was arrested for robbery. After a year of fruitless correspondence in an effort to expunge the arrest record through the administrative process, Menard filed suit.

The case discusses the record keeping of the FBI and most local police departments. The court ordered the FBI to remove Menard's record from its criminal file.

Menard v. Saxbe
498 F.2d 1017 (D.C. Cir. 1974)
Leventhal, C.J.

Despite Menard's insistence that he knew nothing of the wallet, and despite the subsequent arrival of Menard's friend, who corroborated his account, Menard was placed under arrest, booked and fingerprinted at the station-house, and held in police custody for over two days. No criminal complaint was ever filed; no evidence was found indicating that the wallet had been stolen; and no information was adduced that tied Menard to any crime. Nevertheless, the Los Angeles police routinely forwarded to the FBI a fingerprint card, containing Menard's fingerprints and the notation that he had been arrested for burglary and two days later "Released—Unable to connect with any felony or misdemeanor at this time." The FBI has retained a record of Menard's arrest.

· · · · ·

With the apparent exception of the bureau's action in alerting plaintiff's record in the instant case, the FBI has never returned a fingerprint record on its motion. Moreover, the Bureau will not amend, alter, or even reveal a record at the instance of a private individual . . . taking the position not only that the decision to expunge must be made at the local level, but also that disclosure to an individual of the contents of his record will not be permitted, "inasmuch as data contained in our files is confidential and cannot be furnished to private individuals."

· · · · ·

The disabilities flowing from a record of arrest have been well documented. There is an undoubted "social stigma" involved in an arrest record.

The arrest record is used outside the field of criminal justice. Most significant is its use in connection with subsequent inquiries on applications for employment and licenses to engage in certain fields of work. An arrest record often proves to be a substantial barrier to employment. It appears, inter alia, that Menard's FBI record was supplied, subsequent to the filing of the complaint in this case, to the Marine Corps and the National Agency Check Center.

We note that we are focusing here on the FBI's "arrest records" and "criminal files," and we do not prohibit the maintenance of neutral identification records. When the FBI is apprised that a person has been exonerated after initial arrest, released without charge and a change of record to "detention only," the FBI has the responsibility to expunge the incident from its criminal identification files.

Certainly most clients of social work agencies would not have the time and money to engage in litigation to correct an inaccurate record as Menard did. Other bureaucracies probably have procedures concerning records that "have evolved over time," as had those of the FBI. Would it be easy for a client to correct an inaccuracy in a social services record? Would it be possible?

COMPENSATION TO VICTIMS OF VIOLENT CRIME

As society becomes more complex, the controls that were adequate to a smaller population in which most of the members knew each other become insufficient. As violent crime becomes more prevalent, concern about the damage, injury, and social wreckage left by the crime grows. Often the victim is unable to identify the perpetrator, and even if found and convicted, the attacker is usually judgment-proof should the victim sue for civil damages. The remedy the law provides for injury and damages—a civil suit—is of no avail if the criminal is never caught or if the indigent criminal is incarcerated and so not earning wages. Prosecution, conviction, and incarceration provide a remedy for society as a whole but do not benefit the victim with actual damages for wages lost, medical bills, and pain and suffering.

Throughout the centuries humankind has struggled with the idea of reparation, from the primitive "eye for an eye and tooth for a tooth" through payment to the king or chief as reparation for harm to one of his clan. During the mid-20th century, there was a revival of interest in compensating victims of crime, much of it attributable to the work of Margery Fry (1951), an English magistrate and social reformer. There are two philosophical bases for this legislation: (1) the community's duty to provide for those who suffer misfortune, and (2) society's agreement to give basic protection in return for the individual's giving up the right to active self-help.

The Criminal Injuries Compensation Act of 1963 of New Zealand was the first modern attempt to provide reparation for the damages caused by crime. Great Britain and Sweden also have such programs (Foulkes, 1966). The idea has spread to some Canadian provinces and various U. S. states. The statutes vary in their scope and coverage (Hoelzel, 1980). Typically they set up a commission to examine claims and pay damages. Most exclude property damage but include payments for medical expenses, loss of wages, and loss of support to dependents of the victim. Damages may include both physical and mental injuries, including pregnancy in the case of rape. Many statutes establish minimum and maximum payments, presumably on the theory that public support is available for injuries that incapacitate for a long time. Some statutes exclude victims whose attacker is a member of their immediate family; others exclude those who do not report the attack within a certain period of time. These provisions are designed to prevent collusion (Childers, 1964; Rothstein, 1974).

An interesting legal administrative problem is the eligibility of a non-resident injured in a state that has a compensation program. The specter of residence requirements may rise, as it has in other social legislation. Statutes in some states single out certain groups for payment of compensation, for instance, dependents of state employees killed in the line of duty.

In 1984 Congress passed the Victims of Crime Act, which provides funds for victims of federal crimes and for state victim reparations programs. The Victims' Rights and Restitution Act of 1990 added coverage. Services include identifying victims and providing information about where they can receive emergency medical and social services. If you work in the criminal justice system, check federal and state laws.

REFERENCES

Andreony, P. A. (1989). Juvenile extradition: Denial of due process. *Journal of Juvenile Law, 10,* 193–220.

Ankersmit, E. (1976). Setting the contract in probation. *Federal Probation, 40,* 28–33.

Ares, C. E., Ranken, A., & Sturz, H. (1963). The Manhattan Bail Project: An interim report on the use of pre-trial parole. *New York University Law Review, 38,* 67–95.

Balkin, S. (1980). Prisoners by day: A proposal to sentence non-violent offenders to non-residential work facilities. *Judicature, 64,* 154–164.

Birns, H. (1976). Diversion from the criminal process. *American Bar Association Journal, 62,* 1145–1148.

Black's law dictionary (4th ed., rev.). (1968). St. Paul, MN: West Publishing.

Caplan, L. (1984, July 2). The insanity defense. *New Yorker,* pp. 45–78.

Carr, J. J. (1970). An administrative retrospective on police crisis teams. *Social Casework, 60,* 416–422.

Childers, R. D. (1964). Compensation for criminally inflicted personal injury. *New York University Law Review, 39,* 444–471.

Clark, M. E. (1992). The immutable command meets the unknowable mind: Deific decree claims and the insanity defense after *People v. Serravo. Denver University Law Review, 7,* 161–183.

Easterbrook, F. H. (1992). Plea bargaining as compromise. *Yale Law Journal, 101*, 1969–1978.

Employment of social investigation reports in criminal and juvenile proceedings. (1958). *Columbia Law Review, 58*, 707–727.

Foulkes, D. L. (1966). Compensating victims of violence. *American Bar Association Journal, 52*, 237–239.

Fry, M. (1951). *Arms of the law.* London: Gollancz, Ltd.

Gibelman, M., & Schervish, P. H. (1993). *Who we are: The social work labor force as reflected in the NASW membership.* Washington, DC: NASW Press.

Henderson, H. E. (1976). Helping families in crisis: Police and social work intervention. *Social Work, 21*, 314–315.

Hoelzel, W. E. (1980). A survey of 27 victim compensation programs. *Judicature, 63*, 485–496.

Hudson, J., Galaway, B., & Chesney, S. (1977). When criminals repay their victims: A survey of restitution programs. *Judicature, 60*, 313–321.

Lewis, A. (1964). *Gideon's trumpet.* New York: Random House.

Michzels, R. A., & Treger, H. (1973). Social work in police departments. *Social Work, 18*, 67–75.

Mounts, S. E. (1982). Public defendant programs: Professional responsibility and competent representation. *Wisconsin Law Review*, pp. 473–533.

Ogletree, C. J., Jr. (1993). Beyond justifications: Seeking motivations to sustain public defenders. *Harvard Law Review, 106*, 1239–1294.

Parisi, N. (1980). Part-time imprisonment: The legal and practical issues of periodic confinement. *Judicature, 63*, 385–395.

Project: Temporary release in New York State correctional facilities. (1974). *Albany Law Review, 38*, 691–761.

Read, B. (1977). How restitution works in Georgia. *Judicature, 60*, 323-328.

Richards, D. J. (1994, Fall). The public defender defendant: A model statutory approach to public defender malpractice liability. *Valparaiso University Law Review, 29*, 511–556.

Roberts, A. R. (1976). Police social workers: A history. *Social Work, 21*, 294–299.

Rothstein, P. F. (1974). How the Uniform Crime Victims Reparations Act works. *American Bar Association Journal, 60,* 1531–1535.

Schroeder, L. O. (1985). The warrant clause: The key to the castle. *Federal Probation, 49,* 65–69.

Schulhofer, S. J. (1992). Plea bargaining as disaster. *Yale Law Journal, 101,* 1979–2009.

Scott, R. E., & Stuntz, W. J. (1992a). Plea bargaining as contract. *Yale Law Journal, 101,* 1909–1968.

Scott, R. E., & Stuntz, W. J. (1992b). Reply. *Yale Law Journal, 101,* 2011–2015.

Senna, J. J. (1975). Social workers in public defender programs. *Social Work, 20,* 271–277.

Sheridan, W. J. (1967, March). Juveniles who commit noncriminal acts: Why treat in a correctional system? *Federal Probation,* pp. 26–30.

Sheridan, W. J. (1967, June). New directions for the juvenile court. *Federal Probation,* pp. 15–20.

Sheridan, W. J. (1967, September). Structuring services for delinquent children and youth. *Federal Probation,* pp. 51–56.

Stanford, P. (1979, September 1). A model clockwork-orange prison. *New York Times Magazine,* p. 9.

Sullivan, B. (1975, February 24). Male chromosome theory on criminality being challenged. *State-Times,* p. 106.

Treger, H. Police social work. In R. L. Edwards (Ed.-in-Chief), *Encyclopedia of social work* (19th ed., Vol. 3, pp. 1843–1848). Washington, DC: NASW Press.

Uniform law annotated (Suppl., Vol. 2, 1994). St. Paul, MN: West Publishing.

Waldo, G. P., Chiricos, T. G., & Dobrin, L. E. (1973). Community contact and inmate attitudes: An experimental assessment of work release. *Criminology, 11,* 345–381.

Winock, B. J. (1985). Restructuring competency to stand trial. *U.C.L.A. Law Review, 32,* 921–985.

Wolfe, L. (1975, April 12). Clockwork gray. *New York,* pp. 80–83.

Woolf, D. A., & Rudman, M. (1977). A police–social service cooperative program. *Social Work, 22,* 62–63.

STATUTES CITED

Bail Reform Act of 1984. P.L. 98-473, 18 U.S.C.S. § 3041 et seq.

Civil Rights Act of 1964. P.L. 88-352, 78 Stat. 241.

Colorado Sex Offenders Act. C.R.S.A. § 16-13-201 et seq.

District of Columbia Wrongful Death Act. D.C. Code § 16-2701–2703.

Federal Youth Corrections Act of 1950. Ch. 1115, 64 Stat. 1085, 18 U.S.C.S. §§ 5005 et seq.

Illinois Sexually Dangerous Persons Act of 1955. 725 ILCS 205/0.01 et seq.

Omnibus Crime Control and Safe Streets Act of 1968. P.L. 90-351, 82 Stat. 197, 42 U.S.C.A. § 3701 et seq.

Sentencing Reform Act of 1984. P.L. 98-473, 18 U.S.C.S. § 3551.

Speedy Trial Act of 1974. P.L. 93-619, 18 U.S.C.A. § 3161–3174.

Uniform Criminal Extradition Act of 1979. 11 ULA 51.

Victims of Crime Act of 1984. P.L. 98-473, 42 U.S.C. § 10601 et seq.

Victims' Rights and Restitution Act of 1990. P.L. 98-473, 98 Stat. 2170, 42 USC § 10601.

STUDY QUESTIONS

1. How does the U.S. Constitution apply to state criminal justice systems?

2. What are some of the rights lost by conviction of a felony?

3. Is an individual accused of a crime entitled to an attorney?

4. What rights do confined prisoners have?

8

The Juvenile Justice System

The theory of the juvenile justice system is the *parens patriae* doctrine—the idea that the state, as a good parent, can interfere in the lives of children and of their parents for the welfare of children. Philosophically, this interference seems a noble effort to divert children from the possible abuses of the criminal justice system. But what of the child whose misbehavior is not criminal? Is judicial intervention a gross invasion of family rights to control of children (Marks, 1980)?

Many children come to the attention of the juvenile justice system through their parents, who either cannot or will not discipline them. The complaints range from "incorrigibility" to "running away from home." In earlier centuries the "incorrigible" ran away from home to sea or to a pioneer life in another country. These avenues are not open today. For a child whose parents do not have the emotional or financial resources to cope with disruptive behavior, the courts offer a solution, but at times this solution seems worse than doing nothing (Harris, 1978; Nelson, Sanders, & Landsman, 1993).

Many state juvenile laws differentiate between children whose misbehavior is noncriminal and those who commit delinquent acts. These are laudable attempts to ensure that nondelinquent children are not incarcerated with those who have committed criminal acts and to provide special guidance in the minors' own homes so that they remain outside traditional juvenile court jurisdiction. Whether to treat these children within or without the juvenile justice system remains controversial. Many communities do not have the social agencies available to handle the additional caseload.

114

The joint Institute of Judicial Administration/American Bar Association Commission on Juvenile Justice Standards worked for a decade preparing 21 volumes of proposed juvenile justice standards designed to reform the existing system. Social workers, physicians, and other experts worked with judges and lawyers preparing these standards, which will be presented to the states for their consideration. Commission chairman Irving Kaufman, chief judge of the United States court of appeals for the second circuit, urged the 1980 midyear meeting of the house of delegates of the American Bar Association to adopt the final volume of *Non-Criminal Misbehavior* that would remove these "status offenders" from the juvenile justice system. Judge Kaufman argued in vain, "Judges shouldn't be nursemaids for children who cross the street"; the house of delegates deferred action on the volume (Slonim, 1980). For the current status, refer to Rieffel's (1984) handbook. According to Rieffel, the standards contribute to making juvenile justice fair—fair to those who work in the courtroom, fair to society, and fair to youngsters. He provided a brief chronology of the major events in the development of the juvenile justice system, including cases cited in the text.

Children who are "status offenders" may be responding to emotional abuse not apparent to the casual observer. One court has described *status offenders* as "children who, by virtue of their age, are confined for going beyond parental control or running away from home" (*D.B. v. Tewksbury*, 1982). Should society respond to these symptoms of maladjustment, if that is what they are, and if so, how?

HISTORY OF THE JUVENILE COURTS

Juvenile courts are clearly a part of the judicial system but are neither criminal nor civil; they are sui generis. An act of delinquency is not a crime. However, many of the acts that are considered delinquent would be crimes if they were committed by an older person. Recent jurisprudence has emphasized the judicial nature of these courts and the constitutional and other legal constraints binding them.

The first juvenile court was created in 1899 in Illinois (705 ILCS 405/23 et seq.). It was an outgrowth of a reform movement seeking to deal with children informally at the first sign of delinquent behavior without conferring the stigma of a criminal conviction. For its first half-century, there was disagreement over whether this institution was more a social agency than a court (National Conference of Lawyers and Social Workers, 1967, 1968). Sometimes juvenile court judges were not even lawyers. During that first 50 years, not a single juvenile case reached the Supreme Court. However, since *Kent v.*

United States (1966) several major decisions have tried to apply constitutional safeguards to juvenile courts.

In addition to juvenile courts' handling of cases dealing with delinquent and negligent children, family courts have been created in some jurisdictions. These courts handle not only juvenile delinquency and neglect but also separation, divorce, custody, and adoption—all the legal problems of the family.

In some jurisdictions, judges are permanently assigned to family or juvenile court; in others, judges rotate through other courts as well (see Rubin, 1985). Judges who are assigned or elected directly to these courts better understand the emotional charge inherent in family problems and become familiar with community resources for troubled children and families. Where responsibility for juvenile matters is rotated among all the judges on the bench, including those whose specialty is criminal or civil law rather than juvenile or family law, the judge may not have time to appreciate the competence of the probation officers, social workers, and other personnel attached to the court. The advantage to rotation is that all judges become familiar with the limitations of treatment facilities and can influence the electorate to improve them.

JURISDICTION

State law grants jurisdiction to juvenile courts. The laws are similar in most details, commonly defining delinquency as any act that would be criminal if committed by an adult and adding acts like truancy that are not criminal. The jurisdictional statutes also define neglect; Minnesota's is a good example:

> *M.S.A. § 260.015: Subd. 10 "Neglected child" means a child:*
> *(a) Who is abandoned by his parent, guardian, or other custodian; or*
> *(b) Who is without proper parental care because of the faults or habits of his parent, guardian, or other custodian; or*
> *(c) Who is without necessary subsistence, education or other care necessary for his physical or mental health or morals because his parent, guardian or other custodian neglects or refuses to provide it; or*
> *(d) Who is without the special care made necessary by his physical or mental condition because his parent, guardian, or other custodian neglects or refuses to provide it; or*
> *(e) Whose occupation, behavior, condition, environment or associations are such as to be injurious or dangerous to himself or others; or*
> *(f) Who is living in a facility for foster care which is not licensed as required by law, unless the child is living in the facility under court order; or*

(g) Whose parent, guardian, or custodian has made arrangements for his placement in a manner detrimental to the welfare of the child or in violation of law; or
(h) Who comes within the provisions of subdivision 5, but whose conduct results in part from parental neglect.

The definitions are typically vague. An attorney representing a client accused of criminal neglect of a child would certainly try to use the ambiguity as a defense.

In a neglect proceeding, the family's social history and the parent's or guardian's potential for change become very important—at least as important as the evaluation of a criminal seeking probation or parole. Social history is also important in delinquency determinations. Once a minor is adjudicated as a delinquent, the judge will frequently rely on the social worker's recommendations for appropriate treatment. If the history suggests serious delinquency, the judge may waive jurisdiction and transfer the child for trial as an adult. Because of the rise in juvenile crime, many states now allow a juvenile accused of committing such serious crimes as murder, rape, aggravated kidnapping, armed robbery, or aggravated burglary to be transferred to criminal court for trial as an adult. If the child is over a certain age, often 15 years, a transfer hearing is held to determine whether there is probable cause to believe the child committed the offense and whether there is substantial opportunity for rehabilitation through the resources of the juvenile court.

The age cutoff for juvenile court jurisdiction may range from 16 to 21 years. The usual age for treating the individual as an adult is 18 years, the age of majority in many states. Thus, an act may be called delinquent one week before the culprit's 18th birthday and a crime a week after. Even if the offender is under the age limit, the court must still determine whether the facts indicate a need for juvenile court intervention.

Many states are now discussing juvenile and family court jurisdiction over "families in need of supervision." Children in such families may include not only those delinquent or neglected but also runaways and children who need other treatment or disposition different from placement in a training institution or foster home. (See 705 ILCS 405/5-1 et seq. for a statute relating to delinquent minors.) These families come to the attention of the court when expert opinion considers that the children are emotionally or socially disturbed although not necessarily engaging in overt delinquency. If the conduct of the parents is contributing to this condition, supervision and assistance may avert a minor's slide into delinquency and adult criminality. The following case illustrates how a family may come to the attention of the juvenile court and whether a judge must accept jurisdiction.

In re Vulon Children
288 N.Y.S.2d 203, 56 Misc.2d 19 (1968)
[A caseworker initiated the neglect proceeding. Evidence showed that the parents were hardworking and devoted, with an intact family in a well-kept apartment. The three children—Maurice, age 13; Marie, 10; and Michelle, age eight—had good school records. On weekdays the children were left alone from 3:30 P.M. to 5:30 P.M., when their mother returned from work. On the afternoon of the incident, Michelle, who was taking a bath, had vaginal bleeding. A physician attributed it to a laceration, stating that rape was probably not the cause, but that trauma, possibly self-inflicted, was more probable. The mother, who emigrated from Haiti in 1958, and the father refused to consider the possibility of rape and refused psychiatric examination of the children.]
Dembitz, J.

Once determination of neglect is made the court acquires not only a broad authority to control the life of the family but even to deprive the parents of their cardinal right to the custody of their children. . . . Accordingly, a finding of neglect cannot be made lightly; the court should exercise "its jurisdiction to interfere with parental guardianship reluctantly, and only upon strong and convincing proof of unfitness on the part of the parent or material benefit to the child."

It is questionable whether it would constitute "neglect" to leave habitually well-behaved children of ages 13, 10 and eight unattended in an apparently secure apartment in the afternoon for the two hours alleged in the petition; possibly self-responsibility to this limited extent, in a family where parents show an over-all affection and concern, may not only be harmless but beneficial. In any event, Mrs. Vulon testified without contradiction that since the troubling incident here involved she had secured someone to stay in the apartment in the afternoons until she returns from work.

According to petitioner, the parents "refused to believe that their child had been raped. They stated that they would not go into any conversation about rape with their children. They explained that in their country, a child did not learn about sex until the child was about 15 years of age; nor did the mother want me to discuss this with the child."

No doubt Mrs. Vulon's perturbation (described by petitioner) about the erroneous rape theory was due in part to the great damage that this charge would have inflicted on Maurice, the only suspect, who was an exemplary student in a Catholic school, aspiring to the priesthood. Though Mrs. Vulon apparently was herself concerned and frustrated that she was unable to ascertain the exact source of Michelle's bleeding, it was to the benefit rather than the detriment of her children that she refused to succumb to the mistaken suspicion of rape or to give it further currency.

Prosecution of this petition was largely attributable, it is clear, to the parents' refusal of the bureau's request that they consent to their children's examination by the court psychiatrist. Such examination apparently was viewed in part by the bureau as a possible method of determining whether Maurice committed the non-existent rape. So intent was the bureau on its proposal that its attorney approached the court ex parte before the hearing to ask it to order such examinations.

This judge personally has confidence in the psychiatric method and in free discussion with children of sex-related experiences. However, one cannot say that this approach has been so successful with our youth that the state can force parents—particularly in a family with a distinctive cultural pattern—to accept it, unless the need and the likelihood of benefit is clear.

A good faith appraisal by responsible and concerned parents, such as the Vulons, of the best way to handle a problem of child development on which reasonable men can differ in their value judgments, is not neglect.

This case illustrates forcefully that a juvenile court *is* a court and that the judge *is* in charge of the future of the child and parents before him. Social workers may disagree with the judge's decision here and consider that the children were neglected. However, there also may be disadvantage to a recommendation of psychiatric examination. It is interesting that the judge, more than the social worker, looks at the social factors in this situation—ages of the children and ethnic and cultural background—and gives them considerable weight. In any case, the judge, who may only see the parents at one hearing, is in a position to overrule the social worker, who has made a study of the family.

Some juvenile courts authorize the intake worker to decide whether to refer a child for further court proceedings, but once the jurisdiction of the juvenile court attaches, the judge is the final arbiter. The judge decides a case on the law, considering all the facts. Among the facts are experts' testimony, which may sometimes be conflicting. The law sometimes requires a solution other than the one a social worker thinks is optimal for the child.

DUE PROCESS RIGHTS OF JUVENILES

There has been dramatic recognition over the past several decades that juvenile courts are not social agencies but are courts—with all the constitutional protections that implies. *Application of Gault* (1967) is the landmark case in the juvenile court field.

On June 8, 1964, Gerald Gault, 15, was picked up at home by a juvenile officer on complaint of a neighbor that he had made an obscene telephone call to her. His parents were at work, and no notice was left to inform them where their son was. When a neighbor told his mother where Gerald was, she went to the detention home, where she was told that a hearing would be held the next day.

The day of the hearing a deputy filed a petition that was not served on the Gaults. At the hearing, no one was sworn. The complaining witness was not there. No record was made of the proceedings. Information about the hearing and a subsequent one on June 15 was derived from testimony at a habeas corpus proceeding conducted two months later; the testimony is equivocal as to whether Gerald admitted making the call. The probation officers gave the judge a report that was not disclosed to the Gaults. At the conclusion of the hearing the judge committed Gerald as a juvenile delinquent to the state industrial school until age 21, unless sooner discharged. The penalty for the same act, if committed by an adult, would have been a fine of $5 to $40 or imprisonment for not more than two months.

The entire case should be read for the information it gives on the history, development, and current practice in juvenile courts. The excerpts that follow give some of the court's reasoning in applying the due process clause of the Fourteenth Amendment to juveniles.

Application of Gault
387 U.S. 1, 87 S. Ct. 1428 (1967)
Fortas, J.

The highest motives and most enlightened impulses led to a peculiar system for juveniles, unknown to our law in any comparable context. The constitutional and theoretical basis for this peculiar system is—to say the least—debatable.

Due process of law is the primary and indispensable foundation of individual freedom. It is the basic and essential term in the social compact which defines the rights of the individual and delimits the power which the state may exercise.

It is claimed that juveniles obtain benefits from the special procedures applicable to them which more than offset the disadvantages of denial of the substance of normal due process. As we shall discuss, the observance of due process standards, intelligently and not ruthlessly administered, will not compel the states to abandon or displace any of the substantive benefits of the juvenile process. But it is important, we think, that the claimed benefits of the juvenile process should be candidly appraised. Neither sentiment nor folklore should cause us to shut our eyes, for example, to such startling findings as that reported in an exceptionally reliable study of repeaters or recidivism conducted by the Stanford Research Institute for the President's Commission on Crime in the District of Columbia.

Certainly, these figures and the high rates among juveniles to which we have referred . . . could not lead us to conclude that the absence of constitutional protections reduces crime, or that the juvenile system, functioning free of constitutional inhibitions as it has largely done, is effective to reduce crime or rehabilitate offenders. We do not mean by this to denigrate the juvenile court process or to suggest that there are not aspects of the juvenile system relating to offenders which are valuable. But the features of the juvenile system which its proponents have asserted are of unique benefit will not be impaired by constitutional domestication. For example, the commendable principles relating to the processing and treatment of juveniles separately from adults are in no way involved or affected by the procedural issues under discussion. Further, we are told that one of the important benefits of the special juvenile court procedures is that they avoid classifying the juvenile as a "criminal." The juvenile offender is now classed as a "delinquent." There is, of course, no reason why this should not continue.

In any event, there is no reason why, consistently with due process, a state cannot continue if it deems it appropriate, to provide and to improve provisions for the confidentiality of records of police contacts and court action relating to juveniles.

Further, it is urged that the juvenile benefits from informal proceedings in the court. . . . But recent studies have, with surprising unanimity, entered sharp dissent as to the validity of this gentle conception. They suggest that the appearance as well as the actuality of fairness, impartiality and orderliness—in short, the essentials of due process—may be a more impressive and more therapeutic attitude so far as the juvenile is concerned. For example, in a recent study, the sociologists Wheeler and Cottrell observed that when the procedural laxness of the "parens patriae" attitude is followed by stern discipline, the contrast may have an adverse effect upon the child, who feels that he has been deceived or enticed.

A boy is charged with misconduct. The boy is committed to an institution where he may be restrained of liberty for years. It is of no constitutional consequence—and of limited practical meaning—that the institution to which he is committed is called an industrial school.

In view of this, it would be extraordinary if our Constitution did not require the procedural regularity and the exercise of care implied in the phrase "due process." Under our Constitution, the condition of being a boy does not justify a kangaroo court. . . . The essential difference between Gerald's case and a normal criminal case is that safeguards available to adults were discarded in Gerald's case.

Notice, to comply with due process requirements, must be given sufficiently in advance of scheduled court proceedings so that reasonable opportunity to prepare will be afforded, and it must "set forth the alleged *misconduct with particularity." It is obvious . . . that no purpose of shielding the child from the public stigma of knowledge of his having been taken into custody and scheduled for hearing is served by the procedure approved by the court below. The "initial hearing" in the present case was a hearing on the merits. Notice at that time is not timely; and even if there were a conceivable purpose served by the deferral proposed by the court below, it would have to yield to the requirements that the child and his parents or guardian be notified, in writing, of the specific charge or factual allegations to be considered at the hearing, and that such written notice be given at the earliest practicable time, and in any event sufficiently in advance of the hearing to permit preparation.*

We conclude that the due process clause of the Fourteenth Amendment requires that in respect of proceedings to determine delinquency which may result in commitment to an institution in which the juvenile's freedom is curtailed, the child and his parents must be notified of the child's right to be represented by counsel retained by them, or if they are unable to afford counsel, that counsel will be appointed to represent the child.

We shall assume that Gerald made admissions of the sort described by the juvenile court judge. . . . Neither Gerald nor his parents were advised that he did not have to testify or make a statement, or that an incriminating statement might result in his commitment as a "delinquent."

The privilege against self-incrimination is, of course, related to the question of the safeguards necessary to assure that admissions or confessions are reasonably trustworthy, that they are not the mere fruits of fear or coercion, but are reliable expressions of the truth. The roots of the privilege are, however, far deeper. They tap the basic stream of religious and political principle because the privilege reflects the limits of the individual's attornment to the state and—in a philosophical sense—insists upon the equality of the individual and the state. In other words, the privilege has a broader and deeper thrust than the rule which prevents the use of confessions which are the product of coercion because coercion is thought to carry with it the danger of unreliability. One of its purposes is to prevent the state, either by force or by psychological domination, from overcoming the mind and will of the person under investigation and depriving him of the freedom to decide whether to assist the state in securing his conviction.

· · · · ·

Against the application to juveniles of the right to silence, it is argued that juvenile proceedings are "civil" and not "criminal," and therefore the privilege should not apply.

It would be entirely unrealistic to carve out of the Fifth Amendment all statements by juveniles on the ground that these cannot lead to "criminal" involvement. In the first place, juvenile proceedings to determine "delinquency," which may lead to commitment to a state institution, must be regarded as "criminal" for purposes of the privilege against self-incrimination. To hold otherwise would be to disregard substance because of the feeble enticement of the "civil" label-of-convenience which has been attached to juvenile proceedings.

In fact, evidence is accumulating that confessions by juveniles do not aid in "individualized treatment," as the court below put it, and that compelling the child to answer questions, without warning or advice as to his right to remain silent, does not serve this or any other good purpose.

We conclude that the constitutional privilege against self-incrimination is applicable in the case of juveniles as it is with respect to adults.
[Justice Black and White concurred. Justice Harlan concurred in part and dissented in part. Justice Stewart dissented.]
Stewart, J.

The court today uses an obscure Arizona case as a vehicle to impose upon thousands of juvenile courts throughout the nation restrictions that the Constitution made applicable to adversary criminal trials. I believe the court's decision is wholly unsound as a matter of constitutional law, and sadly unwise as a matter of judicial policy.

The inflexible restrictions that the Constitution so wisely made applicable to adversary criminal trials have no inevitable place in the proceedings of those public social agencies known as juvenile or family courts. And to impose the court's long catalog of requirements upon juvenile proceedings in every area of the country is to invite a long step backwards into the nineteenth century. In that era there were no juvenile proceedings, and a child was tried in a conventional criminal court with all the trappings of a conventional criminal trial. So it was that a 12-year-old boy named James Guild was tried in New Jersey for killing Catharine Beakes. A jury found him guilty of murder, and he was sentenced to death by hanging. The sentence was executed. It was all very constitutional.

In *Gault* the Supreme Court used the due process clause of the Fourteenth Amendment to provide juveniles with some of the protections of the Bill of Rights. Due process for juveniles now includes rights to notice, rights to confront and cross-examine witnesses, rights to counsel and, a privilege against self-incrimination. Whether these due process rights will limit the rehabilitative and corrective purposes of the juvenile courts remains to be seen (Teitelbaum & Ellis, 1978). They will certainly require more formal procedures in courts where practice has been lax. The decision lays to rest once and for all the question of whether juvenile courts are truly courts or the "public social agencies" Justice Stewart talks about.

Judge Martin (1992) discussed the dissatisfaction with treatment in juvenile courts, which leads to transfer of serious juvenile offenders for trial as adults. He cited the state statutes that deal with this issue and the various state procedures for transfer. He also reported studies that gave promising indications that rehabilitation in juvenile courts does work.

Still *Gault* left some unanswered questions. For instance, how many of the due process rights afforded adults should apply to juveniles? Subsequent decisions have given partial answers.

In re Winship (1970) dealt with the narrow question of whether due process requires proof beyond a reasonable doubt when a juvenile is charged with an act that would constitute a crime if committed by an adult. After discussing the history of the requirement and its importance considering what the accused has at stake—the possible loss of liberty and the stigma if convicted—the Court held that the standard does apply to juvenile adjudicatory proceedings, saying

> *Nor will there be any effect on the informality, flexibility, or speed of the hearing at which the fact finding takes place. And the opportunity during the post-adjudicatory or dispositional hearing for a wide-ranged review of the child's social history and for his individualized treatment will remain unimpaired.* (p. 366)

The precise issue in *McKeiver v. Pennsylvania* (1970) was whether the due process clause assures the right to trial by jury in a state delinquency proceeding in deciding whether a delinquent act has been committed. The Court said that the juvenile court proceeding is not a "criminal prosecution" within the meaning and reach of the Sixth Amendment, and calling the proceeding either "civil" or "criminal" would be simplistic. The requirement of a jury trial would remake the proceeding into an actual adversary process, putting an effective end to "the idealistic prospect of an intimate, informal protective proceeding." The Court held that due process did not require a jury trial in juvenile proceedings.

> *If the formalities of the criminal adjudicative process are to be superimposed upon the juvenile court system, there is little need for its separate existence. Perhaps the ultimate disillusionment will come one day, but for the moment we are disinclined to give impetus to it.* (p. 545) [Justices Douglas, Black, and Marshall dissented.]

There is certainly disillusionment with the juvenile court system. Many states are lowering the age ceiling for juvenile court jurisdiction and increasing the availability of transfer of adolescents to trial as adults. Perhaps more of the formalities of the criminal adjudicative process will be imposed in the future; this will raise further problems. If a jury trial is a due process requirement, when the accused is eight years old, must the jury of peers come from that age group?

Moss v. Weaver (1976) found unconstitutional under the Fourth Amendment the practice of imposing pretrial detention on accused delinquents without first determining whether there is probable cause to believe that the juvenile has committed the offense. If distinct advantages derive from the informality of juvenile tribunals, are they lessened by requiring a probable cause hearing? Informality is not destroyed because the judge determines whether there is a reasonable belief that the juvenile committed the act. This simply protects the juvenile from unnecessary detention in facilities that may be less than salutary.

The court of appeals was careful to conclude that in a juvenile predetention hearing there is no guaranteed right to hear and cross-examine witnesses. Does this make a predetention hearing similar to the pretermination hearing ordered by the Court in *Goldberg v. Kelly* (1970), where welfare benefits were at stake? The Supreme Court decided the issue in *Schall v. Martin* (1984), a class action suit, using a habeas corpus action to challenge pretrial detention as a violation of due process. Several 14-year-old youths had been charged with robbery and assault. The case gives a good description of how a juvenile court, in this case the New York family court, acts. The court held that the section of the statute authorizing detention based on a finding of "serious risk" that the juvenile "may before the return date commit an act which if committed by an adult would constitute a crime" did not violate due process. The juvenile's liberty may be subordinated to the state's *parens patriae* interest in promoting the welfare of the child. Every state permits juvenile pretrial detention.

In *United States v. Fowler* (1973) a 16-year-old boy was accused of participating in the burglary of a United States Post Office. The court of appeals held that the oral *Miranda* warnings (those warnings that grew out of the *Miranda v. State of Arizona* [1966] case, requiring that, on arrest, suspects be warned that information they give can be used against them in a judicial proceeding and that they have the right to consult with an attorney before answering questions) applied to juvenile proceedings by virtue of *Gault*. Consequently, the boy's answers to questions and his signed affidavit could not be used against him later.

In *Fare v. Michael C.* (1979) the Supreme Court was faced with the question of whether a juvenile's request for his probation officer was a per se invocation of his Fifth Amendment rights. His mother was in prison, his father's whereabouts unknown, and the grandmother he lived with was elderly and blind. Whether statements made during interrogation without advice of counsel are admissible is resolved on the totality of the circumstances. In a 5 to 4 decision the Court upheld the juvenile court's finding that the defendant waived his rights and his statements were voluntary. But *State v. Belton* (1988) held that appointment of the probation officer to act as a "concerned adult" was inadequate and prevented a finding of voluntary waiver of the juvenile's constitutional rights in making a statement.

In *Breed v. Jones* (1975) the Supreme Court held that a prisoner, prosecuted as an adult after an adjudicatory finding in juvenile court that he had violated a criminal statute but was unfit for treatment as a juvenile, had been put in jeopardy at the juvenile court hearing. Subsequent trial as an adult for the same offense violated the double jeopardy clause of the Fifth Amendment. (*Rios v. Chavez*, 1980, made *Breed* retroactive.) However, in *Tuten v. United States* (1983) the court had not exercised its discretion to discharge the youthful offender after completion of his probation. He was later convicted, at age 19, of carrying a pistol without a license. That felony conviction was enhanced by his juvenile court conviction. Cornish (1982) discussed trying children as adults and suggested that the offense alone should not be the deciding factor, but prior records and amenability to rehabilitation should be considered.

In *Davis v. Alaska* (1974) the Supreme Court obliquely modified a juvenile right. It held that the refusal to allow the defendant to cross-examine the key prosecution witness, a juvenile, about the witness's probation after an adjudication of juvenile delinquency denied defendant his constitutional right to confront witnesses. State policy protecting the anonymity of juvenile offenders is outweighed by the defendant's right effectively to cross-examine a witness (see Costikyan, 1976).

In *Nelson v. Heyne* (1974), a class action was brought for relief against certain procedures used in a boy's school, part of a medium-security correctional institution. The court held that corporal punishment and the use of tranquilizing drugs administered intramuscularly by staff, who ignored more moderate medication and worked without adequate medical guidance, constituted cruel and unusual punishment in violation of the Eighth Amendment.

Within the constraints of these cases, the juvenile courts attempt to rehabilitate the young person who runs afoul of the law. The juvenile judge has great leeway in fashioning treatment programs. He may impose regular school attendance as a condition for probation, for instance, but may not validly require summary detention in the event of noncompliance (*Matter of Gerald Allen B.*, 1980). Although *Gault* and its progeny have established certain due process rights of juveniles, these need not weaken, as the courts have been careful to point out, the rehabilitative function of the juvenile justice system. Careful attention to procedures may indeed help the court and its personnel do a better job and minimize charges of malpractice by social workers (Levine, 1977). The juvenile is also assured of constitutional protection against arbitrary treatment, however well-intentioned.

If concerned relatives live in another state, or if an institution specializing in the juvenile's problem is located outside the state, a social worker should not be limited by state boundaries in planning for supervision and placement. In making treatment plans, social workers have available the Interstate Compact on Juveniles, which establishes procedures for out-of-state supervision and for the return of juveniles from a receiving state. All 50 states and the District of Columbia have enacted the compact, so that planning may be truly nationwide.

FEDERAL STATUTES

The federal judicial system has no separate juvenile court. With the Amendments to the Juvenile Delinquency Act in 1994, Congress expressed its interest in dealing with juveniles in a rehabilitative manner, outside the criminal justice system. If those accused of a federal crime are tried under the statute, they are adjudged juvenile delinquents rather than criminals; the disclosure of their records is severely limited; they are given a special speedy trial; and they may be detained in a juvenile facility, a foster home, or a community-based facility rather than a jail. In *United States v. Hill* (1976) the issue was whether the juvenile, tried under the act, must be indicted by a grand jury and tried by a jury. The court of appeals, citing *McKeiver*, said that he did not need to undergo these procedures.

The Federal Youth Corrections Act was repealed in 1984 and no longer directs how convicted juveniles will be treated in the federal system. The United States Sentencing Commission has authority to set guidelines for sentencing to probation, fine, or imprisonment. The guidelines consider age, education, prior record, family ties, and other factors that probation officers would consider. Before a dispositional hearing the court can order observation by an appropriate agency if it is indicated.

CHILD ABUSE

A social problem of alarming proportions is that of abused children, that is, those abused, either physically or emotionally, by parents or other guardians. When children are hurt by someone not responsible for their welfare, such as another child, a neighbor, or a criminal, the ordinary processes of criminal law can be called into play, and the children so abused may be helped by their parents and resources in the community. When children are abused by parents, the trauma of the attack is compounded by the children's removal from the home for their own safety.

The Louisiana definition of child abuse is typical:

Louisiana Revised Statutes, Title 14, Section 403

(3) "Abuse" is the infliction of physical or mental injury or the causing of the deterioration of a child and shall include exploitation or overwork of a child to such an extent that his health, moral or emotional well-being is endangered.

Sexual abuse, along with mental injury, is often difficult to determine. Either because of increased reporting or greater frequency, the numbers of reported incidents of sexual abuse of children is rising. These cases present difficult treatment problems (Gentry, 1978). A recent symposium of the Secretarial Initiative on Child Abuse and Neglect, developed by the U.S. Department of Health and Human Services, reports a dramatic increase in the number and severity of cases of child abuse and neglect in the past decade. According to the report, at least 33 states and the District of Columbia require joint investigations by law enforcement and child protection agencies in such cases (Dinsmore, 1993).

One encouraging phenomenon in this area is the swift response of society in marshalling resources when its attention is called to a social problem needing community action. Once abused child syndrome was identified by physicians, legislative response was swift. Within a decade after the first articles about battered children appeared, every state in the country had passed laws to address the problem (Gil & Noble, 1967; Paulsen, 1966, 1967). The statutes typically mandate that certain professionals—physicians, nurses, social workers, and teachers—report suspected child abuse and keep discretionary reports by others. The statutes also give immunity from civil and criminal liability to those reporting in good faith. Circumstantial evidence must often be used to establish the criminal liability of the abusing parent because the parent may not confess the crime and the child's testimony is often unavailable or unreliable. The right of privileged communication between the child and a professional person, which would include social workers, is not grounds for excluding evidence at a proceeding to determine abuse, as the Louisiana statute shows:

Louisiana Revised Statutes, Title 14, Section 403 E.

Any privilege between husband and wife, or between any professional person and his client, such as physicians and ministers, with the exception of the attorney and his client, shall not be grounds for excluding evidence at any proceeding regarding the abuse or neglect of the child or the cause therefore.

Few cases dealing with child abuse reach the appellate level in the judicial system. Many abusing adults agree to psychiatric treatment for themselves and placement for their children after pleading guilty to a criminal charge and receiving a suspended sentence, conditional on treatment. Therefore, the facts of child abuse cases generally do not reach the attention of the public, except when a child dies or when particularly brutal treatment makes the headlines. The *State v. Hunt* (1965) case did reach an appellate court and shows how the attorney defended his clients, the abusing parents.

Christina Hengsteler, who did housework for the defendants, discovered their 5-year-old daughter, Tina, tied up in the furnace room. Her hands were tied behind her back, she was bleeding, and her nose was flattened. Christina went home; her mother called the sheriff's office; and Ben Bernal, a deputy sheriff assigned to juvenile work, went to her home. He and Ms. Hengsteler then went to the home of Dr. and Mrs. Hunt, asked to see Tina, and followed Mrs. Hunt to the furnace room. Detective Bernal did not have a warrant.

When asked, Tina stated that her mother had "beat her with a hose," although she later agreed with her mother that the bruises had happened when her brother threw a rope around her and pulled her up as if she were a cow. Tina was taken first to the sheriff's office, where she was photographed, and then to a hospital. Thirty days later the Hunts were arrested for aggravated assault. After six days of trial, the jury returned guilty verdicts against both defendants on one count of aggravated assault and battery and all three child neglect counts.

State v. Hunt

2 Ariz. App. 6, 406 P.2d 208 (1965)
Gordon, J.

Defendants assign as error the trial court's denial of their pretrial motion to suppress the evidence compiled by Detective Bernal.

We cannot agree with defendants' contention that Officer Bernal's entry into their home and his conduct therein was unlawful, and therefore cannot agree that the evidence he obtained therein was illegally obtained and should be excluded.

If his purpose is to remove the child from surroundings endangering its health, etc., he is neither arresting the child for a crime nor its parents nor anyone else who might have physical custody of the child at the time. . . . The officer is not investigating the commission of a crime, or gathering evidence for the prosecution of a crime, but is exercising lawful authority to take the child into protective custody, subject to the future disposition of the child under the juvenile courts' authority, should the same be invoked by petition.

We hold that Officer Bernal was on the premises lawfully in a noncriminal proceeding, regardless of the consent or nonconsent of Dr. and

Mrs. Hunt. The remaining question is—Does this give him the authority to obtain from the premises evidence which would be admissible later in a criminal action against the parents of Tina? We believe it does. Being on the premises lawfully in performance of his lawful duty, the obtaining of the evidence was not illegal, hence not within the protection of the exclusionary principle of the Fourth Amendment.

Defendants also assign as error the lower court's permitting Christina Hengsteler and Detective Ben Bernal to testify over hearsay objections concerning the conversations they had with Tina . . . when each of them first saw Tina in the furnace room.

These statements would obviously be hearsay unless they are admissible under the "excited utterance" or "spontaneous exclamation" exception to the hearsay rule.

Applying these guidelines to the facts in this case, we believe the requisites and thus the foundation for the "excited utterance" exception were satisfied.

If the court so found, the only remaining question would be whether sufficient time had expired thereafter in which Tina could have reflected and fabricated. It is not unreasonable to imagine that a child under circumstances as are apparent from the evidence here could have been so excited or terror-stricken from her beating and confinement in the dark furnace room that both requisites were present and satisfied, even though several hours may have passed from time of the beating.

Over defendants' objection of physician–patient privilege Dr. Charles Pullen and Dr. Everett Czerny . . . were allowed to testify.

The reason behind the physician–patient privilege is to encourage freedom of disclosure by the patient so as to aid in the effective treatment. We do not believe its purpose is to exclude otherwise admissible evidence obtained from a third party whose interests in suppressing the evidence are patently adverse to the patient, merely because the declarant holds a close family relationship to the patient. We feel that the relationship of natural father or mother does not confer upon the holder of that title the right to claim the physician–patient exclusionary privilege if in doing so the claimant is excluding otherwise valid evidence of the parent having committed a crime against his or her child. Where such a conflict exists, a guardian of the person or estate would seem to be the more appropriate holder of the privilege.

[The final argument of the defendants concerned denial of a change of venue because of adverse pretrial publicity. The court remanded the case for a new trial, stating that the court would support a courageous bench that could step in to prohibit publicity prejudicial to the rights of the defendants.]

Although the facts of the abuse would be familiar to professionals, the case is interesting because it illustrates the difference in goals and techniques between the lawyer and the social worker. The attorney, certainly, is concerned about the child and the entire family, but only the parents are his clients, and for them he performs the best professional services possible. Although this may involve recommending psychiatric treatment for the client, the awesome questions of guilt and innocence are determined by the factfinder.

The attorney is concerned with the disposition of the case but considers it in terms of impact on the client, which is not necessarily the social worker's focus. The attorney tries to place the facts—of abuse or whatever else—in the best light possible for a client, using whatever defenses are available, as *Hunt* shows, while leaving to the judge and the jury the determination of guilt. If the physician–patient privilege can be used to exclude damaging evidence, the attorney will use it. The excerpt from the Louisiana statute shows that legislatures have anticipated and sought to prevent the use of privilege in this way. (The reasoning for admitting evidence obtained without a search warrant is reminiscent of that in *Wyman v. James* [1971], where the Supreme Court decided that a caseworker's home visit was not a search.)

The Constitution applies to all citizens, even those accused of the most heinous crime, as some would characterize child abuse. The attorney for the accused is the person our criminal justice system allows to use those constitutional protections in the best interest of the client. The philosophical question of what is ultimately in a client's "best interest" is not a question we should expect attorneys to ask themselves.

A recent Alabama case, *H.R. v. State Dept. of Human Resources* (1992) reported that the mother refused to allow entry to her house or interviews with her four children. The court held that two anonymous reports of abuse and neglect were unsworn hearsay and insufficient for probable cause to authorize entry without her consent.

Although it is seldom possible to find out what happened after cases are reported, there are two follow-up cases to *Hunt: In re Adoption of Luke* (1966) and *In re Anonymous* (1966). In one, Tina was permanently removed from the custody of the Hunts; in the other, an interlocutory adoption order for another Hunt child, placed privately, was revoked because the adoptive parents had previoulsy abused an adopted child.

The child abuse statutes typically impose sanctions on those individuals required by law to report child abuse who fail to do so. The Louisiana statute provides for a $500 fine, imprisonment for six months, or both.

The mandatory reporting statutes have not accomplished their purpose of bringing all child abuse to the attention of the criminal authorities. Under the statutes, however, there have been civil suits for damages against physicians who failed to report incidents and thus permitted further abuse. In an unreported case, a suit for $5,000,000 in damages was brought when a child suffered serious brain damage after being returned to parents after the first instance of abuse came to the physician's attention (*Robinson v. Wickl*, 1970, reported in McDonald, 1977). The case was settled out of court for $600,000. In a second case, a physician was sued for malpractice on the basis of not performing his statutory reporting function (*Landeros v. Flood*, 1976; see also Isaacson, 1975). The state supreme court remanded the case to determine, as a question of fact, whether the ability to recognize battered child syndrome is within the skill of an ordinary physician.

A recent Florida case, *Fischer v. Metcalf* (1989), held that minor children could not sue the psychiatrist who had treated their father as a voluntary outpatient. They alleged that the psychiatrist's failure to report his knowledge or suspicion of physical and mental abuse resulted in physical and emotional injuries. The court felt an implied civil remedy was inconsistent with the purposes of helping abused children, preserving family life, and providing treatment.

A 1985 Maine child abuse reporting statute (22 M.R.S.A. § 3872) contains a provision encouraging treatment. The investigating social service workers consult with the therapist and may agree that the perpetrator and child should be shielded from the trauma of an investigation (Myers, 1986).

Although physicians are the more likely target of civil damage suits, social workers who are in a position to observe cases of child abuse must be sure that they report it promptly. At least one social services agency has been held civilly liable for the death of a child abused by his foster mother, when a contributing factor was the negligence of the social worker in not examining more diligently the reports of abuse (*Vonner v. State Dept. of Public Welfare*, 1974). Criminal liability is also more than a remote possibility. In an unreported case, a social worker was found guilty of second degree official misconduct after the death of an abused child under her supervision (*People v. Steinberger*, 1981).

DeShaney v. Winnebago County (1989) is an example of what might happen. The mother of a child beaten by his father to such an extent that he had serious brain damage brought a civil rights action against social workers and local officials. In a 5 to 4 decision, the Supreme Court held that the state had no constitutional duty to protect the child from his father after receiving reports of possible abuse. The caseworker had visited the home and noted suspicious injuries, which she recorded, but took no further action (Schroeder, 1986).

Once it is determined that a child has been abused and must be removed from the home, the social worker uses the same methods as those used in planning for and treating neglected and delinquent children. The individualized social history, the consideration of the needs of all parties, and the search for the best possible placement are familiar to all members of the profession. If the parents are incarcerated, the child's home is temporarily or perhaps permanently disrupted; other living arrangements must be made. This has led to discussion of freeing abused children for adoption (the Hunt children were adopted by private placement) by declaring parental rights terminated.

A termination proceeding should provide ample legal protections, not only for the child but also for the parents. Indigent parents will need appointed counsel to represent their interests. If the parents are not incarcerated, but are receiving treatment, the value of returning the child to their home must be weighed against the possible physical or emotional danger. The ramifications of disposition are of concern to everyone (Musavichick, 1972). Abused children frequently become abusing parents; therefore, society as a whole has a great stake in what happens to them, and social workers are understandably cautious about recommending return of a child to an abusing parent.

In child dependency proceedings, typically civil in nature, counsel may not be appointed for indigent parents because the Supreme Court's decisions require assistance of counsel only in criminal proceedings. However, in *Cleaver v. Wilcox* (1974), a federal court required appointed counsel for indigent parents in such dependency hearings. An excerpt indicates the thinking of the court:

> *When an agency of the state seeks to remove a child from the custody of parents who say they are qualified to rear the child, both the parents and the state have interest in accurate findings of fact and informed juvenile-court supervision. The state's interest in saving public money does not outweigh society's interest in preserving viable family units and the parent's interest in not being unfairly deprived of control and custody of a child. Protection of a right as fundamental as that of child custody cannot be denied by asserting that counsel in civil litigation has always depended upon the free-enterprise generalization that one usually gets what one pays for. The "civil litigation" generalization overlooks the nature of the rights in question and the relative powers of the antagonists. Despite the informality of the juvenile dependency hearings, the parent, untutored in the law, may well have difficulty presenting his or her version of disputed facts, cross-examining witnesses, or working with documentary evidence.*
>
> *Without undertaking to write a manual for state judges on when to appoint counsel in particular cases, we note some of the general factors*

which should be considered: One such factor is the length of the separa-
tion which the parents may face. . . . The greater the probability of
removal, based upon the facts of the case and the social-service worker's
recommendation, the more pressing will be the need for appointed coun-
sel. A second factor is the presence or absence of parental consent or of
disputed facts. Also relevant is the parent's ability to cope with relevant
documents and the examination of witnesses. The more complex the
case, the more counsel can contribute to the hearings. Finally, should
the judge refuse a request for counsel, it is important that the grounds
for the refusal be stated in the record so that meaningful judicial review
of the refusal can be had in the state courts.

This court does not believe it necessary to impose upon an excellent
state court system an inflexible constitutional rule which requires ap-
pointed counsel in every dependency proceeding. . . . Parents are en-
titled to a judicial decision on the right to counsel in each case. The
determination should be made with the understanding that due process
requires the state to appoint counsel whenever an indigent parent, un-
able to present his or her case properly, faces a substantial possibility of
the loss of custody or of prolonged separation from a child. Application
of these guidelines can and should be made by the state courts on a
case-by-case basis. (p. 945)

The fifth circuit has held that due process requires that parents in a
Florida child dependency proceeding be advised of their right to assistance of counsel immediately after service of petition for an adjudication
of dependency or seizure of the child, and, if indigent, that counsel be
appointed unless the parents knowingly and intelligently waive their rights
to counsel (*Davis v. Page*, 1980). But a year later in *Lassiter v. Department of Soc. Serv. of Durham City* (1981), the Supreme Court held that
failure to appoint counsel for indigent parents in a proceeding for termination of parental status did not deprive the parent of due process. In
Lassiter, the petition contained no allegations on which a criminal charge
could be based, no expert witnesses testified, the case presented no
troublesome points of law, and the presence of counsel could not have
made a difference for petitioner. The Constitution does not require appointment of counsel in every parental termination proceeding, and
whether due process calls for such appointment is determined case by
case by the trial court.

If the appointment of counsel for indigents is required increasingly
often in custody proceedings, where are the attorneys coming from? Should
we ask the organized bar to assume this responsibility, or must over-
worked public defender or legal aid offices take it on? These proceedings

affect the future of many individuals and can strengthen or break already tenuous family ties. Adequate legal representation is more than a luxury.

CHILDREN'S RIGHTS

Children are people with the constitutional rights of adults, but the child's rights are limited even more than are adults', because of the rights of parents to exercise authority over them. This limitation concerns activist groups working to eliminate child abuse, warehousing of children in institutions, locking children up for noncriminal activities, and leaving children in limbo, drifting from one foster home to another. These problems are discussed in other chapters.

Some believe that giving children a more active decision-making role would solve some of the problems of frustration and incompatibility between parent and child. One controversial direction these activities have taken is shown by the "divorce" between parent and child in *In re Snyder* (1975). The parents were very strict; the 16-year-old girl was an above-average student. The father sought help from the juvenile court, and the girl herself petitioned to be named a dependent child to prevent a return to the hostile environment of her home. The Supreme Court upheld the juvenile court commissioner, ruling that the parent–child relationship had dissipated to the point where parental control was lost and the child need not return. For children able to support themselves, emancipation permits active exercise of their rights. *Emancipation* means freeing the child from the custody of the parents and the obligation to render services to them. The term is not exact, because not all parental ties have to be severed. The death of a parent does not automatically emancipate a minor, although the marriage of the minor usually does. In some states emancipation requires a legal proceeding in which the minor is judicially declared an adult, with the rights and responsibilities of that status. Before the age of majority was reduced from 21 to 18 years, the proceeding was not uncommon in settling the estate of a deceased parent. Emancipation enables the minor to accept the estate, without the expense of appointment of a guardian for the brief time before the minor reaches adulthood.

Attorneys *ad litem* (appointed to prosecute or defend a lawsuit for a minor) can represent children when their rights may be adverse to those of their parents; custody and adoption are examples (Bernstein, 1979). However, the implications of the state stepping in to overrule parental decisions need careful consideration. To protect children from abusive parents and from an indifferent criminal system is one thing; to replace family ties with government authority is quite another (Hafen, 1977). The "liberty" interests of children in an area of the law that is in flux, and protection for established interests, present constitutional questions of some difficulty (Teitelbaum & Ellis, 1978). Children's liberty interests are protected by due process, so procedural requirements are necessary for intervention by the state in decisions to commit to institutions for people with mental retardation.

Practice in juvenile courts promises dynamic changes in the coming years. One change on the horizon is an attack on the confidentiality of the proceedings (Winter, 1980). Social workers may need to rethink their attitudes toward closed juvenile courts and decide how publicity about these hearings can best be used to protect the children.

REFERENCES

Bernstein, B. E. (1979). The attorney *ad litem:* Guardian of the rights of children and incompetents. *Social Casework, 60,* 463–470.

Cornish, T. R. (1982). Where have all the children gone? Reverse certification. *Oklahoma Law Review, 35,* 373–402.

Costikyan, E. N. (1976, May 13). Assault with intent to maim. *New York, 9,* 7–8.

Dinsmore, J. (1993, July). *Joint investigations of child abuse* (Report of symposium of the Secretarial Initiative on Child Abuse and Neglect developed by the U.S. Department of Health and Human Services). Washington, DC: U.S. Government Printing Office.

Gentry, C. E. (1978). Incestuous abuse of children: The need for an objective overview. *Child Welfare, 57,* 355–365.

Gil, D. G., & Noble, J. H. (1967, September). Public knowledge, attitudes and opinions about physical child abuse in the United States. *Brandeis University Papers in Social Welfare.* Waltham, MA: Brandeis University.

Hafen, B. C. (1977). Puberty, privacy, and protection: The risks of children's rights. *American Bar Association Journal, 63,* 1383–1388.

Harris, L. (1978, August 14). A reporter at large: Persons in need of supervision. *New Yorker,* pp. 55–89.

Isaacson, L. B. (1975). Child abuse reporting status: The case for holding physicians civilly liable for failing to report. *San Diego Law Review, 12,* 743–777.

Levine, R. S. (1977). Social worker malpractice: A new approach toward accountability in the juvenile justice system. *Journal of Juvenile Law, 1,* 101–109.

Marks, R. D. (1980). Juvenile noncriminal misbehavior and equal protection. *Family Law Quarterly, 13,* 461–503.

Martin, G. A. (1992). The delinquent and the juvenile court: Is there still a place for rehabilitation? *Connecticut Law Review, 25,* 57–93.

McDonald, R. A. (1977). Civil action against physicians for failure to report cases of suspected child abuse. *Oklahoma Law Review, 30,* 482–490.

Musavichick, M. (1972, October 10). The child abusers: The story of one family. *World,* pp. 28–32.

Myers, J.E.B. (1986). A survey of child abuse and neglect reporting statutes. *Journal of Juvenile Law, 10,* 1–72.

National Conference of Lawyers and Social Workers. (1967). *Lawyer–social worker relationships in family court intake process.* New York: Author.

National Conference of Lawyers and Social Workers. (1968). *Lawyer–social worker relationships in the family court: Hearing and disposition.* New York: Author.

Nelson, K. E., Sanders, E. J., & Landsman, M. J. (1993). Chronic child neglect in perspective. *Social Work, 38,* 661–676.

Paulsen, M. G. (1966). The legal framework for child protection. *Columbia Law Review, 66,* 679–717.

Paulsen, M. G. (1967). Child abuse reporting law: The shape of the legislation. *Columbia Law Review, 67,* 1–49.

Rieffel, A. B. (1984). *The juvenile justice standards handbook.* Chicago: American Bar Association, Juvenile Justice Implementation Project.

Rubin, H. T. (1985). *Juvenile justice: Policy, practice, and law* (2nd ed.). New York: Random House.

Schroeder, L. O. (1986). Negligence in placement and supervision of children in foster care: Are social workers liable? *Children and Youth Services Review, 8,* 219–226.

Slonim, S. (1980). ABA delegates defer "runaways" proposal. *American Bar Association Journal, 60,* 281.

Teitelbaum, L. E., & Ellis, J. W. (1978). The liberty interest of children: Due process rights and their application. *Family Law Quarterly, 12,* 153–202.

Winter, B. (1980). Juvenile courts: Access gains cited. *American Bar Association Journal, 66,* 947–948.

STATUTES CITED

Federal Youth Corrections Act of 1950. Ch. 1115, 64 Stat. 1085.

Juvenile Delinquency Act of 1994. 18 U.S.C. § 5031–5042.

STUDY QUESTIONS

1. Do juveniles have constitutional rights to a fair trial similar to those of adult criminals?

2. Can social workers give evidence of abuse obtained when they enter a house without a warrant?

3. Should probation officers explain their responsibilities to juveniles under their supervision?

PART II

Legal Problems
of Clients

*I returned, and saw under
the sun, that the race is not
to the swift, nor the battle to
the strong, neither yet bread
to the wise, nor yet riches
to men of understanding,
nor yet favour to men of
skill, but time and chance
happeneth to them all.*

—ECCLESIASTES 9:11

9

Marriage and Filiation Problems

W ho are you? What are you? A father or a mother and a child? A husband or a wife? Free or a slave? That is what status is all about: your relationship to others. Status is the place in the scheme of things that the law assigns to us by virtue of the accidents of our birth, sex, race, nationality, economic level, and genetic makeup.

The importance of the accidents of birth is reflected in the importance our society accords to the institution of the family. From your place in a family comes your legal identity, with all the rights and obligations that flow from it.

MARRIAGE

Marriage is a matter of public concern. It creates legal status not only for the spouses but also for their children and for their ascendants and collaterals. Marriage is therefore not a matter of concern to the couple alone because the new relationship controls property rights, obligations of support, and inheritance.

The state regulates marriage, determining who may marry and what formalities they must follow to do so. Because marriage is a contract, the parties must be able to agree freely. If either party does not know what he or she is doing, there is no marriage, and the party may seek an *annulment,* a formal declaration that no marriage ever existed. In addition, the law says that certain parties may not marry: Brother and sister, although of age and normally capable of consenting to a contract, may not marry each other because they are within a prohibited degree of *consanguinity* or blood relationship. This is different from *affinity*, the connection that exists between a married person and relatives of his or her spouse.

Loving v. Commonwealth of Virginia
388 U.S. 1, 87 S. Ct. 1817 (1967)
Warren, C. J.

This case presents a constitutional question never addressed by this Court: whether a statutory scheme adopted by the State of Virginia to prevent marriages between persons solely on the basis of racial classifications violates the equal protection and due process clauses of the Fourteenth Amendment. For reasons which seem to us to reflect the central meaning of those constitutional commands, we conclude that these statutes cannot stand consistently with the Fourteenth Amendment.

In June, 1958, two residents of Virginia, Mildred Jeter, a Negro woman, and Richard Loving, a white man, were married in the District of Columbia pursuant to its laws. Shortly after their marriage, the Lovings returned to Virginia and established their marital abode in Caroline County. At the October term, 1958, of the circuit court of Caroline County, a grand jury issued an indictment charging the Lovings with violating Virginia's ban on interracial marriages. On January 6, 1959, the Lovings pleaded guilty to the charge and were sentenced to one year in jail; however, the trial judge suspended the sentence for a period of 25 years on the condition that the Lovings leave the state and not return to Virginia together for 25 years, stating that:

> *"Almighty God created the races white, black, yellow, malay, and red, and placed them on separate continents. And but for the interference with his arrangement there would be no cause for such marriages. The fact that he separated the races shows that he did not intend for the races to mix."*

After their convictions, the Lovings took up residence in the District of Columbia. On November 6, 1963, they filed a motion in the state trial court to vacate the judgment and set aside the sentence on the ground that the statutes which they had violated were repugnant to the Fourteenth Amendment. The motion not having been decided by October 28, 1964, the Lovings instituted a class action in the United States district court for the eastern district of Virginia requesting that a three-judge court be convened to declare the Virginia antimiscegenation statutes unconstitutional and to enjoin state officials from enforcing their convictions. On January 22, 1965, the state trial judge denied the motion to vacate the sentences, and the Lovings perfected an appeal to the supreme court of appeals of Virginia. On February 11, 1965, the three-judge district court continued the case to allow the Lovings to present their constitutional claims to the highest state court.

The supreme court of appeals upheld the constitutionality of the anti-miscegenation statutes and, after modifying the sentence, affirmed the convictions. The Lovings appealed this decision, and we noted probable jurisdiction on December 12, 1966.

• • • • •

The two statutes under which appellants were convicted and sentenced are part of a comprehensive statutory scheme aimed at prohibiting and punishing interracial marriages. . . . The Lovings have never disputed in the course of this litigation that Mrs. Loving is a "colored person" or that Mr. Loving is a "white person" within the meanings of those terms by the Virginia statutes.

Virginia is now one of 16 states which prohibit and punish marriages on the basis of racial classifications. Penalties for miscegenation arose as an incident to slavery and have been common in Virginia since the colonial period. The present statutory scheme dates from the adoption of the Racial Integrity Act of 1924, passed during the period of extreme nativism which followed the end of the First World War. The central features of this act, and current Virginia law, are the absolute prohibition of a "white person" marrying other than another "white person," a prohibition against issuing marriage licenses until the issuing official is satisfied that the applicants' statements as to their race are correct, certificates of "racial composition" to be kept by local and state registrars, and the carrying forward of earlier prohibitions against racial intermarriage.

• • • • •

While the state court is no doubt correct in asserting that marriage is a social relation subject to the state's police power . . . the state does not contend in its argument before this Court that its powers to regulate marriage are unlimited notwithstanding the commands of the Fourteenth Amendment. Nor could it do so. . . . Instead, the state argues that the meaning of the equal protection clause, as illuminated by the statements of the framers, is only that state penal laws containing an interracial element as part of the definition of the offense must apply equally to whites and Negroes in the sense that members of each race are punished to the same degree. Thus, the state contends that, because its miscegenation statutes punish equally both the white and the Negro participants in an interracial marriage, these statutes, despite their reliance on racial classifications, do not constitute an invidious discrimination based upon race. The second argument advanced by the state assumes the validity of its equal application theory. The argument is that, if the equal protection clause does not outlaw miscegenation statutes because of their reliance on racial classifications, the question of constitutionality would thus become whether there was any rational basis for a state to treat interracial marriages *differently from other marriages. On this question, the state argues, the scientific evidence is substantially in doubt, and consequently, this Court should defer to the wisdom of the state legislature in adopting its policy of discouraging interracial marriages.*

Because we reject the notion that the mere "equal application" of a statute containing racial classifications is enough to remove the classifications from the Fourteenth Amendment's proscription of all invidious racial discriminations, we do not accept the state's contention that these statutes should be upheld if there is any possible basis for concluding that they serve a rational purpose. . . . [In cases] involving distinctions not drawn according to race, the Court has merely asked whether there is any rational foundation for the discriminations, and has deferred to the wisdom of the state legislatures. In the case at bar, however, we deal with statutes containing racial classifications, and the fact of equal application does not immunize the statute from the very heavy burden of justification which the Fourteenth Amendment has traditionally required of state statutes drawn according to race. . . . The equal protection clause requires the consideration of whether the classification drawn by any statute constitutes an arbitrary and invidious discrimination. The clear and central purpose of the Fourteenth Amendment was to eliminate all official state sources of invidious racial discrimination in the states.

. . . . .

There can be no question but that Virginia's miscegenation statutes rest solely upon distinctions drawn according to race. The statutes proscribe generally accepted conduct if engaged in by members of different races. Over the years, this Court has consistently repudiated "distinctions between citizens solely because of their ancestry" as being "odious to a free people whose institutions are founded upon the doctrine of equality." . . . At the very least, the equal protection clause demands that racial classifications, especially suspect in criminal statutes, be subjected to the "most rigid scrutiny," . . . and, if they are ever to be upheld, they must be shown to be necessary to the accomplishment of some permissible state objective, independent of racial discrimination which it was the object of the Fourteenth Amendment to eliminate.

. . . . .

There is patently no legitimate overriding purpose independent of invidious racial discrimination which justifies this classification. The fact that Virginia only prohibits interracial marriages involving white persons demonstrates that the racial classifications must stand on their own justification, as measures designed to maintain white supremacy. We have consistently denied the constitutionality of measures which restrict the rights of citizens on account of race. There can be no doubt that restricting the freedom to marry solely because of racial classifications violates the central meaning of the equal protection clause.

These statutes also deprive the Lovings of liberty without due process of law in violation of the due process clause of the Fourteenth Amendment. The freedom to marry has long been recognized as one of the vital personal rights essential to the orderly pursuit of happiness by free men.

Marriage is one of the "basic civil rights of man," fundamental to our very existence and survival. . . . To deny this fundamental freedom on so unsupportable a basis as the racial classification embodied in these statutes, classifications so directly subversive of the principle of equality at the heart of the Fourteenth Amendment, is surely to deprive all the state's citizens of liberty without due process of law. The Fourteenth Amendment requires that the freedom of choice to marry not be restricted by invidious racial discriminations. Under our Constitution, the freedom to marry or not marry, a person of another race resides with the individual and cannot be infringed by the state.

These convictions must be reversed. It is so ordered.

Reversed.

Miscegenation statutes rested solely on considerations of race; therefore, they were subject to strict scrutiny. Even though both parties are treated the same, that is, there is equality in denying interracial marriage to both, the statutes cannot stand. Marriage has been a status traditionally regulated by the states, but a state cannot violate the Constitution, even in an area under its control.

Only parties of different sexes may marry. Homosexual liaisons lead to no legally enforceable rights, whereas a heterosexual liaison might result in a valid common-law marriage in the 14 jurisdictions that still recognize such marriages (Horsburgh, 1992). There may be changes in this area as gay and lesbian couples press for legal recognition of their relationship. In fact, although in *Baker v. Nelson* (1971) the court held that Minnesota law does not authorize marriage between persons of the same sex, in Hawaii in 1993 the Supreme Court held that refusing marriage licenses to gay men or lesbians violated Hawaii's due process clause (Waihee, 1994). The case *Baehr v. Lewin* (1993) held that the statute restricting marital relations to male or female establishes sex-based classification, which is subjected to "strict scrutiny" test in an equal protection clause. This is particularly true when one of the female partners in a lesbian relationship is artificially inseminated and wants her partner to be able to adopt the child (Zuckerman, 1986). Heel (1993) discussed the issue and cited cases where states have extended protections to homosexual couples. She mentioned adult adoption, domestic partnership, and contract as alternatives to marriage. Social workers may be asked to advise the courts on the best interest of the child in these instances.

SEPARATION AND DIVORCE

The grounds for separation and divorce are similar in most states—adultery, alcoholism, mental and physical cruelty, and abandonment. There has been a trend throughout the country to establish no-fault divorces. These are granted when the parties can prove they have lived apart for a certain period. Another trend is the granting of a separation or divorce on the grounds of "irreconcilable differences." These no-fault concepts in divorce avoid the unpleasant and for some devastating experience of testifying in court to the acts of hate, hostility, and even violence that led to the rupture of the marriage. In some states there can be no alimony after divorce unless the wife is free from fault and is in need. This separates the spouse's need from child support: a burden that both parents share in most states. Elrod and Walker (1994) discussed the current status of family law.

Divorce terminates marital rights and duties, has support implications, and determines present and future property rights. Because divorce is crucial in freeing the parties to enter another marriage, it should be available to everyone who can prove the grounds, as the *Boddie v. Connecticut* (1971) case illustrates.

Boddie v. Connecticut
401 U.S. 371, 91 S. Ct. 780 (1971)
Harlan, J.
Appellants, welfare recipients residing in the State of Connecticut, brought this action in the federal district court for the district of Connecticut on behalf of themselves and others similarly situated, challenging, as applied to them, certain state procedures for the commencement of litigation, including requirements for payment of court fees and costs for service of process, that restrict their access to the courts in their effort to bring an action for divorce.

It appears from the briefs and oral argument that the average cost to a litigant for bringing an action for divorce is $60.

· · · · ·

There is no dispute as to the inability of the named appellants in the present case to pay either the court fees required by statute or the cost incurred for the service of process. The affidavits in the record establish that appellants' welfare income in each instance barely suffices to meet the costs of the daily essentials of life and include no allotment that could be budgeted for the expense to gain access to the courts in order to obtain a divorce. Also undisputed is appellants' "good faith" in seeking a divorce.

· · · · ·

Appellants thereafter commenced this action in the federal district court seeking a judgment declaring that Connecticut's statute and service of process provisions, "requiring payment of court fees and expenses as a condition precedent to obtaining court relief [are] unconstitutional [as] applied to these indigent [appellants] and all other members of the class which they represent." As further relief, appellants requested the entry of an injunction ordering the appropriate officials to permit them "to proceed with their divorce actions without payment of fees and costs."

. . . . .

Our conclusion is that, given the basic position of the marriage relationship in this society's hierarchy of values and the concomitant state monopolization of the means for legally dissolving this relationship, due process does prohibit a state from denying, solely because of inability to pay, access to its courts to individuals who seek judicial dissolution of their marriages.

. . . . .

Perhaps no characteristic of an organized and cohesive society is more fundamental than its erection and enforcement of a system of rules defining the various rights and duties of its members, enabling them to govern their affairs and definitively settle their differences in an orderly, predictable manner. . . . It is this injection of the rule of law that allows society to reap the benefits of rejecting what political theorists call the "state of nature."

American society, of course, bottoms its systematic definition of individual rights and duties, as well as its machinery for dispute settlement, not on custom or the will of strategically placed individuals, but on the common-law model. It is to courts, or other quasi-judicial official bodies, that we ultimately look for the implementation of a regularized, orderly process of dispute settlement. Within this frame-work, those who wrote our original Constitution, in the Fifth Amendment, and later those who drafted the Fourteenth Amendment, recognized the centrality of the concept of due process in the operation of the system. . . . Only by providing that the social enforcement mechanism must function strictly within these bounds can we hope to maintain an ordered society that is also just. It is upon this premise that this Court has through years of adjudication put flesh upon the due process principle.

Such litigation has, however, typically involved rights of defendants— not, as here, persons seeking access to the judicial process in the first instance. This is because our society has been so structured that resort to the courts is not usually the only . . . legitimate means of resolving private disputes. . . . Thus, this Court has seldom been asked to view access to the courts as an element of due process. The legitimacy of the state's monopoly over techniques of final dispute settlement, even where some are

*denied access to its use, stands unimpaired where recognized, effective al-
ternatives for the adjustment of differences remain.*

*Recognition of this theoretical framework illuminates the precise issue
presented in this case. As this Court on more than one occasion has recognized, marriage involves interests of basic importance in our society. . . . It
is not surprising, then, that the states have seen fit to oversee many aspects
of that institution. Without a prior judicial imprimatur, individuals may
freely enter into and rescind commercial contracts, for example, but we are
unaware of any jurisdiction where private citizens may covenant for or
dissolve marriages without state approval. Even where all substantive requirements are concededly met, we know of no instance where two consenting adults may divorce and mutually liberate themselves from the
constraints of legal obligations that go with marriage, and more fundamentally the prohibition against remarriage, without invoking the
state's judicial machinery.*

*Thus, although they assert here due process rights as would-be plain-
tiffs, we think appellants' plight, because resort to the state courts is the
only avenue to dissolution of their marriages, is akin to that of defendants
faced with exclusion from the only forum effectively empowered to settle
their disputes. Resort to the judicial process by these plaintiffs is no more
voluntary in a realistic sense than that of the defendant called upon to defend
his interests in court. For both groups this process is not only the paramount
dispute-settlement technique, but, in fact, the only available one.*

· · · · ·

*Due process does not, of course, require that the defendant in every civil
case actually have a hearing on the merits. A state can, for example, enter
a default judgment against a defendant who, after adequate notice, fails
to make a timely appearance, . . . or who, without justifiable excuse, violates a procedural rule requiring the production of evidence necessary for
orderly adjudication. . . . What the Constitution does require is an opportunity. . . . The formality and procedural requisites for the hearing can
vary, depending upon the importance of the interests involved and the nature of the subsequent proceedings. That the hearing required by due process is subject to waiver, and is not fixed in form, does not affect its root
requirement that an individual be given an opportunity for a hearing before he is deprived of any significant property interest.*

· · · · ·

*Just as a generally valid notice procedure may fail to satisfy due
process because of the circumstances of the defendant, so too a cost
requirement, valid on its face, may offend due process because it operates
to foreclose a particular party's opportunity to be heard.*

· · · · ·

Drawing upon the principles established by the cases just canvassed, we conclude that the state's refusal to admit these appellants to its courts, the sole means in Connecticut for obtaining a divorce, must be regarded as the equivalent of denying them an opportunity to be heard upon their claimed right to a dissolution of their marriages, and, in the absence of a sufficient countervailing justification for the state's action, a denial of due process.

The arguments for this kind of fee and cost requirement are that the state's interest in the prevention of frivolous litigation is substantial, its use of court fees and process costs to allocate scarce resources is rational, and its balance between the defendant's right to notice and the plaintiff's right to access is reasonable.

In our opinion, none of these considerations is sufficient to override the interest of these plaintiff-appellants in having access to the only avenue open for dissolving their allegedly untenable marriages. Not only is there no necessary connection between a litigant's assets and the seriousness of his motives in bringing suit, but it is here beyond present dispute that appellants bring these actions in good faith. Moreover, other alternatives exist to fees and cost requirements as a means for conserving the time of courts and protecting parties from frivolous litigation, such as penalties for false pleadings or affidavits, and actions for malicious prosecution or abuse of process, to mention only a few. In the same vein we think that reliable alternatives exist to service of process by a state-paid sheriff if the state is unwilling to assume the cost of official service.

$$\bullet \;\; \bullet \;\; \bullet \;\; \bullet \;\; \bullet$$

In concluding that the due process clause of the Fourteenth Amendment requires that these appellants be afforded an opportunity to go into court to obtain a divorce, we wish to re-emphasize that we go no further than necessary to dispose of the case before us, a case where the bona fides of both appellants' indigency and desire for divorce are here beyond dispute. We do not decide that access for all individuals to the courts is a right that is, in all circumstances, guaranteed by the due process clause of the Fourteenth Amendment so that its exercise may not be placed beyond the reach of any individual, for as we have already noted, in the case before us this right is the exclusive precondition to the adjustment of a fundamental human relationship. The requirement that these appellants resort to the judicial process is entirely a state-created matter. Thus, we hold only that a state may not, consistent with the obligations imposed on it by the due process clause of the Fourteenth Amendment, preempt the right to dissolve this legal relationship without affording all citizens access to the means it has prescribed for doing so.
Reversed.

[Justice Douglas's concurring opinion and Justice Black's dissenting opinion are omitted.]

Justice Douglas, concurring, stated that distinctions made on the basis of poverty are invidious. Justice Black, dissenting, would leave regulation of this important status to the states. If it is a violation of due process to forbid indigent people a divorce because they cannot pay a fee, how can it not also be a violation of due process to deny indigent people some other privilege, such as declaring bankruptcy, because of their inability to pay the fee? In *United States v. Kras* (1973), the Court made the distinction that unlike other contract-dispute situations, in divorce the courts are the only dispute resolution mechanism available.

Separation in matrimonial law is a cessation of cohabitation of the spouses by mutual consent or by judicial decree. If a state's policy in administering Aid to Families with Dependent Children calls for a judgment of legal separation to prove absence of the parent, would a divorce be necessary when separation accomplishes the purpose of qualifying for assistance? However, the policy of requiring a legal separation may contradict the Aid to Families with Dependent Children program policy of trying to keep families together. Legal separation as a necessary requirement for public assistance is one more step away from an intact family.

Putative and Common-Law Marriage

A putative marriage is not a true marriage because the parties cannot legally contract (because one of the parties is married to someone else, for instance) or because the parties do not follow prescribed formalities, such as license and ceremony. At least one of the parties must have married in good faith and at all times continue to think that he or she has a valid marriage. The parties must have gone through some of the steps necessary to contract marriage, by having a ceremony, for instance. For policy reasons, the law treats a putative marriage as a valid marriage as far as the "innocent party" is concerned. The attempted marriage may be rendered null because of some impediment, but it can produce civil effects in favor of one who entered it in good faith; for both, if both are in good faith. Those civil effects include legitimacy of children and certain property rights (such as a half interest in property acquired during the marriage in community property states).

Common-law marriage still exists in Alabama, the District of Columbia, Colorado, Georgia, Idaho, Iowa, Kansas, Montana, Ohio, Oklahoma, Pennsylvania, Rhode Island, South Carolina, and Texas (Freed & Foster, 1977; Horsburgh, 1992; Weyrauch, 1980). It occurs when parties live together and hold themselves out as husband and wife, provided no impediment exists to a valid marriage, even though the parties have not satisfied the requirements of a valid marriage. In states that recognize common-law marriages, the parties are as validly married as if they had secured a license and gone through a marriage ceremony. If they wish to marry someone else, even in a state where common-law marriage does not exist, the parties must get a divorce.

If a social history reveals a relationship that has features of either a putative or a common-law marriage, the parties should be referred for legal consultation. The existence of a putative or common-law marriage may have important effects on the receipt of social insurance benefits, such as workers' compensation and social security.

Informal living arrangements may or may not produce legal consequences. In *Marvin v. Marvin* (1976) the female member of the arrangement sued for a division of property acquired by the actor, Lee Marvin, during the time they lived together, on the basis of an alleged oral contract to divide it. The California supreme court held that such express contracts between nonmarital partners could be enforced unless the contract was explicitly founded on consideration for sexual services. If the consideration was for sexual services, the relationship would have an illegal object and be invalid. The court further held that, in the absence of an express contract, the trial court should inquire whether the conduct of the parties demonstrated an implied contract, an agreement of partnership or joint venture, *quantum meruit* (the amount deserved), or a reason for other equitable remedies, such as a constructive or resulting trust. When parties to informal living arrangements do not have any agreement, difficulties in determining ownership of property acquired during the relationship may result.

Conciliation in Court

Marriage counseling, a traditional social work service, is often offered by private agencies supported through charitable campaigns and occasionally through church-related agencies, particularly those of denominations that prohibit divorce. More and more social workers in private practice specialize in marriage counseling. In some jurisdictions, the courts offer marriage counseling, requiring it when couples considering divorce have minor children. Possible invasion of the right to privacy by mandatory counseling must be weighed against the societal policy of encouraging marriage and family stability (Barteau, 1980; Seidelson, 1967). Social workers will be interested in *Yaron v. Yaron* (1975), a New York custody dispute in which the judge upheld the wife's objection to admission into evidence of a family counseling agency's record. The agency had provided marital counseling for the couple in the past. The court said, "Privilege granted by the legislature was not meant to be a myth. It was meant to cure the evil which had resulted from social workers either voluntarily or by court direction being forced to disclose communications given to them of the most intimate nature by people desperately in need of help" (p. 524).

Custody

A marriage that terminates in separation or divorce involves troublesome decisions on custody of any children. This is an area undergoing reexamination as the right of the father vis-à-vis the mother as preferred custodial parent, and the right of parents living in irregular arrangements come before the courts.

Traditionally, the courts have awarded custody of young children to the mother in separation and divorce cases (Foster & Freed, 1978; Goldstein, Freud, & Solnit, 1973). Except in unusual circumstances, when she is morally or physically unfit, the mother is still considered the preferred parent. An act of adultery may not deprive a mother of custody, although open and frequent adultery may. As current newspaper accounts illustrate, the courts may consider other factors, such as a mother's need to place the child in day care while she goes to school. A recent article (Skowron, 1995) reported that a court ordered a child who had been raised by adoptive parents for all of his three and one-half years returned to the biological father he has never met.

A parent is preferred because the parent has a natural right to custody of his or her child. If neither parent is fit, the judge may place the child elsewhere, using the rationale of the "best interest of the child," although courts may pay lip service to this rationale rather than really examine all the placement alternatives. Although the court does not always accept a social worker's recommendation on appropriate custody, judges are usually willing to seek every assistance in making these troublesome decisions.

An example of such a decision is *Duncan v. Duncan* (1976), in which both parents were considered unfit and the choice was between paternal or maternal grandparents and a foster home. Contrary to the recommendation of the welfare investigators, the trial judge granted custody to the paternal grandparents, with visitation rights to the maternal grandparents.

Appellant urges that the trial court erred in granting custody to the paternal grandparents since this result was contrary to the testimony of welfare investigators who appellant considers the court's own expert witnesses. These welfare investigators were not called by either side to this controversy, but rather by the court as the employees of the appropriate government agency charged with the responsibility of child welfare. We do not find that these investigators were tendered as expert

*witnesses, nor do we consider them to be the court's witnesses, thus plac-
ing the trial judge in the position of not being able to disregard their
testimony. Therefore, we find no error on the part of the trial judge.* (p.
381; see also Killacken, 1992)

If social work advice is to be effective in custody disputes, it must be
based on significant facts. In *State in the interest of Johnson* (1973) the
court of appeals disagreed with the trial judge, saying:

> *When an adjudication is based almost entirely on a social worker's rec-
> ommendation (as the judge stated he did in this case) rather than on
> the facts developed by the officer's investigation and on other relevant
> evidence, there are no facts in the record for purposes of appellate re-
> view. More importantly, the losing party has been denied the proce-
> dural due process requirement of an opportunity to be heard.*
>
> *In the present case the social worker on direct examination presented
> meager facts and stated her conclusion. Counsel for the grandparents
> was deprived of full cross-examination and thus of the opportunity to
> develop facts favorable to their position.* (p. 335)

Decisions on custody are often difficult. In *Harris v. Harris* (1977) the
trial court granted custody to the father because the mother's religious
beliefs involved handling poisonous snakes. Because the court had no
authority to dictate to the mother what religion she should teach her
child and because there was no proof that the mother's attendance at her
church exposed the child to the risk of being bitten by a poisonous snake,
the appeals court reversed the decision. Similarly, *Palmore v. Sidat* (1984)
held that private biases and the possible injury they might inflict were
not enough to deprive a mother of custody.

Such esoteric custody decisions do not arise often, but decisions on
the basis of the parent's sexual preference or living arrangements do.
The question of granting custody to a lesbian mother is not unknown
(Riley, 1975; *Schuster v. Schuster*, 1978), and the problem of the parent
who lives with a member of the opposite sex without being married has
become more common. A recent case (*Blew v. Verta*, 1992) held that an
order prohibiting a lesbian mother from visiting her son in the presence
of her female partner was unsupportable. The child enjoyed being in the
home of the mother's partner. These are legal questions of interest to any
social worker counseling a client who is in a custody battle. When the
best living arrangements for a client may have far-reaching legal consequences, the client should be advised to seek legal advice. Although it
may seem calculating to one who seeks counseling to save a marriage, it
is a good practice to recommend legal advice early. A wife who has been

living at subsistence level to give her husband time to "find himself" may find herself and her children entitled only to subsistence alimony and child support if the marital counseling is unsuccessful. In making custody decisions, judges may resort to outside assistance, as in *Duncan*, including conciliation services (Flener & Farber, 1980).

Usually a child has a home and one custodial parent, who has authority to make all major decisions concerning a child's life. The noncustodial parent may have extensive visitation rights, but once custody has been granted, proof of a change in circumstances detrimental to the child's welfare is required to change it. Thus, even a mother who is psychiatrically ill *may* retain custody.

If the parents agree between themselves about custody, the court will usually go along with them. When the father, for instance, has had physical custody of the child for some time, courts are extremely reluctant to upset the living arrangement with a change of custody. There is sometimes a conflict between the rights of the parents and the best interest of the child, which is not always well-defined, given the need for flexibility. Suppose you are advising a mother of young children who needs time to get on her feet before assuming full responsibility for them. Be aware that an award of custody to the father, or even an agreement between them that he assume their care for a time, may lead to her losing custody permanently.

For parents who are mature enough and who live near each other, joint custody may offer benefits to them and the children (Baum, 1976; Miller, 1979). In 1991 all but Alabama, Arkansas, the District of Columbia, Georgia, Nebraska, New York, North Dakota, Rhode Island, South Carolina, South Dakota, Virginia, Washington, West Virginia, Wyoming, Puerto Rico, and the Virgin Islands provided for joint custody. Although the custodial parent has the legal right to decide where the children will live, go to school, and get needed medical or psychological help, amicable joint decisions are certainly in the children's best interest. Kubie (1964) recommended that when they are unable to agree, the parents select a committee to make decisions on major issues. Members might include clergy, pediatricians, psychiatrists, lawyers, or educators.

Burke (1994) discussed a broad range of custody problems involving stepparents, same-sex partners, and unmarried heterosexual partners. A nonlegal parent has to show that custody with the legal parent is detrimental to the child; this can be difficult to prove. The article mentions that Oregon permits anyone who has established a child–parent relationship to petition for custody or visitation. A Michigan court established an equitable parenthood doctrine that serves a similar purpose. In advising clients about custody disputes, social workers should check the law in their state.

Dissatisfied noncustodial parents occasionally keep their children beyond the authorized visitation period or remove them from the jurisdiction in an effort to get custody themselves. This "child snatching," which sometimes constitutes kidnapping or at the least is contempt of court, traumatizes both children and parents. Legal efforts to eliminate it already existed (Coombs, 1978; Hoff, 1986) when President Carter signed a bill in 1981 permitting use of the FBI and the Parent Locator Service to help find a missing child.

The Uniform Child Custody Jurisdiction Act (1968), adopted in some form by every state, provides for enforcement of child custody determinations by sister state courts. The Parental Kidnapping Prevention Act (1980) mandated state court enforcement of sister state decrees made consistently with the act's provisions. The federal courts can hear these cases under federal question jurisdiction. Diversity of citizenship jurisdiction (28 USC §1332) has been used in child-snatching tort litigation. Federal courts may give money damages for tortious interference with custody or visitation.

Alimony and Child Support

Alimony is the financial support due one spouse, usually the wife, from the other after a separation or divorce. Child support is awarded separately. There are tax consequences to designating a monetary award as either alimony or child support, which lawyers for both parties consider in the negotiations. *Alimony pendente lite* is an award made while the divorce is pending in court.

Alimony is based on the dependence of one spouse on the resources of the other and an attempt to maintain the former standard of living. The court will also consider the length of the marriage, the spouse's expectation of continued support, and the spouse's viability in the labor market (Inker, Walse, & Perocchi, 1978). Thus, a younger woman who has not been married long can expect little or no permanent alimony, because she could easily return to her former occupation or find another.

The Supreme Court in *Orr v. Orr* (1979) held that the Georgia law permitting award of alimony only to the wife was a constitutionally invalid denial of equal protection. Although it is rare that a husband is entitled to support because he is not self-supporting, alimony should certainly be as available to him as it is to his wife. Most states allow alimony awards to either spouse (Eden, 1981). Property settlements at the time of divorce will often award to each party of the marriage sufficient resources to make alimony unnecessary.

Is the parent obligated to continue financial support beyond the age of majority of a child? With the age of majority reduced to 18 in many states, a parent's obligation may terminate before the child has completed high school, much less college. *Price v. Price* (1974) held that the Age of Majority Act in Michigan (M.C.L.A. 722.51 et seq.) effectively terminated child support at age 18. However, continuing support for a child's education after age 18 can be negotiated in the divorce settlement.

Wisconsin attempted to sanction nonpayment of child support by prohibiting a later marriage, but in *Zablocki v. Redhail* (1978) the U.S. Supreme Court struck down the attempt. The Court held that the statute impinged on marital and equality interests and that the legislative means did not achieve the desired end of benefiting children of a previous marriage. In *Jones v. Helms* (1981), the Supreme Court upheld a Georgia statute providing that a parent who willfully and voluntarily abandons a dependent child is guilty of a misdemeanor and that parents who commit the offense in Georgia and leave the state are guilty of a felony, stating that it does not impermissibly infringe on a constitutionally protected right of travel or violate the equal protection clause, because it applies equally to all parents residing in Georgia. A carefully designed statute allowing for good-cause exceptions may provide some sanctions for nonpayment of support.

One legislative attempt to reach the erring parent is the Uniform Reciprocal Enforcement of Support Act (Fox, 1978). Enforcing a judgment for alimony and child support against a spouse and parent who has left the state is difficult. To obtain a money judgment against someone, including an order for past-due alimony, the court must have jurisdiction over the person. This is acquired by *service of process,* that is, formal notification to the person that the suit has been filed. In most cases the jurisdiction of a court extends only to the geographical boundaries of its state.

When the spouse is known to be in another state, the Uniform Reciprocal Enforcement of Support Act or one of the parallel statutes adopted by all states plus Guam, the District of Columbia, Puerto Rico, and the Virgin Islands is invoked. These statutes allow the state to which the nonsupporting spouse and parent has gone to assert personal jurisdiction over that person at the request of the state of former residence and permit the state in which the nonsupporting person now resides to order the payment of support. The mechanics of these proceedings are handled by local law enforcement personnel. The Parent Locator Service, created by a 1988 amendment to the Social Security Act, is an aid in finding deserting parents so that a local court can order support. Enforcement of this act has resulted in savings in the use of tax funds from the Aid to Families with Dependent Children program.

One policy question in enforcing support across state lines is whether the primary obligation of support belongs to the immediate family alone or to society as a whole. Our society has a legal system that recognizes small family units, each owing its members mutual care and support that can be enforced legally by the courts even across state lines. Thus, an abandoning spouse may be kept from creating a new family with the subsequent legal obligation of support, or support laws that make the creation of this new unit more difficult because of the prior support obligation. When the family unit has become disrupted, should the legal system be used to enforce mutual care and support, or should society, as a larger family, step in to provide it?

Dissatisfaction with the operation of the Uniform Reciprocal Enforcement of Support Act led to the drafting of the Uniform Interstate Family Support Act. It may attack some of the difficult problems of establishment, enforcement, and modification of child support (Haines, 1993).

FILIATION

Legal identity is a creation both of birth and of legal acts, such as the marriage of parents and their *filiation*—acknowledgment of the child's relationship to them before and subsequent to the child's birth (Schroeder, 1973, 1974). Status is often created arbitrarily by the birth certificate, which documents the child's biological parents (in contrast to the lack of identification for the foundling) and the child's status as legitimate or illegitimate; male or female; black, white, or Asian; and so on. Although the birth certificate is not conclusive, for most of us it establishes filiation. This status as a member of a family establishes certain rights of support and property.

Identifying a biological parent is a problem when a man alleged to be a child's father attempts to disavow paternity. Proof is difficult. To protect the innocent child, courts have required a high degree of proof of nonpaternity to permit bastardization. Terasaki (1977–1978) and Kaye and Kanwischer (1988) discussed the testing of alleged fathers using blood tests. Kaye (1990) also discussed the procedures and concluded that DNA analysis can exclude or include an alleged father as the biological father. The burden of proof is easier to meet now in states that have adopted the Uniform Act on Blood Tests to Determine Paternity. Although blood tests cannot conclusively determine paternity, they can conclusively establish nonpaternity (*Dufrene v. Dufrene*, 1978). (In *Little v. Streater*, 1981, the Supreme Court struck down as a denial of due process a Connecticut law allocating the costs of blood tests in paternity actions to the party requesting them, who in this case was indigent.) The marriage or failure to marry of the biological parents determines not only the race listed on the birth certificate and filiation but also whether a child is under *paternal authority*—the authority of the parent over a minor child that permits control over the property and the person of the child. In early Rome the father's control was supreme: Paternal authority carried with it the power of life and death. This is not true today. The state can interfere with a child's discipline, education, and general development by asserting a higher right to protect a child from ill-considered parental decisions. However, parents retain some rights, such as choosing a child's religious affiliation, even after physical custody of the child has been transferred from the parent to a social agency.

Illegitimacy

When a child is born to parents who are not married or when, although born to a married couple, a subsequent legal proceeding determines that the mother's husband is not the child's father, the child is considered illegitimate. On rare occasions legal proceedings may hold that a woman alleged to be the mother of a child is not. Filiation in the United States is determined by state law. In most jurisdictions, bastardizing a child born during a valid marriage is difficult because there is a strong legal presumption that the child is legitimate. The process has been somewhat eased by the availability of blood tests.

The courts are reluctant to permit the disavowal of paternity of a child born during a legal marriage, because the social stigma and the legal disabilities associated with illegitimacy are real. In *Zepeda v. Zepeda* (1963), an illegitimate child sued his father for damages for the tort of "wrongful life," on the basis of social stigma and economic deprivation inflicted by the child's illegitimate birth. The father of the child, a married man, had seduced the future mother on promise of marriage.

The court found the elements of a tort to be present—duty, breach, proximate cause, and injury—and recognized that the seduction of unmarried women on the promise of marriage had no social utility that would immunize it from liability. However, the court refused to create the new tort although it had the power to do so. Stating that creating a "wrongful life" tort would open a Pandora's box of litigation, the court deferred to the legislature, which could, if it wished, recognize this as a legal wrong. The court said, however, that a child born deformed because its mother had German measles but did not abort, a child born to poor parents or parents of color, and a child born with a tendency to an inherited disease might all have an action for "wrongful life."

Kush v. Lloyd (1992) was a Florida case involving a woman who gave birth to a son with deformities. The woman and her husband underwent genetic testing, the results of which were never transmitted to the pediatrician. After the birth of a second child with deformities, the parents sued the various practitioners and medical entities involved for wrongful life and wrongful birth. Claims against most of the defendants were barred by the statute of response, leaving only Kush, who had rendered care and treatment within the four years preceding the lawsuit. The Florida court said that the tort of wrongful life was not cognizable, but the tort of wrongful birth encompasses all extraordinary expenses caused by the impairing condition for the duration of the child's life expectancy. Damages were put in trust for the child. The tort of wrongful life has continued to be used (Schroeder, 1991). States also provide legal proceedings for determining paternity. In *King v. Tanner* (1989) the court held that results of DNA testing on the alleged father indicated with 99.993 percent certainty that the man was the child's father.

Inheritance. Except in a few states, for many years the illegitimate child could not inherit from the biological parents. In *Trimble v. Gordon* (1977), the Supreme Court dealt with the problem of inheritance by illegitimate children in *intestate successions,* in which the deceased parent did not leave a will and the property must descend according to state law. *Trimble* altered the law of every state that had a statute like that of Illinois, and many other states later changed their laws of descent and distribution, either by legislation or by judicial decision.

Trimble v. Gordon

430 U.S. 762, 97 S. Ct. 1459, 52 L.Ed.2d 31 (1977)
Powell, J.
At issue in this case is the constitutionality of § 12 of the Illinois Probate Act, which allows illegitimate children to inherit by intestate succession only from their mothers. Under Illinois law, legitimate children are allowed to inherit by intestate succession from both their mothers and their fathers.

Appellant Deta Mona Trimble is the illegitimate daughter of appellant Jessie Trimble and Sherman Gordon. Trimble and Gordon lived in Chicago with Deta Mona from 1970 until Gordon died in 1974, the victim of a homicide. On January 2, 1973, the circuit court of Cook County, Ill., ordered a paternity order finding Gordon to be the father of Deta Mona and ordering him to pay $15 per week for her support. Gordon thereafter supported Deta Mona in accordance with the paternity order and openly acknowledged her as his child. He died intestate at the age of 28, leaving an estate consisting only of a 1974 Plymouth automobile worth approximately $2,500.

Shortly after Gordon's death, Trimble, as the mother and next of kin of Deta Mona, filed a petition for letters of administration, determination of heirship and declaratory relief in the probate division of

the circuit court of Cook County, Ill. That court entered an order de-
termining heirship, identifying as the only heirs of Gordon his father,
Joseph Gordon, his mother, Ethel King, and his brother, two sisters,
and half-brother.

· · · · ·

If Deta Mona had been a legitimate child, she would have inherited her
father's entire estate under Illinois law. In rejecting Deta Mona's claim of
heirship, the court sustained the constitutionality of § 12.

· · · · ·

In a case like this, the equal protection clause requires more than the
mere incantation of a proper state purpose. No one disputes the appropri-
ateness of Illinois' concern with the family unit, perhaps the most funda-
mental social institution of our society. The flaw in the analysis lies else-
where. . . . In subsequent decisions, we have expressly considered and
rejected the argument that a state may attempt to influence the ac-
tions of men and women by imposing sanctions on the children born of
their illegitimate relationships.

The more serious problems of proving paternity might justify a more
demanding standard for illegitimate children claiming under their moth-
ers' estates or for legitimate children generally. We think, however, that the
Illinois supreme court gave inadequate consideration to the relation be-
tween § 12 and the state's proper objective of assuring accuracy and effi-
ciency in the disposition of property at death. The court failed to consider
the possibility of a middle ground between the extremes of complete exclu-
sion and case-by-case determination of paternity. For at least some sig-
nificant categories of illegitimate children of intestate men, inheritance
rights can be recognized without jeopardizing the orderly settlement of
estates or the dependability of titles to property passing under intestacy
laws. Because it excludes those categories of illegitimate children unnec-
essarily, § 12 is constitutionally flawed.

· · · · ·

The judicial task here is the difficult one of vindicating constitutional rights
without interfering unduly with the state's primary responsibility in this area.

· · · · ·

Although the present case arises in a context different from that in Lucas,
the question of whether the statute "is carefully tuned to alternative
considerations" is equally applicable here. We conclude that § 12 does not
meet this standard. Difficulties of proving paternity in some situations do
not justify the total statutory disinheritance of illegitimate children whose
fathers die intestate. The facts of this case graphically illustrate the con-
stitutional defect of § 12. Sherman Gordon was found to be the father of

Deta Mona in a state court paternity action prior to his death. On the strength of that finding, he was ordered to contribute to the support of his child. That adjudication should be equally sufficient to establish Deta Mona's right to claim a child's share of Gordon's estate, for the state's interest in the accurate and efficient disposition of property at death would not be compromised in any way by allowing her claim in these circumstances. The reach of the statute extends well beyond the asserted purposes.

. . . . .

For the reasons stated above, we conclude that § 12 of the Illinois Probate Act cannot be squared with the command of the equal protection clause of the Fourteenth Amendment. Accordingly, we reverse the judgment of the Illinois supreme court and remand the case for further proceedings not inconsistent with this opinion.

. . . . .

The chief justice, Mr. Justice Stewart, Mr. Justice Blackmun, and Mr. Justice Rehnquist dissent. Like the supreme court of Illinois, they find this case constitutionally indistinguishable from Labine v. Vincent, *401 U.S. 572 (1971). They would, therefore, affirm the judgement.*

The *Labine v. Vincent* (1971) case, which the dissenters felt determined the outcome of the case at hand, dealt with Louisiana's unique system of *forced heirship*, which denotes certain classes of individuals, usually descendants, who will inherit a fixed portion of the decedent's estate. The testator may not by will deprive children of this portion, although it is possible, for specified reasons, to disinherit a forced heir. Disinheritance is practically never done successfully in Louisiana, in contrast to other states. In states other than Louisiana, certain classes of individuals automatically inherit in the absence of a will, usually the children and the spouse. However, by making a will, testators may deliberately and legally omit a child and leave the estate to a friend, neighbor, or institution, excluding family members entirely.

In *Labine* the acknowledged illegitimate child was denied the right to inherit in intestate succession from her father. Louisiana now permits the parent to bequeath by will to illegitimate children. Establishing inheritance rights of illegitimate children presents real problems for attorneys, for example, in searching title to real estate. Illegitimate heirs whose existence is not apparent may, after the settling of a succession and transfer of property to third persons, seek to enforce their rights.

The Supreme Court used the equal protection clause to decide *Trimble*. The Court felt that the Fourteenth Amendment proscribed a state statute that discriminated between illegitimate and legitimate descendants of a deceased father but not of a deceased mother. Although not holding illegitimacy a "suspect" class requiring "strict scrutiny," nevertheless the scrutiny is not "toothless" and resulted in a holding that the statute was unconstitutional. Note that the Supreme Court decided a major constitutional issue in a case concerning an estate worth $2,500—further proof of the protection of the Constitution for all members of society (Compensation, 1966; Stenger, 1978).

The Supreme Court mentioned the problem of proof of paternity in actions to determine inheritance rights of illegitimate children. In *Lalli v. Lalli* (1978) the Court held that a state may create a statute of limitations requiring filiation to be determined by acknowlegment or declared in a proceeding some time before the alleged father's death.

Support. For many individuals, lack of support is a more immediate problem than inheritance. Support is a corollary of status as a legitimate child; parents are expected to, and usually plan to, support legitimate children. When they do not, the law makes them do so, or society assumes the obligation for them. Illegitimate children traditionally have not had the status to command that obligation, although many states now require support of illegitimate children from parents who have acknowledged them.

In *S. v. D.* (1973) the mother of an illegitimate child brought a class action on behalf of herself, her illegitimate daughter, and others similarly situated to enjoin the "discriminatory application" of a provision of the Texas Penal Code making willful nonsupport of a child under age 18 a misdemeanor. The Texas courts consistently construed the statute to apply solely to the parents of legitimate children.

The Court determined that the plaintiff had not presented the court with a "case" or a "controversy" in the constitutional sense; that is, she had not alleged "such a personal stake in the outcome of the controversy as to assure that concrete adverseness which sharpens the presentation of issues upon which the court so largely depends for illumination of difficult constitutional questions." The Court held that she had not alleged a sufficient nexus between her injury and the government action under attack to justify judicial intervention; the mere existence of an abstract "injury" does not meet the "standing" requirement.

In *Pickett v. Brown* (1983) the Supreme Court held that a Tennessee statute imposing a two-year limitation period on paternity and child support on behalf of certain illegitimate children denied them equal protection. If a parent is disabled and the child receives social security benefits, those benefits may satisfy the support obligation.

The following case was decided about the same time as *S. v. D.* (1973).

Gomez v. Perez
409 U.S. 535, 93 S. Ct. 872 (1973)

Per Curiam [Per curiam means that it was a decision by the entire court, rather than an opinion written by one judge to which the others assented.] *The issue presented by this appeal is whether the laws of Texas may constitutionally grant legitimate children a judicially enforceable right to support from their natural fathers and at the same time deny that right to illegitimate children.*

In 1969, appellant filed a petition in Texas district court seeking support from appellee on behalf of her minor child. After hearing, the state trial judge found that appellee is "the biological father" of the child, and that the child "needs the support and maintenance of her father," but concluded that because the child was illegitimate "there is no legal obligation to support the child and the plaintiff takes nothing." The court of civil appeals affirmed this ruling over the objection that this illegitimate child was being denied equal protection of law. . . . The Texas supreme court refused application for a writ of error finding "No reversible error." We noted probable jurisdiction.

· · · · ·

We have held that under the equal protection clause of the Fourteenth Amendment a state may not create a right of action in favor of children for the wrongful death of a parent and exclude illegitimate children from the benefit of such a right. . . . Similarly, we have held that illegitimate children may not be excluded from sharing equally with other children in the recovery of workmen's compensation benefits for the death of their parent. . . . Under these decisions, a state may not invidiously discriminate against illegitimate children by denying them substantial benefits accorded children generally. We therefore hold that once a state posits a judicially enforceable right on behalf of children to needed support from their natural fathers there is no constitutionally sufficient justification for denying such an essential right to a child simply because her natural father has not married her mother. For a state to do so is "illogical and unjust.". . . We recognize the lurking problems with respect to proof of paternity. Those problems are not to be lightly brushed aside, but neither can they be made into an impenetrable barrier that works to shield otherwise invidious discrimination.

· · · · ·

The judgment is reversed and the case remanded for further proceedings not inconsistent with this opinion. . . .

[The dissenting opinion of Mr. Justice Stewart, with whom Mr. Justice Rehnquist joined, is omitted.]

The cases seem to come to opposite conclusions. However, in *S. v. D.* the Court is saying that a private citizen lacks a judicially cognizable interest in the criminal prosecution of someone else; in the latter, the Court is discussing the violation of equal protection when a right is granted to a legitimate child but denied to an illegitimate one. Since *Gomez v. Perez*, an illegitimate child whose paternity is established may sue for nonsupport if the state allows a legitimate child to do so.

REFERENCES

Barteau, B. (1980). How to create a conciliation court. *Family Advocate, 2*, 6.

Baum, C. (1976, October 13). The best of both parents. *New York Times Magazine*, pp. 45–48.

Burke, K. L. (1994). Redefining parenthood: Child custody and visitation when nontraditional families dissolve. *Golden Gate University Law Review, 24*, 223–258.

Compensation for the harmful effects of illegitimacy. (1966). *Columbia Law Review, 66*, 127–149.

Coombs, R. M. (1978). The "snatched" child is halfway home in Congress. *Family Law Quarterly, 11*, 407–426.

Elrod, L. D., & Walker, T. B. (1994). Family law in the fifty states. *Family Law Quarterly, 27*, 515–745.

Eden, E. E. (1981). Alimony for men: The thrust of recent decisions of the Supreme Court of the United States. *Oklahoma City University Law Review, 6*, 493–511.

Flener, R. D., & Farber, S. S. (1980). Social policy for child custody: A multidisciplinary framework. *American Journal of Orthopsychiatry, 50*, 341–347.

Foster, H. H., & Freed, D. J. (1978). Life with father: 1978. *Family Law Quarterly, 11*, 321–363.

Fox, W. F. (1978). The Uniform Reciprocal Enforcement of Support Act. *Family Law Quarterly, 12*, 113–145.

Freed, D. J., & Foster, H. H. (1979). Divorce in the fifty states: An overview as of 1978. *Family Law Quarterly, 13*, 105–128.

Freed, D. J., & Walker, T. B. (1991). Family law in the fifty states: An overview. *Family Law Quarterly, 25*, 313.

Goldstein, J., Freud, A., & Solnit, A. J. (1973). *Beyond the best interests of the child.* New York: Free Press.

Haines, M. C. (1993). Supporting our children: A blueprint for reform. *Family Law Quarterly, 27,* 7–29.

Heel, J. L. (1993). Homosexual marriage, the changing American family, and the heterosexual right to privacy. *Seton Hall Law Review, 24,* 347–393.

Hoff, P. M. (1986). Federal court remedies in interstate child custody and parental kidnapping cases. *Family Law Quarterly, 19,* 443–459.

Horsburgh, B. (1992). Redefining the family: Recognizing the altruistic caretakers and the importance of relational needs. *University of Michigan Law Journal, 25,* 423.

Inker, M. L., Walse, J. H., & Perocchi, P. P. (1978). Alimony orders following short-term marriage. *Family Law Quarterly, 12,* 91–111.

Kaye, D. H. (1990). DNA paternity probabilities. *Family Law Quarterly, 24,* 279–308.

Kaye, D. H., & Kanwischer, R. (1988). Admissibility of genetic testing in paternity litigation: A survey of state statutes. *Family Law Quarterly, 22,* 109–116.

Killacken, E. (1992). Kinship foster care. *Family Law Quarterly, 26,* 211–220.

Kubie, L. S. (1964). Provisions for the care of children of divorced parents: A new legal instrument. *Yale Law Journal, 73,* 1197–2000.

Miller, D. J. (1979). Joint custody. *Family Law Quarterly, 13,* 345–412.

Riley, M. (1975). The avowed lesbian mother and her right to child custody: A constitutional challenge that can no longer be denied. *San Diego Law Review, 12,* 799–864.

Schroeder, L. O. (1973). Renaissance for the transsexual: A new birth certificate. *Journal of Forensic Sciences, 18,* 237–245.

Schroeder, L. O. (1974). New life: Person or property? *American Journal of Psychiatry, 131,* 541–544.

Schroeder, L. O. (1991). Social work and genetic services: Legal road blocks on the road less traveled. *International Social Work, 34,* 97–108.

Seidelson, D. E. (1967). Systematic marriage investigation and counseling in divorce cases: Some reflections on its constitutional propriety and general desirability. *George Washington Law Review, 36,* 60–94.

Skowron, S. (1995, January 26). Court again orders adopted child returned to his biological father. *The Advocate*, p. 4A.

Stenger, R. L. (1978). The Supreme Court and illegitimacy: 1968–1977. *Family Law Quarterly, 11*, 365–405.

Terasaki, P. I. (1977–1978). Resolution by HLA testing of 1000 paternity cases not excluded by ABO testing. *Journal of Family Law*, pp. 543–557.

Waihee, J. (1994, June 24). New Hawaiian law bans gay marriage. *New York Times*, p. A18.

Weyrauch, W. O. (1980). Metamorphoses of marriage. *Family Law Quarterly, 13*, 415–440.

Zuckerman, E. (1986). Second parent adoption for lesbian-parented families: Legal recognition of the other mother. *U.C. Davis Law Review, 19*, 729–759.

STATUTES CITED

Parental Kidnapping Prevention Act of 1980. P.L. 96-611, 94 Stat. 3568.

Social Security Act Amendment of 1988. P.L. 100-300, 102 Stat. 441, 42 U.S.C. § 663.

Uniform Act on Blood Tests to Determine Paternity. Uniform Parentage Act, 9 ULA 315, Sec. 11 (blood test).

Uniform Child Custody Jurisdiction Act of 1968. 9 ULA 115.

Uniform Interstate Family Support Act of 1988, 9 ULA Part 1 (pocket part 112).

Uniform Reciprocal Enforcement of Support Act of 1991. 42 U.S.C. § 666.

STUDY QUESTIONS

1. Are interracial marriages illegal?

2. What are the grounds for divorce?

3. What are some problems with custody of children after divorce?

10

Foster Parenting and Adoption

Foster care is a child welfare service designed to provide temporary substitute family care when a child's own family is unable to care for him or her because of illness, abuse, abandonment, or other reasons. Care in a foster-family setting is thought to facilitate the child's emotional maturation by duplicating, as much as possible, a family environment.

Children placed in foster care are often those for whom adoption is neither desirable nor feasible. Ideally, the placement is temporary while efforts are made either to strengthen the natural family so that the child may be returned to it or to free the child for adoption. The reality is often different.

The idea of placement of children in homes other than their own is not new. In the 19th century, the Children's Aid Society placed orphaned children in homes throughout the country by taking them in groups to an area like the Midwest where the children were parceled out to those who would take them, often farmers in need of another pair of hands. Instances of neighborhoods taking in orphaned children to raise are not unique to the 20th century (Fry, 1974).

However, the organized government effort to provide homelike care for children who cannot remain in their own homes is a 20th-century phenomenon. By 1977 there were an estimated 420,000 foster children in the United States (Senate Committee on Finance, 1977). Although foster placements are expected to be temporary, 50 percent of all foster children remain in foster care for two or more years; 26 percent, more than five years; and 12 percent, more than 10 years (see also Areen, 1975; Geiser, 1974; National Association of Attorneys General, 1976).

Long stays in foster care are expensive in every sense. The children and the foster parents inevitably develop emotional ties that are hard to break and that create fear that the relationship could end at any time. A 1972 study stated that it cost the state of New York $122,500 to raise a foster child to the age of 18 compared with the estimated $25,560 it cost parents to raise each of their children (Van Name, Settles, & Culley, 1977). The costs, emotional and economic, should be a strong impetus to arranging permanent placement for children (Howe, 1979).

Everett (1995) updated the status of foster care in this country. The federal appropriations continue to rise. Killackey (1992) discussed one program that might help the foster care program and be in the best interests of children: the placement of a child under custody of a child protective agency in the home of a relative. She also discussed the problems with foster care payments to a relative and other factors such as licensing requirements.

Children are placed in foster care either voluntarily by their parents or involuntarily by order of a court. The relationship between foster parent and foster child does not create a new legal status, although parties in the following case argued that it does create a protected interest.

Smith v. Organization of Foster Families for E. and Reform

431 U.S. 816, 97 S. Ct. 2094, 53 L.Ed.2d 14 (1977)

Mr. Justice Brennan

Appellees, individual foster parents and an organization of foster parents, brought this civil rights class action pursuant to 42 U.S.C. § 1983 in the United States district court for the southern district of New York, on their own behalf and on behalf of children for whom they have provided homes for a year or more. They sought declaratory and injunctive relief against New York State and New York City officials, alleging that the procedures governing the removal of foster children from foster homes provided in New York Social Services Law § 383 (2) and 400, . . . and in Title 18, New York Code Rules and Regulations § 450.14 . . . violated the due process and equal protection clauses of the Fourteenth Amendment. The district court appointed independent counsel for the foster children to forestall any possibility of conflict between their interests and the interests asserted by the foster parents. A group of natural mothers of children in foster care were granted leave to intervene on behalf of themselves and others similarly situated.

· · · · ·

The expressed central policy of the New York system is that

"it is generally desirable for the child to remain with or be returned to the natural parent because the child's need for a normal family life will

usually best be met in the natural home, and . . . parents are entitled to bring up their own children unless the best interests of the child would be thereby endangered."

But the state has opted for foster care as one response to those situations where the natural parents are unable to provide the "positive, nurturing family relationships" and "normal family life in a permanent home" that "offer the best opportunity for children to develop and thrive."

. . . . .

Foster care has been defined as "(a) child welfare service which provides substitute family care for a planned period for a child when his own family cannot care for him for a temporary or extended period and when adoption is neither desirable nor possible." . . . Thus, the distinctive features of foster care are first, "that it is care in a family, it is noninstitutional substitute care," and second, "that it is for a planned period—either temporary or extended. This is unlike adoptive placement, which implies a permanent substitution of one home for another."

. . . . .

Under the New York scheme children may be placed in foster care either by voluntary placement or by court order. Most foster care placements are voluntary. They occur when physical or mental illness, economic problems, or other family crises make it impossible for natural parents, particularly single parents, to provide a stable home life for their children for some limited period. Resort to such placements is almost compelled when it is not possible in such circumstances to place the child with a relative or friend, or to pay for the services of a homemaker or boarding school.

Voluntary placement requires the signing of a written agreement by the natural parent or guardian, transferring the care and custody of the child to an authorized child welfare agency.

. . . . .

The agency may maintain the child in an institutional setting . . . but more commonly acts under its authority to "place out and board out" children in foster homes. . . . Foster parents, who are licensed by the state or an authorized foster care agency . . . provide care under a contractual arrangement with the agency, and are compensated for their services. . . . The typical contract expressly reserves the rights of the agency to remove the child on request. . . . Conversely, the foster parent may cancel the agreement at will.

The New York system divides parental functions among agency, foster parents and natural parents, and the definitions of the respective roles are often complex and often unclear. The law transfers "care and custody" to the agency . . . but day-to-day supervision of the child and his activities, and most of the functions ordinarily associated with legal custody, are the responsibility of the foster parent. Nevertheless, agency supervision of the performance of the foster parents takes forms indicating that the foster parent does not have the full authority of a legal custodian. Moreover, the natural parent's placement of the child with the agency does not surrender legal guardianship; the parent retains authority to act with respect to the child in certain circumstances. The natural parent has not only the right but the obligation to visit the foster child and plan for his future; failure of a parent with capacity to fulfill the obligation for more than a year can result in a court order terminating the parent's rights on the grounds of neglect.

· · · · ·

Children may also enter foster care by court order. The family court may order that a child be placed in the custody of an authorized child-care agency after a full adversary judicial hearing . . . if it is found that the child has been abused or neglected by his natural parents. . . . In addition, a minor adjudicated juvenile delinquent, or "person in need of supervision" may be placed by the court with an agency. . . . The consequences of foster care placement by court order do not differ substantially from those of children voluntarily placed, except that the parent is not entitled to return of the child on demand; termination of foster care must then be consented to by the court.

The provisions of the scheme specifically at issue in this case come into play when the agency having legal custodianship determines to remove the foster child from the foster home, either because it has determined that it would be in the child's best interests to transfer him to some other foster home, or to return the child to his natural parents in accordance with the statute or placement agreement.

· · · · ·

The agency is required, except in emergencies, to notify the foster parents in writing 10 days in advance of any removal. . . . The notice advises the foster parents that if they object to the child's removal they may request a "conference" with the social services department. . . . The department schedules requested conferences within 10 days of the receipt of the request. . . . The foster parent may appear with counsel at the conference, where he will "be advised of the reasons . . . and be afforded an opportunity to submit reasons why the child should not be removed." . . . The official must render a decision in writing within five days after the close of the conference, and send notice of his decision to the foster parents and the agency. . . . The proposed removal is stayed pending the outcome of the conference.

· · · · ·

If the child is removed after the conference, the foster parent may appeal to the Department of Social Services for a "fair hearing," that is, a full adversary administrative hearing . . . the determination of which is subject to judicial review . . . however, the removal is not automatically stayed pending the hearing and judicial review.

· · · · ·

Under SSC Procedure No. 5 . . . in place of or in addition to the conference provided by the state regulations, the foster parents may request a full trial-type hearing before the child is removed from their home. This procedure applies, however, only if the child is being transferred to another foster home, and not if the child is being returned to his natural parents.

One further preremoval procedural safeguard is available. Under Soc. Serv. Law § 392, the family court has jurisdiction to review, on petition of the foster parent or the agency, the status of any child who has been in foster care for 18 months or longer. The foster parents, the natural parents, and all interested agencies are made parties to the proceeding. . . . After hearing, the court may order that foster care be continued, or that the child be returned to his natural parents, or that the agency take steps to free the child for adoption. . . . Moreover, § 392 (8) authorizes the court to issue an "order of protection" which "may set forth reasonable conditions of behavior to be observed for a specified time by a person or agency who is before the court." . . . In other words, § 392 provides a mechanism whereby a foster parent may obtain preremoval judicial review of an agency's decision to remove a child who has been in foster care for 18 months or more.

Foster care of children is a sensitive and emotion-laden subject, and foster-care programs consequently stir strong controversy.

· · · · ·

From the standpoint of natural parents, such as the appellant intervenors here, foster care has been condemned as a class-based intrusion in the family life of the poor. . . . Disproportionate resort to foster care by the poor and victims of discrimination doubtless reflects in part the greater likelihood of disruption of poverty stricken families. Commentators have also noted, however, that middle and upper-income families who need temporary care services for their children have the resources to purchase private care. . . . The poor have little choice but to submit to state-supervised child care when family crises strike.

· · · · ·

The extent to which supposedly "voluntary" placements are in fact voluntary has been questioned on other grounds as well. For example, it has been said that many "voluntary" placements are in fact coerced by threat of neglect proceedings and are not in fact voluntary in the sense of the product of an informed consent. . . . Studies also suggest that social workers of middle-class backgrounds, perhaps unconsciously, incline to favor continued placement in foster care with a generally higher-status family rather than return the child to his natural family, thus reflecting a bias that treats the natural parents' poverty and lifestyle as prejudicial to the best interests of the child. . . . This accounts, it has been said, for the hostility of agencies to the efforts of natural parents to obtain the return of their children.

Appellee foster parents as well as natural parents question the accuracy of the idealized picture portrayed by New York. They note that children often stay in "temporary" foster care for much longer than contemplated by the theory of the system. . . . The district court found as a fact that the median time spent in foster care in New York was over four years. . . . Indeed, many children apparently remain in this "limbo" indefinitely. . . . The district court also found that the longer a child remains in foster care, the more likely it is that he will never leave: "the probability of a foster child being returned to his biological parents declined markedly after the first year in foster care." . . . It is not surprising then that many children, particularly those that enter foster care at a very early age and have little or no contact with their natural parents during extended stays in foster care, often develop deep emotional ties with their foster parents. Yet such ties do not seem to be regarded as obstacles to transfer of the child from one foster placement to another. The record in this case indicates that nearly 60% of the children in foster care in New York City have experienced more than one placement, and about 28% have experienced three or more. . . . The intended stability of the foster-home management is further damaged by the rapid turnover among social work professionals who supervise the foster-care arrangements on behalf of the state. . . . Moreover, even when it is clear that a foster child will not be returned to his natural parents, it is rare that he achieves a stable home life through final termination of parental ties and adoption into a new permanent family.

· · · · ·

The parties and amici devote much of their discussion to these criticisms of foster care, and we present this summary in the view that some understanding of those criticisms is necessary for a full appreciation of the complex and controversial system with which this lawsuit is concerned. But the issue presented by the case is a narrow one. . . . The relief sought in this case is entirely procedural.

Our first inquiry is whether appellees have asserted within the Fourteenth Amendment's protection of "liberty" and "property."

· · · · ·

The appellees' basic contention is that when a child has lived in a foster home for a year or more, a psychological tie is created between the child and the foster parents which constitutes the foster family the true "psychological family" of the child. . . . That family, they argue has a "liberty interest" in its survival as a family, protected by the Fourteenth

Amendment. . . . Upon this premise they conclude that the foster child cannot be removed without a prior hearing satisfying due process. Appointed counsel for the children . . . however, disagrees, and has consistently argued that the foster parents have no such liberty interest independent of the interest of the foster children, and that the best interest of the children would not be served by procedural protections beyond those already provided by New York law. The intervening natural parents of children in foster care . . . also oppose the foster parents, arguing that recognition of the procedural right claimed would undercut both the substantive family law of New York, which favors the return of children to their natural parents as expeditiously as possible . . . and their constitutionally protected right of family privacy, by forcing them to submit to a hearing and defend their rights to their children before the children could be returned to them.

It is of course true that "freedom of personal choice in matters of . . . family life is one of the liberties protected by the due process clause of the Fourteenth Amendment." . . . But is the relation of foster parent to foster child sufficiently akin to the concept of "family" recognized in our precedents to merit similar protection?

• • • • •

First, the usual understanding of "family" implies biological relationships, and most decisions treating the relation between parent and child have stressed this element.

• • • • •

A biological relationship is not present in the case of the usual foster family. But biological relationships are not exclusive determination of the existence of a family. The basic foundation of the family in our society, the marriage relationship, is of course not a matter of blood relations.

• • • • •

Thus the importance of the familial relationship, to the individuals involved and to the society, stems from the emotional attachments that derive from the intimacy of daily association, and from the role it plays in "promot[ing] a way of life" through the instruction of children . . . as well as from the fact of blood relationship. . . . At least where a child has been placed in foster care as an infant, has never known his natural parents, and has remained continuously for several years in the care of the same foster parents, it is natural that the foster family should hold the same place in the emotional life of the foster child, and fulfill the same socializing functions, as a natural family. For this reason, we cannot dismiss the foster family as a mere collection of unrelated individuals.

• • • • •

But there are also important distinctions between the foster family and the natural family. . . . Unlike the property interests that are also protected by the Fourteenth Amendment . . . the liberty interest in family privacy has its source, and its contours are ordinarily to be sought, not in state law, but in intrinsic human rights, as they have been understood in "this nation's history and tradition." . . . Here, however, whatever emotional ties may develop between foster parent and foster child have their origins in an arrangement in which the state has been a partner from the outset. While the Court has recognized that liberty interests may in some cases arise from positive law sources . . . in such a case, and particularly where, as here, the claimed interest derives from a knowingly assumed contractual relation with the state, it is appropriate to ascertain from state law the expectations and entitlements of the parties. In this case, the limited recognition accorded to the foster family by the New York statutes and the contracts executed by the foster parents argue against any but the most limited constitutional "liberty" in the foster family.

Ordinarily procedural protection may be afforded to a liberty interest of one person without derogating from the substantive liberty of another. Here, however, such a tension is virtually unavoidable. Under New York law, the natural parent of a foster child in voluntary placement has an absolute right to the return of his child in the absence of a court order obtainable only upon compliance with rigorous substantive and procedural standards, which reflect the constitutional protection accorded the natural family. . . . Moreover, the natural parent initially gave up his child to the state only on the express understanding that the child would be returned in those circumstances. These rights are difficult to reconcile with the liberty interest in the foster family relationship claimed by appellees. It is one thing to say that individuals may acquire a liberty interest against arbitrary governmental interference in the family-life associations into which they have freely entered, even in the absence of biological connection or state-law recognition of the relationship. It is quite another to say that one may acquire such an interest in the face of another's constitutionally recognized liberty interest that derives from blood relationship, state law sanction, and basic human rights—an interest the foster parent has recognized by contract from the onset.

· · · · ·

As this discussion suggests, appellees' claim to a constitutionally protected liberty interest raises complex and novel questions. It is unnecessary for us to resolve those questions definitely in this case, however, for, like the district court, we conclude that "narrower grounds exist to support" our reversal. We are persuaded that, even on the assumption that appellees have a protected "liberty interest," the district court erred in holding that the preremoval procedures presently employed by the state are constitutionally defective.

First, the court held that the "independent review" administrative proceeding was insufficient because it was only available on the request of the foster parents. In the view of the district court, the proceeding should be provided as a matter of course, because the interests of the foster parents and those of the child would not necessarily be coextensive, and it could not be assumed that the foster parents would invoke the hearing procedure in every case in which it was in the child's interest to have a hearing. Since the child is unable to request a hearing on his own, automatic review in every case is necessary. We disagree. As previously noted, the constitutional liberty, if any, sought to be protected by the New York procedures is a right of family privacy or autonomy, and the basis for recognition of any such interest in the foster family must be that close emotional ties analogous to those between parent and child are established when a child resides for a lengthy period with a foster family. If this is so, necessarily we should expect that the foster parents will seek to continue the relationship to preserve the stability of the family; if they do not request a hearing, it is difficult to see that right or interest of the foster child is protected by holding a hearing to determine whether removal would unduly impair his emotional attachments to a foster parent who does not care enough about the child to contest the removal. . . . Moreover, automatic provision of hearings as required by the district court would impose a substantial additional administrative burden on the state.

· · · · ·

Second, the district court faulted the city procedure on the ground that participation is limited to the foster parents and the agency, and the natural parent and the child are not made parties to the hearing. This is not fatal in light of the nature of the alleged constitutional interests at stake. When the child's transfer from one foster home to another is pending, the interest arguably requiring protection is that of the foster family, not that of the natural parents. Moreover, the natural parent can generally add little to the accuracy of factfinding concerning the wisdom of such a transfer, since the foster parents and the agency, through its caseworkers, will usually be most knowledgeable about conditions in the foster home. Of course, in those cases where the natural parent does have a special interest in the proposed transfer or particular information that would assist the factfinder, nothing in the city's procedure prevents any party from securing his testimony. . . . Nothing in the New York City procedure prevents consultation of the child's wishes, directly or through an adult intermediary. We assume, moreover, that some such consultation would be among the first steps that a rational factfinder, inquiring into the child's best interest, would pursue. Such consultation, however, does not require that the *child or an appointed representative must be a party with full adversary powers in all preremoval hearings.*

The other two defects in the city procedure found by the district court must also be rejected. One is that the procedure does not extend to the removal of a child from foster care to be returned to his natural parent. But as we have already held, whatever liberty interest may be argued to exist in the foster family is significantly weaker in the case of removal preceding return to the natural parent, and the balance of due process interests must accordingly be different.

· · · · ·

Finally, the § 392 hearing is available to foster parents, both in and outside of New York City, even where the removal sought is for the purpose of returning the child to his natural parents. Since this remedy provides a sufficient constitutional preremoval hearing to protect whatever liberty interest might exist in the continued existence of the foster family when the state seeks to transfer the child to another foster home a fortiori, the procedure is adequate to protect the lesser interest of the foster family in remaining together at the expense of the disruption of the natural family.

We deal here with issues of unusual delicacy, in an area where professional judgments regarding desirable procedures are constantly and rapidly changing. In such a context, restraint is appropriate on the part of courts called upon to adjudicate whether a particular procedural scheme is adequate under the Constitution. Since we hold that the procedures provided by New York State in § 392 and by New York City's SSC Procedure No. 5 are adequate to protect whatever liberty interests appellees may have, the judgement of the district court is reversed.

Mr. Justice Stewart, with whom the chief justice and Mr. Justice Rehnquist join, concurring in the judgment.

Rather than tiptoeing around this central issue, I would squarely hold that the interests asserted by the appellees are not of a kind that the due process clause of the Fourteenth Amendment protects.

· · · · ·

What remains of the appellees' argument is the theory that the relationship of the foster parent to the foster child may generate emotional attachments similar to those found in natural families.

· · · · ·

But under New York's foster care laws, any case where the foster parents had assumed the emotional role of the child's natural parents would represent not a triumph of the system, to be constitutionally safeguarded from state intrusion, but a failure. The goal of foster care, at least in New York, is not to provide a permanent substitute for the natural or adoptive home, but to prepare the child for his return to his real parents or placement in a permanent adoptive home by giving him temporary shelter in a family setting.

The case is presented at length for its discussion of a foster care system that is similar in operation and consequences to those of other states; many social workers will find the entire opinion useful. Due process would entitle the foster parents to notice, a hearing, and the right to appeal. The Court never really answers the appellees' contention, although it does say that the parties had all the due process to which they were entitled.

The concurring justices would simply say that the foster parents have no protected interest. Justice Stewart makes it plain that the assumption of an emotional role in the foster child's life is a failure rather than a triumph of the system. These "failures" are all too common.

Since *Smith,* other courts have held that foster parents do not have a constitutionally protected interest in their relationship with the foster child (*Kyees v. County Dept. of Public Welfare,* 1979). However, in *Rivers v. Marcus* (1982), the court held that a half sister had a liberty interest in preserving a familial relationship with her half brother and half sister. Although she had signed a standard foster care agreement, she was entitled to procedural due process before termination of the foster care agreement.

If the Supreme Court does not find that the relationship between foster parent and foster child creates a new status, can the nature of the relationship be defined more clearly? An Alaska court was presented with the question of whether foster parents were agents of the state for the purposes of the constitutional proscription against unreasonable searches and seizures (*J.M.A. v. Alaska,* 1976). Suspecting that the foster child was trafficking in drugs, the foster mother searched the child's room, listened in on telephone calls, and turned over to the police a plastic bag of marijuana that she found in his room. Asking whether the person's duties are related to law enforcement, the court held that the foster mother was not an agent of the state, so that the evidence she discovered was admissible in court. Although the activities of a private citizen acting on behalf of the police would be subject to the Fourth Amendment, the foster mother was a substitute for a natural parent and was no more an agent of the police than any natural parent.

Certainly if children in need of care outside their own homes can be cared for in the homes of relatives, that is desirable. It strengthens blood relationships and helps maintain ties with the extended family. But the lack or weakness of an extended family may prevent this. Even if there are relatives who would assist with the care of the child, economic considerations may make placement impossible. The U.S. Supreme Court clarified the option in *Miller v. Youakim* (1979), a class action suit brought by the older sister of four children in foster care and the children for themselves and everyone similarly situated. The four children originally had been placed in foster homes in 1969, but in 1972 two of them were placed with the Youakims, who were under no legal obligation to support them. The Youakim home was approved as a foster home for the children. The sister refused to take the other children, because the $63 Aid to Families with Dependent Children benefit for each child, less than the $105 rate for children in foster care, was insufficient.

Justice Marshall, for a unanimous Court, held that the Aid to Families with Dependent Children–Foster Care (AFDC-FC) program encompasses foster children who, pursuant to a judicial determination of neglect, have been placed in the homes of relatives who meet a state's licensing requirement for unrelated foster homes; such children are therefore entitled to the support of the foster care program. The Court said, "The purpose of the AFDC-FC program was not simply to duplicate the AFDC program for a different class of beneficiaries . . . the Foster Care program was designed to meet the particular needs of all eligible neglected children, whether they are placed with related or unrelated foster parents" (p. 964). This decision may encourage care by family members whom children already know and who presumably have an emotional stake in their future.

In 1980 Congress passed the Adoption Assistance and Child Welfare Act to respond to problems of children lost in foster care by providing services to families at risk. It provides for partial reimbursement of foster care maintenance payments.

ADOPTION

Adoption is a legal proceeding that creates a new status of legitimate filiation. It is a creature of the law. Without strict adherence to the letter of the law, there is no adoption, in contrast to other legal transactions that although initially irregular may be ratified later. Adoption bestows a status that did not exist before and gives an individual a legal relationship to a new set of individuals.

In ancient times adoption was seen as an institution for the benefit of parents. Adoption then provided an heir, cemented alliances with other families and nations, and assured the performance of rituals after the elders died. Although the benefits for adoptive parents continue, the institution is now seen as designed for the benefit of children, providing them with a loving home and a family in which to grow and thrive. Therefore, the current emphasis in adoptions is on the best interest of the child. Professional practice emphasizes searching for a home in which the child can be perceived as a natural child and seeks adoptive parents similar in genetic background and in other ways to the child.

Some states have developed an equitable adoption doctrine that creates an adoptive status in the absence of legal formalities to avoid inequitable results. The doctrine is used to create inheritance rights for those who assumed they were adopted because foster parents planned to adopt or whose formal adoption was flawed by an irregularity in the process. Rein (1984) described the theoretical bases of equitable adoption, proof of the contract to adopt, suggested criteria for the adoption, and the possible consequences. The article also cited cases from several states in which courts have recognized the doctrine. Clients who are contemplating adoption should not rely on this doctrine; they should be advised to see a lawyer to be sure that the law is strictly complied with. Rein (1984) discussed the legal status of adoptees in intestate successions and some of the problems. According to her, equitable adoption should be the de factoequivalent of statutory adoption, and she suggested more-realistic criteria for judging equitable adoptions claims. Usually the equitably adopted child inherits a child's share. However, the doctrine can open up a Pandora's box of problems.

Locke (1980) listed cases in 27 states and the District of Columbia that held that the equitable doctrine applies. The most important prerequisite to application of the doctrine is proof that a contract of adoption was entered into between foster and natural parents or an institution standing in loco parentis.

Biological parents are often reluctant to relinquish custody. It is not unknown for children to remain in foster care indefinitely when parents are unable to plan for their futures and unwilling to surrender them.

The natural zeal of social workers to prevent children from remaining in foster care indefinitely should not blind them to the rights of natural parents. *In re State ex. rel. Sharp* (1960) concerned a young father who turned to child welfare authorities for help with his infant child after his wife died in an accident. During the nine months that the child was in foster care, the father visited three times and paid three monthly board payments. He married again and requested the return of the child. The agency brought an action to declare the child abandoned and free for adoption. The father regained custody of his child through a habeas corpus action. The decision does not indicate what other factors influenced the agency action to seek termination of parental rights, but social workers should be cautious in this area.

Consent

Obtaining consent from the biological parents to allow adoption is a continuing problem. Tragic cases arose after the Vietnamese orphan "baby lift" as parents and other relatives arrived here and sought to find children airlifted from Vietnam earlier, when the fall of Saigon was imminent. Although many children were validly released under the Vietnam Civil Code, others were probably turned over to agencies in the expectation that the families would be reunited later in the United States.

Nguyen Da Yen v. Kissinger (1975) was a class action against the United States Immigration and Naturalization Service (INS) to determine the whereabouts of a large number of children (see also *Huynh Thi Anh v. Levi*, 1978), detained, according to the complaint, in the custody of persons other than their parents in violation of fundamental human rights and of the Fifth Amendment. The court of appeals determined that it had jurisdiction to order the INS to seek information about the location and circumstances of the potential applicants necessary to litigate the claims. The court recognized the need to proceed quickly, before the children had time to forget their natural families and develop strong affectional ties with adoptive families. A note to the opinion is instructive in warning those who use the courts that they must be careful to develop a proper record, and, as in this case, a ground for jurisdiction of the courts.

> *Without extensively belaboring the point, we would like to point out to plaintiffs that while they have been bombarding us with urgings to haste, we have been substantially delayed filling in various fundamental legal nooks and crannies they have overlooked in their haste. We understand plaintiffs' concerns for speed, and share it. Nevertheless, plaintiffs have invoked the legal process in their aid, and must step by step conform to that process. We would suggest that some deliberate careful attention to legal detail will speed the end of this suit, not delay it.* (p. 1200)

As the Vietnamese cases indicate, courts are reluctant to sever familial ties unless that is clearly in the best interest of the child. In the case of adoption of stepchildren by the spouse of one biological parent, courts have regularized the existing family arrangement of the child without consent of the noncustodial parent when that parent has failed to pay court-ordered child support for a year (*In re Coile*, 1977; see also *Lehr v. Robertson, 1983*). However, if circumstances make it impossible for the natural parent to pay support, failure that is not willful or intentional will not render unnecessary the parent's consent to the adoption by a stepparent (*Steed v. McKenzie*, 1977).

Adoption terminates old relationships and creates new ones. Therefore, the rights of persons other than the natural parents may be terminated as well (Levy, 1993). In *Matter of Adoption of Gardiner* (1980) the Iowa court denied visitation rights to the maternal grandparents of a child adopted by the brother and sister-in-law of his natural father. Louisiana amended its civil code in 1978 to permit visitation rights of grandparents after adoption by the stepparent of their deceased child's children, if "such visitation rights would be in the best interest of the child or children" (La. Rev. Stat. § 1:572). The court may order an investigation and report by social workers to help it reach a conclusion on the interest of the child in such visits.

Agency Adoptions

Adoption through a social services agency protects against a change of heart by the natural parents, who may attempt to remove the child from the custody of adoptive parents (as often happens with private adoptions). If adoptions are arranged by licensed agencies, generally the surrender of the child is irrevocable, and the prospective adoptive parents may receive the child free for placement into their home. Of course, prospective adoptive parents may find that they are unable to obtain a child from an agency because no children are available and so turn to private placements (McTaggart, 1979).

In *Golz v. Children's Bureau of New Orleans, Inc.* (1976), the Louisiana Supreme Court discussed the act of surrender to an agency of a legitimate child by both parents. The parents brought a habeas corpus proceeding to recover the child, alleging that the act of surrender was not irrevocable. The natural parents alleged that the act of surrender was a contract of *adhesion,* one in which, because of disparate bargaining ability and the absence of negotiation, consent is not freely given. Discussing the extensive agency efforts to counsel the parents and the efforts of the attorney who notarized their act of surrender to explain the finality of the act, the court rejected the novel argument that the agency was a party of superior bargaining power implicitly coercing a weaker party. The decision cites cases in other states that maintain the irrevocability of an act of surrender to a licensed adoption agency.

There have been dramatic newspaper and television accounts of the return of children to the natural parents after their surrender for adoption. When the parents are unmarried or separated, the adoption worker should get the release of both parents before placement if possible. In 1988 the National Conference of Commissioners on Uniform State Laws approved the Uniform Putative and Unknown Fathers Act. The American Bar Association followed suit. The act provides guidelines for, among other things, determination of paternity, notice and right to be heard at adoption proceedings, and termination of parental rights (Hroka, 1989).

Adoption agencies should be aware of *Janet G. v. New York Foundling Hospital* (1978), in which a 17-year-old natural mother sued to set aside the surrender of her child for adoption. The court held that this was not a matter of contract law but of constitutional principles. The *parens patriae* obligation of the state imposes an affirmative moral duty on it in dealing with minors, and thus minors such as Janet G. are entitled to legal advice in making such a decision. That result is unusual. The more likely result is that shown in *Good v. Zavala* (1988), where the court held that the natural mother gave informed, intelligent consent to the adoption, and the motion to revoke consent was denied.

Spivey (1976) discussed the rights of parents to withdraw consent generally. Most laws agree that prior to the decree of adoption, consent may be withdrawn if it is in the best interests of the child.

As any adoption worker knows, there are many serious and delicate emotional problems associated with adoption. There are legal problems, as well, as the following discussion indicates.

Interracial Adoptions

Brown v. Board of Education of Topeka (1954) started the series of cases holding that race is a suspect classification under the equal protection clause. But even if it is now legally permissible to place a child in an interracial home, is that necessarily in the child's best interest? In a tragic case, *Green v. City of New Orleans* (1956), a black applicant to adopt sued to compel the Bureau of Vital Statistics to issue a new birth certificate designating the child whom he desired to adopt as black. At that time, Louisiana outlawed interracial adoptions.

The child was born of a white mother who had died of a brain tumor. The mother's sister had initial custody of the child, but later granted custody to the welfare department because the child had obvious black features. The designation of race on the birth certificate had been made at the hospital, with the registrant taking it for granted that the father was white. The child was placed in a black foster home until the adoption proceeding. Change in designation of race from white to black was denied, although testimony in the case revealed the strong possibility of a black father and physical characteristics strongly indicative of black blood. Judge Janvier in dissent said,

> A person of the Negro race has as much right to have such records correctly made as a person of the white race. And I cannot condemn this little girl to the humiliation and embarrassment which must ensue if this incorrect entry is to stand even for the five or six years suggested by my associates. There is no assurance that after the lapse of those five or six years another effort will be made to effect the necessary correction and there will result the most unfortunate situation that the little girl registered as white will continue to associate with Negroes and that her

social life will be only with Negroes and yet she will be unable to marry a Negro since, being registered as a white person, miscegenation laws will make such a marriage impossible. In fact, during the five or six years suggested by my associate she will labor under the embarrassment of associating socially only with Negroes who will no doubt taunt her with being registered as "white." (p. 82)

The *Green* court says "the final cause of law is the welfare of society," although it is difficult to see how the "welfare of society" is involved. Because a civil case need not be proved beyond a reasonable doubt, why does the court seem to require an even more stringent standard for changing the designation of race here? The answer is that in the past, when racial designation carried with it serious social and economic effects, great care in changing the race on the birth certificate was justified. Fortunately, the law and the times have changed.

However, there is now a controversy over placing black children with white families. A *New York Times* article discussed groups opposed to it and the limited statistics available as to how common it is (Jones, 1993). A later *New York Times* article (Williams, 1995) discussed the current controversy about transracial adoption since the film *Losing Isaiah* was released.

According to Auld (1993), all states have statutes providing monetary subsidies for families that adopt "hard-to-place" children, including children from minority groups. He reported a study of transracial adopted children and suggested that the adoption serves a child's best interests rather than remaining institutionalized or in foster care. Auld proposed legislation be passed limiting racial matching so that children can be moved into permanent placement more quickly.

Texas, along with Louisiana, once outlawed interracial adoptions. In *In re Gomez* (1967) a black man who had married a white woman desired to adopt her illegitimate white children. Although the trial court forbade the adoption, the court of appeals held the statute prohibiting interracial adoptions unconstitutional.

Southern states were not alone in forbidding or frowning on interracial adoptions. In *In re Baker* (1962) an Ohio trial court prevented the adoption by a Caucasian and Japanese couple of a child of Puerto Rican and English descent, but the court of appeals disagreed, saying "Under ordinary circumstances a child should be placed in a family having the same racial, religious, and cultural backgrounds [as the parents] but such a placement [as this] is not precluded" (p. 53).

Although race, a suspect classification, cannot be the only factor in making a determination for placement, it can be considered. The social consequences of placement of an Asian child with white parents or of a black child with one white and one Asian parent may still be harmful, even though the placement is perfectly legal. In a landmark decision, the federal court of appeals for the fifth circuit held in *Drummond v. Fulton County Dept. of Family and Child. Serv.* (1977) that race may be considered as a factor in making adoption placements. In that case, a mixed-race child had been placed with white foster parents shortly after birth, but their request to adopt was denied. Although there were other factors in the agency's decision (the age of the parents, their health, and their educational attainments), race was an important factor.

When the demand for children far exceeds the supply of those available for adoption, there is little justification for placing a child in a less-than-perfect setting. However, we live in a heterogeneous society, and children may receive great love and affection in what would seem a less-than-perfect placement. Social workers are occasionally more cautious than necessary in making placements, as the following case illustrates.

In re Bonez

50 Misc.2d 1080, 272 N.Y.S.2d 587 (1966)

Justine Wise Polier, J.

For a century this state has recognized the need and the duty to provide "for a more efficient and constant supervision of all the charitable and reformatory institutions which participate in the public bounty, or are supported by taxation." The state boards created for this purpose and to correct "confusion" in administration have undergone changes of name and have had their jurisdiction enlarged over the years.

• • • • •

By both constitutional and legislative action, successive steps have been taken since 1784 to cope with the problems of children whose parents were unable to support them, who were born out-of-wedlock, who were abandoned, who were abused, or who were in need of adoptive care.

• • • • •

It is significant that the section of the law dealing with Aid to Dependent Children specifically states: "Aid shall be construed to include services, particularly those services which may be necessary for each child in the light of the particular home conditions and his other needs."

The law of this state thus clearly imposes on the state and its subdivisions the primary responsibility for providing the care that a child may need away from home either directly or through an authorized agency. In practice, the state has failed to fulfill its duty to secure services through authorized agencies to meet the needs of dependent, neglected children in foster homes or adoptive homes or to provide direct services where the authorized agencies fail or are unable to meet the needs of individual children.

· · · · ·

While the State Department of Social Welfare has steadily increased direct services for children found to be delinquent or in need of supervision, it provides no direct services for dependent children found to be neglected and in need of care away from their own homes within the City of New York.

· · · · ·

The doctrine under which the New York City Public Welfare District has operated through its Bureau of Child Welfare has been that it will accept for direct care only those children whom the voluntary agencies reject. In accordance with this doctrine, the City of New York has gone so far as to create a congregate child care institution for dependent and neglected children under the fiction that it is a private agency.

· · · · ·

However, in practice, on a finding of neglect it has become the practice of the Department of Welfare to refuse direct service for children through either its foster home or adoption units if the child is in the custody of a private agency. The court, therefore, is in practice made entirely dependent on the decisions of the private agency and is treated as a rubber stamp that is used only to secure continuing tax subsidies.

· · · · ·

In an earlier decision dated January 10, 1966, this court found that this child, born out-of-wedlock, and abandoned by her mother in 1962 when less than one year of age, was in need of adoptive placement. The court noted that this child has been in a congregate shelter and in three successive foster home placements under the auspices of the voluntary agency which had requested extension of placement by this court for still another additional year.

· · · · ·

The continuing lack of effective action by the voluntary agency having custody of Ellen and the failure of the Department of Welfare to take any steps to assure this child appropriate placement in an adoptive home have again forced this court to actively intervene on behalf of this abandoned child. This court has experienced both overt and indirect resistance to the removal of the child from the voluntary agency boarding home unit. Because of the elaborate pattern of resistance by both the voluntary and public agency to taking such action as this court found necessary in the best interest of Ellen, the history of this single case is reviewed. Since it is typical of the tragic history of many children now dragging out their lives on public subsidy in a succession of boarding homes without becoming part of a family, the facts are reviewed in detail.

Ellen, born August 7, 1961, had been remanded by the predecessor court (domestic relations court of the City of New York) in May, 1962,

*when she was abandoned by her mother. After nearly three years of cus-
tody in the voluntary agency and its boarding home division, extension of
placement was requested for an additional 12 month period under the
New York State Family Court Act.*

*On reviewing the application in January, 1965, this court questioned
why this child abandoned in 1962 had not been considered for adoptive
placement. The extension for placement was denied, but the child was
continued on remand for the agency to explore adoptive placement. It was
not until June 21, 1965, that the agency reported that Ellen had been tested
recently in their developmental clinic and that there was no apparent
contraindication to adoptive placement. The report added that the adoption
department, however, was unable to recommend a suitable adoptive couple.*

*On September 9, 1965, the agency reported that Ellen was making an
excellent adjustment in her present foster home and emphasized the importance of placing this child in "a warm, secure, long-term foster home with
a foster family who is similar in coloring and cultural descent to Ellen."
This foster home was described as one "where it is foreseeable that they
may adopt Ellen at a later date." In the same report the agency stated that
it had (on the repeated urging of this court) referred Ellen to the adoption
units of seven agencies and to its own adoption unit. The remand was
continued by this court.*

*On November 18, 1965, the agency reported its adoption department
had begun the study of a family which they felt might be acceptable for
Ellen. No mention was made of the family study reported as nearing completion on September 9, 1965. It was also stated that two of the agencies to
whom referrals had been made had accepted the referral of Ellen.*

*Three weeks later, on December 6, 1965, the agency advised this court
that Ellen's foster parents, who had been described as foreseeable adoptive
parents in October, had decided to move to Puerto Rico and that Ellen was
being prepared for an "unexpected transfer" to another foster home.*

*On December 23, 1965, the agency reported that the most recent foster
home was suitable for Ellen, "similar in both coloring and cultural descent, and predisposed to adoption." The court was also assured that their
adoption department was continuing a search for an adoptive home and
that Ellen was still on referral to the two adoption agencies which had
accepted referrals.*

*Again on January 14, 1966, the agency reported that Ellen had made
a suitable adjustment in her foster home and that "she had been accepted
by the family on the basis of her coloring and genetic origins" and spoke
of the possibility of this family being prospective adoptive parents.*

*On February 4, 1966, the possibility of the use of the foster home as an
adoptive home was reiterated and the agency also promised cooperation*

with one of the adoptive agencies that had expressed interest in finding an adoptive home. However, five days later this adoptive agency advised the court in a letter that they understood that Ellen was in an excellent foster home, and that adoption by this couple was reported to be a "realistic possibility."

On February 25, 1966, the agency again reiterated that the present foster parents remained interested in Ellen as a possible adopted child and added: "Since this is Ellen's fourth placement following six months in our nurseries, we do not feel that a removal from the home for adoptive placement through our or any interested agency should be considered until we have had the opportunity to fully explore the potentials of her present home in respect to her adoption." The agency now requested a further remand for an additional six month period.

On June 8, 1966, without explanation as to what had happened to negate the foster home as an adoptive home, the agency stated: "We have explored the use of an adoptive family from our agency for Ellen but they felt that although she is socially appealing and intellectually curious, her darker skin tone would create conflicts within the home and the community." Again, a further six month remand was requested to work out possible plans with a Syracuse agency through the Statewide Adoption Exchange, and secure a decision to have the child freed for adoptive placement. Ellen had already been in the custody of this agency for over four years since she had been abandoned, and no legal steps had been taken to free her for adoption.

In the light of the record, this court wrote on July 11, 1966, directly to the three adoptive agencies that had agreed to accept a referral to ask whether they would review their files and advise the court directly if they were able to accept this child for adoptive placement.

On July 15, 1966, Spence Chapin advised this court that they had withdrawn only because the agency having custody had advised them orally that no assistance was needed. In a letter dated July 19, 1966, the State Department advised this court that although they had been able to locate a potential adoptive home, the agency having custody was unwilling to participate in an interagency meeting to discuss placement as required by the procedures of the Statewide Adoption Exchange. In a letter dated July 25, 1966, Louise Wise Services, the third agency that had agreed to accept a referral also reported it had withdrawn from the case when informed by the agency having custody that its services were not needed.

The agency having custody had in no way informed the court of any of these occurrences, and, in fact, on June 8, 1966, had written to advise the court that it was requesting a further six month remand while "we will continue to work out plans with the Syracuse agency."

During this entire period the Public Welfare District for New York City had remained silent and uncooperative. Its lack of responsiveness, together *with the resistance to adoptive placement by the agency having custody has resulted in this superior, attractive child being placed in a shelter, a congregate institution and three successive foster homes. It has forced this court to assume direct and personal responsibility for finding an adoptive home. It has caused the taxpayer to continue to pay for foster care for this child at the rate of over $3,000 a year for the three years following the 12 months' period required for adoptive placement of an abandoned child.*

This case illustrates that without the development of public services for children or the enforcement of accountability by private agencies to either the State Department of Welfare or its subdivision, children will continue to be left in inappropriate care at great expense to the taxpayer and irreparable damage to the children. This court to fulfill its obligation under law is entitled to receive that assistance and cooperation of the State Department and its political subdivision in far different fashion.

Fortunately in the instant case, Spence Chapin Adoption Service is able to provide an appropriate pre-adoptive home without further delay. The remand to the New York Foundling Hospital is terminated. Placement is made to Spence Chapin Adoption Service effective July 25, 1966, with the privilege to place in a pre-adoptive home pending action to free Ellen for adoption.

The case is adjourned to October 17, 1966, for report by Spence Chapin Adoption Service on Ellen's adjustment in adoptive home and for filing of adoption petition.

Is this case unusual? If not, what can be done about it? Is the only solution an outraged judge? A child who has not been surrendered may remain in a series of foster homes until the age of majority. In such a case, is it better practice to opt for a less-than-perfect placement? Probably a searching examination of the entire question should be made, as well as a review of any policy denying foster parents the right to adopt.

Religion

Social workers have traditionally considered prospective parents' religious affiliation, or lack thereof, in determining the strength and desirability of an adoptive home. Religious affiliation and the strength of parents' ties to their church are certainly factors in evaluating a placement. However, placing a child only in a home where the parents are affiliated with a particular religious denomination is somewhat controversial.

We live in a pluralistic society. There are potential adoptive couples who espouse different religions or different denominations within the same religion, and there are probably a great many prospective adoptive parents who have no religious affiliation whatsoever. Are they to be denied a child simply by the fact or lack of their religion? Would not such a denial immediately raise constitutional questions? Such questions are rarely raised in a legal proceeding, because prospective parents must meet the "best interest of the child" requirement of most adoption statutes. In the following case the question of religion as a placement factor was raised.

Petitions of Goldman
121 N.E.2d 843 (Mass. 1954), cert. denied, 348 U.S. 942 (1955)
QUA, C.J.

The petitioners obtained the children when they were about two weeks old from the hospital where they were born and have had them ever since. [The children were three-year-old twins at the time of the suit; one was mentally retarded.] All of the evidence bearing on the ability of the petitioners to care for the twins, including that contained in the reports mentioned above, tended to show that the petitioners have a good home and sufficient means, are fond of the twins, and are giving them adequate care. . . . The judge further found that the mother and "the natural father" of the twins are Catholics. There was ample evidence to support this finding. The mother did not cease to be a Catholic, even if she failed to live up to the ideals of her religion. The petitioners are of the Jewish faith and intend to bring the twins up in that faith. The mother has consented in writing on both petitions to the adoptions prayed for. She has never seen or spoken to the petitioners, but she had stated that she knew they were Jewish and was satisfied that the twins should be raised in the Jewish faith. . . . The petitioners have dark complexions and dark hair. The twins are blond, with large blue eyes and flaxen hairs.

· · · · ·

This finding was in effect a finding that it was "practicable," in the meaning of that word in Sec. 5B, to "give custody only to persons" of the Catholic faith. The finding rests upon detailed evidence from persons connected with Catholic charities as to many applications to adopt Catholic children by Catholic couples who had been investigated and found in good financial condition with good homes, "who are ready and willing to adopt these two children." It is true that objection was made to the oral part of the evidence which follows that just quoted, and that it would have been desirable if more definite proof could have been had that suitable Catholic persons had actually seen these particular children and stood ready to adopt both of them at one time.

· · · · ·

It is contended that Sec. 5B is unconstitutional as a law "respecting an establishment of religion, or prohibiting the free exercise thereof," contrary to the First Amendment of the Constitution. . . . There is no "subordination" of one sect to another. . . . It is argued that there is

*interference with the mother's right to determine the religion of her off-
spring, and that in these cases she has determined that it shall be Jewish.
Passing the point that so far as concerns religion she seems to have consented rather than commanded and seems to have been "interested only
that the babies were in a good home" there is clearly no interference with
any wish of hers as long as she retains her status as a parent. It is only on
the assumption that she is to lose that status that Sec. 5B becomes opera-
tive. . . . We do not attempt to discuss the philosophy underlying the concept that a child too young to understand any religion, even imperfectly,
nevertheless may have a religion. We have no doubt that the statute was
intended to apply to such children, and that in such instances the words
"religious faith of the child" mean the religious faith of the parents, or in
the case of "dispute" the faith of the mother.*

This case raises a number of questions. Children who have mental
disabilities are often hard to place. If there had been no prospective
adoptive parents for the child with mental disabilities, would the Court
then be justified in denying the adoption by parents of another religion?
Should the natural parent be able to determine the religious affiliation of
the child? The Catholic mother had approved of the placement with a
Jewish couple. If the stated religious preference is for a nontraditional
religion, does it control? If a child is left as a foundling with an orphan-
age run by a religious denomination, should the child automatically be
declared to be of that religion? A later case, *In re Adoption of Child*
(1971), following the best interests of the child, allowed Mormon parents
to adopt a Catholic child; nor were their ages (59 and 47) an impediment
because they were in good health.

The inherent difficulty in determining the child's religion is demonstrated by *In re Glauas* (1953), where the father of a four-year-old child
was Greek Catholic and the mother was Jewish. The court concluded
that "the baptism of the child did not supersede the circumcision." Although an older case, *Re Korte* (1912), denied an adoption to a man who
was a "freethinker," current cases usually deal with differences in denominations. *In re McKenzie* (1936) reversed a lower court denial of a
petition for adoption on the grounds that the adoptive parents were Prot-
estant and the child was Catholic. After four years of custody by the
adoptive couple, the court held that the agency's refusal to consent to the
adoption was in such complete contradiction to the welfare of the child
as to make such denial arbitrary and capricious. In *Eggleston v. Landrum*
(1951) the trial court denied adoption on the sole basis that the adoptive
parents were Christian Scientists. The appellate court reversed, holding
that although the state will not permit modern medical treatment to be

denied a child regardless of religious belief, there was no evidence that the adoptive parents were opposed to medical treatment because of religious beliefs. Many states currently limit the role of religion in custody decisions, although several require the adoptive placement to be with parents of the same religion as the child or natural parents. Comparative judgments between religions must be avoided. Religion is only one factor of many in deciding the best interest of the child.

Beschle (1989) discussed the problem and wrote that religion may be a factor in determining the best interest of the child. This is true not just in the case of a mature child with religious beliefs but in assessing the quality of a family environment.

Single Parents

In dealing with adoption of illegitimate children, social workers have traditionally dealt with the natural mother. Statutes have required only her consent to an act of surrender; the natural father of an illegitimate child had no rights. Of course, when an illegitimate child was surrendered for adoption, the natural father usually had no interest in preventing the adoption and may not even have known of the birth of the child. Newspapers have carried stories of children returned to their natural parents after the illegitimate father has said he did not sign a surrender because he did know of the child's birth and placement for adoption. However, in *Michael H. v. Gerald D.* (1989), there was a challenge to a California provision that a child born to a married woman living with her husband who is neither impotent nor sterile is presumed a child of the marriage. Michael showed a 0.07 percent probability that he was the natural father through an adulterous affair, but the court upheld the provision stating that the case rests on the historic respect accorded the relationship that develops within the unitary family.

The situation has changed dramatically since the decision in *Stanley v. Illinois* (1972). That case involved not actual adoption but the custody of illegitimate children. Stanley lived with and supported his illegitimate children. After their mother died, the children were removed from the home without a hearing as to Stanley's fitness to retain custody. In Illinois a hearing on fitness was required before illegitimate children could be removed from the custody of the natural mother. The Supreme Court held the Illinois statute to be an unconstitutional denial of equal protection.

Since *Stanley*, several cases have required the consent of the natural father to an adoption. One was *In re Johnson* (1977); the father had repeatedly tried to see his son and had offered to marry the mother. The court thought he had exhibited a reasonable degree of interest (see also *In re Gerald*, 1978).

Social workers may worry about the veto power of the natural father over adoption plans for his illegitimate child. *Quilloin v. Walcott* (1978), a case that attacked the constitutionality of the Georgia adoption law that denied the father power to prevent an illegitimate child's adoption, is instructive. The natural mother had married, and her husband petitioned to adopt her child, which the natural father attempted to prevent. The Supreme Court held that an illegitimate father has no natural rights to the child, only earned rights, distinguishing the case from *Stanley* because the father had never shown an interest in the child or accepted any responsibility for his support.

"Earned rights" introduces a new concept into family law. *Caban v. Mohammed* (1979) offers clarification. In that case the natural father had supported his illegitimate children. The case was a contest between the natural parents, each of whom had married a spouse who was willing to adopt the children. The New York statute gave the unwed mother authority to block adoption of her child simply by withholding consent but denied such rights to the father. The court found the statute unconstitutional because the distinction between mothers and fathers was not substantially related to an important state interest. In *Adoption of Walker* (1976) the Pennsylvania court struck down a similar statute as a denial of equal rights on the basis of sex. In a case of first impression, *Matter of Adoption of Evan* (1992), the lesbian partner of the biological mother of a 6-year-old boy was allowed to adopt. The child was conceived by artificial insemination. The opinion discusses at length the advantage to the child of the adoption.

Open Records

A reflection of the concern for the best interests of the child is the sealing of adoption records so that all public documents indicate that a child is the natural child of adoptive parents. Sealing the records reinforces the adoptive family as the only family, cutting ties to natural parents. The concern that natural parents may interfere is perhaps unjustified, but certainly sealed records prevent curiosity seekers, as well as natural parents, from interfering with the new family.

A trend in the United States is the movement by adult adoptees to attempt to become reunited with their natural parents, if only briefly. Social workers have a better appreciation than others of the problems in identity and the natural curiosity that lead adult adoptees to this search. Still, the search is frequently beset with legal problems because state laws require that adoption records remain confidential.

In Louisiana, in *Spillman v. Parker* (1976), *Chambers v. Parker* (1977), and *Massey v. Parker* (1978), courts have allowed adoptees to see the sealed records, even after the legislature amended the adoption laws to provide that records "be opened only on the order of a Louisiana court of competent jurisdiction only to the extent necessary to satisfy such compelling necessity" (LA.R.S. 40:73, 1993). The compelling reason for the court was the Louisiana law of forced heirship, giving children a certain portion of the deceased parent's estate even if the will leaves them nothing. This right, which is enshrined in the Louisiana constitution, is not lost by adoption. Adult adoptees can only know whether they are entitled to an inheritance if they can use the records to identify their natural parents.

The arguments adult adoptees use to see records are basically constitutional. They argue that treating them differently from natural children, who can see their records, denies them equal protection. Because no court has held that adoptees are a suspect class, this different classification is not entitled to "strict scrutiny." Although the classification may require support greater than mere rationality, it probably could survive constitutional attack. Courts use rational relationship, intermediate, and strict scrutiny tests for various classifications depending on their importance. The first would be a classification bearing some rational relationship to a legitimate governmental interest, such as a different tax on four-wheeled vehicles than that on two-wheeled vehicles because of the different harm they cause to roads. Under the intermediate test, the classification must have a substantial relationship to a governmental objective. This test was used in invalidating an Alabama law that granted alimony only to wives and not to husbands. The strict scrutiny test is applied when governmental action affects fundamental rights or involves suspect classifications, including most provisions of the Bill of Rights. Suspect classifications include those based on race or national origin.

Another argument is that the right to privacy of the adopted person includes the right to search for one's roots. However, both the natural parents and the adoptive parents also have a right to privacy, and no court has yet held that this right alone entitles the adult adoptee to inspect sealed records. These arguments, and the assertion that the statutes violate the Thirteenth Amendment by imposing a "badge or incident of slavery," were urged in *Alma Soc. Inc. v. Mellon* (1979), which challenged the constitutionality of the New York statute. The court held that statutes sealing adoption records did not violate substantive due process inasmuch as the state appropriately recognizes the privacy interests of natural and adoptive parents. Certainly, the need to know medical history may cause changes. Perhaps requiring the filing of medical histories with agencies should be urged. For a further discussion of this subject, see DeLorme (1992–1993), which reviews state laws about accessing sealed adoption records.

This is a troublesome area of the law and one in which social workers may be able to advise lawmakers on desirable changes. Social workers facing these decisions, which involve delicate emotional and psychological issues, should give careful attention to the underlying policy of the laws (Scheppers, 1975; Sorosky, Baran, & Pannor, 1978). What are the disadvantages of having adoptive and natural parents know each other's identity? What is the nature of a family? Are there features of it outside the legal boundaries?

Subsidized Adoptions

For some children adoption is not a viable alternative; their special problems are an obstacle to finding an adoptive home. The child with special medical or emotional problems, the older child, the child with a racial or ethnic background unlike most prospective adoptive parents, and the child with siblings seeking common placement all present special problems to adoption agencies. Some children remain in foster homes for so long that their affectional ties with the foster parents grow strong. In difficult cases, parents could be found more readily if the state continued financial support to offset the extraordinary financial burdens entailed in adopting such children.

Subsidized adoptions are a possible solution. Foster parents who desire to adopt the children in their care could be given financial aid, so that foster care payments would continue in whole or in part. Prospective adoptive parents might be more willing to assume the responsibility of a child with mental or physical difficulties knowing that future financial problems would be shared.

The need for subsidized adoptions is particularly apparent when some children remain in foster care for years. The great advantage of foster care is that it provides a substitute family arrangement. Because foster parents are discouraged and often prohibited from adopting, the deep emotional ties children develop are undermined by the fear that the relationship could end at any moment, causing emotional and psychological problems for the child. Foster parents who need the foster children's board payments are further discouraged from adopting children who have been in their homes for a long time because of the hardship of managing without the income (McCarty, 1974; Seelig, 1976; Senate Committee on Labor and Public Welfare, 1975).

In the 1970s states began to deal with this problem by passing subsidized adoption acts. The Children's Bureau of the Office of Child Development, through a grant to the Child Welfare League of America, developed the Model State Subsidized Adoption Act and Regulations, which were approved for dissemination by the Secretary of Health, Education, and Welfare in 1975 (U.S. Department of Health, Education, and Welfare, 1976).

All states except Hawaii, the District of Columbia, and the Virgin Islands now have adoption subsidy statutes. In Hawaii adoption assistance is handled administratively. The states cannot require a means test but can take into account the circumstances of the adoptive parents and the needs of the child. The law provides for children in interstate placements and those whose adoptive family moves from state to state (Bussrere, 1985). Not all parents of an adoptive child with disabilities are happy with the subsidy, as *State in Interest of Martorana* (1993) indicates. The child had a congenital heart defect and cystic fibrosis. Despite the parents' argument that the subsidy should be determined by the needs of the individual child, the court allowed the Office of Community Services to set ceilings on the subsidies.

The problem of race or religion in placing children for adoption, a procedure already fraught with constitutional issues, is further complicated in state-subsidized adoptions. Certainly, both race and religion can be considered in determining the best interest of the child, if these are not the only factors. However, if a sectarian adoption agency denies placement of a child not of the "right" religion, while placing it with parents of another denomination who need the subsidy to accept the child, there is a concern that there may be "state action" in the use of tax funds. The concern of some black people that black children not be placed with other than black families because of the loss of "identity" that such a placement may entail raises the issue of a "suspect" classification and "state action" in the subsidy.

President Carter signed the Adoption Assistance and Child Welfare Act of 1980 on June 17th of that year. It provides matching funds for adoption subsidies for children eligible for public assistance or who have other special needs. Federal matching funds are available for adoption subsidies to children in foster care who are hard to place because of ethnic background; race; color; language; age; physical, mental, or emotional handicap; or membership in a sibling group.

REFERENCES

Areen, J. (1975). Intervention between parent and child: A reappraisal of the state's role in child abuse and neglect cases. *Georgetown Law Journal, 63,* 887–937.

Auld, J. P. (1993). Transracial adoption: Proposing a compromise in the best interests of minority children. *Family Law Quarterly, 27,* 447–460.

Beschle, D. L. (1989). God bless the child? The use of religion as a factor in child custody and adoption proceedings. *Fordham Law Review, 58,* 383–426.

Bussrere, A. (1985). Federal adoption assistance for children with special needs. *Clearinghouse Review, 19,* 586–599.

DeLorme, S. (1992–1993). Accessing sealed adoption records: Considering adoptees' needs and judicial integrity. *Gonzaga Law Review, 28,* 103–120.

Everett, J. E. (1995). Child foster care. In R. L. Edwards (Ed.-in-Chief), *Encyclopedia of social work* (19th ed., Vol. 1, pp. 375–389). Washington, DC: NASW Press.

Fry, A. R. (1974). The children's migration. *American Heritage, 26,* 5–10, 79–81.

Geiser, R. L. (1974, May–June). The shuffled child and foster care. *Trial, 10,* 27–35.

Howe, R. W. (1979). Development of a model act to free children for permanent placement: A case study in law and social planning. *Family Law Quarterly, 13,* 257–344.

Hroka, D. K. (1989). The Uniform Putative and Unknown Fathers Act: Should putative fathers have an absolute right to notice in adoption proceedings? *Tulsa Law Review, 25,* 315–335.

Jones, C. (1993, October 24). Role of race in adoption: Old debate is being reborn. *New York Times,* pp. 1, 13.

Killackey, E. (1992). Kinship foster care. *Family Law Quarterly, 26,* 211–220.

Koman, L. E. (1976). *Legal issues in foster care.* Washington, DC: National Association of Attorneys General.

Levy, R. J. (1993). Rights and responsibilities for extended family members. *Family Law Quarterly, 27,* 191–210.

Locke, G. A. (1980). Modern status of laws as to equitable adoption or adoption by estoppel. *American Law Reports 3d, 97,* 347–400.

McCarty, D. C. (1974). The foster parents dilemma: Who can I turn to when somebody needs me? *San Diego Law Review, 11,* 376–414.

McTaggart, L. (1979, November 10). Babies for sale: The booming adoption racket. *Saturday Review,* pp. 15–20.

Rein, J. E. (1984). Relatives by blood, adoption, and association: Who should get what and why (The impact of adoptions, adult adoptions, and equitable adoptions on intestate succession and class gifts). *Vanderbilt Law Review, 37,* 711–810.

Sampson, J. J. (1993) Uniform Interstate Family Support Act (with unofficial annotations by Sampson). *Family Law Quarterly, 27,* 93–173.

Scheppers, R. C. (1975). Discovery rights of the adoptee. *San Fernando Valley Law Review, 4,* 65–83.

Seelig, G. G. (1976). The implementation of subsidized adoption programs: A preliminary survey. *Journal of Family Law, 15,* 732–769.

Senate Committee on Finance. (1977). *Public assistance amendments of 1977: Hearings on H.R. 7200 before the subcommittee on public assistance.* 95th Congress, 1st Session, Statement of Joseph Califano at 107.

Senate Committee on Labor and Public Welfare. (1975). *Adoption and foster care, 1975: Hearings on S. 1539 before the subcommittee on children and youth.* 94th Congress, 1st Session 283.

Sorosky, A. D., Baran, A., & Pannor, R. (1978). *The adoption triangle.* Garden City, NY: Anchor Press.

Spivey, G. D. (1976). Right of natural parent ot withdraw valid consent to adoption of child. *American Law Reports 3d, 74,* 421–475.

U.S. Department of Health, Education, and Welfare, Office of Human Development, Children's Bureau. (1976). *Subsidized adoption in America* (OHD 76-30087). Washington, DC: Author.

Van Name, J. B., Settles, B. H., & Culley, J. D. (1977). Measuring the cost of caring for a foster child. *Child Welfare, 56,* 431–439.

Williams, L. (1995, March 23). Transracial adoption: The truth comes in shades of gray. *New York Times,* p. B1.

STATUTES CITED

Adoption Assistance and Child Welfare Act of 1980. P.L. 96-272, 94 Stat. 500.

Uniform Putative and Unknown Fathers Act of 1973. 9b ULA 295.

STUDY QUESTIONS

1. Does the status of illegitimacy carry with it any constitutional protections?

2. Is adoption a viable alternative for hard-to-place children?

11

Family Planning

The United States has no consistent family policy on the federal level. Efforts to outlaw child labor and to provide mothers' allowances have had their ups and downs. Anyone who has followed the vicissitudes of the Aid to Families with Dependent Children program recognizes the ambivalence of taxpayers who want to provide for children and keep families together but who vehemently denounce "welfare chiselers." Contrast this with family allowances in Canada and mothers' vacations in Sweden—both examples of comprehensive programs of government support for families. In a heterogeneous society such as ours, however, flexibility is desirable, so family policy is often left primarily to the states.

Social workers struggle with inadequate provision for the indigent parents of wanted children and know only too well about insufficient provision for unwanted children. No children, too many children, and children too close together in age cause many of the problems we see, not only economic but social and psychological as well. Preventing both unwanted pregnancies and childlessness can assist in satisfactory individual adjustment. Judicial decisions in these areas have changed the legal climate for family planning.

CONTRACEPTION

Contraception, the keystone of any family planning program, was outlawed in most states until the mid-20th century. Laws forbidding the sale and use of contraceptives were an outgrowth of the Comstock laws of the 1880s. Anthony Comstock fought pornography and sexual license by buttonholing legislators and writing tracts against vice. Contraception was included by a kind of guilt-by-association. The punitive laws that grew out of his fanatic efforts are not atypical of morality in the Victorian era, honored more in the breach than in the observance. The following two cases legitimized practices that were widespread even though illegal.

Griswold v. State of Connecticut
381 U.S. 497, 85 S. Ct. 1678 (1965)

[The executive director of the Planned Parenthood League of Connecticut and the medical director of the League in New Haven, who was a professor at the Yale Medical School, were arrested for violating a Connecticut law that made it a crime for anyone to use a contraceptive and for anyone to assist or counsel someone else in the use of contraceptives.]

Douglas, J.

We think that appellants have standing to raise the constitutional rights of the married people with whom they had a professional relationship. . . . Certainly the accessory should have standing to assert that the offense which he is charged with assisting is not, or cannot constitutionally be, crime. . . . The rights of husband and wife, pressed here, are likely to be diluted or adversely affected unless those rights are considered in a suit involving those who have this kind of confidential relation to them.

Coming to the merits, we are met with a wide range of questions that implicate the due process clause of the Fourteenth Amendment. . . . We do not sit as a super-legislature to determine the wisdom, need, and propriety of laws that touch economic problems, business affairs, or social conditions. This law, however, operates directly on an intimate relation of husband and wife and their physician's role is one aspect of that relation.

[The Court then discussed certain cases on freedom of association.]

The foregoing cases suggest that specific guarantees in the Bill of Rights have penumbras, formed by emanations from those guarantees that help give them life and substance. . . . Various guarantees create zones of privacy. The right of association contained in the penumbra of the First Amendment is one, as we have seen. The Third Amendment in its prohibition against the quartering of soldiers "in any house" in time of peace without the consent of the owner is another facet of that privacy. The Fourth Amendment explicitly affirms the "right of the people to be secure in their persons, houses, papers and effects, against unreasonable searches and seizures." The Fifth Amendment in its Self-Incrimination Clause enables the citizen to create a zone of privacy which government may not force him to surrender to his detriment. The Ninth Amendment provides: "The enumeration in the Constitution, of certain rights, shall not be construed to deny or disparage others retained by the people."

· · · · ·

The present case, then, concerns a relationship lying within the zone of privacy created by several fundamental constitutional guarantees. And it concerns a law which, in forbidding the use of contraceptives rather than regulating their manufacture or sale, seeks to achieve its goals by means having a maximum destructive impact upon that relationship. Such a law cannot stand in light of the familiar principle, so often applied by this Court, that a "governmental purpose to control or prevent activities constitutionally subject to state regulation may not be achieved by means which sweep unnecessarily broadly and thereby invade the area of protected freedoms."... Would we allow the police to search the sacred precincts of marital bedrooms for telltale signs of the use of contraceptives? The very idea is repulsive to the notions of privacy surrounding the marriage relationship.

We deal with a right of privacy older than the Bill of Rights—older than our political parties, older than our school system. Marriage is a coming together for better or for worse, hopefully enduring, and intimate to the degree of being sacred. It is an association that promotes a way of life, not causes; a harmony in living, not political faiths; a bilateral loyalty, not commercial or social projects. Yet it is an association for as noble a purpose as any involved in our prior designs.

Reversed.

Mr. Justice Goldberg, with whom the Chief Justice and Mr. Justice Brennan join, concurring.

I believe that the gift of privacy in the marital relation is fundamental and basic—a personal right "retained by the people" within the meaning of the Ninth Amendment. Connecticut cannot constitutionally abridge this fundamental right, which is protected by the Fourteenth Amendment from infringement by the States. I agree with the Court that petitioners' convictions must therefore be reversed.

· · · · ·

Mr. Justice Stewart, with whom Mr. Justice Black joins, dissenting.

Since 1879 Connecticut has had on its books a law which forbids the use of contraceptives by anyone. I think this is an uncommonly silly law. As a practical matter, the law is obviously unenforceable, except in the oblique context of the present case. As a philosophical matter, I believe the use of contraceptives in the relationship of marriage should be left to personal and private choice, based upon each individual's moral, ethical, and religious beliefs. As a matter of social policy, I think professional counsel about methods of birth control should be available to all, so that each individual's choice can be meaningfully made. But we are not asked in this case to say whether we think this law is unwise, or even asinine. We are asked to hold that it violated the United States Constitution. And that I cannot do.

This "uncommonly silly law" evoked strong feelings among members of the Supreme Court, if the length of both the concurring and dissenting opinions is evidence. Justice Douglas, who wrote the majority opinion, had first to decide whether the parties before the court had "standing," that is, enough interest in the outcome that a "case or controversy" is presented. He then identified a "right of privacy" that, although nowhere mentioned in the Constitution, he found in the penumbra of various amendments, particularly the First Amendment's provision for freedom of association. Justice Goldberg preferred the Ninth Amendment as the rationale for decision, considering the right to privacy one of the certain rights "retained by the people" in that amendment.

You may wonder whether this new right to privacy will apply in other areas. If the majority of the people of a state believe that abortion for any reason should be outlawed, must the victim of rape or incest bow to the wishes of the majority and either seek an illegal abortion or move to a state that permits it? Does this right of privacy prevent a caseworker from demanding a home visit to allow an evaluation of a client's living conditions? Should it? The decision holds that a state may not outlaw contraception—can a state require it? If a 14-year-old girl has had two illegitimate children, can the state require her, notwithstanding the difficulties of enforcement, to use birth control to prevent conception of additional illegitimate children?

Declaring unconstitutional statutes that outlawed the use of contraceptives by married people was only the beginning of the struggle, as the next case illustrates.

Eisenstadt v. Baird
405 U.S. 438, 92 S. Ct. 1029, 31 L.Ed.2d 349 (1972)
[William Baird was convicted of violating a Massachusetts statute that provided for a maximum 5-year term of imprisonment for giving any drug or article for the prevention of conception. The statute provided exceptions for physicians who prescribed for married persons and pharmacists who filled prescriptions for married persons. Massachusetts justified the law as one to promote health and to deter fornication.]
Brennan, J.
We cannot agree that the deterrence of premarital sex may reasonably be regarded as the purpose of the Massachusetts law.

It would be plainly unreasonable to assume that Massachusetts has prescribed pregnancy and the birth of an unwanted child as punishment for fornication, which is a misdemeanor under Massachusetts general law. . . . Aside from the scheme of values that assumption would attribute to the state, it is abundantly clear that the effect of the ban on distribution of contraceptives to unmarried persons has at best a marginal relation to the preferred objective. . . .Like Connecticut's laws [in Griswold*] § 21 and 21A do not at all regulate the distribution of contraceptives when they are to be used to prevent, not pregnancy, but the spread of disease. . . . Nor, in making contraceptives available to married persons without regard to their intended use, does Massachusetts attempt to deter married persons from engaging in illicit sexual relations with unmarried persons. Even on the assumption that the fear of pregnancy operates as a deterrent to fornication, the Massachusetts statute is thus so riddled with exceptions that deterrence of premarital sex cannot reasonably be regarded as its aim.*

· · · · ·

Even conceding the legislature a full measure of discretion in fashioning remedies for fornication, and recognizing that the state may seek to deter prohibited conduct by punishing more severely those who facilitate than those who actually engage in its commission, we, like the court of appeals, cannot believe that in this instance Massachusetts has chosen to expose the aider and abetter who simply gives away *a contraceptive to 20 times the* 90-day *sentence of the offender himself.*

· · · · ·

If the Massachusetts statute cannot be upheld as a deterrent to fornication or as a health measure, may it, nevertheless, be sustained simply as a prohibition on contraception? . . . We need not and do not. . . decide that important question in this case because, whatever the rights of the individual to access to contraceptives may be, the rights must be the same for the unmarried and the married alike.

If under Griswold *the distribution of contraceptives to married persons cannot be prohibited, a ban on distribution to unmarried persons would be equally impermissible. It is true that in* Griswold *the right of privacy in question inhered in the marital relationship. Yet the marital couple is not an independent entity with a mind and a heart of its own, but an association of two individuals each with a separate intellectual and emotional make-up. If the right of privacy means anything, it is the right of the* individual, *married or single, to be free from unwarranted governmental intrusion into matters so fundamentally affecting a person as the decision whether to bear or beget a child.*

· · · · ·

On the other hand, if Griswold *is not a bar to a prohibition on the distribution of contraceptives, the state could not, consistently with the equal protection clause, outlaw distribution to unmarried but not to married persons. In each case the evil, as perceived by the state, would be identical and the underinclusion would be invidious. . . . We hold that by providing*

dissimilar treatment for married and unmarried persons who are similarly situated, Massachusetts. . . violate[s] the equal protection clause.
Mr. Justice Douglas, concurring.
While I join the opinion of the Court, there is for me a narrower ground for affirming the court of appeals. This to me is a simple First Amendment case.

• • • • •

Had Baird not "given away" a sample of one of the devices whose use he advocated, there could be no question about the protection afforded him by the First Amendment. A state may not "contract the spectrum of available knowledge." . . . However obnoxious Baird's ideas might have been to the authorities, the freedom to learn about them, fully to comprehend their scope and portent, and to weigh them against the tenets of the "conventional wisdom," may not be abridged. . . . Our system of government requires that we have faith in the ability of the individual to decide wisely, if only he is fully apprised of the merits of a controversy.

The right of privacy is not that of the married couple as an entity, but of the individual, with all that implies. These two cases disposed of questions concerning use of and information about contraceptives for adults. There remained the question of whether physicians could prescribe birth control pills for minor youths without the knowledge or consent of their parents. *Carey v. Population Services Inter.* (1977) resolved the matter by striking down a provision of the New York Education Law that made it a crime for anyone to sell or distribute contraceptives to a minor under 16 years of age (see also Jaffe, 1971). Because the regulation imposed a significant burden on individual decisions in the matter of childbearing, with no compelling state interest served, it was unconstitutional.

Norplant is a five-year contraceptive composed of six capsules that are inserted into a woman's arm. These capsules release contraceptive hormones. Several bills have been introduced that would require women receiving public welfare benefits to use Norplant (Hand, 1993).

The trend now is to provide contraceptives for everyone. School social workers may be involved in sex education programs that include passing out condoms to prevent the spread of the human immunodeficiency virus and acquired immune deficiency virus and unwanted pregnancies.

STERILIZATION

Sterilization is a drastic method of contraception; if successful, it prevents future conception entirely. It involves surgical procedures, some more complicated than others, and with more initial risks than is usual in contraception. Because the long-term results of using birth control pills are still unknown, sterilization may be the best method of preventing pregnancy when the individual is sure that children are not desired.

A vasectomy is a procedure in which the male sperm ducts are tied off; the procedure is simple enough to be done in a physician's office. The two procedures by which a woman is sterilized are more complicated. In salpingectomy the woman's fallopian tubes are closed; in hysterectomy the uterus is removed. Results in vasectomy and in salpingectomy are very occasionally reversible (*Harten v. Coons,* 1974/1975). The tubes or ducts may be surgically reopened, but no one contemplating such a procedure should consider that a viable option. For both men and women, and particularly for women, the procedure should be considered irreversible. Consequently, clients should think through the ramifications of the decision very carefully.

Historically, once the decision for sterilization was made, clients might have faced a problem in finding a hospital that was willing to perform the procedure (although this is rarely true today). In *McCabe v. Nassau County Medical Center* (1971) a woman sought injunctive relief against the hospital's refusal to sterilize a woman unless she had at least five children. Mrs. McCabe, who was 25, had been pregnant six times and had four small children. Because of a thyroid condition, she could not take birth control pills, and she and her husband had decided not to have any more children. Although the medical center changed its mind and permitted the sterilization, the court remanded the case to determine whether the rule had violated her constitutional rights so as to entitle her to damages.

The medical center was a public hospital acting "under color of state law." When a private hospital was supported by a religious denomination that does not approve of contraception or sterilization, the result was different (*Taylor v. St. Vincent's Hosp.,* 1975). Even though the private hospital was the only one in a community with certain facilities, and even though it received advantageous state and federal tax benefits, it was not acting "under color of state law" and was therefore not performing a public function for Fourteenth Amendment purposes.

In 1978 Congress passed the Church Amendment of the Health Programs Extension Act, which prohibits a court from finding that any hospital that receives Hill–Burton funds is acting under color of state law. This avenue of legally redressing a hospital's refusal to sterilize is thus closed.

If a woman is competent to make the decision for sterilization, her husband cannot veto it. One court has said that it was not prepared to create a right in a husband to have a fertile wife nor to allow recovery for damage to such a right (*Murray v. Vandevander,* 1974).

Therefore, a wife's major problem is to find a physician and a hospital to perform the sterilization.

To permit sterilization for those who request it is quite different from forcing it on individuals who do not. *Buck v. Bell* (1927) is a landmark case dealing with involuntary sterilization.

Buck v. Bell
274 U.S. 200, 47 S. Ct. 584 (1927)
Holmes, J.

Carrie Buck is a feeble minded white woman who was committed to the state Colony. . . . She is the daughter of a feeble minded mother in the same institution, and the mother of a feeble minded child. She was 18 years old at the time of the trial of her case in the circuit court, in the latter part of 1924. An act of Virginia, approved March 20, 1924 . . . recites that the health of the patient and the welfare of society may be promoted in certain cases by the sterilization of mental defectives, under careful safeguards, etc; that the sterilization may be effected in males by vasectomy and in females by salpingectomy, without serious pain or substantial danger to life; that the Commonwealth is supporting in various institutions many defective persons who if now discharged would become a menace but if incapable of procreating might be discharged with safety and become self-supporting with benefit to themselves and to society; and that experience has shown that heredity plays an important part in the transmission of insanity, imbecility, etc. The statute then enacts that whenever the superintendent of certain institutions. . . shall be of opinion that it is for the best interests of the patients and of society that an inmate under his care should be sexually sterilized, he may have the operation performed upon any patient afflicted with hereditary forms of insanity, imbecility, etc., on complying with the very careful provisions by which the act protects the patients from possible abuse.

. . . . .

The attack is not upon the procedure but upon the substantive law. It seems to be contended that in no circumstances could such an order be justified. It certainly is contended that the order cannot be justified upon the existing grounds. The judgment finds the facts that have been recited and that Carrie Buck "is the probable potential parent of socially inadequate offspring, likewise afflicted, that she may be sexually sterilized without detriment to her general health and that her welfare and that of society will be promoted by her sterilization," and thereupon makes the order. In view of the general declarations of the legislature and the specific findings of the Court, obviously we cannot say as a matter of law that the grounds do not exist, and if they exist they justify the result. We have seen more than once that the public welfare may call upon the best citizens for their lives. It would be strange if it could not call upon those who already sap the strength of the state for these lesser sacrifices, often not felt to be such by those concerned, in order to prevent our being swamped with incompetence. It is better for all the world, if instead of waiting to execute degenerate offspring for crime, or to let them starve for their imbecility, society can prevent those who are manifestly unfit from continuing their kind. The principle that sustains compulsory vaccination is broad enough to cover cutting the Fallopian tubes. . . . Three generations of imbeciles are enough.

But, it is said, however it might be if this reasoning were applied generally, it fails when it is confined to the small number who are in the institutions named and is not applied to the multitudes outside. It is the usual last resort of constitutional arguments to point out shortcomings of this sort. But the answer is that the law does all that is needed when it does all that it can, indicates a policy, applies it to all within the lines, and seeks to bring within the lines all similarly situated so far and so fast as its means allow. Of course so far as the operations enable those who otherwise must be kept confined to be returned to the world, and thus open the asylum to others, the equality aimed at will be more nearly reached.

The requirements of procedural due process—notice, right to counsel, and hearing—were all met in *Buck v. Bell*. Justice Holmes decided the case on substantive due process, which means the Court approved the purpose of the act and the method of carrying it out. In the final paragraph, he answers the argument about equal protection.

In a subsequent sterilization case, *Skinner v. Oklahoma* (1942), the requirement of equal protection was not met. There the Supreme Court held unconstitutional an Oklahoma statute providing for sterilization of "habitual criminals": those convicted two or more times of "felonies involving moral turpitude." Embezzlement was expressly excepted. The Court noted that because the statute applied to a person convicted of stealing chickens and of robbery—Skinner's crimes—but not to embezzlement, which is also a felony and theft, the classification violated the equal protection clause.

Sterilization of people with mental disabilities continues to be a valid exercise of the state's police power (Bligh, 1964; *In re Sterilization of Moore*, 1976; Munro, 1982; and *Wyatt v. Aderholt*, 1974) although most courts hold that unless legislatures specifically authorize it, courts lack jurisdiction to authorize sterilization. However, the courts of both Alabama and Alaska have held that, absent statutory authority, a probate or juvenile court may not order such surgery, even if the guardian considers it necessary for the incompetent person's health and welfare (*Hudson v.*

Hudson, 1979). In *Cox v. Stanton* (1975) the plaintiff was an unmarried 18-year-old mother of a 10-week-old girl. The plaintiff's mother was a welfare recipient. Ms. Cox alleged that the social worker threatened to strike the family from the welfare rolls unless the mother consented to her daughter's temporary sterilization. Rather than a usually reversible tubal ligation, an irreversible bilateral salpingectomy was performed. The court said the suit was filed timely, allowing the plaintiff to sue the doctor.

In a controversial claim for damages, a 15-year-old girl was sterilized on the petition of her mother stating that she was "somewhat retarded" and stayed out at night with men. On discovering that she had not had her appendix out as she thought, the girl sued the judge who had ordered the sterilization. The Supreme Court held that the judge was immune from damages even if his approval of the petition was in error (*Stump v. Sparkman,* 1978), saying, "A judge will not be deprived of immunity because the action he took was in error, was done maliciously, or was in excess of his authority; . . . he will be subject to liability only when he has acted in the clear absence of all jurisdiction" (pp. 356–357). Generally, then, a judge has absolute immunity for damages in a sterilization suit, although others may be sued. The social worker advising parents or other guardians of people with mental disabilities about sterilization should also cover the possible legal consequences. Dugan (1993) discussed involuntary sterilization of people with mental retardation and wrote that after *Buck v. Bell* 30 states passed laws permitting the procedure.

ABORTION

Abortion is an emotionally charged procedure that has legal, social, ethical, and moral implications. Until 1973 it was outlawed in most states, with a very few states permitting abortion to save the life of the mother. Although illegal, abortions were performed in significant numbers. Because the procedure was clandestine, it carried with it the risks attendant on any furtive activity, with the risk of infection and death of the woman added to the risk of arrest and disgrace if discovered. Social workers who have dealt with rape victims or the mothers of incest victims may consider abortion a reasonable alternative in family planning for such clients.

Two decisions of the Supreme Court have made abortion a viable option for individuals who have been unable to plan the number and timing of their children by contraception. The lengthy opinion of the court in *Roe v. Wade* (1973) discusses much that is of historical interest in the development of the legal prohibitions of abortion; these sections, omitted here, will interest many social workers. The crucial point, however, is that abortion has been legal in all states since the case was decided.

Roe v. Wade
410 U.S. 113, 93 S. Ct. 705, 35 L.Ed.2d 147 (1973)
Blackmun, J.
The Texas statutes under attack here are typical of those that have been in effect in many states for approximately a century.

• • • • •

Jane Roe, a single woman who was residing in Dallas County, Texas, instituted this federal action in March 1970 against the district attorney of the county. She sought a declaratory judgment that the Texas criminal abortion statutes were unconstitutional on their face, and an injunction restraining the defendant from enforcing the statutes.

Roe alleged that she was unmarried and pregnant; that she wished to terminate her pregnancy by an abortion "performed by a competent, licensed physician, under safe, clinical conditions"; that she was unable to get a "legal" abortion in Texas because her life did not appear to be threatened by the continuation of her pregnancy; and that she could not afford to travel to another jurisdiction in order to secure a legal abortion under safe conditions.

• • • • •

Viewing Roe's case as of the time of its filing and thereafter until as late as May, there can be little dispute that it then presented a case or controversy and that, wholly apart from the class aspects, she, as a pregnant single woman thwarted by the Texas criminal abortion laws, has standing to challenge those statutes.

• • • • •

The appellee notes, however, that the record does not disclose that Roe was pregnant at the time of the district court hearing on May 22, 1970, or on the following June 17 when the court's opinion and judgment were filed. And he suggests that Roe's case must now be moot because she and all other members of her class are no longer subject to any 1970 pregnancy.

The usual rule in federal cases is that an actual controversy must exist at stages of appellate or certiorari review, and not simply the date the action is initiated.

• • • • •

But when, as here, pregnancy is a significant fact in the litigation, the normal 266-day gestation period is so short that the pregnancy will come to term before the usual appellate process is complete. If that termination makes a case moot, pregnancy litigation seldom will survive much beyond the trial stage, and appellate review will be effectively denied. Our law should not be that rigid. Pregnancy often comes more than once to the same woman, and in the general population, if man is to survive, it will always be with us. Pregnancy provides a classic justification for a conclusion of nonmootness. It truly could be "capable of repetition, yet evading review." . . . We therefore agree with the district court that Jane Roe had standing to undertake this litigation, that she presented a justiciable controversy, and that the termination of her 1970 pregnancy has not rendered her case moot.

· · · · ·

The principal thrust of appellant's attack on the Texas statutes is that they improperly invade a right, said to be possessed by the pregnant woman, to choose to terminate her pregnancy. Appellant would discover this right in the concept of personal "liberty" embodied in the Fourteenth Amendment's due process clause; or in personal, marital, family and sexual privacy said to be protected by the Bill of Rights or its penumbras . . . or among those rights reserved to the people by the Ninth Amendment.

· · · · ·

It perhaps is not generally appreciated that the restrictive criminal abortion laws in effect in a majority of states today are of relatively recent vintage. Those laws, generally proscribing abortion or its attempt at any time during pregnancy except when necessary to preserve the pregnant woman's life, are not of ancient or even of common law origin. Instead, they derive from statutory changes effected, for the most part, in the latter half of the 19th century.

[The Court then discussed ancient attitudes toward abortion, the history of the Hippocratic oath, abortion under common law, English statutory law, and American law, and the position of such organizations as the American Medical Association, the American Public Health Association, and the American Bar Association.]

Three reasons have been advanced to explain historically the enactment of criminal abortion laws in the 19th century and to justify their continued existence.

It has been argued occasionally that these laws were the product of a Victorian social concern to discourage illicit sexual conduct. Texas, however, does not advance this justification in the present case, and it appears that no court or commentator has taken the argument seriously. The appellants and amici contend, moreover, that this is not a proper state purpose at all and suggest that, if it were, the Texas statutes are overbroad in protecting it since the law fails to distinguish between married and unwed mothers.

A second reason is concerned with abortion as a medical procedure. When most criminal abortion laws were first enacted, the procedure was a hazardous one for the woman. This was particularly true prior to the development of antisepsis. . . . Abortion mortality was high. Even after 1900, and perhaps until as late as the development of antibiotics in the 1940s, standard modern techniques such as dilation and curettage were not nearly so safe as they are today.

· · · · ·

Modern medical techniques have altered this situation. Appellants and various amici refer to medical data indicating that abortion in early pregnancy, that is, prior to the end of the first trimester, although not without its risk, is now relatively safe. Mortality rates for women undergoing early abortions, where the procedure is legal, appear to be as low as or lower than the rates for normal childbirth. . . . The state has a legitimate interest in seeing to it that abortion, like any other medical procedure, is performed under circumstances that insure maximum safety for the patient. This interest obviously extends at least to the performing physician and his staff, to the facilities involved, to the availability of after-care, and to adequate provision for any complication or emergency that might arise. The prevalence of high mortality rates at illegal "abortion mills" strengthens, rather than weakens, the state's interest in regulating the conditions under which abortions are performed. Moreover, the risk to the woman increases as her pregnancy continues. Thus the state retains a definite interest in protecting the woman's health and safety when an abortion is proposed at a late state of pregnancy.

The third reason is the state's interest—some phrase it in terms of duty— in protecting prenatal life. Some of the argument for this justification rests on the theory that a new human life is present from the moment of conception. This state's interest and general obligation to protect life then extends, it is argued, to prenatal life. Only when the life of the pregnant mother herself is at stake, balanced against the life she carries within her, should the interest of the embryo or fetus not prevail. Logically, of course, a legitimate state interest in this area need not stand or fall on acceptance of the belief that life begins at conception or at some point prior to live birth. In assessing the state's interest, recognition may be given to the less rigid claim that as long as at least potential life is involved, the state may assert interests beyond the protection of the pregnant woman alone.

[The] right of privacy, whether it be founded in the Fourteenth Amendment's concept of personal liberty and restrictions upon state action, as we feel it is, or as the district court determined, in the Ninth Amendment's reservation of rights to the people, is broad enough to encompass a woman's decision whether or not to terminate her pregnancy. The detriment that the state would impose upon the pregnant woman by denying this choice altogether is apparent.

· · · · ·

We therefore conclude that the right of personal privacy includes the abortion decision, but that this right is not unqualified and must be considered against important state interests in regulation.

• • • • •

Where certain "fundamental rights" are involved, the Court has held that regulation limiting these rights may be justified only by a "compelling state interest" . . . and that legislative enactments must be narrowly drawn to express only the legitimate state interest at stake.

• • • • •

The Constitution does not define "person" in so many words. Section 1 of the Fourteenth Amendment contains three references to "person." The first, in defining "citizens," speaks of "persons born or naturalized." . . . "Person" is used in other places in the Constitution. . . . But in nearly all these instances, the use of the word is such that it has application only postnatally. None indicates, with any assurance, that it has any possible prenatal application.

All this, together with our observation, supra, that throughout the major portion of the 19th century prevailing legal abortion practices were far freer than they are today, persuades us that the word "person," as used in the Fourteenth Amendment, does not include the unborn.

[The Court then discusses the divergent views on when life begins.]

In areas other than criminal abortion the law has been reluctant to endorse any theory that life, as we recognize it, begins before live birth or to accord legal rights to the unborn except in narrowly defined situations and except when the rights are contingent upon live birth. For example, the traditional role of tort law had denied recovery for prenatal injuries even though the child was born alive. That rule has been changed in almost every jurisdiction. In most states recovery is said to be permitted only if the fetus was viable, or at least quick, when the injuries were sustained, though few courts have squarely so held. In a recent development, generally opposed by the commentators, some states permit the parents of a stillborn child to maintain an action for wrongful death because of prenatal injuries. Such an action, however, would appear to be one to vindicate the parent's interest and is thus consistent with the view that the fetus, at most, represents only the potentiality of life. Similarly, unborn children have been recognized as acquiring rights or interests by way of inheritance or other devolution of property, and have been represented by guardians ad litem. Perfection of the interests involved, again, has generally been contingent upon live birth. In short, the unborn have never been recognized in the law as persons in the whole sense.

• • • • •

With respect to the state's important and legitimate interest in the health of the mother, the "compelling" point, in the light of present medical knowledge, is at approximately the end of the first trimester.

. . . . .

With respect to the state's important and legitimate interest in potential life, the "compelling" point is at viability. This is so because the fetus then presumably has the capability of meaningful life outside the mother's womb. State regulation protective of fetal life after viability thus has both logical and biological justifications. If the state is interested in protecting fetal life after viability, it may go so far as to proscribe abortion during that period except when it is necessary to preserve the life or health of the mother.

In summary, the Supreme Court held that a criminal statute such as the one challenged violates the due process clause of the Fourteenth Amendment. Before the end of the first trimester of a pregnancy, the abortion decision is left to the medical judgment of the pregnant woman's attending physician. After that point, states may regulate abortion procedures to protect maternal health. In the final trimester the state may proscribe abortion except if it is necessary, in appropriate medical judgment, for the preservation of the life or health of the mother.

Doe v. Bolton (1973), a companion case to *Roe v. Wade,* was decided at the same time, the Court holding that a Georgia statute violated the Fourteenth Amendment. The statute required that the physician performing the abortion be licensed in Georgia; that the woman be a Georgia resident; and that the abortion be necessary either to preserve the life or health of the mother, to prevent the birth of a defective child, or to terminate a pregnancy resulting from forcible or statutory rape. Two Georgia-licensed physicians who based their decision on separate personal medical examinations of the woman had to concur in the recommendation for abortion. The Court held that the interposition of the hospital abortion committee was unduly restrictive of the patient's rights and needs, which had already been medically substantiated by her physician. The allegations in Mary Doe's petition substantiating her desire for the abortion read like a social worker's case record:

She was a 22-year-old Georgia citizen, married, and nine weeks pregnant. She had three living children. The two older ones had been placed in a foster home because of Doe's poverty and inability to care for them. The youngest, born July 19, 1969, had been placed for adoption. Her husband had recently abandoned her and she was forced to live with her indigent parents and their eight children. She and her husband, however, had become reconciled. He was a construction worker employed only sporadically. She had been a mental patient at the state hospital.

She had been advised that an abortion could be performed on her with less danger to her health than if she gave birth to the child she was carrying. She would be unable to care for or support the new child. (p. 185; see also Dudar, 1973; Young, Berkman, & Rehr, 1973)

The right of privacy that the Court found in *Griswold* in the context of the use of contraceptives by married people led inevitably to a right of privacy for a woman deciding to terminate her pregnancy during the first trimester. Questions involving others who might have a stake in this decision have been raised, as they were in the sterilization cases and with similar results. In *Planned Parenthood of Central Missouri v. Danforth* (1976) the Supreme Court held unconstitutional a requirement of spousal consent before abortion, saying that the state cannot delegate to a spouse a veto power the state itself is absolutely prohibited from exercising during the first trimester. The requirement of parental consent to abortion for a minor has also been held unconstitutional (*Bellotti v. Baird,* 1979).

The right to an abortion does not mean that facilities are always readily available. In *Beal v. Doe* (1977) the Supreme Court held that Title XIX of the Social Security Act of 1935 does not require a state to fund nontherapeutic abortions as a condition of participation in the Medicaid program, although the state may provide the coverage if it desires. *Maher v. Roe* (1977), decided at the same time, held that even though a state chooses to use Medicaid funds to pay expenses incident to childbirth, it need not pay expenses incident to nontherapeutic abortions. The state is not required to show a compelling interest for its policy choice of favoring normal childbirth, because financial need alone does not identify a suspect class. As the Court said, "The case involves no discrimination against a suspect class. An indigent woman desiring an abortion does not come within the limited category of disadvantaged classes so recognized by our cases" (pp. 470–471).

The Court's most recent pronouncements in the financing area came in a First Amendment attack on the Hyde Amendment (1988), which forbids the use of federal matching funds in state Medicaid programs to fund abortions. In *Harris v. McRae* (1980), a 5 to 4 decision, Justice Stewart wrote for the majority that the fact that the funding restrictions coincide with the religious tenets of the Roman Catholic Church does not, without more support, contravene the establishment clause. The dissenters discussed the disproportionate impact the amendment has on indigent women of color. At the state level, in *D. R. v. Mitchell* (1981) an unmarried pregnant woman challenged a Utah statute denying public assistance for the costs of an abortion unless the mother's life was endangered. The court upheld the statute, finding no denial of equal protection. On the other hand, in *Dodge v. Department of Soc. Serv.* (1982) the Colorado court denied a taxpayer request for an injunction against the use of state funds for abortions; the department was allowed to pay because Medicaid did not.

In *Williams v. Zbaraz* (1980), the Court held that a participating state is not obligated under Title XIX to pay for medically necessary abortions for which federal reimbursement is unavailable under the Hyde Amendment. However, in *D. R. v. Mitchell*, (1980), the court of appeals struck down as unconstitutional a Utah statute limiting use of public funds for abortions to those necessary to save the life of the mother; the plaintiff's physician had determined that the abortion was medically necessary in the second trimester.

Further funding restrictions were upheld in *Rust v. Sullivan* (1991), also a 5 to 4 decision. In 1970 Congress had enacted Title X of the Public Health Service Act to provide federal funding for family planning services. The U.S. Department of Health and Human Services issued regulations prohibiting the use of Title X funds in abortion counseling, referral, and activities advocating abortion as a method of family planning. The Supreme Court held that the regulations were based on a permissible construction of the statute prohibiting the use of Title X funds in programs in which abortion is a method of family planning and did not violate First Amendment free speech rights of fund recipients, their staffs, or their patients.

Two cases prior to the Supreme Court decisions dealing with the use of Medicaid funds may still be good law. In *Doe v. Poelker* (1975/1976) a policy of the city of St. Louis prohibiting all nontherapeutic abortions in its *public* hospitals was held unconstitutional as an unwarranted infringement on a pregnant woman's right to privacy and a denial of equal protection to indigent pregnant women. The appellant, who was the mother of two and in severe financial straits, feared that her husband might be sent to prison. She had miscarried five times and suffered from cervical fibroid tumors and polyps, an extremely retroverted uterus, and trichomoniasis. The obstetrics–gynecology clinic was staffed entirely by faculty and students from the St. Louis University School of Medicine, a Roman Catholic institution. Thus, only physicians with moral objections to abortion were available to serve indigent women. However, in *Doe v. Bellin Mem. Hosp.* (1973) the court held that by accepting Hill–Burton funds, a *private* hospital did not surrender its right to establish a rule against performing abortions.

In addition to refusing to provide funds and facilities for indigent women, state legislatures have tried other measures to discourage abortions. Against a contention that it infringed a right of privacy, the New York court of appeals upheld New York City's right to require on pregnancy termination certificates the names and addresses of patients obtaining abortions; these were included in the city health department's computerized records (*Schulman v. New York City Health & Hospitals Corp.*, 1975). However, a Pennsylvania statute subjecting physicians to criminal liability for performing an abortion without using a prescribed technique when the fetus "is viable" or when there was "sufficient reason to believe that the fetus may be viable" was held void for reasons of vagueness (*Colautti v. Franklin*, 1979).

In any case, no one can be required to submit to an abortion or to participate in obtaining one for another if that person has religious or moral scruples against it. At least one statute makes that abundantly clear:

> *No worker or employee in any social service agency, whether public or private, shall be held civilly or criminally liable, discriminated against, dismissed, demoted, in any way prejudiced or damaged, or pressured in any way for refusal to take part in, recommend or counsel an abortion for any woman.* (Louisiana Revised Statutes 40: 1299.31, 1973; see also Ambuel & Rappaport, 1992)

ARTIFICIAL INSEMINATION

Artificial insemination is a procedure by which a man's sperm is medically inserted into a woman's uterus. This noncoital conception is performed for various reasons: A wife has a blocked oviduct, a husband's sperm has low motility, the husband is sterile, or some incompatibility makes fertilization of the ovum by the husband's sperm undesirable or impossible. When the procedure uses the husband's sperm, it is called *homologous* artificial insemination; when it uses the sperm of a donor, it is called *heterologous* artificial insemination. A donor may be a medical student or an intern whose genetic background most closely resembles that of the husband. A donor is unknown to the couple, as they are to him. Medical social workers may be advising clients about this option (Schroeder, 1974).

The procedure is apparently common, although the statistics are not reliable. Many children may be born from this procedure and never know it; members of the immediate family may have no knowledge that the procedure was used (Smith, 1970; Treppa, 1992). However, bitter divorce proceedings occasionally bring out the fact, when the mother refuses the father visitation rights or the father challenges the obligation to support. Several decisions have declared children born of artificial insemination to be illegitimate, even though they were born during marriage and the procedure was carried out with the husband's consent. In one case, although the child was considered illegitimate, the former husband was required to pay child support (*Gursky v. Gursky,* 1964). The court used a contract theory, theorizing that the husband had consented to the procedure and so implicitly agreed to support the child (Special Issue on Surrogacy, 1988). A social worker who recommends such a procedure should advise clients, in case the physician does not, of possible legal difficulties to raise with their attorney. Some states have resolved the problem by declaring that any children born during marriage as the result of such a procedure are the legitimate children of the husband (Louisiana Civil Code Article 188). Shaman (1979–1980) cites the 19 states with statutes creating a legal presumption of legitimacy for children conceived by artificial insemination during a couple's marriage.

Not all women seeking artificial insemination are married. Increasingly, single women are choosing to have children, and some conceive their children by artificial insemination, as do many lesbians in relationships. Social workers may be counseling women who face a variety of legal issues surrounding artificial insemination (Schroeder, 1974).

CREATION OF NEW LIFE

In experimenting with methods to overcome female infertility, scientists have developed ways to remove the ovum from the female and fertilize it outside the womb for various medical reasons. The embryo can then be implanted in the same or another woman.

This procedure raises a host of legal and emotional problems. For instance, if a woman who carries the child to term for another woman refuses to give the child up, can the woman whose egg has been used go to court and claim the child? If the woman uses the sperm of a donor who is now dead, the sperm having been successfully frozen, will the child be considered illegitimate? These are only a few questions such procedures raise (Schroeder, 1974). In addition to the legal problems, there may be social and emotional problems inherent in such a procedure.

Instances of problems with surrogate mothers have made newspaper headlines. One happier case involved a woman who carried her daughter's fertilized eggs to term and so became mother to her grandchildren (Special Issue on Surrogacy, 1988).

At its January 1988 meeting, the Council of the American Bar Association's Section of Family Law approved the Model Surrogacy Act (Special Issue on Surrogacy, 1988). It will be interesting to see which states adopt it and which states pass legislation outlawing the procedure (Field, 1988).

ADOPTION

The legal process of adoption by which a new family relationship is created does require planning. The new status achieved through adoption is discussed more fully in chapter 10.

The U.S. Department of Health, Education, and Welfare drafted a Model Adoption Act and model adoption procedures. The act contains some controversial provisions, such as permitting adult adoptees the right to open confidential adoption records on demand regardless of the desires of the birth parents. It also provides that the natural mother cannot sign a surrender until the child is 72 hours old and may revoke the surrender within 14 days. Critics allege such provisions will delay adoption placement. The Section of Family Law Adoption Committee of the American Bar Association presented a Model State Adoption Act in 1984 (Special Issue on Adoption, 1985).

Social workers in licensed adoption agencies should be familiar with the laws in the state where they work and may testify before legislative committees on proposed improvements and on changes that they oppose. Other social workers who deal with clients anticipating adoption should refer them to agencies or, if the adoption is an intrafamily one, to lawyers.

REFERENCES

Ambuel, B., & Rappaport, J. (1992). Developmental trends in adolescents' psychological and legal consent to abortion. *Law and Human Behavior, 16,* 129–154.

Bligh, R. (1964). Sterilization and mental retardation. *American Bar Association Journal, 51,* 1059–1063.

Dudar, H. (1973, March 19). Abortion for the asking. *Saturday Review of the Society, 1,* 30–36.

Dugan, J. C. (1993). The conflict between "disabling" and "enabling." Paradigms in law: Sterilization, developmentally disabled, and the Americans with Disabilities Act of 1990. *Cornell Law Review, 78,* 501–542.

Field, M. (1988). *Surrogate motherhood.* Cambridge, MA: Harvard University Press.

Hand, J. R. (1993). Buying fertility: Constitutionality of welfare bonuses for welfare mothers who submit to Norplant insertion. *Vanderbilt Law Review, 46,* 715–754.

Jaffe, F. S. (1971, October 8). Towards the reduction of unwanted pregnancy. *Science, 174,* 119–127.

Munro, A. B. (1982). The sterilization rights of mental retardates. *Washington and Lee Law Review, 39*, 207–221.

Schroeder, L. O. (1974). The new life controversy. *Social Casework, 55*, 51–52.

Shaman, J. M. (1979–1980). Legal aspects of artificial insemination. *Journal of Family Law, 18*, 331–351.

Smith, G. P. (1970). For unto us a child is born—legally. *American Bar Association Journal, 56*, 143–146.

Special issue on adoption. (1985, Summer). *Family Law Quarterly, 19*.

Special issue on surrogacy. (1988, Summer). *Family Law Quarterly, 22*.

Treppa, J. M. (1992). In vitro fertilization through egg donation: A prospective view of legal issues. *Golden Gate University Law Review, 22*, 777–794.

Young, A. T., Berkman, B., & Rehr, H. (1973). Women who seek abortions. *Social Work, 18*, 60–65.

STATUTES CITED

Health Programs Extension Act of 1973. P.L. 93-45, 87 Stat. 91, 42 U.S.C.A. § 242b et seq.

Hyde Amendment of 1988. 102 Stat. 1645 et seq.

Public Health Service Act of 1944. Ch. 373, 58 Stat. 682, 42 U.S.C.A. § 201 et seq.

Social Security Act of 1935. Ch. 351, 49 Stat. 620, 42 U.S.C.A. § 301 et seq.

STUDY QUESTIONS

1. Could a state ever order sterilization of an individual with mental disabilities?

2. Is abortion illegal anywhere in the United States?

12

Mental and Emotional Problems and Developmental Disabilities

Mental and emotional diseases, brain disorders and defects, and mental retardation are major problems that absorb tremendous resources in time, money, and energy. Social workers often dispense these resources, deploying their own limited numbers as well as they can and planning the delivery of services by others. Many of these resources go to the areas that have the most vocal advocates. Exceptional children whose parents participate in potent political organizations are more likely to get a large share of limited resources than are the people with senility, elderly people, and poor people of color in nursing homes. The fact is that society's resources are spent in a particular way because of political pressure.

The legal principles of due process and equal protection and other legal constraints do have a bearing on resource allocation. As you become aware of legal rights and legal methods of enforcing them, you will discover new tools for arriving at a more equitable division of resources. Just think of the possibilities for plenty that the "right to treatment" introduces in a desert of scarce resources.

MENTAL ILLNESS

A dearth of resources is a common complaint of professionals working with people with mental illness. But why should society concern itself with people with mental illness? Why should we worry about spending tax money for their treatment? Mental illness is not contagious. Protecting public health, a rationale for control of tuberculosis and venereal disease and for immunization against communicable disease, is not a rationale with mental illness. Because the illness is usually of long duration and the treatment expensive, we explain our concern as reflecting society's responsibility to help others with these overwhelming burdens. But can we justify interference with the liberty and rights of people with mental illness and the locking away of involuntary patients merely because the state provides a public treatment facility for this expensive illness?

Under the *parens patriae* doctrine, the state is considered the good parent that can force treatment on unwilling individuals for their own good and for the protection of society. This doctrine is used to rationalize differences between treatment afforded to a juvenile offender and that given to an adult criminal. The doctrine is not used, however, to force a person with acute appendicitis to have an operation. Why then force a person with mental illness to undergo treatment?

Generally, the individual with a physical illness is no threat to the public's peace or safety. A person who has a contagious disease or is the carrier of one can be restrained under the state's police power, although this is rarely done. However, people with mental illness may be forced to receive unwelcome treatment even when they present no threat to peace or safety.

One explanation for this difference in treatment is a recognition that people with a physical illness are able to make a rational choice whether to receive medical treatment, whereas people with mental illness cannot. In cases where supposedly rational adults refuse needed blood transfusions on religious grounds, the courts do not interfere unless the interests of a minor child or a fetus supersede. But if there is no violation of a positive prohibitory law, is there justification for deprivation of liberty? Certainly, the state's power to act swiftly and without court proceedings when public safety is at stake is justified, as in the commitment of people with mental illness who are violent. But that condition is rare. Does involuntary hospitalization deprive a person of liberty without sufficient legal justification?

Admission to an Institution

Voluntary admission. Individuals with physical illness themselves arrange with their physicians for hospitalization, except in rare emergencies. However, voluntary admission to a mental hospital is the exception rather than the rule. There is usually a determination that the patient is competent to make the decision. Given the nature of mental illness, patients often do not recognize the need for hospitalization. Therefore, relatives and friends force hospitalization and treatment on them.

Involuntary commitment. Legal procedures of varying complexity are used to protect the individual's due process rights in involuntary commitment (see *In re Fisher*, 1974). Some observers deplore this, saying that a legal proceeding simply makes patients feel even more as though the world is against them and adds to their sense of guilt. In *Heller v. Doe by Doe*, in a 5 to 4 decision, the Supreme Court held that statutory schemes requiring a higher standard of proof for involuntary commitment of people with mental illness, as opposed to people with mental retardation, had a rational basis and did not violate equal protection. The case lists the large majority of states that have separate involuntary commitment laws for the two groups of people. Patients may think the proceeding brands them as criminals. But careful legal procedures protect the individual from "railroading," which is rare but not unknown, and from well-meaning but unnecessary confinement. (Rosenham, 1973, reports on an experiment in which eight pseudopatients admitted to mental hospitals were not recognized as not being mentally ill by the professional staff, although they were so recognized by some of the patients.)

Commitment laws vary from state to state. For a discussion of state laws and cases, see Keville (1993). For suicidal or violent patients, states permit emergency commitment, sometimes without a judicial hearing or a physician's examination. Other types of commitment, which allow for varying periods of involuntary hospitalization, provide for judicial hearings and sometimes for jury trials of the individual's mental condition. *Lynch v. Baxley* (1974) was a class action brought to challenge emergency detention in the county jail and state mental hospitals. The federal court held that ex parte proceedings, on the application of one party only (the state), violated due process. The court set forth standards and safeguards required by due process for the protection of persons whose liberty was placed in jeopardy. *Lessard v. Schmidt* (1972) held that Wisconsin civil commitment procedures were constitutionally defective in a number of areas, particularly in the failure to notify of charges justifying detention and in the failure to notify of rights, including the right to a jury trial. (The opinion is a useful historical survey of the treatment of people with mental illness.)

According to *Jones v. United States* (1983), the due process clause allows the government to confine a defendant found not guilty by reason of insanity in a mental institution for a longer term than he would have served in jail if convicted. Justice Brennan dissented, arguing that confinement without due process is not related to the government's purported purpose of providing psychiatric treatment.

A portion of Hawaii's mental health, mental illness, drug addiction, and alcoholism law was amended in 1994 to read:

H.R.S. § 334-60.2.

A person may be committed to a psychiatric facility for involuntary hospitalization if the court finds:

(A) That the person is mentally ill or suffering from substance abuse;

(B) That the person is imminently dangerous to others, and is gravely disabled or is obviously ill; and

(C) That the person is in need of care or treatment, or both, and there is no suitable alternative available through existing facilities and programs which would be less restrictive than hospitalization.

H.R.S. § 334-60.5.(g).

No individual may be found to require medical treatment unless at least one physician who has personally examined the individual testifies in person at the hearing. This testimony may be waived by the subject of the petition. If the subject of the petition has refused to be examined by a licensed physician, the subject may be examined by a court-appointed licensed physician. If he refuses and there is sufficient evidence to believe that the allegations of the petition are true, the court may make a temporary order committing the subject to a psychiatric facility for a period of not more than five days for the purpose of a diagnostic examination and evaluation. The subject's refusal shall be treated as a denial that the subject is mentally ill or suffering from substance abuse. Nothing herein, however, shall limit the individual's privilege against self-incrimination.

The statute seems to require attention to the findings of a hearing as to a person's dangerousness and need for care, which would comply with due process. In *Suzuki v. Yuen* (1980) the court of appeals held that a now-repealed portion of the statute allowing commitment of someone dangerous to any property was unconstitutionally broad. The court did say,

On balance, we find Hawaii's procedures for the involuntary commitment of dangerous mentally ill individuals in conformity with constitutional rights. . . the statute strikes the proper balance between protection of society from those who might harm others and preservation of the rights of the mentally ill who are dangerous to none. (p. 179)

In their zeal to get treatment for a patient, social workers occasionally neglect rights fundamental to all citizens—the right to a hearing before incarceration, for example. The good motive of trying to help a person with illness gain treatment without the trauma of a court appearance may not be enough to justify this neglect. Workers in the mental health field must find the balance between patients' rights and jeopardizing a treatment plan because of commitment procedures. Some commentators have looked at patients' rights not only in the commitment process but also in the hospital where the patient is not free to come and go (Note, 1974; Rose, 1959; Weihofen & Overholser, 1945–1946). Court decisions consider patients' rights to visitation privileges and access to legal counsel and the use of the mail and telephone. Pennsylvania's Mental Health Procedures Act of 1976 allows a person with mental illness the greatest amount of freedom possible by using the least restrictive type of treatment.

Any social worker in a facility with mentally ill patients as clients should be familiar with state commitment laws. This may protect you from a tort suit for *false imprisonment,* the unlawful detention of another person. You also should be familiar with commitment procedures in case emergency hospitalization is warranted. The *Tarasoff v. Regents of California* (1976) case is instructive in that regard. A patient seen at a university mental clinic threatened to kill a girl whom he had once dated. The therapist attempted unsuccessfully to have the patient committed. The patient subsequently murdered the girl, and her parents brought suit against the university and the therapist (see Schroeder, 1979).

The *Tarasoff* case continues to be discussed (see Hulteng, 1989; Lake, 1994). Hulteng cited the 13 states that enacted statutes designed to clarify or limit the scope of potential liability for those reporting threats. He stated that representatives of mental health professionals also advocate immunity from liability for breach of confidentiality for therapists who pass on a warning they think is required. Hulteng also suggested the concerns that may arise regarding the risk to third parties imposed by patients with acquired immune deficiency syndrome.

One legal problem involved in involuntary commitment is the burden of proof required to deprive individuals of liberty against their will. The Supreme Court decided the issue in *Addington v. Texas* (1979). Addington's mother had filed a petition for his indefinite commitment; he protested. He had a long history of confinement for mental and emotional disorders and had threatened to injure his parents. Although he had caused property damage at his apartment and his parents' home, he attempted to show that there was no substantial factual basis for concluding that he was dangerous to himself or others. The language in the case is instructive because it explains why proof beyond a reasonable doubt is not required in commitment cases.

Addington v. Texas

99 S. Ct. 1804 (1979)

White, J.

The function of a standard of proof, as that concept is embodied in the due process clause and in the realm of factfinding, is to "instruct the factfinder concerning the degree of confidence our society thinks he should have in the correctness of factual conclusions for a particular type of adjudication." . . . The standard serves to allocate the risk of error between the litigants and to indicate the relative importance attached to the ultimate decision.

Generally speaking, the evolution of this area of the law has produced across a continuum three standards of levels of proof for different types of cases. At one end of the spectrum is the typical civil case involving a monetary dispute between private parties. Since society has a minimal concern with the outcome of such private suits, plaintiff's burden of proof is a mere preponderance of the evidence. The litigants thus share the risk of error in roughly equal fashion.

In a criminal case, on the other hand, the interests of the defendant are of such magnitude that historically and without any explicit constitutional requirement they have been protected by standards of proof designed to exclude as nearly as possible the likelihood of an erroneous judgment. In the administration of criminal justice our society imposes almost the entire risk of error upon itself.

• • • • •

The intermediate standard, which usually employs some combination of the words "clear," "cogent," "unequivocal" and "convincing," is less commonly used, but nonetheless "is no stranger to the civil law." . . . One typical use of the standard is in civil cases involving allegations of fraud or some other quasi-criminal wrongdoing by the defendant. The interests at stake in those cases are deemed to be more substantial than mere loss of money and some jurisdictions accordingly reduce the risk to the defendant of having his reputation tarnished erroneously by increasing the plaintiff's burden of proof.

• • • • •

Candor suggests that, to a degree, efforts to analyze what lay jurors understand concerning the differences among these three tests or the nuances of a judge's instructions on the law may well be largely an academic exercise; there are no directly relevant empirical studies.

• • • • •

In considering what standard should govern in a civil commitment proceeding, we must assess both the extent of the individual's interest in not being involuntarily confined indefinitely and the state's interest in committing the emotionally disturbed under a particular standard of proof. Moreover, we must be mindful that the function of legal process is to minimize the risk of erroneous decisions.

· · · · ·

This Court repeatedly has recognized that civil commitment for any purpose constitutes a significant deprivation of liberty that requires due process protection.

· · · · ·

Loss of liberty calls for a showing that the individual suffers from something more serious than is demonstrated by idiosyncratic behavior. Increasing the burden of proof is one way to impress the factfinder with the importance of the decision and thereby perhaps to reduce the chance that inappropriate commitments will be ordered.

The individuals should not be asked to share equally with society the risk of error when the possible injury to the individual is significantly greater than any possible harm to the state. We conclude that the individual's interest in the outcome of a civil commitment proceeding is of such weight and gravity that due process requires more than a mere preponderance of the evidence.

· · · · ·

There are significant reasons why different standards of proof are called for in civil commitment proceedings as opposed to criminal prosecutions. In a civil commitment state power is not exercised in a punitive sense.

· · · · ·

The subtleties and nuances of psychiatric diagnosis render certainties virtually beyond reach in most situations. The reasonable doubt standard of criminal law functions in its realm because there the standard is addressed to specific, knowable facts. . . . If a trained psychiatrist has difficulty with the categorical "beyond a reasonable doubt" standard, the untrained lay juror—or indeed even a trained judge—who is required to rely upon expert opinion could be forced by the criminal law standard of proof to reject commitment for many patients desperately in need of institutionalized psychiatric care. . . . Such "freedom" for a mentally ill person would be purchased at a high price.

The Supreme Court in *Addington* held that the burden of proof in involuntary commitment proceedings is somewhere between the two legal standards of a preponderance of the evidence and proof beyond a reasonable doubt; involuntary commitment requires clear, convincing proof. In *Heller v. Doe by Doe* (1993) the Supreme Court upheld the constitutionality of Kentucky's different standard of proof for involuntary commitment of people with mental illness and mental retardation. The standard for mental illness is proof beyond a reasonable doubt and that for mental retardation is clear and convincing evidence. In the *Thomas v. State Dept. of Mental Health* (1992), *Mink v. State Dept. of Mental Health* (1992), and *Thompson v. State Dept. of Mental Health* (1992) cases, the Alabama court reviewed its laws in the context of recommitment, focusing on expert testimony of a recent overt act evidencing the patient's dangerousness. A social worker who is helping to prepare an involuntary commitment the patient will contest should be aware of the standard. Is this a satisfactory compromise between the rights of the individual and the welfare of society? Is there any "right" of society to require treatment of an unwilling patient?

In 1979 the Supreme Court heard two challenges to state statutes permitting the commitment of minor children to mental hospitals by their parents and guardians (*Parham v. J. R.; Secretary, Etc. v. Institutionalized Juveniles*). The Court held that the risk of error inherent in a parental decision to have a child institutionalized for mental health care is sufficiently great that some kind of inquiry should be made by a "neutral factfinder" to determine whether requirements for admission are satisfied. The inquiry does not need to be a formal, judicial-type hearing, but it must be done by a neutral party, probably by a medical professional.

Right to Treatment

If the purpose of restraining an individual's liberty is to provide unwanted treatment, the deprivation of liberty has no justification if the patient receives no treatment. The idea that an individual has a right to treatment was advanced by Birnbaum in 1960 and has been gaining ground ever since. A compelling argument can be made that when a state has deprived an individual of liberty, not as punishment for crime but for treatment, unwanted or even wanted, the state must justify this deprivation by a treatment plan designed to lead to the individual's improvement and eventual release.

People with mental retardation and people with mental illness have the right to treatment. If custodial care is the best treatment for a particular degree of retardation, that care should at least be provided in clean, pleasant surroundings (see *Wyatt v. Stickney,* 1971). If the treatment desirable in a particular case is special education in the community, the right to treatment presumably extends to that.

The opinion in *Rouse v. Cameron* (1966) illustrates judicial thinking in right-to-treatment cases.

Rouse v. Cameron
373 F.2d 451 (D.C. Cir. 1966)

[Appellant was found not guilty by reason of insanity of carrying a dangerous weapon, a misdemeanor for which the maximum imprisonment is one year. He was involuntarily committed to Saint Elizabeth's Hospital. At the time he brought the habeas corpus action, he had been confined there for four years.]

Bazelon, C.J.

The principal issues raised by this appeal are whether a person involuntarily committed to a mental hospital on being acquitted of an offense by reason of insanity has a right to treatment that is cognizable in habeas corpus.

The purpose of involuntary hospitalization is treatment, not punishment. The provision for commitment rests upon the supposed "necessity for treatment of the mental condition which led to the acquittal by reason of insanity." Absent treatment, the hospital is transformed . . . into a penitentiary where one could be held indefinitely for no convicted offense, and this even though the offense of which he was previously acquitted because of doubt as to his sanity might not have been one of the more serious felonies or might have been, as it was here, a misdemeanor.

· · · · ·

If the court finds that a mandatorily committed patient, such as appellant, is in custody in violation of the Constitution and laws, it may allow the hospital a reasonable opportunity to initiate treatment. In determining the extent to which the hospital will be given an opportunity to develop an adequate program, important considerations may be the length of time the patient has lacked adequate treatment, the length of time he has been in custody, the nature of the mental condition that caused his acquittal, and the degree of danger, resulting from the condition, that the patient would present if released. Unconditional or conditional release may be in order if it appears that the opportunity for treatment has been exhausted or treatment is otherwise inappropriate.

The controversy over the right-to-treatment continues unabated. For years, people with mental illness and mental retardation have been dumped into overcrowded institutions that provide no semblance of treatment. Social workers have protested the inadequacies of housing and staffing for many years, but legislatures have turned a deaf ear to their pleas for better financing of public institutions. The right-to-treatment cases illustrate that the courts and the legal process may serve to pry tax funds from the public treasury to improve the lot of these unfortunate citizens. Wholesale release of sick individuals unable to plan for themselves is no solution, but the *Wyatt v. Stickney* (1971) case illustrates a possible solution short of that.

Wyatt v. Stickney
324 F.Supp. 781 (M.D. Ala., N.D. 1971)
[This was a class action initiated by guardians of patients confined at Bryce Hospital, Tuscaloosa, Alabama, and by employees of the Alabama Mental Health Board assigned to Bryce Hospital.]
Johnson, J.

The patients at Bryce Hospital, for the most part, were involuntarily committed through noncriminal procedures and without the constitutional protections that are afforded defendants in criminal proceedings. When patients are so committed for treatment purposes they unquestionably have a constitutional right to receive such individual treatment as will give each of them a realistic opportunity to be cured or to improve his or her mental condition. . . . Adequate and effective treatment is constitutionally required because, absent treatment, the hospital is transformed "into a penitentiary where one could be held indefinitely for no convicted offense." . . . The purpose of involuntary hospitalization for treatment purposes is treatment and not mere custodial care or punishment. This is the only justification, from a constitutional standpoint, that allows civil commitments to mental institutions such as Bryce. According to the evidence in this case, the failure of Bryce Hospital to supply adequate treatment is due to a lack of operating funds. The failure to provide suitable and adequate treatment to the mentally ill cannot be justified by lack of staff or facilities.

The federal district court gave Alabama six months to set standards and implement a treatment program, amended the petition to include residents in an institution for people with mental retardation as plaintiffs in the class action, and set out "minimum constitutional standards for adequate habilitation of the mentally retarded" (*Wyatt v. Stickney,* 1971; *Wyatt v. Stickney,* 1972; see also Pringmore & Davis, 1973). You should consult the *Wyatt* appendix to see whether you agree with the numbers of physicians, nurses, social workers, psychologists, and other personnel recommended for a particular patient population and with other suggested standards.

Higher federal courts have affirmed the right to treatment, but it has not reached the Supreme Court. In *O'Connor v. Donaldson* (1975), a former mental patient was permitted to sue the physicians and the administrator of the mental hospital where he was unlawfully confined without treatment, but Chief Justice Burger was careful to point out in his concurring opinion that the court was not finding a constitutional right to treatment (see Glass, 1977).

The lessons of *Wyatt* and *Donaldson* will not be lost on social reformers. Although political action—convincing lawmakers that reforms are necessary—is an avenue for change, this method is often slow and unrewarding. However, the federal court in *Wyatt* indicated that an unmoving legislature will not be a permanent stumbling block to funding needed reform. Federal courts would not normally take over the job of supervising the state's institutions, but *Wyatt* implies that the courts will not shrink from that task if the legislature and state officials refuse or are unable to carry out the demands of the judiciary for reforms.

The most likely vehicle through which right to treatment will be implemented by a court is the class action suit, enabling numerous complainants to share the cost of litigation to remedy a wrong. The *Donaldson* case illustrates another method: There the former patient sued individual physicians for money damages for the deprivation of liberty caused by involuntary hospitalization without treatment. *Spence v. Staras* (1974) is similar. The mother of a nonverbal son with mental illness who had been beaten at least 20 separate times by a fellow patient and who died as a result of beatings was permitted to sue under the Civil Rights Act of 1964 for her son's pain and suffering before his death.

Another action for damages was *Whitree v. State* (1968), where $300,000 was awarded. The court said, "the lack of psychiatric care was the reason for the inordinate length of this incarceration with the concomitant side effects of physical injury, moral degradation, and mental anguish," adding, "In fact the trial record developed clearly and coldly that the claimant received only custodial care during the greater part of his confinement; and that, in part, said custodial care was brutal and callous." A later case, *Rennie v. Klein,* held that a patient could refuse medication in the absence of an emergency. However, citing *Whitree,* a physician testified that failure to treat an acutely psychotic patient with drugs would be malpractice.

As suits for money damages become more prevalent, there may be improvement in state institutions. Physicians and others responsible for providing treatment will be unwilling to risk the notoriety and expense of a lawsuit, as well as any possible liability for damage, for denial of patients' rights. Those concerned with future planning for mental health care should know that right-to-treatment cases, both individual damage suits and class actions, are real possibilities.

Lake v. Cameron (1966) is a challenge to commitment by a writ of habeas corpus. The rehearing on the denial of the petition was *en banc,* which means that all of the judges in the circuit heard the case. Judge Burger, who dissented, became the Chief Justice of the United States.

Lake v. Cameron

364 F.2d 657 (D.C. Cir. 1966)

[Policemen found the appellant, a 60-year-old woman, wandering about the city of Washington and took her to a hospital. From there she was committed to Saint Elizabeth's (a psychiatric treatment facility), where she was diagnosed as suffering from senile brain disease: "chronic brain syndrome with arteriosclerosis with reaction."]

Bazelon, C.J.

Appellant contends in written and oral argument that remand to the district court is required for a consideration of suitable alternatives to confinement in Saint Elizabeth's Hospital in light of the new District of Columbia Hospitalization of the Mentally Ill Act, which came into effect after the hearing in the district court. Indeed, her counsel appointed by this court, who had interviewed appellant, made clear in answer to a question from the bench on oral argument that although appellant's formal prose pleading requests outright release, her real complaint is total confinement in a mental institution; that she would rather be in another institution or hospital, if available, or at home, even though under some form of restraint.

Habeas corpus challenges not only the fact of confinement but also the place of confinement. And the court is required to "dispose of the matter as law and justice require." . . . The court is not restricted to the alternative of returning appellant to Saint Elizabeth's or unconditionally releasing her.

We are not called upon to consider what action we would have taken in the absence of the new act, because we think the interest of justice and furtherance of the congressional objective require the application to the pending proceeding of the principles adopted in that act. It provides that if the court or jury finds that a "person is mentally ill and, because of that illness, is likely to injure himself or other persons if allowed to remain at liberty, the court may order his hospitalization for an indeterminate period, or order any other alternative course of treatment which the court believes will be in the best interest of the person or of the public."

. . . . .

The court's duty to explore alternatives in such a case as this is related also to the obligation of the state to bear the burden of exploration of possible alternatives an indigent cannot bear. This appellant, as appears from the record, would not be confined in Saint Elizabeth's if her family were able to care for her or pay for the care she needs. Though she cannot be given such care as only the wealthy can afford, an earnest effort should be made to review and exhaust available resources of the community in order to provide care reasonably suited to her needs.

. . . . .

Appellant may not be required to carry the burden of showing the availability of alternatives. Proceedings involving the care and treatment of the mentally ill are not strictly adversary proceedings. Moreover, appellant plainly does not know and lacks the means to ascertain what alternatives, if any, are available, but the government knows or has the means of knowing and should therefore assist the court in acquiring such information.

We remand the case to the district court for an inquiry into "other alternative courses of treatment." The court may consider, e.g., whether the appellant and the public would be sufficiently protected if she were required to carry an identification card on her person so that the police or others could take her home if she should wander, or whether she should be required to accept public health nursing care, community mental health and day-care services, foster care, home health aide services, or whether available welfare payments might finance adequate private care. Every effort should be made to find a course of treatment which appellant might be willing to accept.

In making this inquiry, the district court may seek aid from various sources, for example the D.C. Department of Public Welfare, the Metropolitan Police Department, the D.C. Department of Vocational Rehabilitation, the D.C. Association for Mental Health, the various family services agencies, social workers from the patient's neighborhood, and neighbors who might be able to provide supervision. The court can also require the aid of the Commission on Mental Health, which was established "in recognition of the fact that the assistance of unbiased experts was essential to assist courts in dealing with insanity cases."

Burger, C.J., dissenting

We disagree with remanding the case to require the district court to carry out an investigation of alternatives for which appellant has never indicated any desire. The only issue before us is the legality of Mrs. Lake's confinement in Saint Elizabeth's Hospital and the only relief she herself has requested is immediate unconditional release. The majority does not intimate that appellant's present confinement as a patient at Saint Elizabeth's Hospital is illegal, or that there is anything wrong with it except that she does not like and wishes to get out of any confinement. Nevertheless, this Court now orders the district court to perform functions normally reserved to social agencies by commanding search for a judicially approved course of treatment or custodial care for this mentally ill person who is plainly unable to care for herself. Neither this Court nor the district court is equipped to carry out the broad geriatric inquiry proposed or to resolve the social and economic issues involved.

· · · · ·

We can all agree in principle that a series of graded institutions with various kinds of homes for the aged and infirm would be a happier solution to the problem than confining harmless senile ladies in Saint Elizabeth's Hospital with approximately 8,000 patients, maintained at a great public expense. But it would be a piece of unmitigated folly to turn this appellant loose on the streets with or without an identity tag; and I am sure for my part that no district judge will order such a solution. This city is hardly a safe place for able-bodied men, to say nothing of an infirm, senile, and disoriented woman, to wander about with no protection except an identity tag advising police where to take her. The record shows that in her past wanderings she has been molested, and should she be allowed to wander again all of her problems might well be rendered moot either by natural causes or violence.

The problem presented by this case is not an easy one. Inquiry into treatment alternatives concerns knowledgeable social workers. Can court-appointed lawyers do the social planning required here? Should they be asked to? There has been much lively commentary on such questions (Isaacs, 1971; Whitmer, 1980).

Right to treatment involves the right to refuse treatment as well. In *Rogers v. Okin* (1979) hospitalized patients with mental illness brought a class action challenging the hospitals' medication and seclusion policies. The court held that committed patients are presumed competent to make decisions with respect to treatment in nonemergencies and had the right to refuse psychotropic medication based on their right of privacy. The case went to the Supreme Court and was remanded. In the later *Rogers v. Okin* (1984) the court held that the Massachusetts requirements of a judicial decision maker, adversary proceedings, and detailed regulations governing use of chemical restraints provided more than adequate procedural due process protection for patients' liberty interests. This is not an isolated case (Middleton, 1980). Is further judicial intervention in treatment desirable?

Alexander (1989) discussed the cases that have led to right-to-treatment decisions. To protect themselves, social workers practicing in such institutions should ensure that patients who have been civilly committed have a written plan of treatment, documentation of progress, and changes as needed in treatment strategies. Applebaum (1988) discussed the irony of depriving people with mental illness of their liberty and letting them refuse the medication that will restore that freedom.

Interstate Compact on Mental Health

As commitment and treatment near an end, hospital and aftercare workers have the problem of helping the patient readjust to society—finding a job, renting a room, and applying for disability payments of some kind, all involving contracts and the exercise of legal rights. Occasionally the planning is stymied because the individuals have no family or friends who can take an interest in their convalescence and ultimate release. Chronically ill patients may have been hospitalized so far from their family and for so long that they never had visitors and so lost all contact with relatives.

An example is instructive: A middle-aged man who made a marginal, schizoid adjustment all his life ends up in New Orleans as a dishwasher in a cafe. He holds the job successfully for several years. During a particularly rambunctious Mardi Gras celebration with its accompanying tension, inebriation, and crowds, he loses his tenuous control and has a full-blown psychotic episode. If his illness is complicated by physical illness and his only family consists of a brother in Montana and a niece in Vancouver, family planning for his release is almost impossible. In such a case the availability of the Interstate Compact on Mental Health is an aid to planning. He might be transferred under this act to a hospital close enough to his relatives to permit a visit and some supervision from them as he again tries to live outside the institution.

The compact recognizes that the residence or citizenship of a patient bears no relation to the furnishing of care and treatment and that the controlling factors are community safety and humanitarianism. It therefore establishes a procedure for transferring a patient from one state to another when a desirable treatment plan so demands. It also provides for supervision on convalescent status or conditional discharge, which enlarges the scope of planning. In its operation, the compact is not unlike the Compact on Juveniles and the Uniform Act for Out-of-State Parolee Supervision. If treatment or aftercare planning in another state seems desirable, the social worker should contact the state compact administrator to find out the procedure for a transfer. The compact applies to people with mental retardation and those with mental illness.

Aftercare

There is continuing controversy over certain kinds of treatment—psychosurgery and electroshock therapy, for instance—as well as over the best ways to prepare patients for leaving the hospital and resuming a normal life in the community. Neither admission nor commitment to a mental hospital causes a loss of civil rights unless there have also been guardianship or incompetency proceedings. Of course, hospitalization and a diagnosis of mental illness may be used in a civil proceeding to attack an individual's competence in certain areas, for instance, in making a contract or a will, but patients' ability to cope with the legal consequences of life in the community thus depends on their condition, rather than on any legal disabilities associated with hospitalization. Attention to the legal rights of patients should continue (Ginsberg, 1974; Herr, Arons, & Wallace, 1983).

Aftercare workers who place patients in foster homes and halfway houses should explore the legal consequences of these placements. Does the hospital retain any control over the patient? Who pays for these arrangements? The *Semler v. Psychiatric Institute of Washington, D.C.* (1976) case, although a tort case, should be read carefully. Any procedures established for supervision must be closely followed.

Semler v. Psychiatric Institute of Washington, D.C.
538 F.2d 122 (4th Cir. 1976)

[Mrs. Semler brought this negligence action to recover for the death of her daughter, who was killed by John Steven Gilreath, a Virginia probationer who had been a patient at the institute. The district court, sitting without a jury, awarded the plaintiff $25,000 against the psychiatrists and required the probation officer to contribute half the judgment. The court of appeals affirmed.

Gilreath had pleaded guilty to abducting a young girl. He was sentenced to 20 years' imprisonment, but the sentence was suspended on condition of his treatment and confinement at the institute. On the doctor's recommendation and at the probation officer's request, a state judge allowed him holiday passes. The judge subsequently approved a recommendation that he become a day care patient. Because Gilreath was concerned about the financial burden on his parents, the probation officer gave him a three-day pass to go to Ohio to investigate the possibility of moving there to work and attend therapy sessions at a nearby hospital. A further pass, approved by the doctor but not the judge, did not result in firm plans. Although the probation officer recommended that he receive further therapy, Gilreath was not restored to day care status but was enrolled in a therapy group that met two nights a week. He also moved from home, which was reported to the probation officer but not the judge.]
Butzner, C.J.

Confinement of criminals frequently is intended to protect the public as well as to punish and rehabilitate the wrongdoer. But we need not rely on this generality to determine the nature of the duty imposed on Gilreath's custodians by the state court's probation order. The order itself discloses that the state trial judge had a dual purpose in placing Gilreath on probation. The judge's willingness to allow Gilreath to continue his private psychiatric treatment shows concern for his welfare. At the same time, the requirement of confinement until release by the court was to protect the public, particularly young girls, from the foreseeable risk of attack. This is demonstrated by the following facts. The presentence report informed the judge that on three previous occasions Gilreath had molested other young girls. The report also contained information about Gilreath's need for psychiatric treatment, and it specifically mentioned an observation of a physician who had previously treated Gilreath that a "closed psychiatric facility would be best." . . . It concluded with a probation officer's recommendation for continued treatment at the institute. On the basis of the report, the judge imposed a lengthy sentence and, before placing Gilreath on probation, informed the doctor of his concern for the public.

It is apparent that the decision to release Gilreath was not to be simply a medical judgment based on the state of his mental health. The decision would also entail a judgment by the court as to whether his release would be in the best interest of the community. The special relationship created by the probation order, therefore, imposed a duty on the appellants to protect the public from the reasonably foreseeable risk of harm at Gilreath's hands that the state judge had already recognized.

· · · · ·

The restatement measures a custodian's duty by the standard of reasonable care. Here, that standard has been delineated by the precise language of the court order. The appellants were to retain custody over Gilreath until he was released from the institute by order of the court. No lesser measure of care would suffice. This obligation was not absolute, of course. The appellants would not be liable had Gilreath escaped despite their exercise of reasonable care, and they could surrender his custody to the court at any time. But they could not substitute their judgment for the court's with respect to the propriety of releasing him from confinement.

· · · · ·

The second element of actionable negligence is breach of the duty imposed by law on the alleged tortfeasor. This is a factual question. . . . The appellants, complying with the terms of the order, secured the trial judge's permission before transferring Gilreath to day care. Their principal contention is that the transfer from day care to out-patient status was simply a normal progression of treatment that required no additional judicial approval.

The district judge, however, found that there was a significant difference between day care and out-patient care. This finding is well documented by the evidence. As a day care patient, Gilreath was under the supervision of the institute during the day. At night and on weekends he was supervised by his parents. His medication, which was essential to his treatment, could be carefully monitored, his condition readily observed, and perhaps most importantly, the resources of the institute could assist and sustain him in time of stress. In contrast, as an out-patient, Gilreath

*lived alone and attended only two therapy sessions a week. No one effec-
tively monitored his medication, nor was he under constant observation.
Moreover, he lacked the daily psychiatric supervision, which, as the doctor
had emphasized, was available to him as a day care patient. Thus, he did
not have the resources or the environment of the institute to sustain him in
times of mental stress. In light of these important considerations, we perceive no error in the district court's finding that the appellants breached
the duty imposed on them by the order of probation when they failed to
seek the trial judge's permission to transfer Gilreath to out-patient status.*

*The district court also found that the doctor could not justifiably rely
on the probation officer's acquiescence in the transfer. The judge did nothing to clothe the probation officer with apparent authority to approve such
a transfer. The officer never told the doctor that he was empowered to speak
for the state trial judge, nor did he report that the judge had approved.
Similarly, the probation officer could not rely on the doctor's judgment. He
knew that his own authority was limited to granting passes and that the
state judge had reserved to himself the authority to determine whether
more significant changes of status should be allowed.*

· · · · ·

*The last element of proof necessary to establish actionable negligence is, in
the words of Virginia's supreme court, a "subsequent injury." . . . This raises
the issue of proximate cause, which the Virginia court usually treats as a
question of fact. . . . Addressing the issue in this manner, the district judge
found, on the basis of expert psychiatric testimony, that it was less likely that
Gilreath would have killed the plaintiff's daughter had he remained on day
care. He also accepted as "clear and convincing" the expert's testimony that
the tragedy was foreseeable if Gilreath were not kept in day care or closely confined. These subsidiary findings sustain the district judge's ultimate finding
that the breach of the court order was proximate cause of the plaintiff's loss.*

The judge finds the elements of a tort present: a duty and a breach of
that duty that proximately caused the injury. Careful attention to the
judge's orders might not have averted the tragedy, but the orders were
intended to protect the public and provide rehabilitation for Gilreath.
This is a special case because it involves supervision of a probationer
who had been convicted of a crime. The responsibility of most aftercare
workers is not so great.

MENTAL RETARDATION

The controversy over genetic or environmental influences in mental retardation continues unabated (Herrnstein, 1971; Rauch, 1985). Social
workers are naturally impressed by the social factors that hinder

successful use of native intelligence. However, whether the cause is genetic, traumatic, nutritional, or viral, the legal problems connected with mental illness apply equally to retardation. People with mental retardation have due process rights in connection with commitment; social workers retain legal as well as professional responsibilities in supervising them after institutionalization.

People with mental retardation also have the right to treatment. In the *Wyatt* case the parties and amici (those who filed amicus curiae, or friend-of-the-court, briefs) stipulated a broad spectrum of conditions they felt were mandatory for a constitutionally acceptable minimum treatment program. The order defined "qualified mental health professional" to include a psychologist with a doctoral degree from an accredited program and a social worker with a master's degree from an accredited program and two years of clinical experience. The judge's order also stated: "In the interests of continuity of care, one qualified mental retardation professional shall be responsible for supervising the implementation of the habilitation plan, integrating the various aspects of the habilitation program, and recording the resident's progress as measured by objective indicators. This qualified mental retardation professional shall also be responsible for ensuring that the resident is released when appropriate to the least restrictive habilitative setting" (*Wyatt v. Stickney,* 1972, p. 398). The purpose of such a requirement (Skarnulis, 1974) clearly is to make one person responsible for carrying out the treatment plan so that the individual with mental retardation does not get lost in the process, an all-too-common occurrence in institutions short of staff. Everybody's business is nobody's business.

The Supreme Court affirmed constitutionally protected liberty interests for people with mental retardation under the due process clause of the Fourteenth Amendment in *Youngberg v. Romeo* (1982): reasonably safe conditions of confinement, freedom from unreasonable bodily restraints, and such minimally adequate training as may be required with professional judgment exercised. More businesses are hiring people with mental retardation. Social workers should explore this possibility. Although employable, many people with mental retardation cannot live alone, and they may require group homes—sometimes not welcome in residential neighborhoods. A proposed operator of a group home for people with mental retardation challenged an ordinance excluding them from permitted uses in a zoning district. In *City of Cleburne, Tex. v. Cleburne Living Center* (1985), the Supreme Court held that mental retardation is not a quasi-suspect classification calling for a more exacting standard of judicial review than is normally accorded to economic and social legislation. Thus, requiring a special-use permit violated the equal protection clause in the absence of any rational basis in the record for believing the group home would pose a threat to the city's legitimate interests.

Guardianship

The appointment of a guardian (called "interdiction" in Louisiana) is the legal proceeding that declares an individual incompetent to manage day-to-day affairs and appoints someone to have control over the physical person of the individual and over the estate. The same person need not have control over both the person and property of the incompetent individual; one person may take care of the individual while another person or entity, perhaps a bank, manages the estate, if it is large enough to require expert management.

Social workers often work with parents and relatives of people with mental retardation, and occasionally with relatives of people with mental illness, to help them plan for guardianship. Depending on state law, guardianship may remove from an individual all or only a part of legal capacity. An individual declared fully incompetent could not legally buy a car, buy insurance for it, or contract for its repairs, because these actions require capacity to contract.

The parents of children with mental retardation often recognize the child's limitations in legal matters and wish to provide someone who can manage the child's affairs, particularly after their death. Social workers skilled in dealing with the sadness and guilt involved in recognizing a loved one's limitations can help families face the need for guardianship proceedings. They can advise their clients about the solutions the law offers to these problems and can suggest that they consult an attorney about guardianship or a trust, if the estate is large enough to warrant it. Seventeen states provide for limited guardianship, allowing individuals some residual capacity to manage their affairs. This legal flexibility is desirable; social workers should press for needed changes in states without it (Coon, 1980; Hurme, 1991).

Some elderly people suffer from physical, emotional, or mental disabilities that impair their functioning. Guardianship may be the solution for some; for others, community protective services will offer suitable flexible planning devices. Social workers should explore the need for community adult protective services and for a supportive legal framework (National Conference of Lawyers and Social Workers, 1967).

Custody of Children

Children of parents with mental retardation often present perplexing problems for social workers. The law provides for removing children from the custody of abusive or neglectful parents. However, the inadequacies of a parent with mental retardation, who may be helped by careful supervision to become a better parent, pose troublesome problems. When supervision is not possible and the children are placed in foster homes, the court may feel that the best interest of the children is to terminate the parent–child relationship and free the children for adoption (*In re McDonald*, 1972; "The Law Takes Five Sons," 1972; *State in the Interest of L.A.V.*, 1987). Social workers should examine their caseloads carefully and, if termination of the parent–child relationship seems warranted, be sure that the parents have an attorney.

Sterilization

Ever since Justice Oliver Wendell Holmes, Jr., said in *Buck v. Bell* (1927), "Three generations of imbeciles are enough," states have constitutionally sterilized as long as procedural due process standards are met. A few states still permit the sterilization of people with mental retardation to prevent the problem of custody of children of inadequate parents, and as a valid exercise of the state's police power (*In re Sterilization of Moore*, 1976; see also chapter 11). Ask yourself whether this drastic solution is desirable social policy.

ADDICTION

Addiction to alcohol and other drugs is one of the greatest social problems in our country. Various solutions have been tried, the most famous being prohibition. There, an amendment to the United States Constitution provided legal sanctions against liquor in an ineffective attempt to resolve alcohol abuse. The problems spawned by that experiment—the development of organized crime and the widespread flouting of the law—are an object lesson in the problems prohibitory laws can cause.

Anderson (1995) discussed alcohol abuse, including the criteria that lead to its diagnosis and the theories of its etiology. She discussed the significant differences among subgroups of alcohol abusers; this may be of interest to social workers because numbers and percentages of abusers who are women, children and adolescents, elderly people, lesbians and gay men, and others are given. Because the rate of alcoholism among people who are homeless is 20 percent to 33 percent, alcohol abuse should be an immediate concern for those who work with this population. (The rate of alcoholism is similar among American Indians and Alaska Natives.) Because fetal alcohol syndrome is 33 times higher in American Indians than it is in white Americans, social workers should be alert to the possibility of this condition when working with American Indian women of child-bearing age.

However, we continue to use legal sanctions to control addiction to drugs other than alcohol. The possession and distribution of many drugs are made criminal in most states and by the federal government unless their use has been medically prescribed. Drug smuggling diverts the resources of law enforcement in many parts of the country, particularly in border states. The sanctions for drug dealers may be quite strict, involving long prison sentences without benefit of probation or parole. Yet the ineffectiveness of even strict sanctions against the use of some drugs, particularly marijuana, creates controversy. Several state legislatures have reduced the penalties for possession of marijuana, making it a misdemeanor rather than a felony. The policy of handling drug abuse with criminal sanctions while alcohol abuse is not so treated is also controversial (Roffman, 1973; Szasz, 1972). Demleitner (1994) discussed the early history of the war on drugs. She suggested that legalization of drugs would not be a panacea but would curb the profits of organized crime.

Burke (1995) discussed the various drug control strategies that the government has used, including controlling the domestic supply of drugs and disrupting the international drug trade. Although these measures have by no means controlled the problem, drug use has declined after increasing substantially during the 1970s. However, drug abuse remains a serious problem, and the Violent Crime Control and Law Enforcement Act of 1994 included more money for drug treatment and testing.

A social worker's professional contact with drug abuse may come in community education programs, in its impact on other family problems, and in clinical treatment for the abuse itself. Revenue rulings from the Internal Revenue Service clarify the exclusion from taxation of certain treatments. The "sick pay" exclusion includes time lost from work during treatment for alcoholism, which is now considered an illness. Amounts paid for treatment at a therapeutic center for alcoholism are deductible as medical expenses, and transportation costs paid to attend meetings of Alcoholics Anonymous are expenses "primarily for and essential to medical care."

A recent report on cocaine treatment indicates the need for more research on treatment programs and social services (Nunes-Dinis & Barth, 1993). This could be a fertile field for social work practice.

Criminal Responsibility

In the clinical setting questions arise over legal responsibility for an addict's behavior, particularly when an addict in resident treatment has access to an agency automobile or agency cash. If you are treating people with heroin addiction, you may have the uneasy feeling of being either a police informant or an accessory to crime. Remember, however, that those people who come for treatment are trying to relinquish a life of crime; if incorrigible, they are not likely to confide to the therapist sources of supply. Does the confidentiality of the treatment relationship extend to suppressing knowledge of continued illegal possession and use of drugs? Probably not.

Social workers in such treatment settings need to know the procedures to prevent patients from gaining access to drugs and the laws governing treatment of addicts, particularly when treatment may include the use of another restricted drug, such as methadone. Ask the legal staff of the agency to keep you up-to-date.

If you work with people who have addictions, you need to understand the responsibility of these people for their acts. Facing legal responsibility is one way the therapist can help people with addictions appreciate the consequences of illegal behavior. The law in this area developed from the landmark case of *Robinson v. California* (1962). There the Supreme Court held that criminal punishment for the status of being an addict alone would be forbidden by the Eighth Amendment as cruel and unusual. That rationale was extended to the acts of the individual addicted to alcohol in *Driver v. Hinnant* (1966) and *Easter v. District of Columbia* (1966). The direction of the cases seemed inevitable: Anyone under a compulsion to take a drug would be excused from acts primarily caused by that drug (Cutshaw, 1966). Thus, the robber who broke into the drugstore to steal morphine would not be criminally responsible for that act, because it was compelled by addiction. In *Powell v. Texas* (1968) the Supreme Court reversed the trend.

Powell v. Texas
392 U.S. 514, 88 S. Ct. 2145, 20 L.Ed.2d 1254 (1968)
[Powell was convicted of public intoxication. At the trial there was evidence of his repeated arrests for drunkenness, and psychiatric testimony that he was a chronic alcoholic. On the authority of *Robinson,* he claimed that his incarceration would be cruel and unusual punishment in violation of the Eighth Amendment.]
Marshall, J.
The difficulty with that position, as we shall show, is that it goes much too far on the basis of too little knowledge. In the first place, the record in this case is utterly inadequate to permit the sort of informed and responsible adjudication which alone can support the announcement of an important and wide-ranging new constitutional principle. We know very little about the circumstances surrounding the drinking bout which resulted in this conviction, or about Leroy Powell's drinking problem, or indeed about alcoholism itself. The trial hardly reflects the sharp legal and evidentiary clash between fully prepared adversary litigants which is traditionally

expected in major constitutional cases. The state put on only one witness, the arresting officer. The defense put on three—a policeman who testified to appellant's long history of arrests for public drunkenness, the psychiatrist, and appellant himself.

Furthermore, the inescapable fact is that there is no agreement among members of the medical profession about what it means to say that "alcoholism" is a "disease." One of the principal works in the field states that the major difficulty in articulating a "disease concept of alcoholism" is that "alcoholism has too many definitions and disease practically none." This same author concludes that a "disease is what the medical profession recognizes as such." In other words, there is widespread agreement today that "alcoholism" is a "disease," for the simple reason that the medical profession has concluded that it should attempt to treat those who have drinking problems. There the agreement stops.

· · · · ·

Despite the comparatively primitive state of our knowledge on the subject, it cannot be denied that the destructive use of alcoholic beverages is one of our principal social and public health problems. The lowest current informed estimate places the number of "alcoholics" in America (definitional problems aside) at 4,000,000, and most authorities are inclined to put the figure considerably higher. The problem is compounded by the fact that a very large percentage of the alcoholics in this country are "invisible"—they possess the means to keep their drinking problems secret, and the traditionally uncharitable attitude of our society toward alcoholics causes many of them to refrain from seeking treatment from any source. Nor can it be gainsaid that the legislative response to this enormous problem has in general been inadequate.

There is as yet no known generally effective method for treating the vast number of alcoholics in our society. Some individual alcoholics have responded to particular forms of therapy with remissions of their symptomatic dependence upon the drug. But just as there is no agreement among doctors and social workers with respect to the causes of alcoholism, there is no consensus as to why particular treatments have been effective in particular cases and there is no generally agreed-upon approach to the problem of treatment on a large scale. Most psychiatrists are apparently of the opinion that alcoholism is far more difficult to treat than other forms of behavioral disorders, and some believe it is impossible to cure by means of psychotherapy; indeed, the medical profession as a whole, and psychiatrists in particular, have been severely criticized for the prevailing reluctance to undertake the treatment of drinking problems. Thus it is entirely possible that, even were the manpower and facilities available for a full-scale attack upon chronic alcoholism, we would find ourselves unable to help the vast bulk of our "visible"—let alone our "invisible"—alcoholic population.

However, facilities for the attempted treatment of indigent alcoholics are woefully lacking throughout the country. It would be tragic to return large numbers of helpless, sometimes dangerous and frequently unsanitary inebriates to the streets of our cities without even the opportunity to sober up adequately, which a brief jail term provides. Presumably no state or city will tolerate such a state of affairs. Yet the medical profession cannot, and does not, tell us with any assurance that, even if the buildings, equipment and trained personnel were made available, it could provide anything more than slightly higher-class jails for our indigent habitual inebriates. Thus we run the grave risk that nothing will be accomplished beyond the hanging of a new sign reading "hospital" over one wing of the jailhouse.

One virtue of the criminal process is, at least, that the duration of penal incarceration typically has some outside statutory limit; this is universally true in the case of petty offenses, such as public drunkenness, where jail terms are quite short on the whole. "Therapeutic civil commitment" lacks this feature; one is typically committed until one is "cured." Thus, to do otherwise than affirm might subject indigent alcoholics to the risk that they may be locked up for an indefinite period of time under the same conditions as before, with no more hope than before of receiving effective treatment and no prospect of periodic "freedom."

Faced with this unpleasant reality, we are unable to assert that the use of the criminal process as a means of dealing with the public aspects of problem drinking can never be defended as rational. The picture of the penniless drunk propelled aimlessly and endlessly through the law's "revolving door" of arrest, incarceration, release and re-arrest is not a pretty one. But before we condemn the present practice across-the-board, perhaps we ought to be able to point to some clear promise of a better world for these unfortunate people. Unfortunately, no such promise has yet been forthcoming. If, in addition to the absence of a coherent approach to the problem of treatment, we consider the almost complete absence of facilities and manpower for the implementation of a rehabilitation program, it is difficult to say in the present context that the criminal process is utterly lacking in social value. This court has never held that anything in the Constitution requires that penal sanctions be designed solely to achieve therapeutic or rehabilitative effects, and it can hardly be said with assurance that incarceration serves such purposes any better for the general run of criminals than it does for public drunks.

· · · · ·

On its face the present case does not fall within that holding, since appellant was convicted, not for being a chronic alcoholic, but for being in public while drunk on a particular occasion. The state of Texas thus has *not sought to punish a mere status, as California did in Robinson; nor has it attempted to regulate appellant's behavior in the privacy of his own home. Rather, it has imposed upon appellant a criminal sanction for public behavior which may create substantial health and safety hazards, both for appellant and for members of the general public, and which offends the moral and esthetic sensibilities of a large segment of the community. This seems a far cry from convicting one for being an addict, being a chronic alcoholic, being mentally ill, or a leper.*

· · · · ·

It is suggested in dissent that Robinson stands for the "simple" but "subtle" principle that "criminal penalties may not be inflicted upon a person for being in a condition he is powerless to change."

· · · · ·

In that view, appellant's "condition" of public intoxication was "occasioned by a compulsion symptomatic of the disease" of chronic alcoholism, and that, apparently, his behavior lacked the critical element of mens rea. Whatever may be the merits of such a doctrine of criminal responsibility, it surely cannot be said to follow from Robinson. The entire thrust of Robinson's interpretation of the cruel and unusual punishment clause is that criminal penalties may be inflicted only if the accused has committed some act, has engaged in some behavior, which society has an interest in preventing, or perhaps in historical common law terms, has committed some actus reus. It thus does not deal with the question of whether certain conduct cannot constitutionally be punished because it is, in some sense, "involuntary" or "occasioned by a compulsion."

· · · · ·

Traditional common-law concepts of personal accountability and essential considerations of federalism lead us to disagree with appellant. We are unable to conclude, on the state of this record or on the current state of medical knowledge, that chronic alcoholics in general, and Leroy Powell in particular, suffer from such an irresistible compulsion to drink and to get drunk in public that they are utterly unable to control their performance of either or both of these acts and thus cannot be deterred at all from public intoxication. And in any event this Court has never articulated a general constitutional doctrine of mens rea.

We cannot cast aside the centuries-long evolution of the collection of interlocking and overlapping concepts which the common law has utilized to assess the moral accountability of an individual for his antisocial deeds. The doctrines of actus reus, mens rea, insanity, mistake, justification, and duress have historically provided the tools for a constantly shifting adjustment of the tension between the evolving aims of the criminal law and changing religious, moral, philosophical, and medical views of the nature of man. This process of adjustment has always been thought to be the province of the states.

• • • • •

But formulating a constitutional rule would reduce, if not eliminate, that fruitful experimentation, and freeze the developing productive dialogue between law and psychiatry into a rigid constitutional mold. It is simply not yet the time to write into the Constitution formulas cast in terms whose meaning, let alone relevance, is not yet clear either to doctors or to lawyers.

The decision in *Powell* was 5 to 4, with the dissenters urging that the case had the same essential constitutional defect as *Robinson:* In both the defendant was accused of being in a condition that he had no capacity to change or avoid. You may disagree with Justice Marshall's assessment of treatment facilities in this country, but at least the decision makes clear that people with addictions can be held criminally responsible for criminal behavior associated with their condition.

Alcoholics and others who abuse alcohol are often accused of driving while intoxicated. The Baton Rouge, Louisiana, city police department was the first in the world to operate a *photoelectric intoximeter,* a mobile breath-testing device that measures the amount of alcohol in the blood. Requiring a breath test when arrested for drunken driving, with loss of the driver's license for refusing to take the test, has been held constitutional. However, any people required to decide whether to submit to a chemical test of their blood-alcohol content have the right to consult with a lawyer before making the decision, provided this does not unreasonably delay administration of the test (*Prideaux v. State,* 1976).

In *South Dakota v. Neville* (1985) the Court held that defendant's privilege against self-incrimination was not impaired by admission into evidence of his refusal to submit to blood-alcohol tests. Nor was it a violation of due process to use the refusal as evidence of guilt, even though the police failed to warn him that his refusal could be used against him at trial. Some years later in Minnesota, *Clough v. Commissioner of Public Safety* (1985) held that the right to counsel provided by state law allowed the motorist to contact his parents to get the name of a lawyer.

SEXUAL ISSUES

Although sexual issues do not belong in the category of emotional illness unless accompanied by neurosis, psychosis, or other psychiatric trouble, they do have legal consequences. For a discussion of the issue, see Wiegand and Farr (1992–1993)

Homosexuality

It is rare that a client comes to a social services agency with homosexuality as the presenting problem. Although the fourth edition of the *Diagnostic and Statistical Manual of Mental Disorders* (American Psychiatric Association, 1994) does not list homosexuality as a disorder, it does contain a section on Sexual and Gender Identity disorders that lists diagnostic criteria that formerly would have been identified as homosexuality. This sexual identity often comes to light as a contributing factor in such problems as interpersonal relations or job discrimination. Many states make homosexual practices criminal, even those between consenting adults. In a challenge to the constitutionality of a Virginia statute making sodomy a crime, the court held the statute valid over contentions that it deprived adult men, engaging in regular homosexual relations consensually and in privacy of their homes, their constitutional rights to due process, freedom of expression, and privacy (*Doe v. Commonwealth's Atty. for City of Richmond,* 1975).

A gay man brought *Hardwick v. Bowers* (1985) to challenge the constitutionality of the Georgia sodomy statute. The court held that because it infringed on a constitutional right of the plaintiff, the state would be required to demonstrate a compelling interest in restricting that right. The case was overturned in *Bowers v. Hardwick* (1986), where the Supreme Court ruled the Georgia statute constitutional. Accounts of discrimination against gay men and lesbians in housing, military service, and employment indicate that the social consequences of this sexual orientation can be grave. In 1979 the Surgeon General declared that homosexuality would "no longer be considered a mental disease or defect," and the Immigration and Naturalization Service ordered its agents to stop preventing foreign gay men and lesbians from entering the country ("Ideas and Trends," 1979). The climate has changed dramatically. The Clinton administration's "don't ask, don't tell" policy to permit gay men and lesbians to serve in the military is evidence of the change.

A serious problem for the gay or lesbian parent is obtaining custody of children after divorce; for either parent proof of homosexuality might be considered by the court as per se evidence that the parent is unfit. Of the few courts that have considered the problem, some merely declare that it is one factor to be considered, whereas others stipulate that custody will be awarded only after an assurance that the gay or lesbian relationship is discontinued. Except in Hawaii, a gay or lesbian union cannot result in a valid marriage with full legal protection (Bernstein, 1977; Heet, 1993; *Jones v. Hallahan,* 1973). For further information, see the section on custody in chapter 9.

Transsexualism

Transvestism, dressing like a member of the opposite sex, is often a manifestation of homosexuality. *Transsexuals* have the identity problem of feeling that they are trapped by a trick of nature in the body of the wrong sex. For them, cross-dressing may be preparatory to surgery. In that case the individual should carry a statement from a physician that dressing like the opposite sex is medically prescribed.

Most physicians will not perform this radical surgery, which involves removing the sex organs, without a trial period to determine whether the individual can make the necessary adjustment to living as a member of the other sex. During this period counseling should involve the many legal problems, including change of name, change of sex on the birth certificate, and change of draft status (*M.T. v. J.T.,* 1976; *Pinneke v. Preisser,* 1980; Schroeder, 1973; Smith, 1971). Advising presurgery transsexual patients may become less frequent as it is recognized that surgery is not a desirable solution to these serious gender problems. The Johns Hopkins University Hospital, a pioneer in the surgery, has phased it out, and the Erickson Educational Foundation has closed.

In 1983 there were an estimated 6,000 postoperative transsexual individuals (Taitz, 1987); the number of male-to-female transsexual people is three to four times the number of female-to-male transsexual people. Although Taitz suggested that legislatures consider the problems associated with transsexual operations and possibly enact legislation, there are no reports that any such consideration has occurred.

Promiscuity and Adultery

Frigidity, impotence, and other sexual problems are often encountered and are frequently symptomatic of other problems. These "symptoms" may be used as grounds for dissolution of a marriage. For instance, denial of marital relations can amount to cruelty, which is grounds for separation.

Promiscuity can become grounds for divorce if adultery is proved. In some jurisdictions, failure to consummate the marriage is grounds for *annulment,* a legal declaration that the presumed marriage was void from the beginning. Proof of adultery may be evidence that the parent is unfit and constitute grounds for denying custody of children after divorce. Many courts hold that the adultery, if not in the presence of the children and if not evidence of continuing promiscuity, is just one element to consider in determining the best interest of the child in the custody decision.

REFERENCES

Alexander, R., Jr. (1989). The right to treatment in mental and correctional institutions. *Social Work, 34,* 109–112.

American Psychiatric Association. (1994). *Diagnostic and Statistical manual of mental disorders* (4th ed.). Washington, DC: Author.

Anderson, S. C. (1995) Alchohol abuse. In R. L. Edwards (Ed.-in-Chief), *Encyclopedia of social work* (19th ed., Vol. 1, pp. 203–215). Washington, DC: NASW Press.

Applebaum, P. S. (1988). The right to refuse treatment with antipsychotic medication: Retrospect and prospect. *American Journal of Psychiatry, 145,* 413–419.

Bernstein, B. E. (1977). Legal and social interface in counseling homosexual clients. *Social Casework, 58,* 36–40.

Birnbaum, M. (1960). The right to treatment. *American Bar Association Journal, 46,* 499–505.

Burke, A. C. (1995). Substance abuse: Legal issues. In R. L. Edwards (Ed.-in-Chief), *Encyclopedia of social work* (19th ed., Vol. 3, pp. 2347–2357). Washington, DC: NASW Press.

Coon, M. A. (1980). The law of interdiction: Time for change. *Louisiana Bar Journal, 27,* 223–228.

Cutshaw, L. O. (1966). Some thoughts on alcoholism as involuntary intoxication. *Louisiana Bar Journal, 14,* 159–167.

Demleitner, N. A. (1994). Organized crime and prohibition: What difference does legalization make? *Whittier Law Review, 15,* 613–646.

Ginsberg, L. H. (1974). The mental patient liberation movement. *Social Work, 19,* 103.

Glass, K. (1977). Right to treatment: *O'Connor v. Donaldson. Health & Social Work, 2,* 27–40.

Heel, J. L. (1993). Homosexual marriage, the changing American family, and the heterosexual right to privacy. *Section Hall Law Review, 24,* 347–393.

Herr, S. S., Arons, S., & Wallace, R. E. (1983). *Legal rights and mental-health care.* Lexington, MA: Lexington Books.

Herrnstein, R. (1971, September). I.Q. *Atlantic, 228*(3–4), 103.

Hulteng, R. J. (1989). Commentary—The duty to warn or hospitalize: The new scope of *Tarasoff. Liability in Michigan, 67,* 1–28

Hurme, S. B. (1991). *Steps to enhance guardianship monitoring.* Chicago: American Bar Association.

Ideas and trends. (1979, August 19). *New York Times,* p. E9.

Isaacs, E. (1971). Social service work for a law firm. *American Business Law Journal, 19,* 166–167.

Keville, T. (1993). The power to confine: Private involuntary civil commitment as state action. *New England Journal on Criminal and Civil Confinement, 19,* 61–102.

Lake, P. F. (1994). Revisiting *Tarasoff. Albany Law Review,* pp. 97–173.

The law takes five sons away from home. (1972, December 1). *Life, 73,* 91–97.

Middleton, M. (1980). Mentally disabled patients win "right of refusal." *American Bar Association Journal, 66,* 1512.

National Conference of Lawyers and Social Workers. (1967). *Adult protective services: Responsibilities and reciprocal relationships of the lawyer and social worker* (Publication No. 5). New York: Author.

Note. (1974). Developments in the law—Civil commitment of the mentally ill. *Harvard Law Review, 87,* 1190–1406.

Nunes-Dinis, M., Barth, R. P. (1993). Cocaine treatment and outcome. *Social Work, 38,* 611–617.

Pringmore, C. F., & Davis, P. R. (1973). *Wyatt v. Stickney:* Rights of the committed. *Social Work, 18,* 10–18.

Rauch, J. B. (1985). *Genetic content for graduate social worker education practice.* Alexandria, VA: Council on Social Work Education.

Roffman, R. A. (1973). Heroin and social welfare policy. *Social Work, 18,* 22–23.

Rose, H. A. (1959). Commitment of the mentally ill: Problems of law and policy. *Michigan Law Review, 57,* 945–1018.

Rosenham, D. L. (1973). On being sane in insane places. *Science, 179,* 250–258.

Sands, L. L. (1990). Mental health law—Limited liability under the Mental Health Procedures Act—*Farago v. Sacred Heart General Hospital,* 522 Pa. 410, 562 A.2d 300 (1989). *Temple Law Review, 63,* 451.

Schroeder, L. O. (1973). Renaissance for the transsexual: A new birth certificate. *Journal of Forensic Sciences, 18,* 237–245.

Schroeder, L. O. (1979). Legal liability: A professional concern. *Clinical Social Work Journal, 7*, 194–199.

Skarnulis, E. (1974). Noncitizen: Plight of the mentally retarded. *Social Work, 19*, 56–62.

Smith, D. K. (1971). Transsexualism, sexual reassignment surgery, and the law. *Cornell Law Review, 56*, 963–1009.

Szasz, T. S. (1972, April 1). The ethics of addiction. *Harper's, 244*, 74–79.

Taitz, J. (1987). Judicial determination of the sexual identity of post-operative transsexuals: A new form of sex discrimination. *American Journal of Law and Medicine, 13*, 53–69.

Weihofen, H., & Overholser, W. (1945–1946). Commitment of the mentally ill. *Texas Law Review, 24*, 307–348.

Whitmer, G. E. (1980). From hospitals to jails: The fate of California's deinstitutionalized mentally ill. *American Journal of Orthopsychiatry, 50*, 65–75.

Wiegand, S., & Farr, S. (1992–1993). Part of the moving stream: State constitutional law, sodomy, and beyond. *Kentucky Law Journal, 81*, 449–482.

STATUTES CITED

Civil Rights Act of 1964. P.L. 88-352, 78 Stat. 241, 42 USCA § 2000 e2.

Interstate Compact on Mental Health. 86 Stat. 126.

Violent Crime Control and Law Enforcement Act of 1994. 10 U.S.C.A. § 2382 et seq.

STUDY QUESTIONS

1. Because alcoholism is a sickness, are alcoholics free of responsibility for criminal acts?

2. Do patients have any constitutional rights in an involuntary commitment?

3. Do patients in public facilities have a right to treatment, or is it available only to those who can pay?

13

Social Security Programs

The United States was the last Western nation to adopt universal social insurance. Although the Social Security Act of 1935 contains several titles establishing such programs as public welfare, what we typically think of as social security are Supplemental Security Income (SSI); Medicare; and Medicaid, the program of Old Age, Survivor's and Disability Insurance. This basic program covers almost nine of every 10 persons in paid private employment. Since the passage of the act in 1935, coverage has been gradually increased. The 1939 amendments made monthly benefits payable first in 1940 instead of 1942 as originally planned. Major changes were made in 1950, when the program was broadened to cover many jobs that had previously been excluded, including regularly employed farm and household workers, and most persons, other than farmers and professional people, who work for themselves. The taxes are paid on wages of domestic workers who earn more than $1,000 per year and on wages of farm workers who earn more than $150. At that time, coverage was made available to employees of state and local governments not under a public employees' retirement system and to employees of nonprofit organizations on a voluntary basis. In 1965 self-employed doctors of medicine, the last self-employed group left, were covered.

The social security program was designed to provide income security for working people and their dependents (Ozawa, 1995). Social security includes the earned income tax credit, child support assurance, the dependent care tax credit, and the refundable tax credit for children. With the new ideology of investment, children will be the target of income security policy, and the government will intervene more directly on behalf of children. The future of this country's income security will be based on social insurance, public assistance, and investment.

SUPPLEMENTAL SECURITY INCOME

SSI is completely funded and administered by the federal government. It provides for those elderly, disabled, or blind individuals once covered under state public welfare programs and others who later become eligible. The program was enacted in 1972 after several years of public debate. SSI represents a compromise between the sweeping changes that the Family Assistance Program sponsored by the Nixon administration would have brought about and more-restrictive legislation aimed at reducing the welfare rolls.

SSI establishes national eligibility requirements and benefits for listed categories of needy individuals. It thus prevents some inequities and discrepancies between different states, although it does not do away with all of them; those states that formerly paid a higher benefit than the current federal benefit may supplement the federal benefits. The current maximum monthly grant is $458. This amount is adjusted periodically to reflect changes in the cost of living (Social Security Act § 1617). The resource limit is still $2,000 for a single person and $3,000 for a couple. This and other facets of the SSI program are found in Title XVI of the Social Security Act.

Meyer (1995) reported on the findings of a panel of experts as to the contemporary problems of social security. Benefits vary among states but are routinely inadequate, and eligibility standards are outdated. The work incentives for people with disabilities are inconsistent, and there are disincentives to marry and live with others, an option that could be desirable for some people in need.

Legal Aspects of the Program

The social security program is financed by what Justice Cardozo described, in upholding the constitutionality of the act, as an income tax on employees and an excise tax on employers (*Helvering v. Davis,* 1937). Employees and employers match contributions calculated as a percentage of a base wage. The percentage and the base to which the percentage is applied have both gradually increased. Recent amendments to the Social Security Act that provide for automatic increases in benefits as inflation increases mean that both the tax and the base will continue to rise. The self-employed person pays a percentage of earnings from self-employment up to the maximum combination of employee and employer contributions.

These contributions go into trust funds that are kept separate from all other funds in the United States Treasury. The Federal Old Age and Survivor's Insurance Trust Fund, the oldest and largest of the four funds, dates from 1939 and finances the payment of retirement and survivor's insurance benefits. The Federal Disability Insurance Trust Fund was set up in 1956 to finance the retirement benefits payable to those insured who become disabled before reaching age 65. The law was later changed to allow benefits for disabled workers to be paid from this fund. The Federal Hospital Insurance Trust Fund and the Federal Supplementary Medical and Insurance Trust Fund, the two newest funds, were established by the 1965 amendments to the Social Security Act. Benefits for people age 65 and older are paid from these two funds. A special payroll contribution goes into the hospital insurance trust fund. The supplementary fund is made up of the premiums of those enrolled in the plan and matching amounts from the federal government. By law, the assets of these four trust funds can be used only for the payment of benefits and administrative expenses. Funds not currently needed for the payment of benefits and operating costs are invested in interest-bearing U.S. government securities.

There has been a great deal written recently about the possible bankruptcy of the social security funds. As benefit payments and the number of recipients increase and the number of contributors declines, there is concern that the programs will not be on the "pay-as-you-go" basis envisioned originally. As pressure continues for coverage of those not now covered—for instance, homemakers—the financial stability of this form of social insurance seems in doubt.

The social security program adheres to certain basic principles. It is *work related:* Security for worker and family grows out of work experience, and both entitlement and amount of benefits are based on past earnings and time worked. There is no "means" test; benefits are paid regardless of passive income from savings, pensions, investments, and the like, and the benefits are tax free. There is a ceiling, however, on the amount that may be earned from employment. Although the ceiling on employment earnings does amount to a means test, that benefits are paid regardless of passive income encourages thrift; it also means that an insured worker knows before retiring that benefits will be paid regardless of need. Coverage is compulsory for all of those who work in "covered employment." All are insured, regardless of "insurability," so that the system is truly one of social insurance, covering those individuals who might be poor risks for private insurance.

The following case says something about the legal aspects of the program itself.

Flemming v. Nestor

363 U.S. 603, 80 S. Ct. 1367, 4 L.Ed.2d 1435 (1960)

Harlan, J.

*From a decision of the district court for the District of Columbia holding §
202(n) of the Social Security Act . . . unconstitutional, the Secretary of
Health, Education, and Welfare takes this direct appeal. . . . The challenged section . . . provides for the termination of old-age, survivor, and
disability insurance benefits payable to, or in certain cases in respect of,
an alien individual, who after September 1, 1954 (the date of enactment
of the section), is deported under § 241(a) of the Immigration and Nationality Act . . . on any one of the certain grounds specified in § 202(n).*

*Appellee, an alien, immigrated to this country from Bulgaria in 1913,
and became eligible for old-age benefits in November 1955. In July 1956
he was deported . . . for having been a member of the Communist Party
from 1933 to 1939. This being one of the benefit-termination deportation
grounds specified . . . appellee commenced this action in the district court
. . . to secure judicial review. On cross-motions for summary judgment, the
district court ruled for appellee, holding § 202(n) unconstitutional under
the due process clause of the Fifth Amendment in that it deprived appellee
of an accrued property right.*

. . . . .

*We think that the district court erred in holding that § 202(n) deprived
appellee of an "accrued property right."*

. . . . .

*The social security system may be accurately described as a form of
social insurance, enacted pursuant to Congress' power to "spend money in
aid of the 'general welfare,'" . . . whereby persons gainfully employed, and
those who employ them, are taxed to permit the payment of benefits to the
retired and disabled, and their dependents. Plainly the expectation is that
many members of the present productive work force will in turn become
beneficiaries rather than supporters of the program. But each worker's benefits, though flowing from the contributions he made to the national
economy while actively employed, are not dependent on the degree to which
he was called upon to support the system by taxation. It is apparent that
the noncontractual interest of an employee covered by the act cannot be
soundly analogized to that of the holder of an annuity, whose right to
benefits is bottomed on his contractual premium payments.*

*It is hardly profitable to engage in conceptualizations regarding "earned
rights" and "gratuities." . . . The "right" to social security benefits is in
one sense "earned," for the entire scheme rests on the legislative judgment
that those who in their productive years were functioning members of the
economy may justly call upon that economy, in their later years, for*

protection from "the rigors of the poor house as well as from the haunting fear that such a lot awaits them when journey's end is near." . . . But the practical effectuation of that judgment has of necessity called forth a highly complex and interrelated statutory structure.

. . . . .

To engraft upon the social security system a concept of "accrued property rights" would deprive it of the flexibility and boldness in adjustment to ever changing conditions which it demands. . . . It was doubtless out of an awareness of the need for such flexibility that Congress included in the original act, and has since retained, a clause expressly reserving to it "the right to alter, amend, or repeal any provision" of the act. . . . It was pursuant to that provision that § 202(n) was enacted.

We must conclude that a person covered by the act has not such a right in benefit payments as would make every defeasance of "accrued" interests violative of the due process clause of the Fifth Amendment.

This is not to say, however, that Congress may exercise its power to modify the statutory scheme free of all constitutional restraint. The interest of a covered employee under the act is of sufficient substance to fall within the protection from arbitrary governmental action afforded by the due process clause.

. . . . .

The remaining, and most insistently pressed, constitutional objections . . . [are] that the termination of appellee's benefits amounts to punishing him without a judicial trial . . . that the termination of benefits constitutes the imposition of punishment by legislative act, rendering § 202(n) a bill of attainder . . . and that the punishment exacted is imposed for past conduct not unlawful when engaged in, thereby violating the constitutional prohibition on ex post facto laws. . . . Essential to the success of each of these contentions is the validity of the characterizing as "punishment" in the constitutional sense the termination of benefits under § 202(n).

In determining whether legislation which bases a disqualification on the happening of a certain past event imposes a punishment, the Court has sought to discern the objects on which the enactment in question was focused.

. . . . .

Appellee cannot successfully contend that the language and structure of § 202(n), or the nature of the deprivation, require us to recognize a punitive design. . . . Here the sanction is the mere denial of a noncontractual governmental benefit. No affirmative disability or restraint is imposed, and certainly nothing approaching the "infamous punishment" of imprisonment.

. . . . .

We observe initially that only the clearest proof could suffice to establish the unconstitutionality of a statute on such a ground. Judicial inquiries into congressional motives are at best a hazardous matter, and when that inquiry seeks to go behind objective manifestations it becomes a dubious affair indeed. Moreover, the presumption of constitutionality with which this enactment, like any other, comes to us forbids us lightly to choose that reading of the statute's setting which will invalidate it over that which will save it.

・・・・・

Appellee argues that this history demonstrates that Congress was not concerned with the fact of a beneficiary's deportation—which it is claimed alone would justify this legislation as being pursuant to a policy relevant to regulation of the social security system—but that it sought to reach certain grounds for deportation, thus evidencing a punitive intent. It is impossible to find in this meager history the unmistakable evidence of punitive intent which. . .is required before a Congressional enactment of this kind may be struck down. . . . The legislative record . . . falls short of any persuasive showing that Congress was in fact concerned alone with the grounds of deportation. To be sure Congress did not apply the termination provision to all deportees. However, it is evident that neither did it rest the operation of the statute on the occurrence of the underlying act. The fact of deportation itself remained an essential condition for loss of benefits, and even if a beneficiary were saved from deportation only through discretionary suspension by the Attorney General under § 244 of the Immigration and Nationality Act . . . § 202(n) would not reach him.

・・・・・

The same answer must be made to arguments drawn from the failure of Congress to apply § 202(n) to beneficiaries voluntarily residing abroad. . . . Congress may have failed to consider such persons; or it may have thought their number too slight, or the permanence of their voluntary residence abroad too uncertain, to warrant application of the statute to them, with its attendant administrative problems of supervision and enforcement. Again, we cannot with confidence reject all these alternatives which imaginativeness can bring to mind, save that one which might require the invalidation of the statute.

Reversed.

Mr. Justice Black, dissenting.

For the reasons stated here and in the dissents of Mr. Justice Douglas and Mr. Justice Brennan I agree with the district court that the United States is depriving appellee, Ephram Nestor, of his statutory right to old-age benefits in violation of the United States Constitution . . . [and that doing so] takes Nestor's insurance without just compensation and in violation of the due process clause of the Fifth Amendment. Moreover, it imposes an ex post facto law and bill of attainder by stamping him, without a court trial, as unworthy to receive that for which he has paid and which the government

*promised to pay him. . . . This, in my judgment, reveals a complete misun-
derstanding of the purpose Congress and the country had in passing that
law. It was then generally agreed, as it is today, that it is not desirable
that aged people think of the government as giving them something for
nothing. . . . The people covered by this act are now able to rely with
complete assurance on the fact that they will be compelled to contribute
regularly to this fund whenever each contribution falls due. I believe they
are entitled to rely with the same assurance on getting the benefits they
have paid for and have been promised, when their disability or age makes
their insurance payable under the terms of the law.*

The real constitutional question in *Flemming v. Nestor* was whether
Congress had passed an ex post facto law, one that changes the legal
consequences of a fact or act after the occurrence of the fact or the commission of the act. Because being a Communist was not a crime at the
time that Nestor was a member of the party, he argued that he was being
punished for something that was not criminal. He also argued that the
statute creates a *bill of attainder*, pronouncing someone guilty of a crime
without trial or conviction, in this case penalizing him by depriving him
of his social security benefits. The court refused to find punishment to
be a congressional purpose, although not everyone who is deported suffers a loss of benefits; social security benefits may even be mailed outside the country.

Flemming v. Nestor has not been overruled, although the legislation it
challenged is a product of the post–World War II communism scare. The
case holds that the right to social security benefits is not a vested property right, but more like a privilege. The rights acquired by individuals
under these programs are mere statutory rights, because there is no express contract of insurance in the traditional meaning of insurance. Except for *Flemming v. Nestor*, Congress has regularly moved to increase
coverage and extend entitlement. Given the political implications of removing a profession from coverage or limiting eligibility, we may expect
that the program will continue to expand.

Status

An individual's right to social security benefits, which is clearly defined
in the law, can be objectively determined: the number of quarters of
coverage—three-month periods of employment covered by the law—the
individual has, the income earned in those quarters, and the rate at which
this income was taxed. Others, such as dependents and survivors, may
be entitled to receive benefits on a particular wage earner's record, depending on their relationship to the wage earner. Thus, a wife who reaches

a certain age may receive a retirement benefit if her husband is also receiving a retirement benefit. *Rosenberg v. Richardson* (1976) illustrates how complicated this may be. The claimant's 36-year marriage to the deceased had been rendered illegal because his prior Mexican divorce was invalid; the court granted her the entire widow's benefit, deducting only that portion being applied to augment the amount the original wife was receiving on her own social security account. Because state family law is often confusing, Congress has authorized payment to a woman "deemed" a wife until a "legal" widow makes application. This case permits payment of the entire benefit even though it is divided between two "wives."

A widow may receive a mother's benefit if her children are receiving survivor's benefits; this depends on the relationship to the wage earner and not on the recipients' dependence. A legitimate minor living with the mother after her divorce may receive survivor's benefits after the father's death on the father's wage record, even though he or she received no child support from the father when he was alive. The same would be true of benefits from a deceased mother. A wife, divorced after 10 years of marriage, may receive benefits when her ex-husband receives his own retirement benefits even though his present wife is also receiving a wife's benefits and even though the divorced wife received no alimony from the ex-husband. Payment of benefits to a divorced wife and illegitimate children also has been liberalized over the years.

Receipt of benefits depends on the relationship to the wage earner and on the age of the recipient. Relationship depends on whether there was a valid marriage and whether a child was legitimate or illegitimate and is usually a matter of state law. However, the Social Security Act provides for illegitimate children. If any of your clients are denied social security benefits on a wage earner's records, refer them to an attorney for examination of current laws.

The following case shows how the court interprets social security provisions for survivors and dependents.

Weinberger v. Wisenfeld
420 U.S. 636, 95 S. Ct. 1225, 43 L.Ed.2d 514 (1975)
Brennan, J.
Social Security Act benefits based on the earnings of a deceased husband and father covered by the act are payable, with some limitations, both to the widow and to the couple's minor children in her care. . . . Such benefits are payable on the basis of the earnings of a deceased wife and mother covered by the act, however, only to the minor children and not to the widower. The question in this case is whether this gender-based distinction violates the due process clause of the Fifth Amendment.

Appellee Stephen C. Wisenfeld and Paula Polatschek were married on November 5, 1970. Paula, who worked as a teacher for five years before her marriage, continued teaching after her marriage. Each year she worked, maximum social security contributions were deducted from her salary. Paula's earnings were the couple's principal source of support during the marriage, being substantially larger than those of appellee.

On June 5, 1972, Paula died in childbirth. Appellee was left with the sole responsibility for the care of their infant son, Jason Paul. Shortly after his wife's death, Stephen Wisenfeld applied at the social security office in New Brunswick, New Jersey, for social security survivor's benefits for himself and his son. He did obtain benefits for his son under 42 U.S.C. § 402(d) and received for Jason $206.90 per month until September, 1972, and $248.30 per month thereafter. However, appellee was told that he was not eligible for benefits for himself, because § 402(g) benefits were available only to women. If he had been a woman, he would have received the same amount as his son as long as he was not working . . . and, if working, that amount reduced by $1.00 for every $2.00 earned annually above $2,400.

· · · · ·

Appellee filed this suit in February, 1973, claiming jurisdiction under 28 U.S.C. § 1331, on behalf of himself and of all widowers similarly situated. He sought a declaration that § 402(g) is unconstitutional to the extent that men and women are treated differently, an injunction restraining appellant from denying benefits under 42 U.S.C. § 402(g) solely on the basis of sex, and payment of past benefits commencing with June, 1972, the month of the original application.

· · · · ·

Section 420(g) was added to the Social Security Act in 1939 as one of a large number of amendments designed to "afford more adequate protection to the family as a unit." . . . Monthly benefits were provided to wives, children, widows, orphans, and surviving dependent parents of covered workers. . . . However, children of covered women workers were eligible for survivor's benefits only in limited circumstances . . . and no benefits whatever were made available to husbands or widowers on the basis of the wives' covered employment.

Underlying the 1939 scheme was the principle that "under a social insurance plan, the primary purpose is to pay benefits in accordance with the probable needs of beneficiaries rather than to make payments to the estate of a deceased person regardless of whether or not he leaves dependents." . . . Thus, the framers of the act legislated on the "then generally accepted presumption that a man is responsible for the support of his wife and child."

· · · · ·

Obviously, the notion that men are more likely than women to be the primary supporters of their spouses and children is not entirely without empirical support. . . . But such a gender-based generalization cannot suffice to justify the denigration of the efforts of the women who do work and whose earnings contribute significantly to their families' support. . . . The Constitution also forbids the gender-based differentiation that results in the efforts of women workers required to pay social security taxes producing less protection for their families than is produced by the efforts of men.

Appellant seeks to avoid this conclusion with two related arguments. First, he claims that because social security benefits are not compensation for work done, Congress is not obliged to provide a covered female employee with the same benefits as it provides to a male. Second, he contends that § 402(g) was "reasonably designed to offset the adverse economic situation of women by providing a widow with financial assistance to supplement or substitute for their own efforts in the market place." . . . and therefore does not contravene the equal protection guarantee.

⁙ ⁙

We do not see how the fact that social security benefits are "non-contractual" can sanction differential protection for covered employees which is solely gender-based. From the outset, social security, old age, disability, and survivor's (OASDI) benefits have been "afforded as a matter of right, related to past participation in the productive processes of the country." . . . It is true that social security benefits are not necessarily related directly to tax contributions, since the OASDI system is structured to provide benefits in part according to presumed need. . . . But the fact remains that the statutory right to benefits is directly related to years worked and amount earned by a covered employee, and not to the need of the beneficiaries directly. Since OASDI benefits do depend significantly upon the participation in the work force of a covered employee, and since only covered employees and not others are required to pay taxes toward the system, benefits must be distributed according to classifications which do not without sufficient justification differentiate among covered employees solely on the basis of sex.

Appellant seeks to characterize the classification here as one reasonably designed to compensate women beneficiaries as a group for the economic difficulties which still confront women who seek to support themselves and their families. . . . But the mere recitation of a beneficial compensatory purpose is not an automatic shield which protects against any inquiry into the actual purposes underlying a statutory scheme. Here, it is apparent both from the statutory scheme itself and from the legislative history of § 402(g) that Congress' purpose in providing benefits to young widows with children was not to provide an income to women who were, because of economic discrimination, unable to provide for themselves. Rather, § 402(g), linked as it is directly to responsibility for minor children, was intended to permit women to elect not to work and to devote themselves to the care of children. Since this purpose in no way is premised upon any special disadvantages of women, it cannot serve to justify a gender-based distinction which diminishes the protection afforded to women who do work.

That the purpose behind § 402(g) is to provide children deprived of one parent with the opportunity for the personal attention of the other could not be more clear in the legislative history.

· · · · ·

Indeed, consideration was given in 1939 to extending benefits to all widows regardless of whether or not there were children. The proposal was rejected, apparently because it was felt that young widows without children can be expected to work, while middle-aged widows "are likely to have more savings than young widows, and many of them have children who are grown and able to help them." . . . Thus, Congress decided not to provide benefits to all widows even though it was recognized that some of them would have serious problems in the job market. Instead, it provided benefits only to those women who had responsibility for minor children, because it believed that they should not be required to work.

The whole structure of survivor's benefits conforms to this articulated purpose. Widows without minor children obtain no benefits on the basis of their husband's earnings until they reach age 60 or, in certain instances of disability, age 50. . . . Further, benefits under § 402(g) cease when all children of a beneficiary are no longer eligible for children's benefits. If Congress were concerned with providing women with benefits because of economic discrimination, it would be entirely irrational to expect those women who had spent many years at home rearing children [to work], since those women are most likely to be without the skills required to succeed in the job market. . . . Similarly, the act now provides benefits to a surviving divorced wife who is the parent of a covered employee's child, regardless of how long she was married to the deceased or of whether she or the child was dependent upon the employee for support. . . . Once again, this distinction among women is explicable only because Congress was not concerned in § 402(g) with the employment problems of women generally but with the principle that children of covered employees are entitled to the personal attention of the surviving parent if that parent chooses not to work.

Given the purpose of enabling the surviving parent to remain at home to care for a child, the gender-based distinction of § 402(g) is entirely irrational. The classification discriminates among surviving children solely on the basis of the sex of the surviving parent. . . . It is no less important for a child to be cared for by its sole surviving parent when that parent is male

*rather than female. And a father, no less than a mother, has a constitu-
tionally protected right to the "companionship, care, custody, and management" of the "children he has sired and raised, [which] undeniably
warrants deference and, absent a powerful countervailing interest, protection."... Further, to the extent that women who work when they have sole
responsibility for children encounter special problems, it would seem that
men with sole responsibility for children will encounter the same child-
care related problems. Stephen Wisenfeld, for example, found that providing adequate care for his infant son impeded his ability to work.*

· · · · ·

*Since the gender-based classification of § 402(g) cannot be explained
as an attempt to provide for the special problems of women, it is indistinguishable from the classification held invalid in Frontiero. Like the statutes
there, "[by] providing dissimilar treatment for men and women who are . . .
similarly situated, the challenged section violated the [due process] clause."*
Affirmed.
Mr. Justice Powell, with whom the chief justice joins, concurring.
Mr. Justice Rehnquist, concurring in the result.

The case gives a good description of the various kinds of benefits
available to orphaned children, widows, and widowers. *Califano v.
Goldfarb* (1977) extended the invalidity of gender-based distinctions,
striking down the requirement that a widower, but not a widow, must
prove dependency to receive retirement benefits as the spouse of a covered worker. When a covered worker retires, a spouse who is at least age
60 is entitled to a retirement benefit. Until *Goldfarb* only wives were
entitled to these benefits; they got the greater of the two benefits related
to their husband's earnings and their own, should they have been in covered employment themselves. Until the Supreme Court struck down the
requirement, a husband was required to prove that he received over half
of his support from his wife, a requirement not demanded of women. In
Goldfarb the husband was covered under a federal retirement plan and
had no social security coverage of his own. The Supreme Court agreed
with the *Flemming v. Nestor* rationale that these are noncontractual benefits, but held that they must not be based on invalid classifications.

In an attempt to prevent sham marriages entered into simply to provide future benefits, Congress has defined "widow" and "child" to exclude wives and stepchildren who had their relationships to a deceased
wage earner for less than nine months before his death. The definition
was upheld in *Weinberger v. Salfi* (1975). The Court said that in social
welfare, the relationship requirement is constitutional if rationally based
and free from invidious discrimination. This was declared to be so in

Salfi, thus permitting the use of a conclusive presumption rather than requiring case-by-case determination of whether the marriage was entered into to receive benefits. Providing benefits for stepchildren who have not had a long relationship with a deceased stepparent may not be as appealing politically as providing benefits to adopted and illegitimate children. This, nevertheless, is the sort of problem that compels legislators to broaden coverage when a particularly tragic case comes to their attention.

The coverage of illegitimate and adopted children has gone through various stages. The rights of adopted children are usually protected, if the adoption has met all the requirements of state law. However, a child adopted after the wage earner became disabled is denied dependent's benefits, apparently to prevent adoption solely to receive benefits.

The treatment of illegitimate children depends on proof of paternity and certain statutory indicia of dependency. Although the Supreme Court in cases dealing with statutory grounds for exclusion from benefits has not held that illegitimacy is a "suspect classification" requiring "strict scrutiny," it has adopted a middle standard of review, first determining the "motivating purpose" of the statute and then measuring "the sufficiency of the justifications advanced for the remaining discrimination against illegitimate children . . . in light of this motivating purpose." This contrasts with the standard in *Dandridge v. Williams* (1970), where classifications in the area of economics and social welfare were upheld if merely rational (*Califano v. Boles*, 1979; Stengler, 1978).

Disability

When the Federal Disability Insurance Trust Fund was set up in 1956, it required an individual to be at least 50 years old before being eligible for disability benefits. The law has since been liberalized; benefits are now payable to anyone at any age who has the requisite amount of coverage and current attachment to the labor market—generally five years of work out of the last 10, although an individual who has worked for less than five years, such as the teenager who bags groceries or parks cars, may be covered with fewer quarters. The young person who is permanently and totally disabled by an automobile accident may be entitled to disability benefits.

To be covered, a disability must have lasted or be expected to last for 12 months or longer or be expected to result in death. The disability, whether physical or mental, must be severe enough to keep a person from engaging in activity that is both substantial and gainful. If an individual, bedridden and helpless, is able to earn some money, the activity may be considered gainful and the individual ineligible. The test is individualized: A social worker who is blinded may be able to engage in substantial gainful activity, whereas a laborer would not. The test is whether *this* individual with *these* limitations can work at any job in the national economy. A coal miner who cannot fulfill that job because of arthritis or emphysema may still be able to hold a sedentary job. Whether such a job is available for him is unimportant; disability benefits are not a substitute for unemployment compensation. As a practical matter, some people who are partially disabled may be unemployable, because despite the Americans with Disabilities Act an employer is likely to prefer a fully abled individual over a person with disabilities.

Determining someone to be disabled by alcoholism or drug abuse is particularly troublesome, because the disability seems self-inflicted and the benefits seem to encourage further addiction. Usually these illnesses are accompanied by other physical or mental disabilities, often the result of the addiction but also disabling in themselves. In *Adams v. Weinberger* (1977), however, Adams seemed to have no significant organ damage that precluded work activity; his entire disability was alcoholism. The case was remanded for consideration of whether his inability to stop drinking or to recognize it was a problem-evidenced illness; the court held that continued payment of benefits could be conditioned on his undertaking treatment. Drug addicts and alcoholics may not receive Supplemental Security Income benefits unless they are undergoing treatment.

Because the test for disability involves looking at the limitations of the particular applicant, social workers can help clients by collecting the kinds of information that will prove disability. Education, types of jobs held, ability to perform household tasks, and testimony verifying the existence of pain all may be necessary to establish disability.

Adult offspring may receive disability benefits from the wage record of a parent, even though they have no work record themselves. These benefits are payable when the parent dies or starts drawing disability or retirement benefits. However, the adult child's disability must have existed before age 22. This social insurance program is available to the eligible adult with mental retardation or others whether or not they receive Supplemental Security Income benefits.

In *Califano v. Jobst* (1977) the Supreme Court held that an adult child receiving disabled child's insurance benefits may be denied them on marriage to a nonbeneficiary. The Court reasoned that Congress could have concluded that a child who marries is no longer dependent on parents but on the spouse and that on the spouse's death the disabled survivor can rely on savings or benefits derived from the spouse. In *McMahon v. Califano* (1979) the court of appeals held constitutional a regulation providing that marriage to a noneligible spouse permanently bars the child from insurance benefits. The facts in both cases are typically heartrending. Ask yourself whether you could advise a disabled client to enter a marital relationship, no matter how personally satisfying, that carries such a price tag.

Asch and Mudrick (1995) discussed the area of disability and included tables giving the age and income of people with disabilities, various demographic characteristics, and the most prevalent disorders. They also discussed the civil rights protections for people with disabilities, including the Architectural Barriers Act of 1968, the Rehabilitation Act of 1973, the Education for All Handicapped Children Act of 1975, and the Americans with Disabilities Act of 1990. Social workers should be familiar with this legislation if they are working to help people with disabilities enter the work force.

MEDICARE AND MEDICAID

The high cost of medical care is a continuing problem. Many Western nations have national health care systems. In the United States, much of a covered individual's medical bill is paid by private health insurance. For those whose jobs do not cover them under a group plan and whose income or current health does not permit coverage by private insurance, states and localities provide public health care. Some states support hospitals that accept patients on a charity basis; others provide for a sliding-scale arrangement, with patients required to pay as much of the medical bill as they can afford.

After the passage of the Hospital Survey and Construction (Hill–Burton) Act of 1946 through the early 1960s, there were efforts to pass comprehensive health insurance without success (McKinney, 1987). The Kerrs–Mills bill passed in 1960. This became the Medical Assistance Act and expanded the public assistance section of the Social Security Act for people ages 65 and over who did not qualify for old-age assistance. Efforts were made during the Kennedy and Johnson administrations to pass non-means-tested benefits for older Americans without much success.

Hospitals receiving Hill–Burton funds were required to provide a certain amount of care to indigent people. Arizona attempted to control its costs by providing that a county hospital need not accept an indigent person for nonemergency hospitalization or medical care at the county's expense unless the individual had one year's residence in the county. In *Memorial Hosp. v. Maricopa County* (1974) the Supreme Court held that the residency requirement created an invidious classification that impinged on the right of interstate travel by denying newcomers the basic necessities of life. Absent a compelling state interest, it was an unconstitutional violation of the equal protection clause.

Funds for building hospital facilities did not meet the spiraling costs of hospitalization and physicians' services; therefore, in 1965, the Social Security Act was amended to create the Federal Hospital Insurance Trust Fund and the Federal Supplementary Insurance Trust Fund to protect workers against the high cost of health care in old age. Benefits for both hospital and medical health insurance for people age 65 and older are paid from these two funds, as well as benefits for certain other groups. Special payroll taxes and voluntary monthly premiums finance the hospital insurance benefits. The Supplementary Medical Insurance Trust Fund is made up of premiums of those people automatically enrolled because of entitlement to hospital benefits, premiums from others who voluntarily enroll, and matching amounts from the federal government. The new funds provided a kind of national health insurance for one group—aged workers and their dependent spouses—but extending national health insurance to other groups has met with political opposition (Harris, 1966)

Medicaid (Title XIX of the Social Security Act) is a program of grants to the states to provide medical assistance to individuals at or below the poverty line, including those receiving Supplemental Security Income because of blindness or disability and those receiving Aid to Families with Dependent Children. States may use the grants to help meet the medical bills of needy individuals not otherwise eligible for public welfare benefits because, for example, their family is intact, or their income is excessive.

Sullivan v. Zebley (1990) was a class action challenging the regulations for determining whether a child is disabled for receipt of SSI Medicaid benefits. Since the decision, the Social Security Administration is using a more realistic evaluation, looking to the impact of the impairment on the normal daily activities of a child of the claimant's age, similar to the way it looks at the impact of an adult's impairment on his or her ability to perform any substantial gainful work. Weishaupt and Rains (1991) discussed the case and federal disability programs in general and referenced the *Code of Federal Regulations* provisions that can be used to evaluate limitations. The authors also discussed the development of new regulatory standards that consider many factors.

A special feature of the Social Security Act is provision for payment of medical bills for individuals under age 65 who receive hemodialysis treatment or a kidney transplant. These medical procedures are especially expensive: Although it singles out only one procedure, the provision seems to step toward a universal medical insurance program, even though it covers only extraordinary medical expenses.

The Medicare supplemental medical insurance provisions were challenged in *Mathews v. Diaz* (1976). The act qualifies for enrollment in the Medicare program residents of the United States who are age 65 or older, but aliens are eligible only if they have been admitted for permanent residence and have resided in the United States for at least five years. The Court pointed out that Congress has the power to make rules regarding aliens that would be unacceptable if applied to citizens and has no constitutional duty to provide all aliens with the welfare benefits provided to citizens.

The Medicaid regulations have been challenged as well as the statute. The Supplemental Security Income assistance program requires the states to supplement these payments with state assistance for recipients who would have less income under the new federal program than they had been receiving as aged, blind, or disabled recipients under the former state program. In *Hayes v. Stanton* (1975) the federal court held that these categorically needy recipients were not required to make a "spend down" payment to use up excess income as a condition for receiving Medicaid benefits. *Hayes* contrasts with *Friedman v. Berger* (1976), where the court distinguished the categorically needy from the medically needy. Medically needy people are those whose annual income is too low to meet their medical expenses, for example, the enormous cost of institutional care, but too high to qualify them for Supplemental Security Income. For those receiving care for chronic illnesses in medical institutions, the "spend-down" requirement, which left them $38 over and above the cost of their care, was permissible.

Note that in *Schweiker v. Gray Panthers* (1981), the Supreme Court held that Medicaid regulations that permit the states to "deem" the spouse's income as "available" to the applicant were reasonable exercises of the power delegated to the Secretary of Health and Human Services.

In *Stanton v. Bond* (1974) welfare recipients and welfare rights organizations alleged denial of civil rights because the state had failed to implement an early and periodic screening, diagnosis, and treatment program in accordance with federal regulations. This requirement was added to the basic services of Medicaid in 1967, providing inpatient hospital services, outpatient hospital services, laboratory and X-ray services, skilled nursing home services, and physicians' services. States are not required to participate. If they do, the state administers the program using grants from the federal government. Early and periodic screening and diagnosis were added because the numbers of American children needing medical help was overwhelming (42 U.S.C. § 1396d(a) (4)(b)). In *Stanton* the court enjoined state officials from continuing to administer the state Medicaid program in violation of the statute, that is, without the screening program.

Health Maintenance Organizations

A health maintenance organization (HMO) is an entity that undertakes to provide substantially all the health care needed by a defined enrolled population. Its purpose is prevention rather than treatment. A single fee is collected in advance from enrollees, who then receive total health care. Proponents of these plans claim that they eliminate the incentive for physicians and hospitals to provide unnecessary services, that they provide for economies of scale and might increase price competition among insurers and providers, and that they make it easier for consumers to gain access to the medical care system because all care comes from a single source.

The Health Maintenance Organization Act of 1975 committed the federal government to trial support of the development of these organizations. Prototypical alternatives to fee-for-service medical care were the Kaiser Foundation health plan established in Oakland, California, in 1942, and the Roos-Loos Medical Clinic established in Los Angeles in 1929.

The federal HMO law overrides certain restrictive state laws, providing money for development and mandating that certain employers make HMO coverage an optional part of their employee benefit plans. The act authorized the U.S. Department of Health, Education, and Welfare to make grants and loans to help cover developmental costs for qualified public and nonprofit HMOs serving medically underserved populations. The act was amended in 1976 to deny Public Health Service grants to any state that did not include a federally qualified HMO option in any health benefit plan offered to state and local government employees. HMOs are now operating in all communities, so both requirements are probably now moot.

It may still be too early to judge the impact of HMOs on the spiraling cost of health care services to the general population. They do, of course, provide medical care in one spot, but they do not address the problem of poor distribution of medical services, in which entire counties go without the services of a physician. A debate among professionals about HMO programs has raised many controversial questions (Havighurst, 1971). Several programs have been created to encourage HMO providers to contract with special needs providers such as Medicare (Trubek & Hoffman, 1994). Antitrust enforcement paved the way for development of HMOs because the McCarran–Ferguson Act exempted the "business of insurance" from the reach of antitrust laws if a state regulates that industry (McDavid, 1994). HMOs are organizations that accept contractual responsibility to ensure delivery of a stated range of comprehensive health care services to voluntarily enrolled patients who pay a prepaid, fixed fee for medical services. There are staff, independent practice, and group models. The defining characteristic is the relationship with participating physicians and the way the HMO finances this relationship (Cooper, 1994). In a recent federal court decision, the court ruled that a nonprofit HMO did not qualify for tax-exempt status because it served only its subscribers and arranged for provision of health care by third parties rather than providing it itself (Levine, 1993). This ruling clearly may retard the progress HMOs can make toward acquiring an equal role in modern health care delivery.

All the problems with the current plans may have become moot if the American Health Security Act President Clinton presented to the Congress in the fall of 1993 had been enacted. The act would have guaranteed comprehensive coverage for all American citizens and legal residents through a system of regional and corporate alliances that would organize the buying power of consumers. It continued the federalism evident in other programs, with a national board overseeing state systems and monitoring compliance. The act's provisions, as well as the health care reform proposals made by conservative and liberal democrats, Senate Republicans, and the House Republican Task Force, were discussed by Rappaport (1994). The problem of health care coverage was also discussed at the symposium "Ensuring (E)qual(ity) Health Care for Poor Americans" (1994).

Everyone would have been enrolled in a health plan unless covered under such government-sponsored health programs as Medicare or the programs offered by the U.S. Department of Defense, the Bureau of Veterans Affairs, and the Indian Health Service. Mental health services, substance abuse treatment, some dental services, and clinical prevention services would have been covered, although services thought to be not medically necessary, such as in vitro fertilization and sex change surgery, would not have been.

Hawaii already has near-universal health care. It may be a model for the rest of the country.

REFERENCES

Asch, A., & Mudrick, N. R. (1995). Disability. In R. L. Edwards (Ed.-in-Chief), *Encyclopedia of social work* (19th ed., Vol. 1, pp. 752–761). Washington, DC: NASW Press.

Cooper, M. G. (1994). A "new" approach in medical malpractice: The liability of HMOs for member physician negligence. *Detroit College of Law Review,* pp. 1263–1292.

Harris, R. (1966, July 2). Annals of legislation—Medicare. Part 1. *New Yorker, 42,* pp. 29–62.

Harris, R. (1966, July 9). Annals of legislation—Medicare. Part 2. *New Yorker, 42,* pp. 30–77.

Harris R. (1966, July 19). Annals of legislation—Medicare. Part 3. *New Yorker, 42,* pp. 35–91.

Harris R. (1966, July 23). Annals of legislation—Medicare. Part 4. *New Yorker, 42,* pp. 35–63.

Havighurst, C. (1971). Health maintenance organizations and the market for health services. *Law and Contemporary Problems, 35,* 716–795.

Levine, K. L. (1993). Geisinger health plan likely to adversely affect HMOs and other health organizations. *The Journal of Taxation, 79,* 90–98.

McDavid, J. L. (1994). Antitrust issues in health care reform. *DePaul Law Review, 43,* 1045–1080.

McKinney, E. A. (1987). Health planning. In A. Minahan (Ed.-in-Chief), *Encyclopedia of social work* (18th ed., Vol. 1, 714–720). Silver Spring, MD: National Association of Social Workers.

Meyer, D. R. (1995). Supplemental security income. In R. L. Edwards (Ed.-in-Chief), *Encyclopedia of social work* (19th ed., Vol. 3, pp. 2379–2385). Washington, DC: NASW Press.

Ozawa, M. N. (1995). Income security overview. In R. L. Edwards (Ed.-in-Chief), *Encyclopedia of social work* (19th ed., Vol. 2, pp. 1447–1484). Washington, DC: NASW Press.

Rappaport, A. M. (1994). Policy environment for health benefits: Implications for employer plans. *DePaul Law Review, 43,* 1107–1131.

Stengler, R. L. (1978). The Supreme Court and illegitimacy: 1968–1977. *Family Law Quarterly, 11,* 365–405.

Symposium: Ensuring (e)qual(ity) health care for poor Americans. (1994). *Brooklyn Law Review, 60,* 1–339.

Truber, L. G., & Hoffman, E. A. (1994). Searching for a balance in universal health care reform: Protection for the disenfranchised consumer. *DePaul Law Review, 43,* 1081–1106.

Weishaupt, R. P., & Rains, R. E. (1991). *Sullivan v. Zebley*: New disability standards for indigent children to obtain government benefits. *Saint Louis University Law Journal, 35,* 539–596.

STATUTES CITED

Architectural Barriers Act of 1968. P.L. 90-480, 82 Stat. 718.

Americans with Disabilities Act of 1990. P.L. 101-336, 42 U.S.C.S. 12101.

Education for All Handicapped Children Act of 1975. P.L. 94-142, 89 Stat. 773, 776, 794.

Health Maintenance Organization Act of 1973. P. L. 93-222, 87 Stat. 914, 12 U.S.C. § 1721.

Hospital Survey and Construction (Hill–Burton) Act of 1946. Ch. 958, 60 Stat. 1040.

Rehabilitation Act of 1973. P.L. 93-112, 87 Stat. 355.

Social Security Act of 1935, 42 U.S.C. § 301 et seq.

STUDY QUESTION

1. Does the right to social security benefits follow an individual all over the world?

14

Other Responses to Economic Problems

Loss of income is the presenting problem of many clients who come to public agencies. In the diagnostic process you discover that medical expenses, poor finance management, and lack of job skills all exacerbate the basic economic problem. The extravagant spouse and compulsive gambler are not unknown to marriage counselors. Impulsive or uninformed purchases contribute to mounting debt, and discriminatory hiring practices limit access to employment and government services. There are myriad causes of indigence.

In some rare instances you may conclude that money alone is the solution, although usually its lack is more a symptom than a cause. Economic issues cut across the range of problems social workers see. Our legal system provides certain programs to ameliorate these problems.

INCOME MAINTENANCE PROGRAMS

Loss of income from a major reversal in life is a risk everyone is exposed to. Both state and federal governments recognize some responsibility for relieving this loss, offering programs for temporary or permanent income replacement when an individual's own resources are inadequate because of unemployment, illness and disability, retirement, and (for dependents) death of the wage earner.

Public responsibility for the care of less-fortunate people has a long history. Imperial Rome had a program for the distribution of free grain; in the days of Augustus Caesar almost a third of the total population of Rome was receiving some kind of public assistance (Tannahil, 1973).

The Judeo–Christian heritage of charity includes the biblical exhortation to leave gleanings in the field for poor people and the development of monasteries whose prime function was caring for poor people and people with disabilities.

Our own concerns are contemporary. The real growth in public income-maintenance programs in the United States began with the passage of the Social Security Act in 1935. This legislation has been continually amended and expanded by Congress and broadened by judicial interpretation. Its basic provisions include a federal unemployment tax, a system of compulsory contributory taxes during the working life of an individual, survivor's benefits for spouse and children if the worker dies, benefits to the disabled worker, retirement income for the worker and spouse, funeral benefits, and grants-in-aid to the states to finance and administer a system of public welfare. This last program has been supplanted, except for Aid to Families with Dependent Children (AFDC), by the Supplemental Security Income (SSI) program, which offers income protection, unrelated to the labor market, for elderly, blind, or disabled individuals.

All the public income-maintenance programs present legal problems of interest to social workers. Because guarantees of due process and equal protection apply in any public program, those that combat particular social problems must do so within a constitutional framework. Administrators responsible for delivering services must consider the legal problems presented by coverage, financing, and individual rights to better use the limited tax funds at their disposal. Are these programs the best possible way to accomplish their purpose? If not, how can we fashion better ones?

Public Welfare

Poor people are extremely heterogeneous. Their poverty may be situational; it may derive from labor market discrimination; or it may be caused by personal traits, emotional disorders, or disability. Industrial accidents, leaving in their wake disabled wage earners and dependent children, can also contribute to the lack of economic security.

In the past, governments have tried various means to care for poor people and people with disabilities. Some governments established almshouses and poor farms; others provided food, shelter, and clothing either through distribution of commodities or surplus clothing or through outright money grants. In addition, private charitable programs grew to meet recognized local needs. For instance, churches developed orphanages to care for children whose parents had died in epidemics or industrial accidents (Rauch, 1976; Trolander, 1973).

Origins of public welfare. Public welfare or public assistance is a program for providing economic security for individuals who, for reasons beyond their control, either are not now or never have been in the labor market. Much American public welfare legislation comes from English laws brought by settlers to this country.

In 1388 during the reign of Richard II, an act was passed to prohibit vagrancy and wandering about the country. The act provided that beggars "impotent to serve" were to remain in the place where they were staying at the time of the proclamation of the act; if they could not be maintained there, they would be sent back to their birthplace.

The Elizabethan Act of 1601, for the relief of poor people, remained in force with countless amendments for nearly 350 years, until it was superseded by the National Assistance Act of 1948. The act required justices of the peace to appoint in every parish overseers of the poor, made tax assessment compulsory, set up methods of caring for certain needy populations, and obliged certain enumerated relatives to support needy members. In 1662 Charles II enacted the law of settlement, an expansion of the 1388 vagrancy law, which empowered justices of the peace to return to their former home any newcomers who the overseer thought might become public charges. Thus, the early English laws for the relief of poor people were essentially the responsibility of local government, safeguarded by the principles of settlement and removal and primary family responsibility (Clarke, 1957). Vestiges of these poor laws remain in our income-maintenance programs and other forms of social legislation (Pumphrey & Pumphrey, 1961).

Modern public welfare. The passage of the Social Security Act in 1935 introduced a new type of cooperative federalism. In mandating public assistance, the act devised a system of grants-in-aid to help the states meet their relief burden (Handler & Goodstein, 1968; Wisner, 1970). A state could receive from the federal government a percentage of the money it spent on public assistance if its plan for meeting the relief burden met federal requirements. The state plan had to

> *(1) be in effect in all political subdivisions of the state, and, if administered by them, be mandatory upon them; (2) provide financial participation by the state; (3) either provide for the establishment or designation of a single state agency to administer the plan or provide for the establishment or designation of a single state agency to supervise the administration of the plan; (4) provide for granting any individual, whose claim for aid is denied, an opportunity for a hearing before such state agency; (5) provide such methods of administration as are found by the board to be necessary for efficient operation of the plan. (Social Security Act, § 454)*

These requirements still exist for grants-in-aid for state medical assistance and Aid to Families with Dependent Children programs. Programs for old age assistance and aid to people who are blind or disabled were subsumed by the federal government into the SSI program.

The current maximum SSI grant, obtained through the social security office, is $458. Income and assets are considered. When real property cannot be sold for some reason, its value is excluded from consideration as a resource in determining SSI benefits. State funds supplemented by federal funds pay for the grants.

Individuals receiving grants because of disability may apply for rehabilitative services; many of these individuals are referred by private agencies, hospitals, schools, or interested persons.

The AFDC regulations require the state to consider the family's income and resources. Minor siblings who reside with children applying for AFDC must be included in the unit and their income, such as child support and social security, must be counted in determining financial eligibility. In *Lukhard v. Reed* (1986) the Supreme Court allowed Virginia to treat personal injury awards as income, denying eligibility for as many months as the income would last if recipients spent an amount equal to the state's standard of need for each month. The goal was to correct any tendency to spend the acquired income rapidly to regain eligibility. If you have clients who anticipate a windfall, explore the state regulations to make sure your advice is current. Note that in *Heckler v. Turner* (1985) the Court held that the state agency must treat mandatory tax withholding from wages as a work expense in calculating a family's need for AFDC.

Residence requirements and other eligibility conditions. All programs of public assistance present policymakers with painful choices. One way to limit coverage and so reduce state tax expenditures is to require that those individuals who receive public welfare be residents of the state, a provision born of the settlement-law portion of the poor laws, which permitted the return to a former home of any newcomer who might become a public charge. This requirement's justification is that the state's taxpayers are willing to support only those indigent people who once may have been state taxpayers themselves. The *Shapiro v. Thompson* case (1969), a landmark in public welfare, consolidated cases from two states and the District of Columbia dealing with the residence requirements.

Shapiro v. Thompson
394 U.S. 618, 89 S. Ct. 1322, 22 L.Ed.2d 600 (1969)
Brennan, J.
Each is an appeal from a decision of a three judge district court holding unconstitutional a state or District of Columbia statutory provision which

denies welfare assistance to residents of the state or district who have not resided within their jurisdictions for at least one year immediately preceding their applications for such assistance. We affirm the judgments of the district courts in the three cases.

· · · · ·

There is no dispute that the effect of the waiting-period requirement in each case is to create two classes of needy resident families indistinguishable from each other except that one is composed of residents who have resided a year or more, and the second of residents who have resided less than a year, in the jurisdiction. On the basis of this sole difference the first class is granted and the second class is denied welfare aid upon which may depend the ability of the families to obtain the very means to subsist—food, shelter, and other necessities of life.

· · · · ·

Primarily, appellants justify the waiting-period requirement as a protective device to preserve the fiscal integrity of state public assistance programs. It is asserted that people who require welfare assistance during their first year of residence in a state are likely to become continuing burdens on state welfare programs. Therefore, the argument runs, if such people can be deterred from entering the jurisdiction by denying them welfare benefits during the first year, state programs to assist long-time residents will not be impaired by a substantial influx of indigent newcomers.

· · · · ·

We do not doubt that the one-year waiting period is well suited to discourage the influx of poor families in need of assistance. An indigent who desires to migrate, resettle, find a new job, and start a new life will doubtless hesitate if he knows that he must risk making that move without the possibility of falling back on state welfare assistance during the first year of residence, when his needs may be most acute. But the purpose of inhibiting migration by needy persons into a state is constitutionally impermissible.

This Court long ago recognized that the nature of our federal union and our constitutional concepts of personal liberty unite to require that all citizens be free to travel throughout the length and breadth of our land uninhibited by statutes, rules, or regulations which unreasonably burden or restrict this movement.

· · · · ·

Alternatively, appellants argue that even if it is impermissible for a state to attempt to deter the entry of all indigents, the challenged classification may be justified as a permissible state attempt to discourage those indigents who would enter the state solely to obtain larger benefits. We observe first that none of the statutes before us is tailored to serve that objective. Rather, the class of barred newcomers is all-inclusive, lumping the great majority who come to the state for other purposes with those who come for the sole purpose of collecting higher benefits. In actual operation, therefore, these statutes enact what in effect are non-rebuttable presumptions that every applicant for assistance in his first year of residence comes to the jurisdiction solely to obtain higher benefits.

· · · · ·

More fundamentally, a state may no more try to fence out those indigents who seek higher welfare benefits than it may pay to fence out indigents generally. Implicit in any such distinction is the notion that indigents who enter a state with the hope of securing higher welfare benefits are somehow less deserving than indigents who do not take this consideration into account. But we do not perceive why a mother who is seeking to make a new life for herself and her children should be regarded as less deserving because she considers, among other factors, the level of a state's public assistance. Surely such a mother is no less deserving than a mother who moves into a particular state in order to take advantage of its better educational facilities.

Appellants argue further that the challenged classification may be sustained as an attempt to distinguish between new and old residents on the basis of the contribution they have made to the community through the payment of taxes. We have difficulty seeing how long-term residents who qualify for welfare are making a greater present contribution to the state in taxes than indigent residents who have recently arrived. If the argument is based on contributions made in the past by the long-term residents, there is some question, as a factual matter, whether this argument is applicable in Pennsylvania where the record suggests that some 40 percent of those denied public assistance because of the waiting period had lengthy prior residence in the state. But we need not rest on the particular facts of these cases. Appellants' reasoning would logically permit the state to bar new residents from schools, parks, and libraries or deprive them of police and fire protection. Indeed it would permit the state to apportion all benefits and services according to the past tax contributions of its citizens. The equal protection clause prohibits such an apportionment of state services.

We recognize that a state has a valid interest in preserving the fiscal integrity of its programs. It may legitimately attempt to limit it expenditures, whether for public assistance, public education, or any other program. But a state may not accomplish such a purpose by invidious distinctions between classes of its citizens. It could not, for example, reduce expenditures for education by barring indigent children from its schools. Similarly, in the cases before us, appellants must do more than show that denying welfare benefits to new residents saves money. The saving of welfare costs cannot be an independent ground for an invidious classification.

The argument that the waiting period requirement facilitates budget predictability is wholly unfounded. The records in all three cases are utterly devoid of evidence that either state or the District of Columbia in fact uses the one-year requirement as a means to predict the number of people who will require assistance in the budget year.

. . . . .

The argument that the waiting period serves as an administratively efficient rule of thumb for determining residency similarly will not withstand scrutiny. The residence requirement and the one-year waiting-period requirement are distinct and independent prerequisites for assistance under these three statutes, and the facts relevant to the determination of each are directly examined by the welfare authorities. Before granting an application, the welfare authorities investigate the applicant's employment, housing, and family situation and in the course of the inquiry necessarily learn the facts upon which to determine whether the applicant is a resident.

Similarly, there is no need for a state to use the one-year waiting period as a safeguard against fraudulent receipt of benefits; for less drastic means are available, and are employed, to minimize that hazard. . . . Since double payments can be prevented by a letter or a telephone call, it is unreasonable to accomplish this objective by the blunderbuss method of denying assistance to all indigent newcomers for an entire year.

Pennsylvania suggests that the one-year waiting period is justified as a means of encouraging new residents to join the labor force promptly. But this logic would also require a similar waiting period for long-term residents of the state. A state purpose to encourage employment provides no rational basis for imposing a one-year waiting period restriction on new residents only.

We conclude therefore that appellants in these cases do not use and have no need to use the one-year requirement for the governmental purposes suggested. Thus, even under traditional equal protection tests a classification of welfare applicants according to whether they have lived in the state for one year would seem irrational and unconstitutional. But, of course, the traditional criteria do not apply in these cases. Since the classification here touches on the fundamental right of interstate movement, its constitutionality must be judged by the stricter standard of whether it promotes a compelling state interest. Under this standard, the waiting period requirement clearly violates the equal protection clause.

Finally, even if it could be argued that the constitutionality of § 402(b) [the argument was that Congress in the Social Security Act had approved state plans with residence requirements] is somehow at issue here, it follows from what we have said that the provision, insofar as it permits the

one-year waiting-period requirement, would be unconstitutional. Congress may not authorize the states to violate the equal protection clause. Perhaps Congress could induce wider state participation in school construction if it authorized the use of joint funds for the building of segregated schools. But could it seriously be contended that Congress would be constitutionally justified in such authorization by the need to secure state cooperation? Congress is without power to enlist state cooperation in a joint federal–state program by legislation which authorizes the states to violate the equal protection clause.
[Chief Justice Warren, and Justices Black and Harlan dissented.]

The description of the situation of the applicants for assistance, which is omitted, contains a history of illness, admission to mental hospitals, and moving to find a better job and to be nearer relatives, that is familiar to any social worker. Notice that the Court used the equal protection clause of the Fourteenth Amendment as the rationale for its decision. When a state must classify, the classification need not always be perfect. This classification distinguished between people who had and had not lived within the state more than a year. If a distinction impinges on a fundamental right, it must be justified by a compelling state interest. The fundamental right here was the right to travel freely throughout the country. The state interest in easing administration and saving money was not considered compelling enough to overcome this basic right.

In dissent Chief Justice Warren wrote: "The Court's decision reveals only the top of the iceberg. Lurking beneath are the multitude of situations in which states have imposed residence requirements including eligibility to vote, to engage in certain professions or occupations or to attend a state-supported university" (89 S.Ct. at 1342). As Chief Justice Warren anticipated, the *Shapiro* rationale has been used to attack such laws.

Residency requirements. Two years after *Shapiro* the Supreme Court had to decide whether a state could condition welfare benefits on United States citizenship or on residency within the United States for a specified number of years (*Graham v. Richardson*, 1971). In a unanimous opinion by Justice Blackmun, the Court said no, because either condition would violate the Fourteenth Amendment: Because an alien is a person for equal protection purposes, state concern for fiscal integrity is no more compelling a justification for the classification than in *Shapiro*.

The Supreme Court has since said that a state may not seek to "fence out" those indigent people who migrate solely in pursuit of larger welfare benefits (*Wyman v. Owens*, 1970) and that durational residency requirements are also impermissible under locally funded general assistance programs (*Pease v. Hansen*, 1971); the Court upheld without opinion invalidation of statutes that the New York and Connecticut legislatures had claimed were "an essential step in protecting . . . the economic and social viability" of their states. Both states had imposed durational residence requirements for five-year "emergency periods" (*Dunn v. Rivera,* 1972; *Wyman v. Lopez,* 1972). (See *Gaddis v. Wyman,* 1969, for a full discussion of the issue.)

The *Shapiro* rationale has been used in areas completely apart from welfare benefits. For instance, residency requirements for voting are now limited to a minimum administrative period—only long enough to permit officials to check the rolls (*Dunn v. Blumstein,* 1972).

The purpose of the National Voter Registration Act of 1993 was to increase the number of eligible citizens who register to vote. Therefore, citizens can register to vote when they apply for a driver's license, by mail, and in person. To ensure that eligible applicants are registered, the act requires that the motor vehicle application be submitted, the form postmarked, or the applicant appear at a registration office not later than the lesser of 30 days or the period provided by state law before the election.

The rationale of *Shapiro* does not invalidate all residency requirements. The Wisconsin Supreme Court upheld the state settlement law in *In re Reitz* (1971). The Reitzes, husband and wife, lived and therefore had legal settlement for general relief purposes in the town of Vanden Broek. They moved to Milwaukee and stayed there for three years without finding work. During this period they received relief from Milwaukee County, which the town of Vanden Broek was required to repay. The town refused to continue reimbursing the county, because it was able to provide employment for the Reitzes. The town alleged that they were not denied benefits on the basis of residence because, regardless of legal settlement, eligible dependents were entitled to assistance. The town further alleged that if a dependent refuses to return to the place of legal settlement when this would not reduce employment and earning opportunities, materially disrupt family ties, or create any material injustice on him or her, that refusal will make the person ineligible for assistance. The Supreme Court dismissed the appeal (*Reitz v. VandenBrock,* 1972).

Cohabitation. Residence requirements, direct descendants of the Elizabethan poor laws, are one way states attempted to limit the number of people eligible for public assistance. Another was by a restrictive definition of a dependent child for the AFDC program. Because adult caretakers of these children are drawn from an age group presumptively employable, the program is especially vulnerable to the criticism that lack of restriction on expenditures increases taxes.

The "man-in-the-house" or "substitute-father" regulations that attempted to narrow the definition of dependent child are discussed in

King v. Smith (1968). The case challenged an Alabama regulation that will be familiar to social workers who have worked in public welfare for any length of time, because many states had similar regulations.

The regulation presumed that a child whose mother "cohabited"— had sexual relations—with a man was not deprived of parental support. The mother's paramour was presumed to be providing support, whether the relationship took place in or out of the home. Although the Court emphasized that regular and actual contributions to a needy child, including those from the person called a "substitute father," could be taken into account, there were no such contributions in *King*. Choosing to *construct*—interpret—the Social Security Act rather than the Constitution, the Court held that the term "parent" in the act included only those persons with a legal duty of support. However, a state can require that a parent must have been absent for a certain period before the child will be eligible for assistance. In *Smith v. Huecker* (1976) a federal court of appeals approved a 30-day period of absence as an eligibility requirement to determine the "continued absence from the home" of the parent.

Lewis v. Martin (1970) is a variation on the same theme. Under a California statute, implemented by administrative regulations, the needs of the dependent child were to be reduced by the income of a stepfather or an adult male assuming the role of spouse to the mother, even one not legally married to her. The Supreme Court held that unless there was proof of actual contributions, California could not consider a child's resources to include such income, because neither person was legally obligated to support the child.

In *Townsend v. Swank* (1971) Illinois extended benefits to needy dependent youths 18 through 20 years old attending high school or vocational training school but denied such benefits to youths attending a college or university. The Supreme Court held that under § 404(a)(10) of the Social Security Act, a state must provide aid to "all eligible individuals." If a state decided to extend benefits to the new age group, youths age 18 through 20, it could not do so in a way that conflicted with the federal statute and the supremacy clause. Eligible 18-year-olds attending college must be treated the same as those attending vocational school. The Supreme Court has also held that the statutory term "dependent child" does not include unborn children (*Burns v. Alcala,* 1975); states may exclude pregnant women from AFDC coverage because their children are not yet born.

In *Carelson v. Remillard* (1972) the court struck down as conflicting with the Social Security Act a California regulation excluding military service from the definition of the "continued absence" of a parent that qualified a child for benefits. In a Minnesota case, *Rosen v. Hursh* (1972), the stepfather, who had neither adopted his wife's children nor accepted legal responsibility for their support, refused to disclose the amount of his income. An AFDC grant was then terminated. The court struck down the regulation, saying "The practice of terminating AFDC benefits to children because their stepparent, over whose behavior they exercise no control, refuses to cooperate with welfare officials imposes a condition upon AFDC eligibility which is not contemplated by the act and which presents a significant obstacle to accomplishment of the act's goals" (464 F.2d at 735).

An attempt to avoid the requirement that states consider only income actually available to the needy child was struck down in *Nolan v. deBaca* (1979). The mother, an unemployed full-time student at the University of New Mexico, had no income of her own. Her husband, also a full-time student, worked part-time. He had not adopted his wife's children and under New Mexico law was not obligated to support them. New Mexico, as a community property state, determined that half of the husband's income was available to the wife. Her children were therefore not needy. The court held that only the husband *received* the income and did not voluntarily or regularly provide the children with support. The decision is important for those in other community property states, where similar attempts might be made to limit the number of AFDC-eligible dependent children.

A different approach to the "man in the house" was taken in New York, where "lodger" regulations required a pro rata reduction in the shelter allowance of a family receiving AFDC solely because a parent allowed someone not legally responsible for the family to reside in the home. New York argued that the presence of the lodger was evidence that the AFDC family had excess room and that its shelter allowance therefore exceeded its needs. The first footnote to the case, *Van Lare v. Hurley* (1975), reads "Petitioner Hurley's lodger was an unrelated male friend, petitioner Taylor's was her sister, and petitioner Otey's was her 23-year-old-son." The Supreme Court held that the New York regulation was invalid under the Social Security Act because it was based on the assumption that the nonpaying lodger was contributing to the welfare household, without any inquiry into whether the lodger in fact did so. The case illustrates the problems in devising a regulation to avoid supporting illicit unions with tax funds. The fact that the "lodgers" in two of the three cases consolidated for trial were relatives compounds the problem. The regulations relating to "households" in the food stamp cases that follow further illustrate the difficulty in drafting regulations distinguishing those to whom the public wishes to deny benefits, such as those involved in illicit unions, from the "deserving poor."

The problem of the "household" would be simplified if state law obligated a stepparent or a paramour to support the natural parent's children. Is this a desirable social policy? Could a state require that any man who *could* be the father of an illegitimate child, having had sexual relations with the mother at the appropriate time, support the child? If there were several men in this category, should all have to pay support? (see Breslin, 1966).

Connecticut adopted a regulation denying assistance to a mother who refused to name the father of her child. The regulation was held invalid; it created an eligibility requirement not authorized by federal statute (*Doe v. Harder*, 1970). Connecticut then enacted a criminal statute penalizing the mother of an illegitimate child who refused to name the father. In *Roe v. Norton* (1975) the Supreme Court vacated a judgment upholding that statute for reconsideration in light of the 1975 amendment to the Social Security Act, which required the parent to cooperate with the state in getting support from the other parent. Although her children may not be denied aid when the mother refuses to name the father, she may be denied aid.

Polls taken during the 1980s concerning public assistance showed a shift in public opinion toward doing more for poor people. A large percentage of people thought that welfare recipients cheat by getting money to which they are not entitled. In 1985, 36 percent of those polled approved of President Reagan's proposal to reduce spending on social services (Shapiro, Patterson, Russell, & Young, 1987).

The 1975 amendment to the Social Security Act was a response to public concern over parents who were failing to support their children. It required the state to demand child support from parents and to set up methods to establish the paternity of illegitimate children, whom the fathers would then be obligated to support. The statute permits the use of the social security number to trace parents who have abandoned their children, so that support proceedings can be brought against them in the new jurisdiction.

The Parent Locator Service (42 U.S.C.A. 653) has been amended several times since it was established in 1975. The secretary of the U.S. Department of Health and Human Services is authorized to obtain and transmit to any authorized person information about the whereabouts of the absent parent for the purpose of enforcing support obligations. The services can access wage and unemployment compensation claims information (Kessinger, 1993). Apparently, the Parent Locator Service has been successful in obtaining from absent parents sizable child-support payments. (If this is desirable social policy, should a similar locator service be established to find children and force them to support aged parents who are receiving SSI?) Although parental support of their minor children is desirable, the parents' responsibility is enforced only in the

AFDC program. The federal statute contains no penalties for a mother who refuses to name the presumed father of an illegitimate child; therefore, the problem the Connecticut statute was attempting to address remains.

The states do have some leeway in determining eligibility. In *Lavine v. Milne* (1976) applicants for New York home relief sought a declaration that the statute was unconstitutional in creating a "rebuttable presumption" that a person who applies for public assistance within 75 days of voluntary termination of employment has terminated employment for the purpose of qualifying. The Supreme Court allowed the state to place on applicants the burden of proving a permissible benefit-seeking motive.

Financing. Although public welfare programs are supported in large part by federal funds, the federal courts have traditionally left to the states decisions on how to use these and local tax funds, within the limits of due process and statutory interpretation of eligibility. A state may recognize a certain level of need for the basic necessities of food, clothing, and shelter and still not give large enough monetary benefits to enable recipients to acquire all these necessities. Besides giving only a percentage of recognized need, states in the past have been permitted to set a different percentage of need in different categories. The following case illustrates the rationale of the court for leaving to the states the method of distributing available funds.

Dandridge v. Williams
397 U.S. 471, 90 S. Ct. 1153 (1970)
Stewart, J.
This case involves the validity of a method used by Maryland, in the administration of an aspect of its public welfare program, to reconcile the demands of its needy citizens with the finite resources available to meet those demands. . . . Under [the AFDC program] a state computes the so-called "standard of need" for each eligible family unit within its borders. . . . Some states provide that every family shall receive grants sufficient to meet fully the determined standard of need. Other states provide that each family unit shall receive a percentage of the determined need. Still others provide grants to most families in full accord with the ascertained standard of need, but impose an upper limit on the total amount of money any one family unit may receive. Maryland, through administrative adoption of a "maximum grant regulation," has followed this last course.

· · · · ·

The operation of the Maryland welfare system is not complex. By statute the state participates in the AFDC program. It computes the standard of need for each eligible family based on the number of children in the family and the circumstances under which the family lives. In general, the *standard of need increases with each additional person in the household, but the increments become proportionately smaller. The regulation here in issue imposes upon the grant that any single family may receive an upper limit of $250 per month in certain counties including Baltimore City, and of $240 per month elsewhere in the state. The appellees all have large families, so that their standards of need as computed by the state substantially exceed the maximum grants that they actually receive under the regulation.*

• • • • •

Thus the starting point of the statutory analysis must be a recognition that the federal law gives each state great latitude in dispensing its available funds.

• • • • •

The states must respond to this federal statutory concern for preserving children in a family environment. Given Maryland's finite resources, its choice is either to support some families adequately and others less adequately, or not to give sufficient support to any family. We see nothing in the federal statute that forbids a state to balance the stresses that uniform insufficiency of payments would impose on all families against the greater ability of large families—because of the inherent economies of scale—to accommodate their needs to diminished per capita payments. The strong policy of the statute in favor of preserving family units does not prevent a state from sustaining as many families as it can and providing the largest families somewhat less than their ascertained per capita standard of need. Nor does the maximum grant system necessitate the dissolution of family bonds. For even if a parent should be inclined to increase his per capita family income by sending a child away, the federal law requires that the child, to be eligible for AFDC payments, must live with one of several enumerated relatives. The kinship tie may be attenuated but it cannot be destroyed.

The appellees rely most heavily upon the statutory requirement that aid "shall be furnished with reasonable promptness to all eligible individuals." . . . But since the statute leaves the level of benefits within the judgment of the state, this language cannot mean that the "aid" furnished must equal the total of each individual's standard of need in every family group. Indeed the appellees do not deny that a scheme of proportional reductions for all families could be used that would result in no individual's receiving aid equal to his standard of need. As we have noted, the practical effect of the Maryland regulation is that all children, even in very large families, do receive some aid. . . . So long as some aid is provided to all eligible families and all eligible children, the statute itself is not violated.

• • • • •

Although a state may adopt a maximum grant system in allocating its funds available for AFDC payments without violating the act, it may not,

*of course, impose a regime of invidious discrimination in violation of the
equal protection clause of the Fourteenth Amendment.*

• • • • •

*In the area of economics and social welfare, a state does not violate the
equal protection clause merely because the classifications made by its laws
are imperfect. If the classification has some "reasonable basis," it does not
offend the Constitution simply because the classification is not made with
mathematical nicety or because in practice it results in some inequality.*

• • • • •

*Under this long-established meaning of the equal protection clause, it
is clear that the Maryland maximum grant regulation is constitutionally
valid. [A] solid foundation for the regulation can be found in the state's
legitimate interest in encouraging employment and in avoiding discrimination between welfare families and the families of the working poor. By
combining a limit on the recipient's grant with permission to retain money
earned, without reduction in the amount of the grant, Maryland provides
an incentive to seek gainful employment. And by keying the maximum
family AFDC grants to the minimum wage a steadily employed head of a
household receives, the state maintains some semblance of an equitable
balance between families on welfare and those supported by an employed
breadwinner.*
[Justices Marshall and Brennan dissented.]

If the "intractable economic, social, and even philosophical problems
presented by public welfare assistance programs" are not the business of
the Supreme Court, whose business are they? Yours and mine?

The report of hearings before a Senate subcommittee on welfare research makes instructive reading ("Welfare Research," 1978). Ten years
of research on the negative income tax did not provide comforting answers to those who wanted a national income maintenance program for
the nation's poor people. Studies were conducted in New Jersey; rural
North Carolina and Iowa; Gary, Indiana; Seattle, Washington; and Denver, Colorado. A guaranteed income, instead of encouraging work and
self-sufficiency, produced substantial reductions in work effort and increased breakup of marriages. Why does welfare produce such results,
when it proceeds with best of intentions (Kristol, 1971)? The results imply that people will not work if provided a subsistence without work, that
teenagers do not seek education when they do not have to work to provide for themselves, and that these unfortunate results are compounded
among people of color.

Money alone is obviously not the answer. What *is* the answer for
social planners? Would social workers better use their professional

efforts in casework among the nation's welfare beneficiaries by encouraging them to develop personal resources and individual strengths to help better their lives?

Since the *Dandridge case*, states can classify with less-than-perfect limits, at least in the area of "economics and social welfare," in contrast to the *Shapiro* decision, where no limits were allowed on the fundamental right to travel freely. There is no fundamental right to public assistance.

In *Bowen v. Gilliard* (1987) the Court said that under the Deficit Reduction Act of 1984, for AFDC purposes families were to include all children living in the same home, including those for whom support payments were being received. Previously the client could exclude from the family unit a child for whom support payments were being made if it was financially advantageous. The change was held to meet Fifth Amendment due process and equal protections requirements because it serves the goals of decreasing federal expenditures and distributing benefits among competing needy families in a fair way.

Recipients of general assistance challenged the time limits on benefits in *Daugherty v. Wallace* (1993). The court held that the time limit did not violate the recipient's equal protection rights because under the state constitution Ohio did not have an affirmative duty to provide assistance.

Many states now mandate the termination of various boards, commissions, or agencies at a certain time unless a review of their operation justifies re-creation by the legislature. Colorado, in 1976, was the first state to pass such a "sunset law." Although programs of public assistance are not affected, the concept of auditing the performance of any public service has merit. Social workers must be prepared to justify the existence of each project, licensing board, or program. Cost–benefit analysis and examination of the results of various administrative techniques should be a continuous process, even when years may be needed to see the positive or negative results of an effort.

In 1968 Congress added to 42 U.S.C.A. § 602(a) the following: "By July 1, 1969, the amounts used by the states to determine the need of the individuals will have been adjusted to reflect fully changes in living costs since such amounts were established and any maximums that the state imposes on the amount being paid to families will have been proportionately adjusted." That seems to indicate that the states must increase their standards of need as the cost of living goes up. However, cases dealing with this amendment suggest the states are not required to increase their grants to needy individuals. Although the state must adjust the minimum amount budgeted for each individual's food and clothing as those costs go up, the state is not required to give the needy individual the full amount (see *Lampton v. Bonin*, 1969; *Shea v. Vialpando*, 1974).

Home visit versus invasion of privacy. Public welfare programs have struggled not only with the question of residency and the definition of "dependent child" but also with the question of controlling the personal conduct of welfare recipients. The concept of "worthy poor" continues to plague us; a review of *King v. Smith* (1968) shows that the state's concern about morals may have been a factor in the "man-in-the-house" regulation (Reich, 1966). Under any scheme of income maintenance, when recipients grossly mismanage benefits, the resulting unfavorable publicity presents difficult questions for policymakers.

Although ours is a heterogeneous society made up of vastly different cultural norms, public welfare administrators are often criticized when the behavior of recipients does not follow preconceived notions of middle-class values. The home visit and its consequent supervision is one way to control personal behavior, although it is not often recognized as having that function. The following case illustrates how the Supreme Court legitimized this casework tool.

Wyman v. James
400 U.S. 309, 91 S. Ct. 381 (1971)
Blackmun, J.
This appeal presents the issue whether a beneficiary of the program for Aid to Families with Dependent Children (AFDC) may refuse a home visit by the caseworker without risking the termination of benefits.

• • • • •

The district court majority held that a mother receiving AFDC relief may refuse, without forfeiting her right to that relief, the periodic home visit which the cited New York statutes and regulations prescribe as a condition for the continuance of assistance under the program. The beneficiary's thesis, and that of the district court majority, is that home visitation is a search and, when not consented to or when not supported by a warrant based on probable cause, violates the beneficiary's Fourth and Fourteenth Amendment rights.

• • • • •

Plaintiff Barbara James is the mother of a son, Maurice, who was born in May 1967. They reside in New York City. Mrs. James first applied for AFDC assistance shortly before Maurice's birth. A caseworker made a visit to her apartment at that time without objection. The assistance was authorized.

Two years later, on May 8, 1969, a caseworker wrote Mrs. James that she would visit her home on May 14. Upon receipt of this advice, Mrs. James telephoned the worker that, although she was willing to supply information "reasonable and relevant" to her need for public assistance, any discussion was not to take place at her home. The worker told Mrs.

James that she was required by law to visit in her home and that refusal to permit the visit would result in the termination of assistance. Permission was still denied. . . . Mrs. James, individually and on behalf of Maurice, and purporting to act on behalf of other persons similarly situated, instituted the present civil rights suit under 42 U.S.C. § 1983.

·　·　·　·　·

When a case involves a home and some type of official intrusion into that home, as this case appears to do, an immediate and natural reaction is one of concern about Fourth Amendment rights and the protection which that amendment is intended to afford. Its emphasis indeed is upon one of the most precious aspects of personal security in the home. "The right of the people to be secure in their persons, houses, papers, and effects."

·　·　·　·　·

This natural and quite proper protective attitude, however, is not a factor in this case, for the seemingly obvious and simple reason that we are not concerned here with any search by the New York social service agency in the Fourth Amendment meaning of that term. It is true that the governing statute and regulations appear to make mandatory the initial home visit and the subsequent periodic "contacts" (which may include home visits) for the inception and continuance of aid. It is also true that the caseworker's posture in the home is perhaps, in a sense, both rehabilitative and investigative. But this latter aspect, we think, is given too broad a character and far more emphasis than it deserves if it is equated with a search in the traditional criminal law context. We note, too, that the visitation in itself is not forced or compelled, and that the beneficiary's denial of permission is not a criminal act. If consent to the visitation is withheld, no visitation takes place. The aid then never begins or merely ceases, as the case may be. There is no entry of the home and there is no search.

If, however, we were to assume that a caseworker's home visit, before or subsequent to the beneficiary's initial qualification for benefits, somehow (perhaps because the average beneficiary might feel she is in no position to refuse consent to the visit), and despite its interview nature, does possess some of the characteristics of a search in the traditional sense, we nevertheless conclude that the visit does not fall within the Fourth Amendment's proscription. This is because it does not descend to the level of unreasonableness. It is unreasonableness which the Fourth Amendment's standard [prohibits].

·　·　·　·　·

There are a number of factors which compel us to conclude that the home visit proposed for Mrs. James is not unreasonable.

1. The public's interest in this particular segment of the area of assistance to the unfortunate is protection and aid for the dependent child whose family requires such aid for that child. The

focus is on the child and, further, it is on the child who is depen-
dent. There is no more worthy object of the public's concern. The
dependent child's needs are paramount, and only with hesitancy
would we relegate those needs, in the scale of comparative val-
ues, to a position secondary to what the mother claims as her
rights.

2. *The agency, with tax funds provided from federal as well as from*
   state sources, is fulfilling a public trust. The state, working through
   its qualified welfare agency, has appropriate and paramount in-
   terest and concern in seeing and assuring that the intended and
   proper objects of the tax-produced assistance are the ones who
   benefit from the aid it dispenses. Surely it is not unreasonable, in
   the Fourth Amendment sense or in any other sense of that term,
   that the state have at its command a gentle means, of limited
   extent and of practical and considerate application, of achieving
   that assurance.

3. *One who dispenses purely private charity naturally has an inter-*
   est in and expects to know how these charitable funds are utilized
   and put to work. The public, when it is the provider, rightly ex-
   pects the same. It might well expect more, because of the trust
   aspect of public funds, and the recipient, as well as the case-
   worker, has not only an interest but an obligation.

4. *The emphasis of the New York statutes and regulations is upon the*
   home, upon "close contact" with the beneficiary, upon restoring the
   aid recipient "to a condition of self support," and upon the relief of
   his distress. The federal emphasis is no different. . . . And it is con-
   cerned about any possible exploitation of the child.

5. *The home visit, it is true, is not required by federal statute or*
   regulation. But it has been noted that the visit is "the heart of
   welfare administration"; that it affords "a personal, rehabilita-
   tive orientation, unlike that of most federal programs"; and that
   the "more pronounced service orientation" effected by Congress
   with the 1956 amendments to the Social Security Act "gave re-
   doubled importance to the practice of home visits."

6. *The means employed by the New York agency are significant.*
   . . . Privacy is emphasized. The applicant–recipient is made the
   primary source of information as to eligibility. Outside informa-
   tion sources, other than public records, are to be consulted only
   with the beneficiary's consent. Forcible entry or entry under false
   pretense or visitation outside working hours or snooping in the home
   are forbidden. . . . All this minimizes any "burden" upon the
   homeowner's right against unreasonable intrusion.

7. *Mrs. James, in fact, on this record presents no specific complaint of any unreasonable intrusion of her home and nothing which supports an inference that the desired home visit had as its purpose the obtaining of information as to criminal activity. . . . What Mrs. James appears to want from the agency which provides her and her infant son with the necessities for life is the right to receive those necessities upon her own informational terms, to utilize the Fourth Amendment as a wedge for imposing those terms, and to avoid questions of any kind.*

8. *We are not persuaded . . . that all information pertinent to the issue of eligibility can be obtained by the agency through an interview at a place other than the home, or, as the district court majority suggested, by examining a lease or a birth certificate, or by periodic medical examinations, or by interviews with school personnel. . . . Although these secondary sources might be helpful, they would not always assure verification of actual residence or of actual physical presence in the home, which are requisites for AFDC benefits, or of impending medical needs. And, of course, little children, such as Maurice James, are not yet registered in school.*

9. *The visit is not one by police or uniformed authority. It is made by a caseworker of some training whose primary objective is, or should be, the welfare, not the prosecution, of the aid recipient for whom the worker has profound responsibility. . . . The caseworker is not a sleuth but rather, we trust, is a friend in need.*

10. *The home visit is not a criminal investigation, does not equate with a criminal investigation, and . . . is not in aid of any criminal proceeding. If the visitation serves to discourage misrepresentation or fraud, such a criminal prosecution should follow, then, even assuming that the evidence discovered upon the home visitation is admissible, an issue upon which we express no opinion, that is a routine and expected fact of life and a consequence no greater than that which necessarily ensues upon any other discovery by a citizen of criminal conduct.*

11. *The warrant procedure, which the plaintiffs appear to claim to be so precious to them, even if civil in nature, is not without its seriously objectionable features in the welfare context. If a warrant could be obtained (the appellees afford us little help as to how it would be obtained), it presumably could be applied for ex parte, its execution would require no notice, it would justify entry by force, and its hours for execution would not be so limited as those prescribed for home visitation. The warrant necessarily would imply*

*conduct either criminal or out of compliance with an asserted gov-
erning standard. Of course, the force behind the warrant argument
welcome to the one asserting it, is the fact that it would have to rest
upon probable cause, and probable cause in the welfare context, as
Mrs. James concedes, requires more than the mere need of the caseworker to see the child in the home and to have assurance that the
child is there and is receiving the benefit of the aid which has been
authorized for it.*

* * * * *

*It seems to us that the situation is akin to that where an Internal Rev-
enue Service agent, in making a routine civil audit of a taxpayer's income
tax return, asks that the taxpayer produce for the agent's review some proof
of a deduction that taxpayer has asserted to his benefit in the computation
of his tax. If the taxpayer refuses, there is, absent fraud, only a disallow-
ance of the claimed deduction and a consequent additional tax. The taxpayer is fully within his "rights" in refusing to produce the proof, but in
maintaining and asserting those rights a tax detriment results and it is a
detriment of the taxpayer's own making. So here Mrs. James has the "right" to
refuse the home visit, but a consequence in the form of cessation of aid, similar
to the taxpayer's resultant additional tax, flows from that refusal. The choice
is entirely hers, and nothing of constitutional magnitude is involved.*

* * * * *

*Our holding today does not mean, of course, that a termination of ben-
efits upon refusal of a home visit is to be upheld against constitutional
challenge under all conceivable circumstances.*

* * * * *

*We therefore conclude that the home visitation as structured by the New
York statutes and regulations is a reasonable administrative tool; that it
served a valid and proper administrative purpose for the dispensation of the
AFDC program; that it is not an unwarranted invasion of personal privacy;
and that it violates no right guaranteed by the Fourth Amendment.*

There were several dissents: Justice Douglas framed the central question
as "whether the government by force of its largesse has the power to 'buy up'
rights guaranteed by the Constitution," and asked whether a search of Mrs.
James's home without a warrant should be "made 'reasonable' merely because she is dependent on government largesse?" In commenting on the
possibility of discovering child abuse, Justice Marshall asked, "Would the
majority sanction, in the absence of probable cause, compulsory visits to all
American homes for the purpose of discovering child abuse? Or is this Court
to hold as a matter of constitutional law that a mother, merely because she is
poor, is substantially more likely to injure or exploit her children?"

The "gentle means" of home visitation assures the state that its tax funds will benefit those for whom they are intended. Thus, the caretaker's constitutional rights must yield to the interest of the dependent child. Do welfare recipients waive their right to privacy and to freedom of association by accepting benefits for themselves and their children? Should they have to?

The Supreme Court legitimized the home visit as "the heart of welfare administration," affording "a personal, rehabilitative orientation, unlike that of most federal programs." What is the valid and proper administrative purpose of the home visit? How can it best be used to accomplish the most effective use of resources? Is there any other way to accomplish that result?

Many of these challenges to the operation of public assistance programs have been possible because of public interest lawyers and law firms. These counselors will take constitutional and statutory challenges to the Supreme Court if necessary. An attorney in a legal aid office may challenge in court practices of welfare departments, with the help of nonprofit organizations created to research legal areas like welfare and child abuse.

Occasionally a client may be stymied in challenging an adverse decision through inability to pay a filing fee or other court costs that an indigent client has to pay even though the attorney is providing free legal service. In *Ortwein v. Schwab* (1973) the Supreme Court, in a 5 to 4 decision, upheld Oregon's appellate filing fee, as applied to indigent people seeking to appeal an adverse welfare decision, as not violating the due process or equal protection clauses of the Fourteenth Amendment.

Food Stamps

The food stamp program is not an income maintenance program per se, although it does increase the amount of disposable income available to low-income people. The concept originated before World War II but did not last long. A pilot program was established in 1961, and in 1964 Congress passed the Food Stamp Act, which allows certain individuals to buy food stamps at less than market value to be used at their face value to buy food.

Generally, households whose members receive AFDC, General Assistance, or SSI payments are eligible to receive food stamps. Other households may be eligible if they meet the standards of income, resources, and work registration. The amount they may buy is based on a complicated formula that includes the income and resources of a particular household and the number of its eligible members. Food stamps have become part of the budgeted resources of many lower-middle-income households. The program has significance for people other than those receiving some kind of public assistance, with consequent political ramifications. Any attempt to repeal the program would affect farmers, students working their way through college, and many others who would fight attempts by Congress to change it.

The following cases illustrate the complications of food stamp distribution. You will also appreciate the legal difficulties facing Congress when it attempts to tighten eligibility.

United States Dept. of Agric. v. Moreno
413 U.S. 528, 93 S. Ct. 2821, 37 L.Ed.2d 782 (1973)
Brennan, J.

The federal food stamp program was established in 1964 in an effort to alleviate hunger and malnutrition among the more needy segments of our society. . . . Eligibility for participation in the program is determined on a household rather than an individual basis. . . . An eligible household purchases sufficient food stamps to provide that household with a nutritionally adequate diet. The household pays for the stamps at a reduced rate based upon its size and cumulative income. The food stamps are then used to purchase food at retail stores, and the Government redeems the stamps at face value, thereby paying the difference between the actual cost of the food and the amount paid by the household for the stamps.

• • • • •

In January 1971, however, Congress redefined the term "household" so as to include only groups of related individuals.

[The court then discussed the situation of appellees who share households with nonrelated persons for various commendable reasons, both economic and charitable.]

Under traditional equal protection analysis, a legislative classification must be sustained, if the classification is rationally related to a legitimate governmental interest.

• • • • •

The challenged statutory classification (households of related persons versus households containing one or more unrelated persons) is clearly irrelevant to the stated purposes of the act.

• • • • •

Thus, if it is to be sustained, the challenged classification must rationally further some legitimate governmental interest other than those specifically stated in the congressional "declaration of policy." Regrettably, there is little legislative history to illuminate the purposes of the 1971 amendment of § 3(e). The legislative history that does exist, however, indicates that the amendment was intended to prevent so-called "hippies" and "hippie-communes" from participating in the food stamp programs. . . . The challenged classification clearly cannot be sustained by reference to this congressional purpose. For if the constitutional conception of "equal protection of the laws" means anything, it must at the very least mean that a bare congressional desire to harm a politically unpopular group cannot constitute a legitimate government interest.

· · · · ·

Although apparently conceding this point, the government maintains that the challenged classification should nevertheless be upheld as rationally related to the clearly legitimate governmental interest in minimizing fraud in the administration of the food stamp program. In essence, the government contends that, in adopting the 1971 amendment, Congress might rationally have thought (1) that households with one or more unrelated members are more likely than "fully related" households to contain individuals who abuse the program by fraudulently failing to report sources of income or by voluntarily remaining poor; and (2) that such households are "relatively unstable," thereby increasing the difficulty of detecting such abuses. But even if we were to accept as rational the government's wholly unsubstantiated assumptions concerning the differences between "related" and "unrelated" households we still could not agree with the government's conclusion that the denial of essential federal food assistance to all otherwise eligible households containing unrelated members constitutes a rational effort to deal with its concerns.

· · · · ·

Thus, in practical operation, the 1971 amendment excludes from participation in the food stamp program, not those persons who are "likely to abuse the program," but, rather, only those persons who are so desperately in need of aid that they cannot even afford to alter their living arrangements so as to retain their eligibility. "Traditional" equal protection analysis does not require that every classification be drawn with precise "mathematical nicety." . . . But the classification here in issue is not only "imprecise"; it is wholly without any rational basis. The judgment of the district court holding the "unrelated person" provision invalid under the due process clause of the Fifth Amendment is therefore affirmed.

United States Dept. of Agric. v. Murry
413 U.S. 508, 93 S. Ct. 2832, 37 L.Ed.2d 767 (1973)
Douglas, J.
These appellees brought a class action to enjoin the enforcement of the tax dependency provision of the act; and, as noted, the three-judge panel granted the relief.

Appellees are members of households that have been denied food stamp eligibility solely because the households contain persons 18 years or older who have been claimed as "dependents" for federal income tax purposes by taxpayers who are themselves ineligible for food stamp relief. Section

5(b) makes the entire household of which a "tax dependent" was a member ineligible for food stamps for two years: (1) during the tax year for which the dependency was claimed and (2) during the next 12 months. During these two periods of time § 5(b) creates a conclusive presumption that the "tax dependent's" household is not needy and has access to nutritional adequacy.

• • • • •

The tax dependency provision was generated by congressional concern about non-needy households participating in the Food Stamp program. The legislative history reflects a concern about abuses of the program by "college students, children of wealthy parents."

• • • • •

Tax dependency in a prior year seems to have no relation to the "need" of the dependent in the following year. It doubtless is much easier from the administrative point of view to have a simple tax "dependency" test that will automatically—without hearing, without witness, without findings of fact—terminate a household's claim for eligibility for food stamps.

• • • • •

We have difficulty in concluding that it is rational to assume that a child is not indigent this year because the parent declared the child as a dependent in his tax return for the prior year. But even on that assumption our problem is not at an end. Under the act the issue is not the indigency of the child but the indigency of a different household with which the child happens to be living. Members of that different household are denied Food Stamps if one of its present members was used as a tax deduction in the past year by his parents even though the remaining members have no relation to the parent who used the tax deduction, even though they are completely destitute, and even though they are 1, or 10 or 20 in number. We conclude that the deduction taken for the benefit of the parent in the prior year is not a rational measure of the need of a different household with whom the child of the tax-deducting parent lives and rests on an irrebuttable presumption often contrary to fact. It therefore lacks critical ingredients of due process.

These cases illustrate the perennial problem of meeting perceived abuses in income maintenance programs within the framework of a constitutional system. The Court uses the due process clause of the Fifth Amendment because the legislation is federal, rather than state, and with it strikes down the legislation as irrational. In challenges to the Fifth Amendment due process clause, the courts apply the traditional equal protection analysis of the Fourteenth Amendment, because due process implies that individuals must be treated equally.

These cases did not deal with a protected right, as *Shapiro* did with freedom to travel, but rather with a traditional equal protection analysis of rationality in classification. There is no protected "right" to public assistance of any kind. The state and federal governments presumably could terminate them entirely. However, if they exist, these programs cannot contain classifications, such as those exempting households containing unrelated people and tax dependents, that are without justification.

The Food Security Act of 1985 reauthorized and extended most of the country's farm programs and improves the Food Stamp Program. It increased the allowances that families can deduct from their gross income and the resource limitations.

Lyng v. Castillo (1986) challenged the practice of treating parents, children, and siblings who live together as a single "household" and applying a different standard when groups of more-distant relatives and unrelated persons live together. The Supreme Court held that the distinction between the two groups was not unequal treatment under the due process clause. In *Lyng v. International Union, UAW* (1988), unions and their members challenged the amendment that made a household ineligible for food stamps if a member was on strike. The amendment also precluded any increase in the allotment of food stamps because the income of the striking worker had decreased. The Supreme Court held that this did not abridge First Amendment rights to associate or express themselves, nor did it violate the Fifth Amendment's equal protection guarantee.

Homeless people are now entitled to food stamps, which can be issued within five days of request instead of the usual 30 days. Homeless people are not required to file monthly verification reports. In contrast to residents of other institutions, residents of a homeless shelter are not ineligible. There are now food stamp outreach programs to provide eligible but nonparticipating people with benefits. In 1986 Congress allowed authorized soup kitchens and shelters to accept food stamps, even though the stamps cannot be used to purchase ready-to-eat foods at restaurants. In 1988 Congress provided that food stamps could be used to purchase prepared meals at concessional prices (Fennell, 1993). For students, the Higher Education Amendments of 1986 greatly expanded the expenses they can exclude from income if they receive Pell Grants, Supplemental Education Opportunity Grants, Guaranteed Student Loans, or other assistance authorized by Title IV of the Higher Education Act of 1965. If you are advising students or homeless people, this may be useful.

Unemployment Compensation
The real impetus for a national program of unemployment compensation was the Great Depression of the 1930s. Several states, recognizing that advances in technology or economic upheavals might lead to job loss through no fault of the workers, had attempted compensation

programs before the depression. But these programs died because of the competitive disadvantage they caused for businesses in those states against other states where employers did not have to pay a tax toward unemployment compensation. The solution was a national program that put all employers on an equal footing.

Congress included within the Social Security Act provision for a tax of 3 percent on the payrolls of employers of eight or more in any 20 weeks of the year, with a great number of exemptions. If a state passed an unemployment compensation program of its own, the employer could deduct 2.7 percent of the federal tax from any tax owed under the state program. All states subsequently passed such programs, and benefits are payable through the states. There are no federal unemployment compensation benefits, although the tax remains. The proceeds of the tax are returned to the states to create employment security offices, where beneficiaries are required to register and which attempt to find jobs for them.

The exemptions to coverage have been reduced considerably over the years. Many states now require payment of unemployment compensation benefits if an employer has employed only one person for a specified time. Employees of nonprofit organizations are now generally covered.

Unemployment compensation, which is designed for the short-term replacement of income denied by job loss, gives an individual some income while looking for another job. To be eligible the individuals must have worked a certain time in covered employment, must register for work, must be able to work and be available for work, and must not have left the last job under certain disqualifying circumstances.

The program is not designed as disability insurance—thus the requirement that the claimant be able to work. Disqualifications that keep a worker from drawing benefits, and in many states mean the individual must work in covered employment for a certain period before becoming eligible again, include leaving a job without good cause, refusing suitable employment, or participating in a labor dispute. The program is designed only to protect those who lose a job without personal fault. The labor dispute disqualification is designed to provide neutrality in labor disputes and has not surprisingly been a fertile field for litigation.

Sherbert v. Verner (1963) challenged the operation of unemployment compensation. The appellant, a member of the Seventh-Day Adventist Church, was discharged when the mill in which she was working went to a six-day week from a five-day week, and she refused to work on Saturday, the Sabbath day of her faith. She also refused to accept other work that would require working on Saturday and was denied unemployment compensation benefits for failing, without good cause, to accept "suitable work when offered." The Court, discussing the free exercise clause of the First

Amendment, asked whether disqualification for benefits imposed a burden on the free exercise of her religion and decided it clearly did.

The problem of accommodating the religious beliefs of employees is a difficult one. In *Verner* the court decided a case where the legislation impinged on a protected right, the free exercise of religion. In the case of protected rights, such as the right to travel involved in *Shapiro,* there must be a compelling state interest to sustain the burden, in contrast to legislation in the "area of economics and social welfare," where the classification must only be rational. The *Verner* Court reasoned that the operation of the statute forced her to choose between following the precepts of her religion and forfeiting benefits, a dilemma forbidden by the First Amendment.

The Civil Rights Act of 1964 prohibits discrimination in employment on the basis of religion, among other things. In cases dealing with charges of religious discrimination, such as having to work on Saturday when it is one's Sabbath, the courts have required employers to make "reasonable accommodation" to the employees' religious beliefs. This has to be decided case by case, although employers are not required to make financial sacrifices, such as paying another employee time and a half to work on Saturday in place of an employee who will not work because of religious beliefs.

Justice Harlan, dissenting in *Verner,* urged that the employee was simply unavailable for work because of personal considerations. Should programs of social insurance consider individual needs? For instance, suppose the mother of young children loses her daytime job and refuses to go on a shift from 3:00 P.M. to 11:00 P.M. because there would be no one to take care of her children. Should she be entitled to unemployment compensation if she refuses to take the job? Or should protections of the Bill of Rights, such as religious freedom, be entitled to greater deference than other personal considerations?

Most decisions in this area hold that personal reasons for refusing suitable work, such as family responsibilities and lack of transportation, will result in disqualification. However, the problems are not simple; nor is it easy to predict what an appeals board or a court will decide.

The Civil Rights Act, which forbids discrimination on the basis of race, color, religion, gender, or national origin, was amended in 1990. The amendment caps damages based on the size of the employing organization. However, the amendment provides compensatory and punitive damages, and jury trials are now available for intentional violations of the act. According to Allen (1992), it is unclear whether the amendment applies to causes of action arising after the effective date of the statute or whether it applies to cases pending at the time the law was enacted.

Many states do not pay AFDC benefits to a family with an unemployed father, even though the Social Security Act permits such payments. If the father is disqualified under unemployment compensation laws, U.S. Department of Health and Human Services regulations allow states to deny AFDC benefits under the unemployed parents program (AFDC-UP). In 1961 Congress expanded the definition of dependent child on an experimental basis to include children whose deprivation was caused by the unemployment of a parent. Congress made the program permanent in 1968 but required that participating states deny aid to families in which a parent is receiving unemployment compensation. In *Philbrook v. Glodgett* (1975) the Supreme Court held that a Vermont regulation completely excluding unemployed fathers even if they were only eligible for unemployment compensation conflicted with the Social Security Act: A family can be excluded from benefits only for each week in which unemployment compensation is actually received by the father.

The Supreme Court considered eligibility for AFDC-UP benefits in two other cases, both 5 to 4 decisions. In *Batterton v. Francis* (1977) the Court held that excluding from the definition of unemployed father one "whose unemployment results from participation in a labor dispute or who is unemployed by reason of conduct or circumstances which result or would result in disqualification for unemployment compensation under the state's unemployment compensation law" was reasonable. In *Califano v. Westcott* (1979) denial of benefits to families in which the children have been deprived of parental support because of the unemployment of the father but not the mother was held an unconstitutional gender classification not substantially related to the attainment of any valid statutory goals. Because AFDC-UP became mandatory under the 1988 Family Support Act, the program may grow (Abramovitz, 1995).

Most unemployment compensation programs are limited, with 26 weeks being the usual period of coverage. After a long period of exceptionally high unemployment, Congress passed the Emergency Unemployment Compensation Act of 1974, which extends benefits for unemployed workers who have exhausted their right to regular benefits. These benefits, although paid by the states, are reimbursed by the federal government. This supplemental benefits program is triggered by the state or national unemployment rate. A state with an industry suffering many layoffs, such as the aerospace industry, could have a higher rate of unemployment than a neighboring state with a healthy textile industry; the extended benefits would be available to workers in the first state and not in the second. If the national rate of unemployment rises to a certain level, workers in all states are eligible.

In 1977 Congress extended the program again and added new eligibility requirements. Those people who refuse suitable work or are not actively seeking work will be disqualified from receiving further supplementary benefits until they have worked at least four weeks and earned at least four times the average weekly benefit amount. "Suitable work" here is defined as "any work which is within the individual's capabilities," in contrast to regular unemployment regulations, which usually permit claimants to refuse a job offer not in their regular line of work or at substantially less pay than they were receiving.

Because extended benefits may now support a recipient for as long as a year, does such a program really get to the problem of loss of income, or is it only a palliative? Would another type of income maintenance program be preferable for the long-term unemployed?

The Current Population Survey was redesigned to better reflect labor market behavior, which has changed radically in the past 30 years. Women, especially mothers with young children, are now major participants in the labor market. The proportion of people of color in the labor market has increased, and the number of part-time and temporary workers has also risen. The data show a decline in adult men's labor force participation and an increase in labor force activity for teenagers and older workers (Norwood & Tanur, 1994).

Workers' Compensation

Industrial accidents are inevitable. The idea of an employer passing on to the consumer the cost of compensating employees for work-related illnesses and accidents is a new one, however. In the past an employee who was hurt on the job had only a tort remedy against the employer, suing the employer for damages if the employer was in some way negligent. Certain defenses became available to the employer when the employee sued. One defense was the fellow–servant rule—the injury was caused by the negligence of a fellow employee. Another was assumption of risk—the employee assumed the risk of injury by knowingly accepting dangerous employment. A third argument was contributory negligence—the employee could not recover if negligent to any degree, although the employer may have been grossly negligent. Of course, if the employer was not at all negligent, the employee could not recover.

Today all states have some form of workers' compensation, usually provided through a state commission administering scheduled amounts of benefits financed by employer insurance premiums. The compensation provides employees with rehabilitation through comprehensive medical care and also protects them and their dependents against loss of income up to scheduled maximum amounts. Originally, only industrial accidents were covered, but coverage has gradually been liberalized to cover occupational disease as well. In some states suicide and alcoholism may be considered job related or rising out of employment, and benefits are awarded to the employee or any dependents. For instance, a Tennessee supreme court case upheld an award of workers' compensation death benefits to the widow of a police officer whose death from chronic alcoholism was allegedly hastened because of increased drinking brought about by the aggravation of degenerative arthritis brought on when he slipped and fell while on duty. The court took judicial notice "that chronic alcoholism can carry with it an irresistible and uncontrollable desire to drink alcohol, and that a substantial school of thought supports the proposition that alcoholism is a disease" (*Wheeler v. Glens Falls Ins. Co.*, 1974).

Michigan has held that it defied logic to declare that a job was responsible for accelerating or aggravating a worker's alcoholism and denied coverage (*Pierce v. General Motors Corp., Fisher Body Div.*, 1993). But in Louisiana two cases broadened coverage. Although one worker had a history of hypertension, obesity, high cholesterol, and high triglycerides, the court held that his heart attack arose out of his work, awarding his widow death benefits (*State of Juneau v. Tudor Const. Co.*, 1993). In the second case, a security guard who was mugged while walking in a high-crime area between a public bus stop and work received compensation for total and permanent disability. The court held that the mugging, which occurred two blocks from the workplace, occurred in the "course of employment" under the threshold doctrine (*Stewart v. Louisiana Plant Serv., Inc.*, 1992). An ill or injured worker can always apply for benefits and let the commission decide if the problem arose in the course of employment.

Some states limit coverage to hazardous employment, a concept that can be broadened by judicial interpretation. Some employment—domestic service, casual labor, and often agricultural labor—has traditionally been excluded, but in these areas coverage is also being broadened. The amount of benefits is often inadequate.

Richardson v. Belcher (1971) challenged the provision of Social Security Act § 224 that requires workers' compensation payments to be offset against benefits payable under federal disability insurance. Congress decided that these payments serve a common purpose and that workers' compensation should take precedence; the Supreme Court sustained the provision. Many individuals who receive workers' compensation are not eligible for social security disability benefits because they are not permanently and totally disabled, a standard not required in workers' compensation. The offset provision ensures that beneficiaries will not receive more in compensation and disability payments than they would have received in wages.

Justice Douglas in dissent said,

Eligibility for social security disability benefits is premised upon a worker's having attained "insured" status in the course of an employment "covered" by the act. It is undisputed that Raymond Belcher, and through him his wife and two minor children, had so qualified in 1968 when he broke his neck while employed by the Pocahontas Fuel Co. in Lynco, West Virginia. Indeed, his application for such benefits has been approved, and the benefits authorized and paid.

Section 224 of the Social Security Act, however, requires that these benefits be substantially reduced solely because Belcher also receives state workmen's compensation payments. It is said that the duplication of benefits "impedes rehabilitation," and may lead to a cutting back of state workmen's compensation programs.

The rehabilitation goal does not explain the special treatment given to workmen's compensation beneficiaries.

Had Belcher's supplemental disability payment come from a Veterans Administration program, a Civil Service Retirement Act or Railroad Retirement Act annuity, a private disability insurance policy, a self-insurer, a voluntary wage-continuation plan, or the proceeds in an action in tort arising from the disabling injury, there would have been no reduction in his social security disability benefits. The offset under § 224 applies only to federal social security disability beneficiaries also receiving workmen's compensation payments, a group which in 1965 totalled only 14 percent of all social security disability beneficiaries. Yet of the 849,000 disabled workers who in 1965 received social security disability benefits, over 16 percent also received overlapping veterans' benefits, and almost 14 percent received benefits from private insurance maintained under the auspices of an employer or a union. Congress is of course not required to address itself to all aspects of a social problem in its legislation. It must, however, justify the distinctions it draws between people otherwise similarly situated. Rehabilitation incentives are not a rational justification for the discrimination worked by § 224. If it is at all rational to argue that duplicating payments "impede rehabilitation," the argument must apply to all such payments regardless of their sources. The nature of a supplemental benefit has no relation to a worker's incentive to return to work. (pp. 84–85)

Does this provision of the Social Security Act violate the equal protection clause? Although it would seem to, because it singles out individuals with disabilities who receive workers' compensation benefits, there is no protected constitutional right and there is a rational basis for the offset. Would this kind of legislation be one way to handle the problem of malingering?

A perennial problem in all social insurance programs is delay in processing applications and in certifying and paying benefits. *Burtton v. Johnson* (1976) dealt with delays in receipt of unemployment compensation benefits. The court discussed the Supreme Court decision in *California Dept. of Human Resources v. Java* (1971) and the requirements in the Social Security Act of "payment when due" of benefits. The case held that withholding compensation while the employer appeals determination of eligibility violates federal requirements. The employee was determined eligible at a hearing that the employer did not atend, despite notification. Payment on the nearest payday following the termination is the goal, because "the unemployed worker needs assistance to tide him over until he finds other work. He needs this assistance to avoid welfare or private charity, and he needs it so that he has the resources to find substantially equivalent employment without having to accept any job no matter how unsuited he may be for it" (p. 768). The same problem, which appears in public assistance programs (*Like v. Carter,* 1971) also plagues social security. *Edelman v. Jordan* (1974) held that a court cannot award retroactive payments of benefits wrongfully withheld because of the delay in processing applications, although an injunction to forbid the delay is possible.

Programs for income maintenance in this country are dynamic. Lawmakers seem willing to change programs, adding experimental elements and deleting others to improve the distribution of benefits and the coverage of those people in need. How best to improve the programs is a matter of public debate. Certain commentators think a negative income tax is the best solution (Friedman, 1967); others recommend different programs (Garfinkel, 1968; Katz, 1973; Ozawa, 1973). Social workers, who so often see the sorry aftermath of income loss, should familiarize themselves with current proposals so they can give valuable assistance to lawmakers struggling with the problem. A knowledge of the politics of welfare reform is instructive, helping the social planner understand not only what is desirable but what is politically possible (Moynihan, 1973).

HOUSING

For most of us, having an attractive, comfortable place to live is one of our major satisfactions. For many people, however, finding a safe and economical place to live is a major problem. Finding "shelter" means not only searching for an apartment, house, mobile home, or condominium but also facing the legal problems presented by a purchase agreement, a lease, or a tenants' or homeowners' cooperative agreement. Any client who has problems with housing documents should be referred to an attorney.

A major problem raised by housing is financing. Federal legislation mandates truth-in-lending disclosures and other protections in the area of consumer credit, although the best protection anyone has is good judgment—taking care to read any document that must be signed and seeking legal advice for an explanation of the legal terms these documents contain.

Public Housing

The first federal public housing law was enacted in 1937 to provide "decent, safe and sanitary housing" for low-income families. This law was supplemented by the Housing Act of 1949, which supported slum clearance and redevelopment. Still, the goal of decent, safe, and adequate housing for low-income families has certainly not yet been met (Ronfeldt & Clifford, 1969–1970; Teafore, 1969–1970). The Federal Housing Administration Act (FHA) Section 235 subsidy program provides subsidies to enable low-income purchasers to acquire homes. The houses are bought from private owners, and represented by private realtors, with mortgages obtained from private lending institutions. The FHA must approve both the house and the purchaser before the subsidy is approved. There have been numerous complaints about abuses in the program; federally subsidized home-buying programs do have some problems, ones social workers may confront in trying to work with local bar association or legal aid offices to educate individuals about buying a home.

Because authorities have state as well as federal funds for public housing construction and operation, their activities are "state action" that must meet constitutional limitations—unlike private landlords, who can discriminate against families with children, those people whose income is below a certain level, and so on. Thus, in *Thorpe v. Housing Auth. of City of Durham, N.C.* (1969) the supreme court held that managers of federally assisted public housing projects must follow U.S. Department of Housing and Urban Development (HUD) guidelines giving tenants the reason for an eviction and an opportunity for reply. Thorpe had a month-to-month tenancy, with the lease providing for termination by either party on 15 days' notice. Thorpe received a notice, with no reason given, the day after being elected president of a tenants' organization. In *Cole v. Housing Auth. of City of Newport* (1970), a two-year residency requirement imposed on applicants for admission to a federally aided, low-rent public housing project was held to violate the equal protection clause. The court cited *Shapiro* and said to the sophisticated argument of defendants:

We are confronted with the assertion that if the two-year durational requirement were declared invalid, voters in city governments elsewhere as well as at Newport would simply not approve new low-income housing. Thus, the purpose and effect of the requirements are not to impair the rights to travel, but to make the voters think the right to travel is being impaired, even though it is not. (p. 812)

In *Wright v. Roanoke Redevelopment and Housing* (1987), another 5 to 4 decision, the Supreme Court held that tenants in low-income housing projects could bring a § 1983 action alleging that the authority over-billed them for utilities and violated the rent ceiling imposed by the Brooke Amendment to the Housing Act and that requiring a "reasonable" allowance for utilities was not too vague or amorphous a phrasing to confer on the tenants enforceable rights (McDougall, 1987).

HUD must consider the racial impact of its housing policies, so that if public housing projects for low-income families continue segregated housing practices, HUD can order facilities to discontinue "ghetto" housing. In *Hills v. Gautreaux* (1976) the Supreme Court upheld a remedial order reaching beyond a city's geographic boundaries but within the housing market for applicants. The Court has also held that either party to a suit brought on charges of violating the fair housing provisions of the Civil Rights Act of 1964 could seek a jury trial (*Curtis v. Leather,* 1974). Conservative members of Congress sometimes seek to reduce funds for public housing, so that tax support may dry up to reflect current political realities.

HUD is decreasing subsidies for rents. Tenants now pay 30 percent of their income for rent and utilities in privately owned housing and the federal government the rest, up to a set "fair-market rent." As the fair-market rent decreases, more subsidized housing will leave the program. See Ramsey et al. (1993) for a discussion of the program signed into law by President Bush in 1990 that will convert public housing projects to tenant-owned and tenant-managed properties.

The problem of homelessness continues. The Stewart B. McKinney Homeless Assistance Act passed in 1987 was the first step in a comprehensive approach to the problem. It provides for emergency and transitional housing, permanent housing for people with mental illness, and supportive housing services along with job training and food assistance. The act also requires HUD to reserve at least 50 percent of McKinney Act funding for the Shelter Plus Care Program.

Rent Strikes

For tenants dealing with landlords unwilling or unable to make necessary repairs, the doctrine of removal or constructive eviction may apply:

The tenant can move out, with no liability for rent payments, when the landlord has violated the warranty of habitability by not repairing the premises. This relief is useful only where other housing is available. For low- and middle-income residents in a tight housing market, this is rarely an option.

Another possible avenue of relief is for the tenant to assume responsibility for repairing the premises, deducting the costs from rent. This is risky, because the courts have discretion whether to allow expenses to be deducted from rent. Suing the landlord for damages and breach of the implied warranty of habitability is another possibility.

Especially in the late 1960s, some tenants used rent strikes to deal with recalcitrant landlords. In this type of action, the tenants withhold all or part of the rent until repairs are made; it is only effective with good organization and determined tenants, because landlords can always evict individuals for nonpayment of rent. Unless there is an organization to fight evictions, with tenants speaking in one voice, withholding rent is usually not effective. Nevertheless, if you are dealing with clients in public housing or low-income private housing you might explore this option with a legal aid office (Blumberg & Robbins, 1976; David & Callan, 1974; Moskovitz, 1970).

Urban Homesteading

Urban homesteading creates interesting housing possibilities for poor and middle-income city dwellers and may spark a renaissance in slum neighborhoods. In homesteading programs, cities sell abandoned property at tax sales for a nominal sum, typically a dollar. The buyer then puts "sweat equity" into the property in the form of personal labor and limited expenditures to bring the property up to the city's housing code. After living on the property for a certain period of time and completing the repairs, the buyer becomes the owner. It is not unlike the Homestead Act of 1862, which triggered a mass movement into frontier areas and the settlement of wilderness lands.

Urban homesteading also has federal help and support. A federal statute (42 U.S.C. § 1706(e)) authorizes HUD to transfer certain of its real estate to local or state governments. There are also attractive federal financing incentives.

Some legal problems are associated with these programs, however. There is a redemption period for property acquired by a city through a tax lien or by purchase at public auction for satisfaction of taxes. This period, usually two to three years, gives the former owner a chance to redeem the property by paying the back taxes; until the redemption period has passed, the city cannot transfer good title to an urban homesteader. In the meantime the building may deteriorate and be vandalized. This problem could be solved by legislative reduction of the redemption period, but this would hurt owners who lose property through inadvertence or financial disaster. Two other possibilities are to have the property declared a public nuisance, which requires the use of a city's police power, or to create a kind of "receivership" program, with the city as receiver taking over the dwelling and performing the necessary repairs, thus establishing a lien on the property for the costs. If the costs remain unpaid, the city can foreclose the lien. This prevents further deterioration but also requires tax funds from some source. An additional problem occurs when a municipality may sell property only at public auction for the highest price. To establish an urban homesteading program, the city charter may have to be amended to avoid these problems. The new urban homesteading program authorizes HUD to acquire single-family properties in bulk from the Resolution Trust Corporation and transfer them to local government units and public agencies that may retransfer them to lower-income families (Ramsey et al., 1993).

In urban areas with deteriorating neighborhoods and a housing crunch—a common coincidence—urban homesteading may offer a possibility for saving downtown areas, raising the tax base, and providing affordable housing. This is a possible project for social action (Drewes, 1974; "From Plans to Pliers," 1974).

DEBT

How society protects creditors' rights reflects its health and maturity. If debt cannot be collected, credit will not be extended; protection for creditors means greater availability of credit generally. We do not imprison for nonpayment of debt in this country, although imprisonment for nonpayment of alimony and child support may seem to be just that. Legally, though, that debtor is imprisoned for disobeying the court's order to support, that is, for contempt of court.

Debt is one of the major economic problems of clients. Individuals may not be covered by an income maintenance program or the coverage may be inadequate to meet their needs. Frequently, clients live beyond their means, a problem many people have and one we might expect to find more often in people living at or near subsistence level. In a society where wants are manufactured by clever marketing, individuals get into debt almost without realizing it. A consumer-oriented society such as ours encourages toleration of debt because the economy depends on it to a great extent (Fiorello, 1975). For clients who are financially overextended, many larger communities offer debt-counseling agencies. Lawyers refer their clients to these agencies for help in managing debt and avoiding bankruptcy, because creditors often wait to file suit when they realize that debtors are trying to get their affairs in order to pay their obligations.

Unconscionable Contracts

Some individuals have entered into contracts that seem unconscionable, with terms so unfavorable that they shock the conscience. Ordinarily, absent an incapacity, a person is held to the terms of any contract not fraudulently entered into, favorable or not. Often, the contracting party is simply improvident. However, the Uniform Commercial Code empowers a court to declare a contract unconscionable, and some courts have done so when the terms are so unreasonable as to indicate that a party had little bargaining power and hence little real choice. However, if the description of a contract seems outrageous to you, it is always a good idea to suggest that the client ask a lawyer about it.

An example of an unconscionable contract is found in *Williams v. Walker Thomas Furniture Company* (1965). There, the contract for the purchase of items on credit provided that each payment be prorated on the outstanding debt, so that a balance was due on every item purchased until the entire outstanding debt was paid. This enabled the creditor to repossess all items, no matter how long the customer had been paying for them, if there was a default in the payment of any monthly installment:

> *Appellant's second argument presents a more serious question. The record reveals that prior to the last purchase appellant had reduced the balance in her account to $164. The last purchase, a stereo set, raised the balance due to $678. Significantly, at the time of this and the preceding purchases appellee was aware of appellant's financial position. The reverse side of the stereo contract listed the name of appellant's social worker and her $218 monthly stipend from the government. Nevertheless, with full knowledge that appellant had to feed, clothe and support both herself and seven children on this amount, appellee sold her a $514 stereo set. We cannot condemn too strongly appellee's conduct. It raises serious question of sharp practice and irresponsible business dealings.* (p. 448, quoting the District of Columbia court of appeals)

The court goes on to describe unconscionability as an "absence of meaningful choice on the part of one of the parties together with contract terms which are unreasonably favorable to the other" (350 F.2d at 449).

Consumer Credit Protection Act

The Consumer Credit Protection Act, the "truth-in-lending" act, was enacted in 1969. Various provisions of the act, including those that require a creditor to list the finance charge, were designed to enable the consumer to shop around to obtain favorable credit rates. Because consumers can now readily ascertain how much the credit will cost, they look for the merchant who offers the best terms. Although the intention is benign, many low-income consumers with limited sources of credit cannot shop around for the best terms. The act has extremely broad provisions for regulating real estate credit transactions and also provides for attorney's fees in cases where provisions of the act are not met. This makes it possible for attorneys to represent low-income clients who could not otherwise afford an attorney.

Certain provisions of the act limit the amount of wages that can be seized by garnishment. *Garnishment* is a judicial proceeding in which the property of a debtor is taken by court order from another's hands to discharge the debt. Although usually thought of in terms of wages, bank accounts can also be garnished. Often employers hold up to two weeks' wages belonging to the judgment debtor, which the judgment creditor can take to settle the outstanding debt. Employers may not release more than 25 percent of *disposable earnings,* the amount left after required deductions like social security and income taxes have been made. There is no limit on the amount banks may release. Some states used to permit garnishment of a much greater portion of a debtor's wages, which inevitably led to more bankruptcies. The act prohibits the employer from firing an employee whose wages are garnished once—formerly a common practice, because the garnishment procedure is troublesome and expensive for the employer.

A 1970 amendment to the act added a new federal law on credit cards, which limits liability of cardholders for unauthorized use, prohibits the issuance of credit cards except in response to request, and establishes criminal penalties for unauthorized use. Although credit card problems usually arise because of misuse by the cardholder, the cards occasionally are lost or stolen and used by others. In those cases, the holder's liability is limited to $50 for illegal use before notification to the issuer of the loss or theft.

In 1977 the Fair Debt Collection Practices Act was added to the statute, creating a private right of action against debt collectors for harassment or abuse, false or misleading representation, or unfair practices in attempting to collect a debt. Low-income consumers have been particularly vulnerable to abusive collection techniques. Because employers may not discriminate against an employee whose wages have been garnished pursuant to judgment, a creditor's contact with an employer could be a problem. The employer might choose to fire the employee immediately rather than wait and have to cope with a garnishment. Because the act provides attorney's fees and damages for abuses in collection practices, low-income consumers now have ways to protect themselves.

Bankruptcy

Bankruptcy is a drastic method of freeing oneself from debt to start fresh. If a debtor is unable to pay obligations, federal law provides a method to turn over to a trustee all nonexempt property. The property is then sold and the proceeds used to pay off as much of the debts as is possible. Any client who has overwhelming debts from a serious illness or an accident should be referred to an attorney to determine whether bankruptcy is an appropriate alternative.

The Bankruptcy Reform Act, the first wholesale revision of the bankruptcy statutes since 1898, was passed in 1978. It allows a husband and wife to commence a joint case by filing a single petition, paying only a single filing fee.

The new act codifies *United States v. Kras* (1973), where the Supreme Court held that there is no right to file a bankruptcy petition in *forma pauperis*. However, the act does provide more-generous exemptions. There is an exemption for a homestead of $7,500; an interest in motor vehicles up to $1,200; and exemptions for household goods, wearing apparel, tools of the trade, and so on. The purpose of exempting certain property from sale by the trustee is to give the debtor the minimum living needs required to start life over without going into debt. Social insurance payments, social security benefits, and disability payments are also exempt. The new act also reforms wage-earner plans that give the debtor a plan for repayment of debts in full or in part. These are improvements over the previous informal out-of-court plans.

REFERENCES

Abramovitz, M. (1995). Aid to families with dependent children. In R. L. Edwards (Ed.-in-Chief), *Encyclopedia of social work* (19th ed., Vol. 1, pp. 183–194). Washington, DC: NASW Press.

Allen, D. (1992). Retroactivity of the Civil Rights Act of 1991. *Baylor Law Review, 44,* 569–592.

Blumberg, R. E., & Robbins, B. Q. (1976). Beyond URLTA: A program for achieving real tenant goals. *Harvard Civil Rights-Civil Liberties Law Review, 11,* 1–47.

Breslin, H. P. (1966). Liability of possible fathers: A support remedy for illegitimate children. *Stanford Law Review, 18,* 859–872.

Clarke, H. I. (1957). *Social legislation* (2d ed.). New York: Appleton-Century-Crofts.

David, H., & Callan, J. M. (1974). Newark's public housing rent strike: The high-rise ghetto goes to court. *Clearinghouse Review, 4,* 581–587.

Drewes, W. C. (1974). Homesteading, 1974: Reclaiming abandoned housing on the urban frontier. *Columbia Journal of Law and Social Problems, 10,* 416–455.

Fennell, M. A. (1993). Hunger and homelessness: Why the homeless need food stamp advocacy and how to pay for it. *Fordham Law Journal, 21,* 127–157.

Fiorello, T. M. (1975, January). Consumer education needed. *Social Work, 18,* 109–110.

Friedman, M. (1967). The case for the negative income tax. *National Review, 19,* 239–241.

From plans to pliers—Urban homesteading in America [Comment]. (1974). *Fordham Urban Law Journal, 2,* 273–304.

Garfinkel, I. (1968, October). Negative income tax and children's allowance programs: A comparison. *Social Work, 13,* 33–39.

Handler, J. F., & Goldstein, A. E. (1968). The legislative development of public assistance. *Wisconsin Law Review,* pp. 414–460.

Katz, A. J. (1973, March). Four income maintenance experiments. *Social Work, 18,* 111–113.

Kessinger, R. A. (1993). *Uniform reciprocal enforcement of support act—A state-by-state guide on child custody and support.* New York: Practicing Law Institute.

Kristol, I. (1971). Welfare: The best of intentions, the worst of results. *Atlantic, 228,* 45–47.

McDougall, H. A. (1987). Affordable housing for the 1990's *University of Michigan Journal of Law Reform, 20,* 727–788.

Moskovitz, M. (1970). Rent withholding and the implied warranty of habitability—Some new breakthroughs. *Clearinghouse Review, 4,* 49, 622–627.

Moynihan, D. P. (1973). *The politics of a guaranteed income.* New York: Random House.

Norwood, J. L. & Tanur, J. M. (1994). Review: Measuring unemployment in the nineties. *Public Opinion Quarterly, 58,* 277–294.

Ozawa, M. N. (1973). Taxation and social welfare. *Social Work, 18,* 66–76.

Pumphrey, R. E., & Pumphrey, M. W. (Eds.). (1961). *The heritage of American social work.* New York: Columbia University Press.

Ramsey, B. C., Broder, J. N., Chiaviella, A. J., Duffy, J. F., Dunnells, G. R., Larson, J. A., Sterling, S. A., & Vernon, L. E. (1993). The Cranston-Gonzalez National Affordable Housing Act—An overview. *Real Property Probate and Trust Journal, 28,* 177–256.

Rauch, J. B. (1976). The charity organization movement in Philadelphia. *Social Work, 21,* 55–62.

Reich, C. (1966). Social welfare in the public–private state. *University of Pennsylvania Law Review, 114,* 487–493.

Ronfeldt, S. F., & Clifford, D. J. (1969–1970). Judicial enforcement of the housing and urban development acts. *Hastings Law Journal, 21,* 317–368.

Shapiro, R. Y., Patterson, K. D., Russel, J., & Young, J. T. (1987). The polls: Public assistance. *Public Opinion Quarterly, 51,* 120–130.

Tannahil, R. (1973). *Food in history.* New York: Stein & Day.

Teafore, S. D. (1969–1970). Homeownership for low-income families: The concomium. *Hastings Law Journal, 21,* 243–286.

Trolander, J. A. (1973). The response of settlements to the Great Depression. *Social Work, 18,* 92–102.

Welfare research and experimentation: Hearings before the Subcommittee on Public Assistance, 95th Cong., 2d Sess. (1978).

Wisner, E. (1970). *Social welfare in the South.* Baton Rouge: Louisiana State University Press.

STATUTES CITED

Bankruptcy Reform Act of 1978. P.L. 99-554, 100 Stat. 3088, 11 U.S.C. § 101–151326.

Civil Rights Act of 1991. 2 U.S.C. § 608, 1201–1224.

Consumer Credit Protection Act of 1968. P.L. 90-321, 82 Stat. 146, 15 U.S.C. § 1601 et seq.

Deficit Reduction Act of 1984. P.L. 98-369, 98 Stat. 494, 26 U.S.C. § 1 et seq.

Emergency Unemployment Compensation Act of 1974. P.L. 93-572, 99 Stat. 1869, 26 U.S.C. §3304 note.

Fair Debt Collection Practices Act of 1977. P.L. 95-109, 91 Stat. 874, 15 U.S.C. § 1692.

Family Support Act of 1988. P.L. 100-485. 102 Stat. 2343.

Federal Housing Administration Act of 1974. 42 U.S.C. § 1441.

Food Security Act of 1985. P.L. 99-198, 99 Stat. 1354, 16 U.S.C. § 3801 et seq.

Food Stamp Act of 1964. P.L. 88-525, 78 Stat. 703, 7 U.S.C. § 2011–2025.

Higher Education Act of 1965. P.L. 89-329, 79 Stat. 1219.

Higher Education Amendments of 1986. P.L. 99-498, 100 Stat. 1268.

Homestead Act of 1862. Ch. 75, 12 Stat. 392.

Housing Act of 1949. Ch. 338, 63 Stat. 413, 12 U.S.C. § 24 et seq.

Parent Locator Service. 42 U.S.C.A. 653, 1988.

Social Security Act of 1935. Ch. 531, 49 Stat. 620, 42 U.S.C. § 301 et seq.

Stewart B. McKinney Homeless Assistance Act of 1987. P.L. 100-77, 101 Stat. 482, 42 U.S.C. § 11301 et seq.

STUDY QUESTIONS

1. Can states require that beneficiaries live in the state five years before receiving AFDC?

2. Is it true that social workers cannot require a home visit if the client does not want one?

15

Special Sociolegal Problems

In a changing world, a dynamic profession must be alert to new areas for intervention and involvement. Energy and discriminating judgment will assist social workers who are dealing with special populations or areas of medical care that present perplexing questions.

MEDICAL PROBLEMS
The spiraling costs of medical care are familiar to everyone. Added to these are the psychological burdens on families in which a member is maintained on life support systems with no hope of recovery. In addition, organ transplantation and experimentation in genetic research are areas in which the correlative rights of society, the family, and the patient must be carefully analyzed.

Informed Consent
Informed consent is a doctrine developed in law to ensure that an individual has the legal capacity to consent to medical procedures and sufficient information to make an informed decision about the treatment. The doctrine presumes voluntary agreement to the recommended procedures. An individual who is legally unable to give consent cannot give informed consent (Somerville, 1979). Without informed consent, medical treatment is considered an assault, a legal wrong. If the next of kin to an unconscious patient cannot be reached to give consent to lifesaving procedures, it is presumed that the patient's consent would be given. For a child or any incompetent adult, consent can be given by the guardian or next of kin.

Informed consent is based on knowledge of the risks of the procedures. In determining how much to tell an individual, the physician takes into account the individual's background; sophistication in scientific matters; and physical, nervous, and mental state. Informed consent presumes that the individual understands the alternatives, although physicians are understandably reluctant to discuss with patients the long odds of success in some procedures (*Karp v. Cooley,* 1974).

Medical procedures may be rejected for a variety of reasons, not just because they are experimental or dangerous. A competent individual who refuses a blood transfusion for religious reasons is capable of understanding the life-threatening risks associated with that decision. If the individual is incompetent or if the state has an overriding concern—for instance, the protection of children who would be left as wards of the state if the parent died—the state may order treatment for an unwilling patient (*In Interest of Ivey,* 1975). These special circumstances override the exercise of the First Amendment freedom of religion.

Informed consent is a problem in medical research. Research results may skew if subjects are given too much information, because they anticipate effects that do not occur. The need for control groups frequently entails the use of a readily available population, for instance prisoners. This raises ethical questions about whether their agreement to participate is voluntary. Should human beings be guinea pigs (Benfell, 1977)?

Formal informed consent from the patient is often not possible in decisions to remove life support systems, because the patient is usually unconscious. Should others make that decision? What others and under what circumstances?

Right to Die

Controversy about the right to die, or death with dignity, reached everyone through publicity surrounding the Karen Quinlan case (*Matter of Quinlan,* 1976). Karen Anne was in a vegetative state sustained by life-support equipment. Her father petitioned the court to be appointed her guardian and made known that he would exercise her constitutional right to privacy and order the equipment removed. The medical staff agreed with his decision, and the court concurred. This was the first case in which a constitutional right of privacy to make such a decision was found. Later cases have concurred. *In the Matter of Dinnerstein* (1978) was a Massachusetts case in which the court agreed that when a hospital patient of advanced age was in an essentially vegetative state as the result of a massive stroke and was irreversibly and terminally ill, the attending physician could lawfully direct, without advance court approval, that resuscitation measures be withheld in case of cardiac or respiratory arrest (see also *Eichner v. Dillon,* 1980). In *Salz v. Perlmutter* (1978) the patient was a competent adult, his condition was terminal, and his family agreed with his wishes to discontinue medical treatment; his refusal of treatment could not be classed as an attempted suicide (Podgers, 1980). His right to refuse medical treatment was based on the constitutional right of privacy found in *Quinlan.*

The exercise of the right to die defined as a constitutional right to privacy depends on state law. In the absence of either informed consent or a court decision, physicians are understandably hesitant to remove life-support systems, fearing liability for "pulling the plug." Liability depends on such esoteric legal distinctions as that the failure to use extraordinary means initially was an omission, whereas later discontinuation of their use is an act; only one, "pulling the plug," has possible criminal consequences (Conway, 1974; see also *Lovato v. District Court,* 1979).

The right to die has collateral consequences in which determining the moment of death becomes crucial, especially if the organs of a terminally ill patient or of one injured in an accident can be transplanted. Cessation of respiration and heartbeat were the traditional signs of death until modern technological methods of maintaining both were developed. Physicians and other medical researchers now argue that a brain-death determination should be the crucial criterion when life is sustained by the use of machines.

In 1990 the Supreme Court heard the case of Nancy Cruzan, who was in a vegetative state after an automobile accident in 1983. Missouri refused her parents' request to withdraw artificial feeding and hydration equipment, saying there must be clear and convincing evidence of the patient's desire to terminate medical treatment. The Court agreed that Missouri could require clear and convincing evidence of the incompetent person's wishes (*Cruzan v. Director Missouri Dept. of Health,* 1990). Such evidence was presented after the decision, and Nancy died after her feeding tube was removed (Powell & Cohen, 1994).

The legal problems associated with organ transplants are not limited to determination of the moment of death, because organs can be removed from a living person for transplant to another. In *Strunk v. Strunk* (1969) a Kentucky court authorized the donation of a healthy kidney from a mentally incompetent adult to his brother. The donation was considered in the best interest of the incompetent brother, who was devoted to his brother. However, a Louisiana case, *In re Richardson* (1973), held the contrary on similar facts (Powell & Cohen, 1994).

The Living Will

Legislation authorizing a living will is one way to solve some of the problems associated with removal of life-support systems. The living will is a document executed by a rational adult that authorizes the removal of life-support systems when an illness is terminal and the individual is no longer able to make that choice. It absolves responsible parties from criminal liability.

California took the lead with this kind of legislation in 1976, and 31 states and the District of Columbia now have such legislation. Kaplan (1995) discussed the state and federal legislation involved in making end-of-life decisions. Forty-five states and the District of Columbia authorize both a living will and durable power of attorney, and 24 states and the District of Columbia authorize surrogate decision making and specify the order in which family members and close friends can be called on to serve as surrogate decision makers. The statutes vary. Some permit execution of the document only after a diagnosis of terminal illness, on the premise that a person cannot make such a serious decision until actually faced with it. Most statutes do not permit the family or attending physician to witness the document, although Arkansas permits listed relatives to execute the document for the terminally ill individual ("The Living Will," 1979; Strand, 1976).

Currently most American states have legislation providing for living wills. After the *Cruzan* decision, Congress passed a statute requiring all hospitals that receive federal funds to inform patients about living wills. Depending on the hospital, this may be done by medical social workers (Schroeder, 1992).

Many states have also enacted durable power of attorney statutes. These allow competent persons to appoint someone to make health care decisions for them. Unlike other powers of attorney, they survive the incompetence of the maker.

Uniform Anatomical Gift Act

The next of kin are not always willing to grant permission for the donation of organs when a relative dies. Competent adults may make the donation themselves by advance decision under the provisions of the Uniform Anatomical Gifts Act.

As of June 1971 the program had been enacted by 43 states and the District of Columbia. The act enables physicians to use organs of individuals who die away from their domiciles and away from those who know of their wish to donate eyes, heart, kidneys, or other organs to the living. If the law of the state where death occurs is similar to that of the state in which the deceased made the donation of organs, legal problems are greatly reduced. The program has been adopted in all 50 states and the District of Columbia.

The wishes of the deceased donor are usually made known by a card (sometimes a driver's license) carried in the wallet that authorizes the use of the organs. Because most organs must be transplanted immediately after death, this procedure is useful. Canada has a Model Human Tissues Act similar to the Uniform Anatomical Gift Act, which five provinces have used as a basis for statutes.

Because the timing of the gift of an organ does not necessarily coincide with need, there should be an organ storage bank and a method of matching need with availability, perhaps through computer storage of the information. Organ transplants and the use of sophisticated prostheses such as pacemakers and plastic arteries are a far cry from the wooden dentures and legs that were the extent of human replacement parts not long ago (Lathem, 1975).

Kurtz and Saks (1993) discussed the proposed cadaveric organ donor act which would establish a National Organ Donor Registry. The article provided the number of transplants that occurred in 1991 and named the 27 states and the District of Columbia that have adopted a form of the Living Organ Donor Act. A controversial part of the act permits the donation of fetal tissue from a spontaneous or legal abortion provided neither parent objects. The authors also attached a minority report criticizing the acts.

Genetic Counseling

Replacement parts may soon include additions to the molecular structure of the human gene, if the revolution in biological research continues. We can dream that the use of recombinant DNA will prevent the transmission of the hereditary characteristics that cause such diseases as Huntington's chorea, Tay-Sachs disease, diabetes, and sickle cell anemia.

At present genetic counseling is limited to helping individuals who suspect genetic problems to learn whether they are carriers of an inherited familial disease. If they are, they may be presented with the alternatives of sterilization, a different mate, or amniocentesis, in which the amniotic fluid containing fetal cells is examined to determine the presence of disease or undesirable genetic traits. None of the alternatives may be acceptable. Genetic counseling occasionally confronts people who are unaware that they are carriers of a particular genetic defect and are unprepared to face the knowledge (Gary, 1974).

Genetic counseling, like medical research, involves the use of medical records, with the accompanying danger of the release of confidential data. The Privacy Act of 1974 created the Privacy Protection Study

Commission, which made recommendations to Congress and the president for record-keeping practices and the use of medical records in research (Privacy Protection Study Commission, 1977; see also "Confidentiality of Health Records," 1980; Gordis & Gold, 1980). All cases, the esoteric as well as the "common" ones, of illness or death of loved ones, require social workers to demonstrate both compassion and expertise (Foster & Pearman, 1978).

SPECIAL GROUPS

The need for a living will or genetic counseling may concern a few of us, but legal problems are a worry for all. Certain groups have special legal problems deserving attention; several of them are targeted here.

Women

Women are not a numerical minority in the United States, but their practical disabilities are as real as those suffered by an actual minority. "Traditionally, such discrimination was rationalized by an attitude of romantic paternalism which, in practical effect, put women not on a pedestal, but in a cage" (411 U.S. at 685; 93 S.Ct. at 1769), said Justice Brennan in *Frontiero v. Richardson* (1973), a case brought by a female U.S. Air Force lieutenant who sought benefits for her husband as her dependent. Benefits were denied because she failed to show that he was dependent on her for more than half of his support. The wives of members of the military were not required to make any showing of dependency.

The government argued that Congress could rationally conclude that most wives of members of the armed services are financially dependent on their husbands. It is cheaper and easier to presume that fact than to have a case-by-case determination of dependency. The Court held that by "according differential treatment to male and female members of the uniformed services for the sole purpose of achieving administrative convenience, the statutes violate the due process clause of the Fifth Amendment insofar as they require a female member to prove the dependency of her husband." The Fifth Amendment was cited in the decision rather than the equal protection clause of the Fourteenth Amendment because the latter clause applies to the states; the discrimination here was by the federal government.

Frontiero followed by one term the decision in *Reed v. Reed* (1971), in which the Supreme Court held unanimously that a provision in the Idaho Probate Court Code was unconstitutional. Because it gave mandatory preference for appointment as administrator of an estate to a male applicant over an equally qualified female applicant within the same entitlement class, it violated the equal protection clause of the Fourteenth Amendment. Administrative convenience was again the rationale. The Court said:

> *To give a mandatory preference to members of either sex over members of the other, merely to accomplish the elimination of hearings on the merits, is to make the very kind of arbitrary legislative choice forbidden by the equal protection clause of the Fourteenth Amendment; and whatever may be said as to the positive values of avoiding intrafamily controversy, the choice in this context may not be lawfully mandated solely on the basis of sex.* (pp. 76–77)

Frontiero seemed to hold that sex is a suspect classification and that any gender discrimination must be subject to strict scrutiny, as is true in racial classifications. However, the Court has retreated from that position. In *Geduldig v. Aiello* (1975) and *General Electric Co. v. Gilbert* (1976), the Court upheld the exclusion of pregnancy from disability insurance programs, absent an indication that the exclusion was a pretext for discriminating against women, but it *did* strike down mandatory maternity leave rules in *Cleveland Bd. of Educ. v. LaFleur* (1974). Administrative convenience in conclusively presuming that all women are physically unfit to teach past the fourth or fifth month of their pregnancy is insufficient to overcome the finding that such rules arbitrarily impinge on the constitutional right of a woman to decide to bear a child. The Pregnancy Discrimination Act of 1978—an amendment to Title VII of the Civil Rights Act of 1964 prohibiting discrimination against women employees because of pregnancy, childbirth, or related conditions—will help resolve many discriminatory practices.

On February 5, 1993, President Clinton signed the Family and Medical Leave Act. It provides that private, state, and federal employers of 50 or more employees within a 75-mile radius of a given workplace must provide for eligible employees 12 weeks of unpaid leave during any 12-month period to care for the employee's child after birth, adoption, or acceptance of a foster care placement; to care for the employee's spouse, son or daughter, or parent who has a serious health condition; or for a serious health condition that makes the employee unable to do the job. After the leave, the employer must reinstate the employee to the same job or one with equivalent status. With so many single working parents and families with both parents employed, this will give individuals more options in planning for family emergencies. Although women will probably use the benefit more, men may use the leave as well. Although employees will be informed of the act, social workers should become familiar with it.

In *Davis v. Passman* (1979) a congressman was charged by a staff member with discrimination on the basis of sex. The Court held that his conduct was not shielded by the speech or debate clause of the Constitution and that the due process clause of the Fifth Amendment was a proper basis for the action. However, in *Personnel Adm'r of Massachusetts v. Feeney* (1979) the Court upheld the Massachusetts veterans preference statute against an attack on the basis of sex discrimination. The Court held that the statute preferred veterans of either sex and not men over women. Because veterans' preferences exist in most civil service states, women will continue to be discriminated against indirectly until more women are veterans.

Displaced homemakers. Women, and occasionally men, who have been at home for a number of years outside the salaried labor market fall into this category. The Displaced Homemakers Act gives the legal definition:

Sec. 802 Definitions. . . .

(7)   The term "displaced homemaker" means an individual who -

(A)   has not worked in the labor force for a substantial number of years but has, during those years, worked in the home providing unpaid services for family members.

(B)   (i)   has been dependent on public assistance or on the income of another family member but is no longer supported by that income, or

(ii) is receiving public assistance on account of dependent children in the home; and

(C)   is unemployed or underemployed and is experiencing difficulty in obtaining or upgrading employment.

Several states have programs to help prepare homemakers for salaried jobs, often using exciting techniques for evaluating skills in homemaking that may carry over to the labor market. Although age discrimination in employment is forbidden, these homemakers rarely have many marketable skills, so that discrimination is impossible to document. Careful attention to documenting unpaid work performed outside the home may bring greater recognition of experience useful to employers (Max & Schulman, 1980).

One area of discrimination against women generally, not just displaced homemakers, was ameliorated with the passage of the Equal Credit Opportunity Act of 1974. Forbidding discrimination against a credit applicant on the basis of sex or marital status, the act makes it possible for women to get loans on the same basis as men. In addition, married women can provide a credit record for themselves by asking creditors to consider payments made by them or their husbands as creating a credit rating for them as well. Divorced or widowed women will thus have a credit rating so that a loan officer can determine their eligibility for credit.

Rape. Rape is defined as "the unlawful carnal knowledge of a woman by a man forcibly and against her will" (*Black's Law Dictionary,* 1968). Black's sixth edition adds to that definition that, under some statutes, the crime embraces unnatural as well as natural intercourse and may include intercourse between two men. In some states only slight penetration is necessary for the crime; emission of semen is not. Rather than being a "sexual" crime, rape is now recognized as a crime of aggression—a violent crime against the person. Some states include homosexual rape within the definition, recognizing rape as a sexual assault of any person against another, regardless of sex. Women have been convicted of rape; when aiding and abetting as principals in its commission, they are guilty, although they are not perpetrators of the act itself.

A great deal has been written about rape concerning both its increase and the inadequacy of the criminal justice system to handle it properly. Conviction is difficult unless the victim is able to identify the assailant. Because the victim *must* be a witness at the criminal trial, she may be subjected to the unpleasant questions necessary to establish the crime and her resistance to it: it is an element of the crime that the act is "against her will" (Brownmiller, 1975). Because of the possibility of blackmail, probing questions are necessary to establish every element of the crime; the accused rapist does have constitutional rights.

Recent cases have focused attention on husbands raping their wives and companions raping unmarried partners. Many state criminal laws have a marital rape exemption that recognizes the common-law principle that a husband cannot, as a matter of law, be guilty of rape. In fact, the exemption is being extended to unmarried cohabitants and "voluntary social companions" (Schulman, 1980). Nineteen states have abolished the marital rape exemption, 17 by legislation and two by judicial decision (Ryder & Kuzmenka, 1991). Data suggest that marital rape occurs in 14 percent of American households, but because of underreporting, this figure may be even higher. Some commentators contend that the exemption violates the equal protection clause because it treats married and unmarried women differently without a rational reason. In response to that argument, five states passed statutes to extend the immunity to cohabitors. Because victims of marital rape suffer long-term effects, social workers should be aware of the crime and its implications. Date rape is also a current concern (Pfeiffer, 1990).

American Indians

Another group with special legal problems is American Indians. Since 1834—when Congress established the Bureau of Indian Affairs through the General Allotment Act of 1887, which made legal the breaking of treaties and destruction of reservations—to the Indian Reorganization Act of 1934—which attempted to restore the autonomy of the tribes— the history of the relationship of the federal government to the American Indians is regrettable and embarrassing (Cingolani, 1973). It was not until 1946 that the Indian Claims Commission was created. This is a judicial tribunal authorized to hear money claims by recognized groups of American Indians against the United States (Pierce, 1977). Proceedings before the commission, in which Indian tribes seek compensation for lands taken from them, review past treatment (see *Oneida Indian Nation of N.Y. State v. County of Oneida*, N.Y., 1974). Excerpts from two cases demonstrate the resulting litigation.

United States v. Oneida Nation of New York
477 F.2d 939 (1973)

Kunzig, J.

In issue in this government appeal from a decision of the Indian Claims Commission (the commission) is whether the government owed and subsequently breached fiduciary duty to protect the Oneida Indians in land dealings with the State of New York when the United States government did not participate in the transactions.

We hold that the federal government did owe a fiduciary duty to the Indians when, with knowledge of the transactions, the government failed to protect the rights of the Indians. We do not hold that actual federal participation is a prerequisite to the imposition of this fiduciary obligation. . . . Between 1785 and 1846 the Oneida Nation and the State of New York were signatories to twenty-seven (27) treaties in which the Indians ceded a vast majority of their lands to the state. The Oneida Nation, as found by the commission, were tribal members of the Iroquoian confederacy located along the shores of Oneida Lake in west-central New York. On June 28, 1785, the Oneida Nation joined with the Tuscarora Tribes to cede certain lands located in the State of New York to the State of New York. Thereafter, by the terms of the treaty of 1788 the Indians ceded all of their lands to the State of New York, except for an area of approximately 100 square miles that was reserved for their own use and was to be held by their posterity forever (hereinafter referred to as the Oneida Reservation). Between 1795 and 1846, the State of New York entered into a series of twenty-five (25) treaties with the Oneidas whereby the State of New York acquired virtually the entire Oneida Reservation. . . . Sales to states were expressly prohibited in the original Trade and Intercourse Act itself. Although this language referring to the states was dropped in subsequent Trading and Intercourse Acts, it was replaced by language which forbids any and all purchases from the Indians absent federal government consent regardless of the parties.

United States v. Creek Nation
476 F.2d 1290 (1973)

Durfee, S. J.

In the year 1790 the Creek Nation exercised the right of occupancy over a wide area of land located in a part of the present states of Alabama, Georgia, and Mississippi. Such right of occupancy was recognized by the United States. By various treaties thereafter made the Creeks ceded most of their tribal domain to the United States, and in 1826 were confined in a comparatively small domain in eastern Alabama and western Georgia. By treaty of January 24, 1826, proclaimed April 22, 1826, the Creek Nation ceded to the United States all of its domain located in the State of Georgia. After the treaty of 1826, these Indians were confined to a small domain in eastern Alabama, containing about 5,200,000 acres. As additional consideration for the cessation of tribal lands in 1826, the United States agreed to purchase lands west of the Mississippi River where a portion of the Creek Nation intimated it would settle. About 1827 or 1828 some of the Creeks did move to and settle upon lands west of the Mississippi in Indian territory assigned to the Creek Nation along and between the Verdigris, Arkansas, and Canadian Rivers. . . . In 1829 the State of Alabama, which had achieved statehood in 1819, extended its jurisdiction over the Creek country and divided the Indian territory. . . . There is no doubt, and appellant has not disputed that these intrusions by the State of Alabama were contrary to federal law. . . . The federal government had ample authority under the intercourse law of March 30, 1802, 2 Stat. 139, to protect the Creek Nation from physical intrusion upon Creek lands by white settlers. Consistent with its own policy of Indian removal from the East, the federal government determined it would not oppose Alabama's actions. The press of white settlers to overtake Indian lands in the eastern United States had found expression in a formal declaration of policy by Congress in the act of May 29, 1830, 4 Stat. 411, that the Indian tribes were to be removed from their ancestral homes in the east to lands west of the Mississippi River by seeking agreement of tribes for the exchange of their eastern lands for land in the west. As a coercive inducement to obtain the agreement of the Creeks, the federal government told the Creeks that it was powerless to prevent the extension of the Alabama laws over (and as a consequence thereof the influx of white settlers into) Creek lands. . . . It should be remembered that the Creeks who had remained in Alabama after 1828 had a fixed intention to remain there rather than move west. The Alabama land was the last enclave of the ancestral lands left the

Creeks and the religious significance of the land cemented the Creek in-
tention to remain there. . . . In an apparent concession to the steadfast
intention of the Creeks to remain in Alabama, the federal government
advanced the idea to the Creek Chiefs that each chief and each Creek
head of family in Alabama would be given fee simple title to separate
sections of the ancestral lands. This idea of promising fee simple title to
individual members of the tribe in return for a tribal cession of the 5,200,000
acres was the outgrowth of a strategy of removal first enunciated by An-
drew Jackson in the address to the Creeks on March 23, 1829.

• • • • •

Following the negotiation of the treaty of 1832 speculators formed com-
panies and entered the Creek country with a view to purchasing individual
Indian reservations. Many schemes were used to obtain these reserves. Of-
fices for the certification of sales of reserves were set up in October 1833,
pursuant to Article III of the treaty. Certifying agents began certifying
contracts as soon as the locations were completed in 1834. Soon after they
began their work, complaints were made that gross frauds were being prac-
ticed upon the Indians by speculators. . . . Other cases contain further
recitals of wretched treatment by the government.

Several of the cases turn on whether the particular Indian community
is a "tribe," a word with a specific legal meaning that establishes a trust
relationship with the United States. A tribe has jurisdiction over its members for some criminal matters and certain other legal disputes (Collins,
Johnson, & Perkins, 1977; *Joint Tribal Council of Passamaquoddy Tribe
v. Morton*, 1975; "Symposium," 1968).

Social workers who work with Indians may have to consider the status
of the individual as a tribal member. Legal disputes reaching the courts
frequently depend on that status and cover a variety of problems: property disputes, domestic relations, crime, and economic problems. In the
Crowe case plaintiff claimed inheritance of her father's holdings against
the tribal council's division of land. The court held that it was without
power to substitute its judgment on the merits for that of the tribe and so
could not restore to plaintiff her holdings. The case was remanded for
reconsideration by the tribe. This excerpt illustrates the different property concepts existing in tribal law and Euro-American law.

Crowe v. Eastern Band of Cherokee Indians, Inc.

506 F.2d 1231 (4th Cir. 1974)

Field, C.J.

The sovereignty of Indian tribes as "distinct, independent, political com-
munities" qualified to exercise the power of self-government was first

definitely recognized in a landmark case, Worcester v. Georgia. . . . *What has been described as "perhaps the most basic principle of all Indian Law" is that the powers invested in an Indian tribe are not powers granted by express acts of Congress, but rather inherent powers of a limited sovereignty which has never been extinguished. . . . Under the Indian concept of tribal property the ownership and use of land is communal. The power of absolute ownership is lodged in the tribe and the interests of the individual members of the tribe are "limited to a mere occupancy of the tracts set apart for homes with the right to free use in common of the unoccupied portion of the reserve." . . . There can be no individual ownership of land and the individual's right of use depends upon tribal law or custom. . . . It would appear that the court was applying Anglo-American principles of real property law, and in so doing adopted an approach that was incompatible with the established principle that lands belong to the Indian tribe as a community and not the members severally or as tenants in common.*

Whether tribal courts can resolve disputes frequently depends on whether the Indian resides on land that is legally recognized as a reservation. In one case that reached the Supreme Court (*DeCoteau v. District Court for Tenth Jud. Dist.,* 1975), a mother brought a habeas corpus action alleging that the South Dakota Welfare Department lacked jurisdiction to remove her children on grounds of neglect. This was a consolidated case (one in which two or more cases are tried together), like *Brown v. Board of Education of Topeka* (1954). In the other cases, Indians challenged their convictions of crimes of South Dakota laws committed on lands presently non-Indian but that were within the 1867 reservation boundaries. The argument was that because in 1867 these were reservation lands, the state had no jurisdiction. The Supreme Court held that the South Dakota state court had civil and criminal jurisdiction over the conduct of members of the tribe on non-Indian, nonallotted lands, even those within the 1867 reservation borders.

In *United States ex rel. Cobell v. Cobell* (1974) the parties were both enrolled members of the Blackfeet tribe. The wife sued for divorce, the husband was awarded temporary custody of the children, and the award was sustained by the Montana supreme court. The wife took her children to visit her mother on the Blackfeet reservation, where the tribal council issued a temporary restraining order enjoining the children's removal from the reservation. The father filed a petition of habeas corpus in federal district court, which granted the writ. The children's grandmother and the tribal judge appealed.

The court of appeals held that the tribal court lacked jurisdiction to determine custody of the children, because the parents, by invoking the state court's jurisdiction for divorce purposes, had submitted questions of custody to the judgment of the state court. In addition, the Tribal Law and Order Code explicitly disclaimed tribal jurisdiction over marriage, divorce, and adoption, deferring to state law. Therefore, matters of status depend on the tribal code and the court in which the proceedings are initiated.

Indians are entitled to social security and state welfare benefits like other citizens of a state, but they may also be entitled to special benefits because of their residence on a reservation. *Morton v. Ruiz* (1974) involved a Papago Indian and his wife who lived in an Indian community a few miles away from the reservation, where he worked in a mine. During a prolonged strike at the mine the husband was out of work and was not entitled to unemployment compensation, because those benefits are denied to strikers. He applied for general assistance benefits under the Snyder Act of 1921, which provides among other things for the Bureau of Indian Affairs to provide for relief of distress and conservation of health. These benefits were denied by the Bureau of Indian Affairs because of a regulation limiting eligibility to Indians living "on reservations." The Supreme Court held that Congress did not intend to exclude from the general assistance program full-blooded, unassimilated Indians living in an Indian community near their native reservation who maintained close economic and social ties with the reservation. The Court quoted from reports of Senate hearings to show that Congress intended the benefits to be for Indians living "on or near" a reservation.

In another economic decision, *Hamilton v. Butz* (1975), the court of appeals held that Congress did not intend that the distribution of funds to individual Alaska natives pursuant to the Alaska Native Claims Settlement Act of 1971 should displace food stamp assistance (Cross & Rath, 1980). These distributions, given in compensation because the act extinguished titles natives had to Alaskan lands, were thus not included in determining resources available to native Alaskans who sought food stamps. Other preferences, for example, preferential treatment for Indians in hiring and promotion in the Bureau of Indian Affairs, have been upheld by a unanimous Supreme Court reasoning from Congress's unique trust obligations toward tribal Indians (*Morton v. Mancari*, 1974).

Tribal councils have a great deal of autonomy, as *Santa Clara Pueblo v. Martinez* (1978) illustrates. There a female member of the pueblo in New Mexico brought a class action suit to challenge a membership ordinance of the pueblo: Male members who marry nonmembers may apply for membership in the tribe for their children; female members who marry nonmembers may not. The ordinance was an economic measure, enacted when the elders became concerned that the population increase from intermarriage would strain the pueblo's economic resources. Although the court of appeals held that the tribe was not justified in deviating from the Fourteenth Amendment standard, the Supreme Court reversed and held that suits against the tribe under the Indian Civil Rights Act of 1968 are barred. Nothing on the face of the Indian Civil Rights Act, the Court said, purported to subject the tribes to the jurisdiction of the federal courts in civil actions for declaratory or injunctive relief. An interesting footnote is that Julia Martinez was married to a full-blooded Navaho. However, she and her husband lived at the Santa Clara Pueblo; their children were reared there; all spoke Tewa, the traditional and official language of the pueblo; and all practiced the traditional religion.

Social work with American Indians requires special attention to the cultural factors operating in this group and the tribal laws under which Indians live (Farris, 1973; Lewis & Ho, 1975). Tribal law may require that ordinary legal problems of an Indian be handled in a different fashion.

Migrant Workers

Indians at least have the protection and services of the Bureau of Indian Affairs; migrant workers may slip through the cracks when social services are provided. When the first programs of social legislation were passed in this country, they generally did not cover agriculture. The reasoning was that the administrative problems and financial costs of coverage for the small farmer were too great. This is the same parochial thinking that for many years excluded domestic workers from social security coverage. As agriculture has evolved from the traditional small family farm to large agribusiness complexes, coverage has been extended more and more, yet the problem of identifying migrant farm workers and providing services for them remains.

A holdover from the Elizabethan poor laws is the tradition of thinking of social programs in terms of localities: the municipality, the county, the state. The advantage, it is thought, is that localities have greater intimacy with people and their problems and can use innovative programs to ameliorate social problems without large-scale upheaval. This is of no value to the transient worker who has no ties to a particular locality. Migrant workers may follow a harvest from Florida to Wisconsin, perhaps remaining in one locality only a few weeks. Theirs are truly national problems.

Providing social and human services—welfare, education, and public health—is traditionally a local task. Until *Shapiro v. Thompson* (1969), states were permitted to condition the receipt of public benefits and services on residence within the state for a certain period of time. *Shapiro* held this to be a denial of equal protection. Therefore, migrant families may receive Aid to Families with Dependent Children (AFDC). However, because their employment is transient, applicants may have to leave a community before processing is complete, and their lack of a fixed address effectively closes this avenue of economic relief. In addition, AFDC is normally designed for one-parent families. Food stamps present the same problems: lack of a fixed address and too little time to process applications.

As for federal social legislation, regularly employed farm workers were covered by old age, survivor's, and disability insurance under social security in 1950; the coverage was extended to certain self-employed farmers and other farm workers in 1954. If a farm worker earns more than $150 during a year, social security taxes are paid. The Farm Labor Contract Registration Act of 1963 was the first attempt by Congress to regulate the practices of "crew leaders," who are often the employers of migrants. The crew leader is required to keep payroll records and deduct for social security. Crew leaders who provide transportation for migrant workers are regulated by the Interstate Commerce Commission. Like all farm workers, migrant workers are not protected by the National Labor Relations Act, and many are excluded from unemployment compensation.

Health problems may be expected in a group of people who typically live in substandard housing and have an inadequate diet. Federal funding for migrant health-care services includes the Migrant Health Act of 1962; Title XX of the Social Security Act of 1935; the Early Periodic Screening, Diagnosis and Treatment Program; Rural Health Initiative; Health for Underserved Rural Areas; and National Health Service Corporation (see *Martinez v. Mathews*, 1976). But migrant workers have the same problem in taking advantage of these programs as with AFDC, because Medicaid benefits and the Early Periodic Screening, Diagnosis and Treatment Program have the same eligibility standards.

If you have a migrant client, rural legal aid societies can often help in giving information and protecting migrant workers' rights.

Health services provided to indigent residents may not be denied to transients. In *Memorial Hosp. v. Maricopa County* (1974) the Supreme Court held it a violation of equal protection to deny county nonemergency medical care to an indigent person who had not resided in the county for a year. The Court applied the equal protection and right to travel arguments used in *Shapiro*.

A major problem for migrant workers is the education of their children. In 1966 Title I of the Elementary and Secondary Education Act was amended to include migrant children as an educationally deprived group. That legislation has been repealed. Other legislation (20 U.S.C.A. § 2743) provides annual funds to the states for educational programs serving the children of migrant workers. Constant disruptions in schooling caused by following the harvest may mean that children are below the average in arithmetic or English as they move into new schools. They will certainly be at a disadvantage moving from a course in Florida history to one in North Carolina politics and then to one in New Jersey geography. The problem of moving from one school system to another includes the trouble of forwarding to the next school copies of a child's records.

In 1970 the Migrant Data Bank Records Transfer System was established in Little Rock. The Arkansas Department of Education has a central computer that records the name, sex, birthdate, birthplace, standardized reading and math test scores, medical data, and student identification number of each registered migrant child. By July 1971 all 48 mainland states were participating in the data bank. These data permit a state to obtain a complete history on any migrant child by submitting the student identification number ("Migrant Legal Action," 1974; Patino, 1987).

People with Disabilities

In 1975 Congress passed Public Law 94-142, the Education for All Handicapped Children Act. The legislation provides grants to state and local educational agencies to provide specialized education in the least restrictive environment for children with disabilities, defined as "mentally retarded, hard of hearing, deaf, speech impaired, visually handicapped, seriously emotionally disturbed, orthopedically impaired, other health–impaired, deaf–blind, multi-handicapped, or as having specific brain difficulties" (Anderson, Freeman, & Edwards, 1977; Englehardt, 1976; Schroeder, 1978). The law requires an individual education plan for each exceptional child, after evaluation by a multidisciplinary team. Social workers who participate in the evaluation process and school social workers who deal with problems associated with conditions of children with disabilities are familiar with the legislation. Evaluation must be free of bias. At least one court has said that lack of funds is no excuse for not educating exceptional children (*Mills v. Board of Education of District of Columbia,* 1972).

The Supreme Court has looked at the act. *Board of Educ., etc. v. Rowley* (1982) was the first time the Court interpreted it. A deaf girl had a special hearing aid and additional instruction from tutors. She progressed well educationally, academically, and socially but was apparently not living up to her potential. Her parents wanted a sign language interpreter in the classroom. The Court held that "free appropriate public education" did not require the state to maximize the potential of each child with a disability commensurate with opportunity provided nondisabled children, so the act did not require that an interpreter be provided. School social workers may look to outside resources for additional help in maximizing the potential of a child with a disability (see *Zobrest v. Catalina Foothills School District,* 1993).

In *Burlington Sch. Comm. v. Department of Educ.* (1985) the child's individualized education plan called for placement in private school. The town refused to pay for it. After several trials and remands the case reached the Supreme Court. The Court held that the court reviewing the plan has the power to order school authorities to reimburse parents for expenditures for private special education.

In 1968 Congress passed the Architectural Barriers Act setting standards for design, construction, and alteration of public buildings to ensure access for those with physical disabilities whenever possible. Many states have followed suit. Providing transportation and access to public buildings for those people with disabilities will be expensive. What should our policy be for bringing everyone into the mainstream of American life?

The most important legislation for people with disabilities was the Rehabilitation Act of 1973 (see Burgdorf & Burgdorf, 1975). Section 504 reads,

> *No otherwise qualified handicapped individual in the United States, as defined in Section 706(7) of this title, shall, solely by reason of his handicap, be excluded from the participation in, be denied the benefits of, or be subjected to discrimination under any program or activity receiving federal financial assistance.*

The Supreme Court decision in *Southeastern Community College v. Davis* (1979) caused some consternation as to the future of mainstreaming children with disabilities (but see *Camenisch v. University of Texas,* 1980). A woman with a hearing loss, already a licensed practical nurse, was refused admission to a program leading to certification as a registered nurse because the college felt that clinical routines like surgery, which require wearing a mask, would prohibit her from lip-reading. The college expressed concern about the safety of her practicing as a registered nurse. The Supreme Court agreed, holding that "an otherwise qualified person is one who is able to meet all of a program's requirements in spite of his handicap." However, a lower federal court has held that people with disabilities may enforce the Section 504 prohibition of employment discrimination regardless of whether the employer receives federal financial assistance to provide employment. The plaintiff, who had epilepsy had worked as a volunteer counselor for a county probation department but was refused employment as a group counselor. Guernsey (1989) discussed the area.

In 1990 President Bush signed the Americans with Disabilities Act, which greatly extends the scope of the Rehabilitation Act. It prohibits discrimination against people with disabilities by employers of 15 or more employees as of July 1994. No medical examination may be required before employment, and qualifications must be consistent with business necessity. *Disability* is defined as a physical or mental impairment that substantially limits one or more of the major life activities of an individual. The disabled person must be qualified to perform the job, with or without reasonable accommodation. The employer need not accommodate the applicant if it would involve undue hardship, defined as significant difficulty and expense. Social workers in rehabilitation may be able to think of inexpensive employer accommodations such as raising or lowering machines.

Examples of physical and mental impairments that the act covers include multiple sclerosis, cancer, heart disease, diabetes, epilepsy, mental retardation, emotional illness, asymptomatic HIV disease, tuberculosis, drug addiction, and alcoholism (LeBlanc, 1992). The following case dealt with a school teacher hospitalized for tuberculosis in 1957. The disease was in remission for the next 20 years, during which she taught elementary school. After relapses in 1977 and 1978, she was suspended with pay. At the end of the 1978–1979 school year she was discharged. She brought suit under the Rehabilitation Act of 1973.

School Board of Nassau County, Fl. v. Arline
480 U. S. 273, 107 S. Ct. 1123 (1987)
Mr. Justice Brennan delivered the opinion of the Court
We do not agree with petitioners that, in defining a handicapped individual under § 504, the contagious effects of a disease can be meaningfully distinguished from the disease's physical effects on a claimant in a case such as this. Arline's contagiousness and her physical impairment each resulted from the same underlying condition, tuberculosis. It would be unfair to allow an employer to seize upon the distinction between the effects of a disease on others and the effects of a disease on a patient and use that distinction to justify discriminatory treatment.

· · · · ·

The fact that some persons who have contagious diseases may pose a serious health threat to others under certain circumstances does not justify excluding from the coverage of the act all persons with actual or perceived contagious diseases. Such exclusion would mean that those accused of being contagious would never have the opportunity to have their condition evaluated in light of medical evidence and a determination made as to whether they were "otherwise qualified." Rather, they would be vulnerable to discrimination on the basis of mythology—precisely the type of injury Congress sought to prevent. We conclude that the fact that a person with a

record of a physical impairment is also contagious does not suffice to re-
move that person from coverage under § 504.

The remaining question is whether Arline is otherwise qualified for the
job of elementary school teacher. To answer this question in most cases, the
district court will need to conduct an individualized inquiry and make
appropriate findings of fact. Such an inquiry is essential if § 504 is to
achieve its goal of protecting handicapped individuals from deprivations
based on prejudice, stereotypes, or unfounded fear, while giving appropri-
ate weight to such legitimate concerns of grantees as avoiding exposing
others to significant health and safety risks.

· · · · ·

In making these findings, courts normally should defer to the reason-
able medical judgments of public health officials. The next step in the
"otherwise qualified" inquiry if the employer could reasonably accommo-
date the employee under the established standards for that inquiry.

The Court held that if the risk of Arline infecting children is trivial,
she must be reinstated. Otherwise, the board must try to offer her another position, such as an administrative job that requires little contact
with children. This case may serve as a guide for courts looking at cases
brought under the Americans with Disabilities Act.

Although we traditionally consider handicapping conditions to be
physical and emotional, the inability to speak English may be a handicapping condition for a child who enters public school. Bilingual–bicul-
tural education programs attempt to ameliorate this problem. The gen-
esis of these programs was the 1968 amendment to the Elementary and
Secondary Education Act of 1965, intended to develop pilot projects to
help children of low-income families who were educationally disadvantaged by their inability to speak English. Stimulus for the growth of these
programs was the suit brought by members of San Francisco's Chinese
community against the local school district on behalf of some 1,800 non-
English-speaking students who were not receiving instruction in English.
In that case, *Lau v. Nichols* (1974), a unanimous court found that the
failure to provide a solution to the language problem violated both the
Civil Rights Act of 1964 and the regulations promulgated by U.S Department of Health, Education, and Welfare under the authority of 42
U.S.C. 2000d-1, the statute that requires the president's approval of rules
and regulations that effectuate the prohibition against discrimination under federally assisted programs on the grounds of race, color, or national
origin. The Court found it obvious that the non–English-speaking Chinese minority were receiving fewer benefits than the English-speaking
majority because of the language barrier.

The Supreme Court did not specify a remedy, and various courts have struggled with programs devised by school districts. In *Guadalupe Organization, Inc. v. Tempe Elementary Sch. Dist. #3* (1978) the court of appeals for the ninth circuit squarely held that there is no constitutional right to this type of program, although there is a statutory right with benign purpose. Does this disadvantage non-English-speaking people who, under bilingual education, would not receive rigorous education in the English language?

Aging

The political clout of elderly people is shown in part by the indexing of social security benefits to the cost of living, although no one supposes that this solves all the economic problems of the elderly. Because many elderly people are newly poor, they must undergo a traumatic readjustment to a drastically reduced standard of living. The Older Americans Act of 1965 brought the federal government into a social service program solely for the country's senior citizen population (Rowse, 1978). It created the Administration on Aging and three grant programs to the states: (1) for community social services projects, (2) for research and demonstration, and (3) for training in the field of aging.

Economic trials are not the only problems of elderly people. Crimes against elderly people prompt indignant responses from lawmakers ("Special Section," 1977). Abuses in life-care contracts should also receive attention. These are contracts in which elderly people turn over all their property and money to a provider in return for a promise of care for life. These are attractive offers, but if they are not backed up by sufficient resources, bankruptcy of the provider leaves the elderly person with no resources and no legal recourse.

Nursing homes present major problems for elderly people, both in availability and in quality. Many elderly people who cannot be maintained in their own homes or those of relatives must turn to long-term care facilities. In 1965 the Illinois Supreme Court's landmark decision in *Darling v. Charleston Hosp.* (1965) allowed the admission of hospital bylaws, industry accreditation standards, and state licensing regulations as evidence of the hospital's duty of care to its patients. It is possible that performance standards of long-term care facilities will similarly be admissible (see 42 C.F.R. 442; Butler, 1980; Rains, 1992). Action for damages by an elderly patient in a nursing home who is injured or otherwise harmed by poor care is a remedy for the individual but does not solve the acute problem of adequate long-term facilities for the many.

Kapp (1991) discussed the traditional underrepresentation of elderly people in malpractice claims and the beginning of interest in the creation of the Nursing Home Litigation Groups in the American Trial Lawyers Association. The largest source of negligence claims against nursing homes comes from injuries associated with falls or wandering. Kapp cited cases where nursing homes have been responsible under various situations. The article also discussed federal Medicare and Medicaid statutes and regulations as they apply to nursing homes and discussed the Health Care Financing Administration (HCFA) and its regulations, which became effective in 1990. These regulations include providing residents with a minimum amount of social work (see 42 C.F.R. 483.15(g) (1990)).

REFERENCES

Anderson, R. J., Freeman, M., & Edwards, R. L. (Eds.). (1977). *School social work and P.L. 94-142: The Education for All Handicapped Children Act.* Silver Spring, MD: National Association of Social Workers.

Benfell, C. (1977, Spring). Abusing the bodies and minds of prisoners. *Barrister, 4,* 27–37.

Black's law dictionary (4th ed., rev.) (1968). St. Paul, MN: West Publishing.

Brownmiller, S. (1975). *Against our will: Men, women, and rape.* New York: Simon & Schuster.

Burgdorf, M. P., & Burgdorf, R. (1975). History of unequal treatment: The qualifications of handicapped persons as a "suspect class" under the equal protection clause. *Santa Clara Lawyer, 15,* 855–910.

Butler, P. A. (1980). A long-term health care strategy for legal services. *Clearinghouse Review, 14,* 613–702.

Cingolani, W. (1973). Acculturating the Indian: Federal policies. *Social Work, 18,* 24–28.

Collins, R. B., Johnson, R. W., & Perkins, K. I. (1977). American courts and tribal self-government. *American Bar Association Journal, 63,* 808–815.

Confidentiality of health records: A symposium on current issues, opportunities, and unfinished business. (1980). *American Journal of Orthopsychiatry, 50,* 639–685.

Conway, D. J. (1974, Winter). Medical and legal views of death: Confrontation and reconciliation. *Saint Louis University Law Journal, 19,* 172–188.

Cross, R., & Rath, B. (1980). Indian monies and welfare eligibility. *Clearinghouse Review, 14,* 120–123.

Englehardt, J. A. (1976). The Education for All Handicapped Children Act: Opening the schoolhouse door. *New York Review of Law and Social Change, 6,* 43–63.

Farris, C. E. (1973). A White House conference on the American Indian. *Social Work, 18,* 80, 86.

Foster, M. G., & Pearman, W. A. (1978). Social work, patient rights, and patient representatives. *Social Casework, 59,* 89–100.

Gary, L. I. (1974). The sickle cell controversy. *Social Work, 19,* 263–272.

Geurnsey, T. F. (1989). The Education for All Handicapped Children Act and section 504 of the Rehabilitation Act of 1973: Statutory interaction following the Handicapped Children's Protection Act of 1986. *Nebraska Law Review, 68,* 564–600.

Gordis, L., & Gold, E. (1980). Privacy, confidentiality, and the use of medical records in research. *Science, 207,* 153–156.

Kaplan, K. O. (1995). End-of-life decisions. In R. L. Edwards (Ed.-in-Chief), *Encyclopedia of social work* (19th ed., Vol. 1, pp. 856–868). Washington, DC: NASW Press.

Kapp, M. B. (1991). Malpractice liability in long-term care: A changing environment. *Creighton Law Review, 24,* 1235–1260.

Kurz, S. F., & Saks, M. J. (1993). Cadaveric Organ Donor Act; Living Organ Act (Drafts and accompanying reports on a proprosed federal law). *The Journal of Corporation Law, 18,* 523–618.

Lathem, A. (1975, February 10). Replaceable you. *New York, 8,* 37–47.

LeBlanc, P. (1992). Introducing the Americans with Disabilities Act: Promises and challenges. *University of San Francisco Law Review, 27,* 149–164.

Lewis, R. G., & Ho, M. K. (1975). Social work with Native Americans. *Social Work, 20,* 379–382.

The living will—Death with dignity or mechanical vitality [comment]. (1979). *Cumberland Law Review, 10,* 163.

Max, E., & Schulman, J. (1980). Legal recognition for the world experience of women. *Clearinghouse Review, 14,* 733–734.

Patino, V. (1987). Migrant farm worker advocacy empowering the invisible labor. *Harvard Civil Rights—Civil Liberties Law Review, 22,* 43–53.

Pfeiffer, M. C. (1990). Date rape: The realities. *Southern University Law Review, 17,* 283–295.

Pierce, M. H. (1977). The work of the Indian Claims Commission. *American Bar Association Journal, 64,* 227–232.

Podgers, J. (1980). "Rational suicide" raises patient rights issues. *American Bar Association Journal, 66,* 1500–1501.

Powell, J. A., & Cohen, A. S. (1994). The right to die. *Issues in Law and Medicine, 10,* 169–182.

Privacy Protection Study Commission. (1977). *Personal privacy in an information society.* Washington, DC: U.S. Government Printing Office.

Rains, R. E. (1992). A pre-history of the Americans with Disabilities Act and some initial thoughts as to its constitutional limitations. *St. Louis University Public Law Review, 11,* 185–202.

Rowse, G. T. (1978). Legal services for the elderly under title III of the Older Americans Act: Utilization of a "means test." *Clearinghouse Review, 12,* 225–230.

Ryder, S. L., & Kuzmenka, S. A. (1991). Legal rape: The marital rape exception. *The John Marshall Law Review, 24,* 393–421.

Schroeder, L. O. (1978, December). Education of exceptional children: Act 754 of 1977. *Louisiana Bar Journal, 26,* 137–143.

Schroeder, L. O. (1992). Where there's a will. *International Journal of Medicine and Law, 516,* 417–422.

Schulman, J. (1980). The marital rape exemption in the criminal law. *Clearinghouse Review, 14,* 538–540.

Somerville, M. A. (1979). *Consent to medical care* [Study paper]. Protection of Life Series. Ottawa, CA: Law Reform Commission of Canada.

Special section on legal problems of the elderly. (1977). *Connecticut Law Review, 9,* 425–487.

Strand, J. G. (1976). The living will: The right to death with dignity? *Case Western Law Review, 26,* 485–526.

Symposium: Indian law. (1968). *Arizona Law Review, 10,* 553–689.

STATUTES CITED

Alaska Native Claims Settlement Act of 1971. P.L. 92-203, 85 Stat. 688, 43 U.S.C.A. §§1601–1624.

Americans with Disabilities Act of 1990. P.L. 101-336, 104 Stat. 327, 42 U.S.C.S. 12101.

Architectural Barriers Act of 1968. P.L. 90-480, 82 Stat. 718, 42 U.S.C.A. § 4151 et seq.

Civil Rights Act of 1964. P.L. 88-352, 78 Stat. 241, 42 U.S.C.A. 88 1971 et seq.

Displaced Homemakers Self-Sufficiency Assistance Act of 1990. P.L. 101-554, 104 Stat. 2751, 29 U.S.C.A. 801 et seq.

Education for All Handicapped Children Act of 1975. P.L. 94-142, 89 Stat. 773.

Elementary and Secondary Education Act of 1965. P.L. 89-10, 79 Stat. 27, 20 U.S.C. § 241 (a).

Equal Credit Opportunity Act of 1974. P.L. 93-495, 88 Stat. 1521, 15 U.S.C.A. 1691 et seq.

Family and Medical Leave Act of 1993. P.L. 103-3, 2 U.S.C.A. §§ 2041–2055.

Farm Labor Contractor Registration Act of 1963. P.L. 88-582, 78 Stat. 920, 7 U.S.C.A. §§ 2041–2055.

Indian Civil Rights Act of 1968. P.L. 90-284, 82 Stat. 77-80, 25 U.S.C.A. §1301 et seq.

Indian General Allotment Act of 1887. Ch. 119, 24 Stat. 388, 25 U.S.C.A. § 331 et seq.

Indian Reorganization Act of 1934. Ch. 576, 48 Stat. 984, 25 U.S.C.A. § 461 et seq.

Migrant Health Act of 1962. P.L. 87-692, 76 Stat. 592, 42 U.S.C.A. §§ 2476, 247b, 247d, 254b.

National Labor Relations Act of 1935. Ch. 372, 49 Stat. 449, 29 U.S.C.A. § 151 et seq.

Older Americans Act of 1965. P.L. 89-73, 79 Stat. 218, 42 U.S.C.A. § 3001 et seq.

Pregnancy Discrimination Act of 1978. P.L. 95-555, 92 Stat. 2076, 42 U.S.C.A. § 200e(k).

Privacy Act of 1974. P.L. 93-579, 88 Stat. 1876, 5 U.S.C.A. § 552a.

Rehabilitation Act of 1973. P.L. 93-112, 87 Stat. 355, 29 U.S.C.A. § 701 et seq.

Snyder Act of 1921. Ch. 115, 42 Stat. 208, 25 U.S.C.A. § 13.

Social Security Amendments of 1974 (Title XX). P.L. 93-647, 88 Stat. 2337, 42 U.S.C.A. §§ 401–433.

Uniform Anatomical Gift Act of 1987. 8A ULA 19.

FURTHER READING

Ginsberg, R. B. (1977). Let's have E.R.A. as a signal. *American Bar Association Journal, 64,* 70–73.

Thompson, J. K. (1976). Fighting discrimination: Up against the ivied wall. *Social Work, 21,* 506–511.

STUDY QUESTIONS

1. What are some legal problems of concern to social workers who work with American Indians?

2. How will the Americans with Disabilities Act affect social work practice?

3. What are some legal problems that medical social workers should consider?

Cases Cited

Abbott v. Owens-Corning Fiberglas Corp., 444 S.E.2d 285, 191 W.Va. 198 (1994).

Abbott v. Thetfort, 534 F.2d 1101 (5th Cir. 1976), *en banc, cert. denied,* 430 U.S. 954, 97 S. Ct. 1598, 51 L.Ed.2d 804 (1977).

Ada C. Pollock-Blundon Assn. v. Heirs of Evans, 273 So.2d 552 (La. App. 1st Cir. 1973).

Adams v. Weinberger, 548 F.2d 239 (8th Cir. 1977).

Addington v. Texas, 99 S. Ct. 1804 (1979).

Adoption of Walker, 360 A.2d 603 (Pa. 1976).

Ake v. Oklahoma, 470 U.S. 68, 105 S. Ct. 1087, 84 L.Ed.2d 53 (1985).

Alicea Rosada v. Garcia Santiago, 562 F.2d 114 (1st Cir. 1977).

Alma Soc. Inc. v. Mellon, 601 F.2d 1225 (2d Cir. 1979), *cert. denied,* 444 U.S. 995 (1979).

Anderson v. Vasquez, 827 F.Supp. 617 (N.D. Cal. 1992).

Application of Gault, 387 U.S. 1, 87 S. Ct. 1428 (1967).

Argersinger v. Hamlin, 407 U.S. 25, 92 S. Ct. 2006 (1973).

Arnett v. Kennedy, 416 U.S. 134, 94 S. Ct. 1633, 40 L.Ed.2d 15 (1974).

Atcherson v. Siebenmann, 605 F.2d 1058 (8th Cir. 1979).

Atlas Roofing Co., Inc. v. Occupational Safety & Health Review, 430 U.S. 442, 97 S. Ct. 1261, 51 L.Ed.2d 464 (1977).

Baehr v. Lewin, 852 F.2d 44 (Hawaii 1993).

Baker v. Nelson, 191 N.W.2d 185, 291 Minn. 310 (1971).

Batterton v. Francis, 432 U.S. 416, 97 S. Ct. 2399, 53 L.Ed.2d 448 (1977).

Baugh v. Woodard, 808 F.2d 333 (1987).

Beal v. Doe, 432 U.S. 438, 96 S. Ct. 2366, 53 L.Ed.2d 464 (1977).

Bearden v. Georgia, 461 U.S. 660, 103 S. Ct. 2064, 716 L.Ed.2d 221 (1983).

Bellotti v. Baird, 99 S. Ct. 3035 (1979).

Belmont v. California State Personnel Board, 36 Cal. App.3d 518, 111 Cal. Rptr. 617 (1974).

Bethea v. United States, 365 A.2d 64 (1976).

Blew v. Verta, 617 A.2d 31 (Pa. Super. 1992).

Blue Shield of Virginia v. McCready, 457 U.S. 466, 102 S. Ct. 2540, 75 L.Ed.2d 149 (1982).

Board of C. of P. of New Orleans v. Splendour S. & E. Co., 273 So.2d 19 (La. 1973).

Board of Educ., etc. v. Rowley, 458 U.S. 176, 102 S. Ct. 3034, 73 L.Ed.2d 690 (1982).

Boddie v. Connecticut, 401 U.S. 371, 91 S. Ct. 780 (1971).

Bolling v. Sharpe, 347 U.S. 497, 74 S. Ct. 693 (1954).

Bowen v. Gilliard, 483 U.S. 587, 107 S. Ct. 3008, 97 L.Ed.2d 485 (1987).

Bowers v. Hardwick, 478 U.S. 186, 106 S. Ct. 2841, 92 L.Ed.2d 140 (1986).

Branti v. Finket, 445 U.S. 507, 100 S. Ct. 1287, 63 L.Ed.2d 574 (1980).

Breed v. Jones, 421 U.S. 519, 95 S. Ct. 1779, 44 L.Ed.2d 346 (1975).

Broadrick v. Oklahoma, 413 U.S. 601, 93 S. Ct. 2908, 37 L.Ed.2d 830 (1973).

Brown v. Board of Education of Topeka, 347 U.S. 483, 74 S. Ct. 686 (1954).

Buck v. Bell, 274 U.S. 200, 47 S. Ct. 584 (1927).

Burlington Sch. Comm. v. Department of Educ., 471 U.S. 358, 105 S. Ct. 1996, 85 L.Ed.2d 385 (1985).

Burns v. Alcala, 420 U.S. 575, 95 S. Ct. 1126, 43 L.Ed.2d 469 (1975).

Burtton v. Johnson, 538 F.2d 765 (7th Cir. 1976).

Caban v. Mohammed, 441 U.S. 380, 99 S. Ct. 1760 (1979).

Califano v. Boles, 99 S. Ct. 2767 (1979).

Califano v. Goldfarb, 430 U.S. 199, 97 S. Ct. 1021, 51 L.Ed.2d 270 (1977).

Califano v. Jobst, 98 S. Ct. 95 (1977).

Califano v. Westcott, 99 S. Ct. 2655 (1979).

California Dept. of Human Resources v. Java, 402 U.S. 121, 91 S. Ct. 1347, 28 L.Ed.2d 666 (1971).

California v. Superior Court of California, 482 U.S. 400, 107 S. Ct. 2433, 96 L.Ed.2d 332 (1987).

Carelson v. Remillard, 406 U.S. 598, 92 S. Ct. 1932, 32 L.Ed.2d 352 (1972).

Camenisch v. University of Texas, 616 F.2d 127 (5th Cir. 1986).

Carey v. Population Services Inter., 431 U.S. 678 97 S. Ct. 2010, 52 L.Ed.2d 675 (1977).

Chambers v. Parker, 349 S.2d 425 (La. App. 4th Cir. 1977).

City of Cleburne, Tex. v. Cleburne Living Center, 473 U.S. 432, 105 S. Ct. 3249, 87 L.Ed.2d 313 (1985).

Cleaver v. Wilcox, 499 F.2d 940 (9th Cir. 1974).

Cleveland Bd. of Educ. v. LaFleur, 414 U.S.632, 39 L.Ed.2d52, 945.Ct.791 (1974).

Clough v. Commissioner of Public Safety, 360 N.W.2d 428 (Minn. App. 1985).

Colautti v. Franklin, 99 S. Ct. 675 (1979).

Cole v. Housing Auth. of City of Newport, 435 F.2d 807 (1st Cir. 1970).

Colorado v. Bannister, 101 S. Ct. 42 (1980).

Community Serv. Soc. v. Welfare Insp. Gen., 398 N.Y.S.2d 92, 91 Misc.2d 383 (N.Y. 1977).

Cottle v. Storer Communications, Inc., 849 F.2d 570 (11th Cir. 1988).

Cox v. Stanton, 529 F.2d 47 (4th Cir. 1975).

Cronier v. Cronier, 540 So.2d 1160 (La. App. 1st Cir. 1989).

Crowe v. Eastern Band of Cherokee Indians, Inc., 506 F.2d 1231 (4th Cir. 1974).

Cruzan v. Director Missouri Dept. of Health, 110 S. Ct. 2841 (1990).

Curtis v. Leather, 415 U.S. 189, 94 S. Ct. 1005, 39 L.Ed.2d 260 (1974).

Dandridge v. Williams, 397 U.S. 471, 90 S. Ct. 1153 (1970).

Darling v. Charleston Hosp., 33 Ill. 2nd 326, 211 N.E.2d 253 (1965), *cert. denied* 383 U.S. 946 (1966).

Daugherty v. Wallace, 621 N.E.2d 1374, 87 Ohio App.3d 228 (1993).

Davis v. Alaska, 415 U.S. 308, 94 S. Ct. 1105, 39 L.Ed.2d 347 (1974).

Davis v. Page, 618 F.2d 374 (5th Cir. 1980).

Davis v. Passman, 99 S. Ct. 2264 (1979).

D. B. v. Tewksbury, 545 F. Supp. 896 at 898 (1982).

Decoteau v. District Court for Tenth Jud. Dist., 404 U.S. 425, 95 S. Ct. 1082, 43 L.Ed.2d 300 (1975).

DeShaney v. Winnebago County DSS, 489 U.S. 189, 109 S. Ct 998, 103 L. Ed2d 249 (1989).

Dodge v. Department of Soc. Serv., 657 P.2d 969 (1982).

Doe v. Bellin Mem. Hosp., 479 F.2d 756 (7th Cir. 1973).

Doe v. Bolton, 410 U.S. 179, 93 S. Ct. 739, 35 L.Ed.2d 201 (1973).

Doe v. Commonwealth's Atty. for City of Richmond, 403 F. Supp. 1199 (E.D. Va. 1975), *aff'd without opinion* 425 U.S. 901, 96 S. Ct. 1489, 47 L.Ed.2d 751 (1976).

Doe v. Harder, 310 F. Supp. 302 (D. Conn. 1970), *appeal dismissed,* 399 U.S. 902, 90 S. Ct. 2202, 26 L.Ed.2d 557 (1970).

Doe v. Poelker, 515 F.2d 541 (8th Cir. 1975), *cert. denied,* 428 U.S. 909, 96 S. Ct. 3220 (1976).

Doe v. Utah Dept. of Public Safety, 782 F.2d 489 (Utah 1989).

Dothard v. Rawlinson, 433 U.S. 321, 97 S. Ct. 2720, 53 L.Ed.2d 786 (1977).

Downs v. Sawtelle, 574 F.2d 1 (1st Cir. 1978), *cert. denied,* U.S. 910, 99 S. Ct. 278 (1978).

D. R. v. Mitchell, 617 F.2d 203 (10th Cir. 1980).

Driver v. Hinnant, 356 F.2d 761 (4th Cir. 1966).

Drummond v. Fulton County Dept. of Family and Child. Serv. 563 F.2d 1200 (5th Cir. 1977).

Dufrene v. Dufrene, 366 S.2d 1016 (La. App., 1st Cir. 1978).

Duncan v. Duncan, 339 S.2d 380 (La. App. 1976).

Dunn v. Blumstein, 405 U.S. 330, 92 S. Ct. 995, 31 L.Ed.2d 274 (1972).

Dunn v. Rivera, 404 U.S. 1054, 92 S. Ct. 742, 30 L.Ed.2d 743 (1972).

Durham v. United States, 214 F.2d 862 (D.C. Cir. 1954).

Durst v. United States, 434 U.S. 542, 98 S. Ct. 849, 55 L.Ed.2d 14 (1978).

Easter v. District of Columbia, 361 F.2d 50 (D.C. Cir. 1966).

Eastern Kentucky Welfare Rights Org. v. Simon, 506 F.2d 1278 (D.C. Cir. 1974).

Edelman v. Jordan, 415 U.S. 651, 94 S. Ct. 1347, 39 L.Ed.2d 662 (1974).

Eggleston v. Landrum, 210 Miss. 645, 50 So.2d 364 (1951).

Eichner v. Dillon, 426 N.Y.S.2d 517 (1980).

Eisenstadt v. Baird, 405 U.S. 438, 92 S. Ct. 1029, 31 L.Ed.2d 349 (1972).

Ennis v. Barg, 509 N.W.2d 33 (N.D. 1993).

Family Counseling Serv., Etc. v. Rust, 462 F.Supp. 74 (1978).

Fare v. Michael C., 442 U.S. 707, 99 S. Ct. 2560, 61 L.Ed. 197 (1979).

Fischer v. Metcalf, 543 So.2d 785 (Fla. App.3d Dist. 1989).

Fitzpatrick v. Bitzer, 427 U.S. 445, 96 S. Ct. 2666, 49 L.Ed.2d 614 (1976).

Flagiello v. Pennsylvania Hospital, 417 Pa. 486, 208 A.2d (Pa. Sup. Ct. 1965).

Flemming v. Nestor, 363 U.S. 603, 80 S. Ct. 1367, 4 L.Ed.2d 1435 (1960).

Frank v. State, 613 P.2d 517 (Utah 1980).

Friedman v. Berger, 547 F.2d 724 (2d Cir. 1976).

Frontiero v. Richardson, 411 U.S. 677, 93 S. Ct. 1764, 36 L.Ed.2d 583 (1973).

Gaddis v. Wyman, 304 F.Supp. 717 (1969).

Gagnon v. Scarpelli, 411 U.S. 778, 93 S. Ct. 1756 (1973).

Garcia v. San Antonio Metro. Transit Auth., 469 U.S. 528, 105 S. Ct. 1005, 831 L.Ed.2d 1016 (1985).

Garlington v. Kingsley, 289 So.2d 88 (La. 1974).

Geduldig v. Aiello, 417 U.S. 484, 94 S. Ct. 2485, 41 L.Ed.2d 256 (1975).

General Electric Co. v. Gilbert, 429 U.S. 125, 97 S. Ct. 401, 50 L.Ed.2d 343 (1976).

Gideon v. Wainwright, 372 U.S. 335, 83 S. Ct. 792 (1963).

Glen Manor Home for the Jewish Aged v. N.L.R.B., 474 F.2d 1145 (6th Cir., 1973).

Goldberg v. Kelly, 397 U.S. 254, 90 S. Ct. 1011 (1970).

Golz v. Children's Bureau of New Orleans, Inc., 326 So.2d 865 (La. 1976).

Gomez v. Perez, 409 U.S. 535, 93 S. Ct. 872 (1973).

Good v. Zavala, 531 So.2d 909 (Ala. Civ. App., 1988).

Graham v. Richardson, 403 U.S. 365, 91 S. Ct. 1848, 29 L.Ed.2d 534 (1971).

Green v. City of New Orleans, 88 So.2d 76 (La. App. Arl. 1956).

Griggs v. Duke Power Company, 401 U.S. 424, 91 S. Ct. 849 (1971).

Griswold v. State of Connecticut, 381 U.S. 497, 85 S. Ct. 1678 (1965).

Guadalupe Organization, Inc. v. Tempe Elementary Sch. Dist. #3, 587 F.2d 1022 (9th Cir. 1978).

Guillory v. Adm'rs of Tulane Educ. Fund, 207 F.Supp. 554 (E.D. La. 1962).

Gursky v. Gursky, 30 Misc.2d 1083, 242 N.Y.2d 835 (1964).

Hamilton v. Butz, 520 F.2d 709 (9th Cir. 1975).

Hardwick v. Bowers, 760 F.2d 1202 (1985).

Harnett v. Ulett, 466 F.2d 113 (8th Cir. 1972).

Harris v. Harris, 343 So.2d. 762 (Miss. 1977).

Harris v. McRae, 100 S. Ct. 2671 (1980).

Harten v. Coons, 502 F.2d 1363 (10th Cir. 1974), *cert. denied,* 420 U.S. 963 (1975).

Hayes v. Stanton, 512 F.2d 133 (7th Cir. 1975).

Heart of Atlanta Motel, Inc. v. United States, 379 U.S. 241, 85 S. Ct. 348, 13 L.Ed.2d 258 (1964).

Heckler v. Turner, 470 U.S. 184, 105 S. Ct. 1138, 84 L.Ed.2d 138 (1985).

Heller v. Doe by Doe, 113 S. Ct. 2637, 125 L.Ed.2d 257 (1993).

Helvering v. Davis, 301 U.S. 619, 57 S. Ct. 904, 81 L. Ed. 1307 (1937).

Herzbrun v. Milwaukee County, 504 F.2d 1189 (7th Cir. 1974).

Hills v. Gautreaux, 425 U.S. 284, 96 S. Ct. 1538, 47 L.Ed.2d 792 (1976).

Hodgson v. Greyhound Lines, Inc., 499 F.2d 859 (7th Cir. 1974), *cert. denied,* 419 U.S. 1122 (1975).

Homemakers H. & H. C. S., Inc. v. Chicago Home for Friend, 484 F.2d 625 (7th Cir. 1973).

Horak v. Biris, 474 N.E.2d 13 (Ill. App. 2d Dist. 1983).

H.R. v. State Dept. of Human Resources, 612 S.2d 477 (Ala. Civ. App. 1992).

Hudson v. Hudson, 373 So.2d 310 (Ala. Sup. Ct. 1979).

Huynh Thi Anh v. Levi, 586 F.2d 625 (6th Cir. 1978).

Illinois State Employee Union, Council 34, Etc. v. Lewis, 473 F.2d 561 (1972).

In Interest of Ivey, 329 So.2d 53 (Fla. App. 1st Dist., 1975).

In re Adoption of Child, 322 N.Y.S.2d 532, 37 A.D.2d 78 (1971).

In re Adoption of Luke, 3 Ariz. App. 327, 414 P.2d 176 (Ariz. Ct. App. 1966).

In re Anonymous, 3 Ariz. App. 351, 414 P.2d 435 (Ariz. Ct. App. 1966).

In re Baker, 117 Ohio App. 26, 185 N.E.2d 51 (1962).

In re Bonez, 50 Misc.2d 1080, 272 N.Y.S.2d 587 (1966).

In re Coile, 343 So.2d 325 (La. App. 1977).

In re Fisher, 39 Ohio St.2d 71, 313 N.E.2d 851 (1974).

In re Gerald, 403 N.Y.S.2d 57, *appeal dismissed* 413 N.Y.S.2d 923, 386 N.E.2d 834 (1978).

In re Glauas, 121 N.Y.S.2d 12 (1953).

In re Gomez, 424 S.W.2d 656 (Tex. Civ. App. 1967).

In re Johnson, 369 N.E.2d 70 (Ill. App. 1st Dist. 1977).

In re McDonald, 201 N.W.2d 447 (Sup. Ct. Iowa 1972).

In re McKenzie, 197 Minn. 234, 266 N.W. 746 (1936).

In re Reitz, 53 Wis.2d 87, 191 N.W.2d 913 (1971).

In re Richardson, 284 So.2d 185 (La. App. 1973).

In re Snyder, 85 Wash.2d 182, 532 P.2d 278 (1975).

In re State ex rel. Sharp, 219 So.2d 317 (1st Cir. La. 1960).

In re Sterilization of Moore, 289 N.C. 95, 221 S.E.2d 307 (1976).

In re Vulon Children, 288 N.Y.S.2d 203, 56 Misc.2d 19 (1968).

In re Winship, 397 U.S. 358, 90 S. Ct. 1068 (1970).

In the Matter of Dinnerstein, 380 N.E.2d 134 (Mass. App. 1978).

Jackson v. Foti, 670 F.2d 516 (5th Cir. 1982).

Jackson v. Statler Foundation, 496 F.2d 623 (2d Cir. 1974).

Janet G. v. New York Foundling Hospital, 403 N.Y.S.2d 646 (1978).

J.M.A. v. Alaska, 542 P.2d 170 (Alaska, 1976).

Johnson v. Avery, 393 U.S. 483, 89 S. Ct. 747 (1969).

Joint Tribal Council of Passamaquoddy Tribe v. Morton, 528 F.2d 370 (1st Cir. 1975).

Jones v. Hallahan, 501 S.W.2d 588 (Ky. App. 1973).

Jones v. Helms, 101 S. Ct. 2434 (1981).

Jones v. Hoffman, 272 So.2d 529 (Fla. App., 4th Dist. 1972).

Jones v. United States, 463 U.S. 354, 103 S. Ct. 3043, 77 L.Ed. 2d 694 (1983).

Karp v. Cooley, 496 F.2d 878 (5th Cir. 1974), *cert. denied,* 419 U.S. 845, 95 S. Ct. 79 (1974).

Katzenbach v. McClung, 370 U.S. 294, 85 S. Ct. 377, 13 L.Ed.2d (1964).

Kent v. United States, 383 U.S. 541, 86 S. Ct. 1045 (1966).

King v. Smith, U.S. 309, 88 S. Ct. 2128 (1968).

King v. Tanner, 539 N.Y.S.2d 617 (Sup. 1989)

Kush v. Lloyd, 616 So.2d. 415 (Fla. 1992).

Kyees v. County Dept. of Public Welfare, 600 F.2d 693 (7th Cir. 1979).

Labine v. Vincent, 401 U.S. 572, 91 S. Ct. 1017 (1971).

Lake v. Cameron, 364 F.2d 657 (D.C. Cir. 1966).

Lalli v. Lalli, 99 S.Ct. 518 (1978).

Lampton v. Bonin, 304 F.Supp. 1384 (E.D. La. 1969).

Landeros v. Flood, 50 Cal. App.2d 189, 123 Cal. Rptr. 713 (1976), *vacated*, 131 Cal. Rptr. 69, 551 P.2d 389 (1976).

Larry v. Lawler, 605 F.2d 954 (7th Cir. 1978).

Lassiter v. Department of Soc. Serv. of Durham City, 101 S. Ct. 2153 (1981).

Lau v. Nichols, 414 U.S. 563, 94 S. Ct. 786 (1974).

Lavine v. Milne, 424 U.S. 577, 96 S. Ct. 1010, 47 L.Ed.2d 249 (1976).

Lehr v. Robertson, 463 U.S. 248, 103 S. Ct. 2985, 77 L.Ed.2d 614 (1983).

Lessard v. Schmidt, 349 F.Supp. 1078 (E.D. Wis. 1972).

Lewis v. Martin, 397 U.S. 552, 90 S. Ct. 1281, 25 L.Ed.2d 561 (1970).

Li v. Yellow Cab Co. of Calif., 119 Cal. Rptr. 858, 532 P.2d 1226 (1975).

Like v. Carter, 448 F.2d 768 (8th Cir. 1971), *cert. denied*, 405 U.S. 1069 (1971)

Little v. Streater, 101 S. Ct. 2202 (1981).

London v. Florida Dep't of Health & Rehab. Serv., 448 F.2d 655 (5th Cir. 1971).

Lovato v. District Court, 601 P.2d 1072 (Colo. 1979).

Loving v. Commonwealth of Virginia, 388 U.S. 1, 87 S. Ct. 1817 (1967).

Lukhard v. Reed, 481 U.S. 368, 107 S. Ct. 1807, 95 L.Ed.2d 328 (1986).

Lynch v. Baxley, 386 F.Supp. 378 (M.D. Ala., N.D. 1974).

Lyng v. Castillo, 477 U.S. 635, 106 S. Ct. 2727, 91 L.Ed.2d 527 (1986).

Lyng v. International Union, UAW, 485 U.S. 360, 108 S. Ct. 1184, 99 L.Ed.2d 380 (1988).

Maher v. Gagne, 100 S. Ct. 2570 (1980).

Maher v. Roe, 432 U.S. 464, 97 S. Ct. 2376, 53 L.Ed.2d 484 (1977).

Maine v. Thibout, 100 S. Ct. 2502 (1980).

Marshall v. Barlow's Inc., 436 U.S. 307, 98 S. Ct. 1816 (1978).

Martinez v. California, 444 U.S. 277, 100 S. Ct. 553, 62 L.Ed.2d 481 (1980).

Martinez v. Mathews, 544 F.2d 1233 (5th Cir. 1976).

Marvin v. Marvin, 134 Cal. Rptr. 815, 557 P.2d 106 (Calif. S. Ct. 1976).

Maryland v. Wirtz, 392 U.S. 183, 88 S. Ct. 2017, 20 L.Ed.2d 1020 (1968).

Massey v. Parker, 362 So.2d 1195 (La. App. 4th Cir. 1978).

Matter of Adoption of Evan, 583 N.Y.S.2d. 997, 153 Misc.2d 844 (1992).

Matter of Adoption of Gardiner, 287 N.W.2d 553 (Iowa S. Ct. 1980).

Matter of Gerald Allen B., 164 Cal. Rptr. 193 (App. Ct. 1980).

Matter of Quinlan, 70 N.J. 10, 355 A.2d 647 (1976).

Matthews v. Diaz, 426 U.S. 67, 96 S. Ct. 19/883, 48 L.Ed.2d 478 (1976).

McCabe v. Nassau County Medical Center, 453 F.2d 698 (2nd Cir. 1971).

McKeiver v. Pennsylvania, 403 U.S. 528, 91 S. Ct. 1976 (1970).

McMahon v. Califano, 605 F.2d 49 (2nd Cir. 1979).

Memorial Hosp. v. Maricopa County, 414 U.S. 250, 94 S. Ct. 1076, 39 L.Ed.2d 306 (1974).

Menard v. Saxbe, 498 F.2d 1017 (D.C. Cir. 1974).

Michael H. v. Gerald D., 491 U.S. 110 (1989).

Miller v. Youakim, 440 U.S. 125, 99 S. Ct. 957, 59 L.Ed.2d 194 (1979).

Mills v. Board of Education of District of Columbia, 348 F.Supp. 864 (D.C. Cir. 1972).

Mink v. State Dept. of Mental Health, 620 So.2d 22 (Ala. Civ. App. 1992).

Miranda v. State of Arizona, 384 U.S. 436, 86 S. Ct. 1602, 16 L.Ed.2d 694 (1966).

Mistretta v. U.S., 109 S. Ct. 647, 102 L.Ed.2d 714 (1989).

Morrissey v. Brewer, 408 U.S. 471, 92 S. Ct. 2593 (1972).

Mortin v. Mancari, 417 U.S. 599, 94 S. Ct. 2474, 41 L.Ed.2d 2900 (1974).

Morton v. Ruiz, 415 U.S. 199, 94 S. Ct. 1055, 39 L.Ed.2d 270 (1974).

Moss v. Weaver, 525 F.2d 1258 (5th Cir. 1976).

M.T. v. J.T., 355 A. 2d 204 (1976).

Murray v. Vandevander, 522 P.2d 202 (Ct. App. Okla. 1974).

Myers v. Drozda, 180 Neb. 183, 141 N.W.2d 852 (Neb. 1966).

National Labor Relations Board v. Florida Memorial College, 820 F.2d 1182 (1987).

National Labor Relations Board v. Yeshiva University, 444 U.S. 672, 100 S. Ct. 856, 63 L.Ed.2d 115 (1980).

National League of Cities v. Usery, 426 U.S. 833, 96 S. Ct. 2465, 49 L.Ed.2d 245 (1976).

National Retired Teachers Ass'n. v. U.S. Post. Serv., 593 F.2d 1360 (D.C. Cir. 1979).

Nelson v. Hayne, 491 F.2d 352 (7th Cir. 1974), *cert. denied,* 417 U.S. 976 (1974).

Newman v. State of Ala., 559 F.2d 283 (5th Cir. 1977).

Nguyen Da Yen v. Kissinger, 528 F.2d 1194 (9th Cir. 1975).

Nolan v. deBaca, 603 F.2d 810 (10th Cir. 1979).

O'Connor v. Donaldson, 422 U.S. 563, 95 S. Ct. 2486, 45 L.Ed.2d 396 (1975).

Oneida Indian Nation of N.Y. State v. County of Oneida, N.Y., 414 U.S. 661, 94 S. Ct. 772, 39 L.Ed. 73 (1974).

Orr v. Orr, 440 U.S. 268, 99 S. Ct. 1102, 59 L.Ed.2d 306 (1979).

Ortwein v. Schwab, 410 U.S. 653, 93 S. Ct. 1172, 35 L.Ed.2d 572 (1973).

Palmore v. Sidat, 104 S. Ct. 1879 (1984).

Parham v. J. R., 99 S. Ct. 2493 (1979).

Parrish v. Civil Service Comm'n. of County of Alameda, 57 Cal. Rptr. 623, 425 P.2d 223 (1967).

Pearce v. Wichita County, City of Wichita Falls, Etc., 590 F.2d 128 (5th Cir. 1979).

Pease v. Hansen, 404 U.S. 70, 92 S. Ct. 318, 30 L.Ed.2d 224 (1971), reversing per curiam 157 Mont. 99, 483 P.2d 720 (1971).

People v. Burwick, 121 Cal. Rptr. 488, 535 P.2d 352 (1975).

People v. Feagley, 121 Cal. Rptr. 509, 535 P.2d 373 (1975).

People v. Steinberger, Dis. Ct., County of Pueblo (Colo.), 422 N.L.2d 843, 440 N.Y.S.2d 1034 (1981).

Perez v. Sugarman, 499 F.2d 761 (2d Cir. 1974).

Personnel Adm'r of Massachusetts v. Feeney, 99 S. Ct. 2282 (1979).

Petitions of Goldman, 121 N.E.2d 843 (Mass. 1954), *cert. denied,* 348 U.S. 942 (1955).

Philbrook v. Glodgett, 421 U.S. 767, 95 S. Ct. 1893, 44 L.Ed.2d 525 (1975).

Phillips v. Phelps, 370 S.2d 898 (La. App. 1st Cir., 1979).

Phillips v. Adult Prob. Dept., City & County of San Francisco, 491 F.2d 951 (9th Cir. 1974).

Pickett v. Brown, 461 U.S. 1, 103 S. Ct. 2199, 76 L.Ed.2d 372 (1983).

Pierce v. General Motors Corp., Fisher Body Div., 504 N.W.2d 648 (1993).

Pinneke v. Preisser, 623 F.2d 546 (8th Cir. 1980).

Planned Parenthood of Central Missouri v. Danforth, 428 U.S. 52, 96 S. Ct. 2831, 49 L.Ed.2d 788 (1976).

Plessy v. Ferguson, 163 U.S. 537, 16 S. Ct. 1138, 41 L.Ed. 256 (1896).

Powell v. Alabama, 287 U.S. 45 (1932).

Powell v. Texas, 392 U.S. 514, 88 S. Ct. 2145, 20 L.Ed.2d 1254 (1968).

Price v. Price, 215 N.W.2d 756 (1974).

Prideaux v. State, 247 N.W.2d 385, 97 A.L.R. 3d 833 (Minn. Sup. Ct. 1976).

Profitt v. State of Colorado, 482 P.2d 965 (Colo. 1971).

Quilloin v. Walcott, 434 U.S. 246, 98 S. Ct. 549 (1978).

Re Korte, 139 N.Y.S. 444 (1912).

Reed v. Reed, 404 U.S. 71, 92 S. Ct. 251, 30 L.Ed.2d 225 (1971).

Reitz v. VandenBrock, 406 U.S. 902 (1972).

Rennie v. Klein, 462 F.Supp. 1131 (N.J. 1978).

Richardson v. Belcher, 404 U.S. 79, 92 S. Ct. 254, 30 L.Ed.2d 231 (1971).

Richardson v. Ramirez, 418 U.S. 24, 94 S. Ct. 2655 (1974).

Richland County Ass'n For Retarded Citizens v. Marshall (1981), 660 F.2d 388 (9th Cir. 1981).

Rieser v. District of Columbia, 563 F.2d 462 (D.C. Cir. 1977).

Riley v. National Fed'n of the Blind of N.C., 487 U.S. 781, 108 S. Ct. 2667, 101 L.Ed.2d 669 (1988).

Rios v. Chavez, 620 F.2d 702 (9th Cir. 1980).

Rivers v. Marcus, 696 F.2d 1016 (1982).

Robinson v. California, 370 U.S. 660 (1962).

Robinson v. Wickl, C.A. No. 37607, Cal. Super. Ct. (San Luis Obispo, *filed* Sept. 4, 1970).

Roe v. Norton, 422 U.S. 391, 95 S. Ct. 221, 45 L.Ed.2d 268 (1975).

Roe v. Wade, 410 U.S. 113, 93 S. Ct. 705, 35 L.Ed.2d 147 (1973).

Rogers v. Okin, 478 F.Supp. 1342 (D.C. Mass. 1979).

Rogers v. Okin, 738 F.2d 1 (1984).

Roseborough v. Scott, 875 F.2d 1160 (1994).

Rosen v. Hursh, 464 F.2d 731 (1972).

Rosenberg v. Richardson, 548 F.2d 487 (2d Cir. 1976).

Rouse v. Cameron, 373 F.2d 451 (D.C. Cir. 1966).

Rust v. Sullivan, 111 S. Ct. 1759, 114 L.Ed.2d 233 (1991).

S. v. D., 410 U.S. 614, 93 S. Ct. 1146, 35 L.Ed.2d 536 (1973).

Salz v. Perlmutter, 362 So. 2d 160 (Fla. App. 1978).

Sampson v. Murray, 415 U.S. 61, 94 S. Ct. 937, 39 L.Ed.2d 166 (1974).

Santa Clara Pueblo v. Martinez, 436 U.S. 49, 98 S. Ct. 1670, 56 L.Ed.2d 106 (1978).

Schall v. Martin, 467 U.S. 253, 104 S. Ct. 2403, 81 L.Ed.2d 207 (1984).

School Board of Nassau County, Fl. v. Arline, 480 U.S. 273 107 S. Ct. 1123 (1987).

Schulman v. New York City Health & Hospitals Corp., 38 N.Y. 2d 234, 342 N.E.2d 501 (1975).

Schuster v. Schuster, 90 Wash.2d 626, 585 F.2d 130 (1978).

Schweiker v. Gray Panthers, 101 S. Ct. 2633 (1981).

Secretary, Etc. v. Institutionalized Juveniles, 99 S. Ct. 2538 (1979).

Semler v. Psychiatric Institute of Washington, D.C., 538 F.2d 122 (4th Cir. 1976).

Senior Citizens Stores, Inc. v. United States, 602 F.2d 711 (5th Cir. 1979).

Shapiro v. Thompson, 394 U.S. 618, 89 S. Ct. 1322, 22 L.Ed.2d 600 (1969).

Shea v. Vialpando, 416 U.S. 251, 94 S. Ct. 1746, 40 L.Ed.2d 120 (1974).

Sherbert v. Verner, 374 U.S. 398, 83 S. Ct. 1790, 10 L.Ed.2d 965 (1963).

Skinner v. Oklahoma, 316 U.S. 535, 62 S. Ct. 1110 (1942).

Smith v. Huecker, 531 F.2d 1355 (6th Cir. 1976).

Smith v. Organization of Foster Families for E. and Reform, 431 U.S. 816, 97 S. Ct. 2094, 53 L.Ed.2d 14 (1977).

South Dakota v. Neville, 459 U.S. 554, 103 S. Ct. 916, 74 L.Ed.2d 748 (1983).

Southeastern Community College v. Davis, 99 S. Ct. 2361 (1979).

Specht v. Patterson, 388 U.S. 605, 87 S. Ct. 1209 (1967).

Spence v. Staras, 507 F.2d 554 (7th Cir. 1974).

Spillman v. Parker, 332 S.2d 573 (La. App. 4th Cir. 1976).

Stanley v. Illinois, 405 U.S. 645, 92 S. Ct. 1243, 22 L.Ed.2d 551 (1972).

Stanton v. Bond, 504 F.2d 1246 (7th Cir. 1974).

State in Interest of Martorano, 619 So.2d 1127 (La. App. 4th Cir. 1993).

State in the Interest of Johnson, 283 So.2d 333 (La. App. 4th Cir. 1973).

State in the Interest of L.A.V., 516 So.2d 1315 (La. App. 2d Cir. 1987).

State of Juneau v. Tudor Const. Co., 621 So.2d 179 (La. App. 3d Cir. 1993).

State v. Belton, 523 So.2d 77 (La. App. 3 Ctr. 1988).

State v. Brown, 366 So.2d 550 (La. 1979).

State v. Hayes, 389 A.2d 1379 (1978).

State v. Hunt, 2 Ariz. App. 6, 406 P.2d 208 (1965).

State v. Jojola, 89 N.M. 489, 553 P.2d 1296 (1976).

State v. Peart, 621 S.2d 780 (La. 1993).

Steed v. McKenzie, 344 So.2d 689 (La. App. 1977).

Stewart v. Louisiana Plant Serv., Inc., 611 So.2d 682 (La. App. 4 Cir. 1992).

Strunk v. Strunk, 445 So.2d 145 (Ky. 1969).

Stump v. Sparkman, 435 U.S. 349, 98 S. Ct. 1099, 55 L.Ed.2d 331 (1978).

Sullivan v. Zebley, 110 S. Ct. 885 (1990).

Suzuki v. Yuen, 617 F.2d 173 (9th Cir. 1980).

Sweeney v. Bd. of Trustees of Keene State College, 604 F.2d 106 (1st Cir. 1979).

Tarasoff v. Regents of California, 731 Cal. Rptr. 14, 551 P.2d 334 (1976).

Taylor v. St. Vincent's Hosp., 523 F.2d 75 (9th Cir. 1975), *cert. denied,* 96 S. Ct. 1420, 47 L.Ed.2d 355 (1976).

Thomas v. State Dept. of Mental Health, 620 So.2d 18 (Ala. Civ. App. 1992).

Thompson v. State Dept. of Mental Health, 620 So.2d 25 (Ala. Civ. App. 1992).

Thorpe v. Housing Auth. of City of Durham, N.C., 393 U.S. 268, 89 S. Ct. 518, 21 L.Ed.2d 474 (1969).

Townsend v. Swank, 404 U.S. 181, 92 S. Ct. 502, 30 L.Ed.2d 448 (1971).

Trimble v. Gordon, 430 U.S. 762, 97 S. Ct. 1459, 52 L.Ed.2d 31 (1977).

Trujillo v. United States, 959 F.2d 1377 (1974).

Tuten v. United States, 460 U.S. 660, 103 S. Ct. 1412, 75 L.Ed.2d 259 (1983).

United States v. Creek Nation, 476 F.2d 1290 (1973).

United States v. Fowler, 476 F.2d 1091 (7th Cir. 1973).

United States v. Hill, 538 F.2d 1072 (4th Cir. 1976).

United States v. Kras, 409 U.S. 434, 93 S. Ct. 631, 34 L.Ed.2d 626 (1973).

United States v. Oneida Nation of New York, 477 F.2d 939 (1973).

United States v. R.L.C., 112 S. Ct. 1329, 117 L.Ed.2d 559 (1992).

United States v. Stine, 675 F.2d 69 (3rd Cir. 1982).

United States Civil Service Comm'n v. National Assn. of Letter Carriers, 413 U.S. 548, 93 S. Ct. 2880, 37 L.Ed.2d 796 (1973).

United States Dept. of Agric. v. Moreno, 413 U.S. 528, 93 S. Ct. 2821, 37 L.Ed.2d 782 (1973).

United States Dept. of Agric. v. Murry, 413 U.S. 508, 93 S. Ct. 2832, 37 L.Ed.2d 767 (1973).

United States ex rel. Cobell v. Cobell, 503 F.2d 790 (9th Cir. 1974), *cert. denied,* 421 U.S. 939, 95 S. Ct. 1667 (1975).

United States ex rel. Stachulak v. Coughlin, 550 F.2d 931 (7th Cir. 1975).

United Way, Etc. v. Department of Industry, 313 N.W.2d 859, 105 Wis.2d 447 (1981).

Usery v. Charleston County Sch. Dist., Etc., 558 F.2d 1169 (4th Cir. 1977).

Van Lare v. Hurley, 421 U.S. 338, 95 S. Ct. 1741, 44 L.Ed.2d 208 (1975).

Virginia Academy of Clin. Psychol. v. Blue Shield of Va., 624 F.2d 476 (4th Cir. 1980).

Vitek v. Jones, 100 S. Ct. 1254 (1980).

Vonner v. State Dept. of Public Welfare, 261 L. 445, 273 So.2d 252 (1974).

Walden v. Wishengrad, 745 F.2d (1984).

Washington v. Davis, 426 U.S. 229, 96 S. Ct. 2040, 48 L.Ed.2d 597 (1976).

Weber v. Aetna Casualty & Surety Co., 406 U.S. 164, 92 S. Ct. 1400, 31 L.Ed. 768 (1972).

Weinberger v. Salfi, 422 U.S. 749, 95 S. Ct. 2457, 45 L.Ed.2d 522 (1975).

Weinberger v. Wisenfeld, 420 U.S. 636, 95 S. Ct. 1225, 43 L.Ed.2d 514 (1975).

Wengler v. Druggists Mutual Ins. Co., 466 U.S. 152, 100 S. Ct. 1540 (1980).

Wheelahan v. State of Louisiana through the Louisiana Claims Review Board, 376 S.2d 576 (La. App. 4th Cir. 1979).

Wheeler v. Glen Falls Ins. Co., 513 S.W.2d 179 (1974).

Whirlpool Corporation v. Marshall, 445 U.S. 1, 100 S. Ct. 883, 63 L.Ed.2d 154 (1980).

Whitree v. State, 56 Misc.2d 693, 290 N.Y.S.2d 486 (1968).

Wilderman v. Nelson, 467 F.2d 1173 (8th Cir. 1972).

Williams v. Edwards, 547 F.2d 1206 (5th Cir. 1977).

Williams v. Walker Thomas Furniture Company, 121 U.S. App. D.C. 315, 350 F.2d 445, 18 A.L.R.3d 1297 (1965).

Williams v. Zbaraz, 100 S. Ct. 2694 (1980).

Wright v. Roanoke Redevelopment and Housing, 479 U.S. 418, 107 S. Ct. 766, 93 L.Ed.2d 781 (1987).

Wyman v. Bowen, 397 U.S. 49, 90 S. Ct. 813 (1970), *affirming per curiam sub nom.* Goddis v. Wyman, 304 F. Supp. 717 (S.D.N.Y. 1969).

Wyman v. James, 400 U.S. 309, 91 S. Ct. 381 (1971).

Wyman v. Lopez, 404 U.S. 1055, 92 S. Ct. 736, 30 L.Ed.2d 743 (1972).

Wyatt v. Aderholt, 368 F.Supp. 1383 (M.D. Ala. 1974).

Wyatt v. Stickney, 344 F.Supp. 387 (M.D. Ala., N.D. 1972).

Wyatt v. Stickney, 344 F.Supp. 373 (M.D. Ala. N.D. 1972).

Yaron v. Yaron, 38 Misc.2d 276, 372 N.Y. S.2d 518 (1975).

Youngberg v. Romeo, 457 U.S. 307, 102 S. Ct. 2452, 73 L.Ed.2d 28 (1982).

Zablocki v. Redhail, 434 U.S. 374, 98 S. Ct. 673 (1978).

Zahn v. Int'l Paper Co., 414 U.S. 291, 94 S. Ct. 505, 38 L.Ed.2d 511 (1973).

Zepeda v. Zepeda, 41 Ill. App.2d 240, 190 N.E.2d 49 (App. Ct., 1st Dist. 1963), *cert denied,* 85 S. Ct. 444 (1963).

Zobrest v. Catalina Foothills School District, 113 S. Ct. 2462 (1993).

Index

Age Discrimination in Employ-
ment Act of 1967, 51
Aid to Families with Dependent
Children (AFDC). *See also*
Welfare programs
assistance provided by, 273
Foster Care program, 178
legal separation as requirement for, 150
unemployed parents program,
299–300
Ake v. Oklahoma (1985), 99
Alaska Native Claims Settlement Act of 1971, 328
Alcohol abuse/alcoholism, 239,
241–245, 264. *See also*
Addicted individuals
*Alicea Rosada v. Garcia
Santiago* (1977), 50
Alimony, 155, 156
Alma Soc. Inc. v. Mellon (1979),
193
American Indians
cases dealing with compensation for, 324–326
custody issues and, 327–328
legal problems of, 323–324
property issues and, 326–327
public assistance for, 328
tribal laws of, 328–329
American Law Institute (ALI)
test, 98
Americans with Disabilities Act
of 1990, 52, 265, 338
Anderson v. Vasquez (1992),
105
Annulment, 247
Appellate courts, state, 28
Application of Gault (1967),
92, 119, 120–123, 124,
125, 126

Arbitration, 33
Architectural Barriers Act of
1968, 265, 332
Argersinger v. Hamlin (1973),
96
Arnett v. Kennedy (1974), 65
Arraignment, 94
Arrest
explanation of, 92
preliminary hearing following, 94
at scene, 92–93
by warrant, 92
Artificial insemination, 145,
215–216
Atcherson v. Siebenmann
(1979), 50
*Atlas Roofing Co., Inc. v.
Occupational Safety &
Health Review* (1977), 53
Attorneys
ad litem, 135
how to find, 22–23
how to work with, 20
payment for, 33–35
role of, 19–20

B
Baehr v. Lewin (1993), 145
Bail, 93–94
Bail Reform Act of 1984, 94
Baker v. Nelson (1971), 145
Bankruptcy, 310
Bankruptcy Reform Act of 1978,
311
Batterton v. Francis (1977), 300
Baugh v. Woodard (1987), 106
Beal v. Doe (1977), 213
Bearden v. Georgia (1983), 103
Bellotti v. Baird (1979), 213

sterilization as method of,
203–204
Contracts
employment, 47
explanation of, 6–7
with minors, 66–67
with restraints of trade, 67
unconscionable, 309
Corporations, 38–39. *See also*
Nonprofit corporations
Cottle v. Slover Communications,
Inc. (1988), 43
Council on Social Work Education, 76
Counseling, marriage, 151–152
Court costs, 34–35
Court system. *See also* Juvenile
justice system
hierarchy in, 28
jurisdiction in, 28–30
lawmaking within, 27–28
Cox v. Stanton (1975), 206
Crime
compensation for victims of,
109–110
criminal responsibility for,
97–99
explanation of, 89
legal capacity for, 97
sex, 104
Criminal charge, 32–33
Criminal justice system. *See also*
Juvenile justice system
arrest, arraignment, and trial
in, 92–95
Constitution and, 90–92
criminal responsibility and,
97–99
expungement of arrest and
conviction records and,
107–109

legal representation and,
96–97
rights of confined individuals
and, 104–107
sentencing and, 99–104
sex crimes and, 104
social workers involved in,
89–90
victim compensation and,
109–110
Criminal responsibility
of addicted individuals,
240–245
for crime, 97–99
Cronier v. Cronier (1989), 83
Crowe v. Eastern Band of
Cherokee Indians, Inc.
(1974), 326–327
Cruzan, Nancy, 317
Cruzan v. Director Missouri Dept.
of Health (1990),
317
Curriculum Policy Statements
(Council on Social Work
Education), 76
Curtis v. Leather (1974), 306
Custody. *See* Child custody
Cy pres doctrine, 40–41

D

Dandridge v. Williams (1970),
15, 263, 284–286
Darling v. Charleston Hosp.
(1965), 335
Daugherty v. Wallace
(1993), 287
Davis v. Alaska (1974), 126
Davis v. Page (1980), 134
Davis v. Passman (1979), 321
D. B. v. Tewksbury (1982), 115

due process clause of, 92,
120–123
equal protection clause in,
15, 55, 92
Frank v. State (1980), 68
Freedom of speech, 63–65
Friedman v. Berger (1976), 267
Frontiero v. Richardson
(1973), 320
Fry, Margaret, 109
Fundraising, by social
workers, 71

G

Gaddis v. Wyman (1969), 280
Gagnon v. Scarpelli (1973), 101
Garcia v. San Antonio Metro.
Transit Auth. (1985), 54
Garlington v. Kingsley
(1974), 40
Garnishment, 310
Gay men. *See* Homosexuality
Geduldig v. Aiello (1975), 321
General Electric Co. v. Gilbert
(1976), 321
Genetic counseling, 319–320
Gideon v. Wainwright (1963), 96
Glen Manor Home for the
Jewish Aged v. N.L.R.B.
(1973), 56
Goldberg v. Kelly (1970), 9–14,
20, 30, 125
Golz v. Children's Bureau of New
Orleans, Inc. (1976), 181
Gomez v. Perez (1973), 163–164
Good v. Zavala (1988), 182
Government Employee Rights
Act of 1991, 48
Graham v. Richardson
(1971), 279
Grand juries, 33–34, 93

Green v. City of New Orleans
(1956), 182–183
Griggs v. Duke Power Company
(1971), 48
Griswold v. State of Connecticut
(1965), 199–200, 213
Guadalupe Organization, Inc. v.
Tempe Elementary Sch.
Dist. #3 (1978), 334
Guardianship, 238
Guillory v. Adm'rs of Tulane
Educ. Fund (1962), 42
Gursky v. Gursky (1964), 215

H

Hamilton v. Butz (1975), 328
Handicapped individuals. *See*
Disabled individuals
Hardwick v. Bowers
(1985), 246
Harnett v. Ulett (1972), 50
Harris v. Harris (1977), 153
Harris v. McRae (1980), 213
Harten v. Coons (1975), 204
Hatch Political Activity Act of
1939, 63, 64, 65
Hayes v. Stanton (1975), 267
Health insurance
background of, 265–266
health maintenance organiza-
tions and, 268–269
private, 265
Health Maintenance Organiza-
tion Act of 1973, 269
Health maintenance organiza-
tions (HMOs), 268–269
Health Programs Extension Act
of 1973, 204
Heart of Atlanta Motel, Inc. v.
United States (1964), 48
Heckler v. Turner (1985), 275

illegitimate children and, 159–164
In Interest of Ivey (1975), 316
In re Adoption of Child (1971), 190
In re Adoption of Luke (1966), 131
In re Anonymous (1966), 131
In re Baker (1962), 183
In re Bonez (1966), 184–188
In re Coile (1977), 180
In re Fisher (1974), 221
In re Gerald (1978), 191
In re Glauas (1953), 190
In re Gomez (1967), 183
In re Johnson (1977), 191
In re McDonald (1972), 239
In re McKenzie (1936), 190
In re Reitz (1971), 280
In re Richardson (1973), 317
In re Snyder (1975), 135
In re State ex rel. Sharp (1960), 179
In re Sterilization of Moore (1976), 206, 239
In re Vulon Children (1968), 118
In re Winship (1970), 124
Institute of Judicial Administration/American Bar Association Commission of Juvenile Justice Standards, 115
Insurance reimbursements, 69–70
International social work, 70–71
Interracial marriage, 145
Interstate Compact on Mental Health, 233
Intestate successions, 159
In the Matter of Dinnerstein (1978), 316

Invasion-of-privacy rules, 25
Involuntary commitment
aftercare and, 233–236
burden of proof for, 223–226
of mentally ill individuals, 221, 222, 224

J

Jackson v. Foti (1982), 99
Jackson v. Statler Foundation (1974), 44, 45
Janet G. v. New York Foundling Hospital (1978), 181
J.M.A. v. Alaska (1976), 177
Johnson v. Avery (1969), 104
Joint Tribal Council of Passamaquoddy Tribe v. Morton (1975), 326
Jones v. Hallahan (1973), 247
Jones v. Helms (1981), 156
Jones v. Hoffman (1972), 27
Jones v. United States (1983), 221
Judges, 25, 116
Jurisdiction
diversity, 29–30
explanation of, 28–29
of juvenile courts, 116–119
Jurisprudence, 27
Justice system. *See* Criminal justice system; Juvenile justice system
Juvenile Delinquency Act of 1994, 127
Juvenile justice system. *See also* Criminal justice system
background of, 115–116
due process and, 119–127
jurisdiction of, 116–119
rehabilitation efforts of, 126, 127

Powell v. Alabama (1932), 96
Powell v. Texas (1968), 241–245
Pregnancy Discrimination Act of 1978, 321
Pretrial detention, 125
Pretrial parole, 94
Price v. Price (1974), 156
Prideaux v. State (1976), 245
Prisoner's rights, 104–107
Privacy Act of 1974, 319
Privacy rights
　abortion and, 213
　of adopted persons, 193
　marriage counseling and, 151–152
Private agencies, 38. *See also* Nonprofit corporations
Private practice social workers
　increase in, 62
　insurance reimbursements and, 69–70
　leases and, 67–68
　legal capacity to contract and, 66–67
　malpractice and, 68–69
　zoning and, 68
Privileged communication
　cases involving, 84–85
　explanation of, 83–84
　legislation concerning, 68
Probable cause, 92, 93
Probation
　conditions placed on, 100–101
　explanation of, 100
　responsibility to public and, 101–102
　revocation of, 101
　role of social workers in, 100
Procedural due process
　explanation of, 8, 9, 15
　prisoners' rights and, 106
Procedural law, 6

Professional education
　continuing, 78
　for social workers, 76
Professional organizations, 78–79
Profitt v. State of Colorado (1971), 27
Promiscuity, 247
Property rights. *See also* Inheritance
　illegitimacy and, 161
　nonmarital partners and, 151
　prisoners and, 106
Pro se cases, 45
Public assistance. *See* Welfare programs
Public defender programs
　background of, 96
　explanation of, 96–97
　social workers in, 97
Public Health Service Act of 1944, 214
Public housing, 305–306. *See also* Housing
Public setting social workers
　civil services rules and, 65–66
　constraints on, 62–63
　freedom of speech limitations on, 63–65
Puerto Rico, 25
Putative marriage, 150–151

Q, R
Quilloin v. Walcott (1978), 192
Quinlan, Karen, 316–317
Rape, 323
Reed v. Reed (1971), 320
Refugee Relief Act of 1953, 70
Rehabilitation Act of 1973, 52, 265, 332, 333
Reitz v. VandenBrock (1972), 280

About the Author

Leila Obier Schroeder, MSW, JD, is professor of business law in the College of Business Administration and special lecturer in the School of Social Work at Louisiana State University, Baton Rouge. She served as psychiatric social work consultant for the state and, during her first year of law school, supervised social workers in community mental health clinics.

The Legal Environment of Social Work

Designed by Anne Masters Design, Inc.

Composed by Patricia D. Wolf, Wolf Publications, Inc., in Bodoni and Futura.

Printed by Boyd Printing Company on 60# Windsor.

Related Texts from the NASW Press

The Legal Environment of Social Work, *by Leila Obier Schroeder.* Focuses on the legal system as it influences the social work profession and highlights the laws that affect the delivery of social work services. Covers the criminal justice system, juvenile courts, filiation and adoption concerns, and new legislation, such as the Americans with Disabilities Act.

ISBN: 0-87101-235-9. Item #2359. $34.95.

Changing Hats: From Social Work Practice to Administration, *by Felice Davidson Perlmutter.* This NASW Press best-seller examines the challenges faced by practitioners making the move into management. The author explores the perspectives of the direct practitioner/administrator, as well as the societal and professional contexts in which management theories inform practice.

ISBN: 0-87101-184-0. Item #1840. $21.95.

Skills for Effective Human Services Management, *Richard L. Edwards and John A. Yankey, Editors.* Describes in crisp, clear language how business wisdom can be applied to effectively manage human services organizations. Provides skills-building techniques and practice exercises to sharpen and increase management skills.

ISBN: 0-87101-195-6. Item #1956. $31.95

(order form on reverse side)

ORDER FORM

Title	Item #	Price	Total
___ The Legal Environ. of Social Work	Item 2359	$34.95	_____
___ Changing Hats	Item 1840	$21.95	_____
___ Skills for Effective Human Svcs Mgt.	Item 1956	$31.95	_____
	+ 10% postage and handling		_____
		Total	_____

❏ I've enclosed my check or money order for $ _____.

❏ Please charge my   ❏ NASW Visa*   ❏ Other Visa   ❏ MasterCard

_____   _____

Credit Card Number   Expiration Date

Signature _____

Use of this card generates funds in support of the social work profession.

Name_____

Address _____

City _____ State/Province _____

Country _____ Zip _____

Phone _____   _____

NASW Member # (if applicable)

(Please make checks payable to NASW Press. Prices are subject to change.)

NASW PRESS

NASW Distribution Center
P.O. Box 431
Annapolis JCT, MD 20701
USA

Credit card orders call
1-800-227-3590
(In the Metro Wash., DC, area, call 301-317-8688)
Or fax your order to 301-206-7989

*LEz 6/95